WHEN COFFEE SPEAKS

Stories from and of
Latin American coffeepeople

recorded
translated
compiled
written
by
Rachel Northrop

Printed in the United States of America at McNally Jackson Books, 52 Prince Street, New York, NY 10012.

www.mcnallyjackson.com/bookmachine/when-coffee-speaks-northrop

First Edition

ISBN 978-1-938022-68-5

For Oskar Schell, Sufiya Zenobia, Teresa Mendoza,
and the broker at 37 Laurier Canal.

May there always be
stories apart.

And for Joseph Campbell.

This Project Made Possible in Part by Generous Support from

In addition to producing high quality coffee, Potenciana Café actively partners with the tax-exempt organization Saplings to enhance educational opportunities, sustain the pristine environment, and develop economic opportunities in remote Costa Rican villages.

This Project Made Possible in Part by Generous Support from

Over 90 Kickstarter backers
around the world

This Project Made Possible in Part by Generous Support from

RedWhaleCoffee.com

Through the Red Whale brand and our coffee, we are determined to positively influence our global community.

Red Whale appreciates the work of Rachel Northrop, bringing her message home from coffee producing countries and beyond. We look forward to hearing more from her.

THANK YOU

UNITED STATES of AMERICA

Don+MJ
Faith+Chris

Julio   Nick   Nina Earl
         Kelsey Ashley
James   Chelsea Adrienne Helena
         Robin+James Fury
Deborah Michael Matt
Mike
Bill

Paulo

GRATITUDE

GRACIAS

AGRADECIMIENTOS

This book would not have been possible without the infinite generosity of the friends I formed and families I adopted along the way, and of course the unfaltering support of friends and family back at home wondering what in the world I was doing.

Thank you to the individuals mentioned on the previous pages, and my deepest thanks to the interviewees whose stories are included in the following pages. Thank you to everyone who contributed to helping transform this from an idea into reality.

This book is not about coffee; it's about people. Words, numbers, and images can only serve to approximate interactions; articles, statistics and photos will never yield flesh and breath. But the longer we spend with the stories of others the more we can hope to understand people we can't see and hear for ourselves.

Este libro no trata del café, sino de las personas. Las palabras, los números, y las fotos solo nos brindan una aproximación, nunca generan carne ni respiración. Pero, lo mas tiempo que pasamos con las historias de los démas, lo mas que podemos esperar entender las personas que no esten frente a nosotros.

Por eso, doy mis gracias a las personas que he conocido en mi camino y a su generosisad sin fin, y gracias a Dios por haberme protegido y guido en mi odisea por tierras anteriormente desconocidas. Ahora yo me cuento con mas hogares, mas familias, mas amigos, y mas conocimientos. Pero mas que la satisfacción que me da todo esto, es la satisfacción de poder compartir las historias de tantas personas y lugares queridas con udstedes lectores.

Gracias.

Table of Contents

Photo Credit: Nina Raman

Foreword

Most coffee growers don't know the luxury of second chances; nature allows no do-overs. The terrain must be properly selected and prepared, the seedlings gingerly cared for until maturity, and the soil must be tended and amended. The ceaseless summer rains must be channeled, pickers must be arranged, and transportation on unmaintained roads completed to realize the results of many a years' labor. And that is just what might be controlled.

So much more is beyond the control of the growers; the price paid for coffee is not established until after the harvest begins, the ebb and flow of rain cycles is predictably unpredictable, and numerous "not if, but when" plant diseases can render emerald green rows of coffee impotent. Even the most robust vehicles fall victim to the brutality of the winding, kidney jarring, frequently disappearing roads, on which growers and communities depend. For many, there is not enough time; there is not enough money to recover from a misstep.

Even among coffee aficionados, there is a knowledge gap that lies somewhere between the discovery of coffee in Ethiopia hundreds of years ago and placing an order for a caffè macchiato at your corner coffee bar every morning. Rachel Northrop has bridged that gap in this seminal effort.

I virtually introduced myself to Rachel in October, 2012 while surfing the internet. I came across a description of the *When Coffee Speaks* project and invited her to visit our small *cafetal* in the remote, pristine Potenciana Mountains of Costa Rica. A month later, the rendezvous took place in the small town of Puriscal, me under the hood trying to get my truck started and she with a back pack and hiking boots. I'm not sure what I was expecting, but she wasn't it! A young, attractive woman, looking like the school teacher she used to be. But, on the roads, climbing the mountains, and in the fields, Rachel appeared as though she had grown up in a neighboring community. The slip and slide ride up to the Potenciana tests nerves and shakes molars on the best days. Appearing still raveled, she asked beau coups spot-on questions while careening about the cab.

Unflapped when we were bogged down in the daily deluge, we waited out the rain taking in the expansive beauty that

1

is the Potenciana. One perk of good coffee is that it's grown in the most beautiful places on the planet. Out in the fields picking coffee, an unspoken competition brewed among the Gringo workforce to fill our *cajuela* baskets with plump red cherries. Rachel's nimble gait steadied her among the trees while her Benihana-like technique plucked plum red cherries. All the while we kept our heads on a swivel; one eye targeting prime cherries, the other scanning the undergrowth for the feared Terciopelo snakes. Smug smiles were quickly erased when our *cajuelas* matched the local efforts. The Gringo team toils combined earned a paltry $2.85! But, in spite of what others might consider hardships, one unquestioned similarity on every farm is the growers' love of their lives, their land, and each other. While in the Potenciana, Rachel showed an innate comfort while talking with our local crew, uncovering stories of coffee, community, and connections.

As impressive as "Rachel of the Fields" was, she had one more surprise. The next time I saw Rachel was several weeks later at an annual, international coffee conference in San Jose, Costa Rica. She had visited at least two other farms in that interim. The inquisitive, daring, fearless, and very personable farmhand had morphed. Rachel, now in business casual, was now asking pointed questions of the coffee authorities, buyers, and policy makers, presenting as elegantly and tastefully as a Vanderbilt. She now had it all, from seed to harvest, from harvest to processing, from processing to what we enjoy every morning. The conference culminated with a formal event. Now, recall, I first saw her with a pair of hiking boots and a back pack. How she stuffed an evening gown and heels into that backpack, I will always wonder.

Rachel was in the fields, at the receivers and processors, and at the dinner tables, experiencing the full palate of what goes into growing coffee. This is a story that started as an earnest attempt to answer a simple question and grew into a fascinating and profound discovery of a way of life.

Mike Pannell, PhD
Potenciana Café, S.A.
Costa Rica

Introduction

Leaving a fulltime job and a more-than-full-time life in NYC to travel through Latin America armed with rubber boots and a voice recorder in pursuit of coffee stories might seem like a crazy choice, but for me it seemed like the obvious one.

Before departing on this odyssey I'd spent two years writing for examiner.com as Manhattan Green Living Examiner. I was finding an increasing tendency among New Yorkers to eschew certified organic products in favor of local ones. I started peeking into locavore movements and quickly realized that, while there was a considerable argument in favor of locavore practices from an environmental standpoint, it was a lifestyle I'd personally never be able to adopt. Coffee comes from the tropics (I urge New Yorkers to check out the one plant in the Brooklyn Botanic Garden's tropical room that inspired me to first wonder about coffee. Free admission all day Tuesdays and Saturdays between 10am-12am!) There's no way I can get it within any of the accepted locavore radii, and there's certainly no way I'm giving it up. Which then lead me to consider, if one of the biggest factors in a food's greenness is the distance it treks to get to your plate (or cup), is there any such thing as sustainable coffee? What would I have to do to find out?

More and more New Yorkers want to know where their food comes from, and ever since I'd seen that one plant at the BBG in 2007 I'd wanted to know more about where coffee comes from. When I first saw that coffee tree I was equal parts shocked that coffee came from a plant and shocked at myself for never having wondered about the source of something I consumed so regularly.

In an effort to find out what all those labels on coffee mean, and thus try to sort out whether "shade grown," "organic," and "fair trade" held any water in actually doing good things for people and planet, I started reading everything I could about coffee. I quickly realized that coffee literature falls into two categories: history of coffee's global distribution two hundred years ago and guides to gourmet preparation. I couldn't find anything at all about where the black deli coffee I drink every morning comes from. There were few references to farmers and references to stories they had told, but there was nothing from the growers themselves. All the authors of these coffee books were North American and European and traveled in the company of translators, usually with the dual goals of researching and buying some coffee.

I saw a hole. Where were the voices of the people who actually did the work to grow all this coffee that percolates on every corner? I decided to try to fill that void. I quit my job, sold my bike, donated my winter coats, and headed south with a backpack and a goal.

I'm obviously also a North American, but I'm less of a writer and more of a compiler. Since I speak Spanish, I'm focusing on coffee in regions that speak a language I do and eliminating the layer of a translator, because, unfortunately, something is always lost in translation.

Not one producer I've spoken to would even consider writing a book; many are incredulous that I'd want to talk to them because "journalists usually want to talk to the bosses." Almost all farmers don't feel like they have anything to tell me that could be remotely interesting. I promise them that the people who drink their coffee do in fact want to know about the people, lives, communities and stories behind what they're drinking.

I've visited over thirty five farms, toured milling and roasting plants, slept in remote fincas, forded rivers, learned to make tortillas, ridden horses, wandered through living agroforestry labs, scaled mountains, picked bushels of ripe coffee cherries, tasted over twenty local harvests, recorded over eighty five conversations, dined with corporate gurus, attended two major industry conferences, gutted fish, and machete hacked away at the jungle.

I've learned more than I imagined was possible and become a sort of unlikely horizontal messenger between farmers; growers want to know what's going on at other *fincas* and at other points in the chain.

This is perhaps the most exciting stage of my journey, the chance to share all that with the world, the opportunity to pass along all stories that I saw, heard, and became a part of.

NB: All interviews are translated from Spanish by Rachel Northrop unless otherwise noted.

A Note on Methods and Form

The Spanish speaking coffee growing world extends from Southern Mexico to Bolivia, so once I'd made the decision to go I was faced with the overwhelming question of, "Where to?" I'm bold and adventurous and independent, but I try not to be stupid and did not want to drop myself in a place where I'd be in danger. The trouble with United Statesian portrayals and perceptions of other places is those portrayals are often skewed and biased (for a host of complex reasons), so I really didn't know which places fell into the "doable" category. Rather than exclude places based on prejudice, I decided to drop a pin in the map in a place where people I knew and trusted had been and could thus vouch that as a 24-year-old white (albeit bilingual, but still really white) rogue writer with a backpack I would in fact be ok and actually get some work done, versus spending excessive time/money/effort trying to assess potential threats.

So I dropped a pin in Costa Rica.

Based on accounts from trusted sources, I figured I wouldn't die if I went there. I started combing through the Worldwide Opportunities on Organic Farms (WWOOF) listserv for a place to start as a volunteer, just to have an address to put on my customs arrival form and guarantee that I'd have a roof over my head for at least a few weeks.

I found a cow farm willing to have me and booked a one-way ticket.

Once I'd make the choice to go, organic things started happening.

My friend Paulo mentioned that his mom's friend Juan had retired to a coffee farm in Panama. My friend Kelsey's coworker Elizabeth was leaving for Nicaragua in a few months to work as a teacher trainer. My friend Julio revealed that he had actually been born on his family's coffee farm in the Colombian mountains where much of his family still lived.

Suddenly, organically, I had one name and one phone number in each of four geographically contingent Spanish speaking coffee growing countries: Nicaragua, Costa Rica, Panama, Colombia. I figured that was as good as a full itinerary.

As soon as I touched down, those initial organically amassed contacts morphed into even more organic connections. I started talking to everyone I met, and nature/a god/the universe/seasonal luck responded by offering up people who were willing to talk to me, house me, feed me, teach me, and share their lives with me.

I followed every lead I had. I also knocked on doors, sent emails to addresses I found on posters, websites, and coffee packaging. I Googled and investigated and cold called and pursued. And people answered.

In this way my organic coffee odyssey unfolded. In pouring the condensed stories from my odyssey into this text, I've left the drops of conversation in the chronological order in which they occurred. I offer footnotes* and superscripts [referencing related explanatory material in the Appendix] and **end-of-interview choices** to let you navigate this text according to your whims and interests.

Is a cup of coffee just a simple thing you drink? Is a book something you just read from front to back?

Maybe. Coffee can be a simple pleasure, and this book can be read from cover to cover, all asterisks and superscripts and choice-offerings ignored.

But, if you're up for the challenge, you'll find that coffee is biologically, monetarily, politically, socially, industrially, logistically, culinarily, and chemically complex. If you're up for the challenge, you can trace patterns and themes and questions and navigate this text in different directions and dimensions. Or you can retrace my footsteps and hear from the people I heard from in the order I heard from them, and then read an appendix of my thoughts and reflections at the end. Or not. The choice is yours.

Drink up.

For more on the influences and rationale behind the investigative project and the structure of the final book, turn to p. 407

(These are what the "choose-your-own-adventure" style end-of-interview choices look like.)

*indicated with an asterisk like this

Coffee Survey

1. Have you ever seen a coffee plant?
   - o Yes
   - o No
2. On what type of plant does coffee grow?
   - o On a root underground
   - o On a low vine
   - o On a leafy bush/tree
   - o On a tall palm-like tree
   - o On a corn-like stalk
3. How does coffee grow?
   - o Inside a nut
   - o Inside small cherries
   - o Inside large, fleshy fruit
   - o Many beans in a pod
4. Where in the world does coffee grow, generally? (Select all that apply)
   - o Africa
   - o Asia
   - o Australia
   - o Caribbean
   - o Europe
   - o Central America
   - o North America
   - o Pacific Islands
   - o South America
   - o The Poles
5. Is coffee grown in the continental United States?
   - o Yes
   - o No
6. Where in the world is coffee grown, specifically? (Select all that apply)
   - o Alaska
   - o Argentina
   - o Austria
   - o Bolivia
   - o Brazil
   - o California

- o China
- o Colombia
- o Costa Rica
- o Ethiopia
- o Germany
- o Guatemala
- o Florida
- o Hawaii
- o Indonesia
- o Italy
- o Jamaica
- o Kenya
- o Nicaragua
- o Rwanda
- o Oregon
- o Panama
- o Spain
- o Vietnam
- o Yemen

7. What climate conditions are necessary to grow coffee?
- o Minimal sun and cold temperatures
- o Sandy soil and high altitude
- o Fertile soil and temperatures above freezing
- o Minimal precipitation and temperatures above 70° F

8. Which factors affect coffee flavor? (Select all that apply)
- o Soil composition
- o Precipitation
- o Altitude
- o Temperature
- o Interplanted species

9. Do you drink coffee?
- o Yes
- o No

10. If so, how often? What's your favorite? Where does it come from?

For answers, turn to "Coffee 101" on p. 344

Coffee Jargon

Finca: Any rural mountain land you own is your finca. A finca is not necessarily a farm, because your finca might not produce anything or have any animals on it. It might have a house or some sort of building, or it might just be wild mountainside, but if it has boundaries and an owner, it's a finca. Across the Spanish-speaking slice of the global coffee production belt, finca is the unanimous term for property someone owns, without referring to what that property is used for.

Cafetal: A cafetal, however, refers only to what a piece of property is used for, and a cafetal is always used for growing coffee. The existing translations are "coffee field," "coffee farm," or "coffee plantation," but none of these is quite accurate. All of these words immediately evoke images of expanses of flat space with homogenous rows of planted things. English's agrarian language is one of amber waves of grain. We in the U.S. don't grow things in our mountains. In Latin America they do. And English has no words for what it looks like.

A cafetal is not a farm because farms don't include forests, and all cafetales are a species of forest—even those with zero shade trees— because coffee plants themselves are trees. A cafetal is not a field because fields are flat and fairly uniform, (maybe coffee growing regions in Kenya or Brazil are flat and fairly uniform, but then they would be called *shambas* or *fazendas*) and here cafetales are never flat and nowhere near uniform. A cafetal is not a plantation because plantations are massive with an owner rocking on the front porch in clean linen and contracted help (be it migrant labor or yesterday's slaves) hard at work, and cafetales are owned by families who work the land themselves, even if they do hire some additional help. And even though all cafetales are a sort of forest, cafetales are not necessarily coffee forests, because "forest" evokes in North American readers the image of towering pines and dense groves of oaks whose leaves change every fall.

Cafetal is the blanket term for the part of a finca where coffee is grown. Spanish does something cool with the suffix "–al" that we can't do in English: it turns any product into the place

9

where that product is grown. *Cañal,* where the *caña* (sugarcane) grows; *maizal,* where the *maíz* (corn) grows; *cedral,* where the *cedros* (cedars) grow; *cafetal,* where the *café* grows. The suffix carries none of the implications that do English's "farm, field, plantation, forest," of the topography or flora or fauna of a place. It just means "place where that grows," whether that place is steep, flat, shaded, small, expansive, overgrown or immaculate.

Caficultor: A caficultor is a person who owns and runs a cafetal. To be a caficultor you have to be in charge, but you have to also get your hands a little dirty. Because most Latin American cafetales are owned by smallholders, almost all landowners either do all of the actual coffee production labor themselves with the help of family members or hire some seasonal labor and one or two year round guys. Caficultores know their fincas and make judgment calls about what to plant where, when, and how. When the money is tight, they're the ones who decide whether it means less fertilization or more macheteing away the weeds by hand instead of buying herbicides. Depending on the country, caficultores may also be the ones who do some steps in processing the coffee (in Colombia, for example), but they're always the ones responsible for coaxing coffee trees out of the ground and cherries off the trees. In Colombia, caficultores are called *cafeteros.*

Caturra/o: There are thousands of varietals of coffee trees, but only a handful are planted for commercial production. The main division in coffee varietals is between Robusta (higher caffeine content, more robust field performance, and less desirable flavor in the cup) and Arabica (lower caffeine content, more finicky field performance, and milder, more desirable flavor). Within Arabica the two main commercial varietals are Typica and Bourbon. The Caturra (in Colombia usually called Caturro) variety is a mutation of Bourbon, one well suited to mountain cultivation offering a high production yield and tasty final product. The one drawback is its extreme susceptibility to the debilitating leaf rust fungus *la roya.*

Catuai: Another common coffee varietal used in commercial production. Catuai is a true-breeding cross between Mondo Novo, itself a cross between Bourbon and Typica, and Caturra.

Catimor: A true-breeding cross between a Robusta varietal (Hibrido de Timor) and Caturra. The Robsuta genes make Catimor resistant to leaf rust, but the consensus among roasters is that it tastes pretty undesirable. Unfortunately, that consensus didn't come until after thousands of hectares across Latin America were thriving with it. As many Catimor trees reach their 20s, most growers are finally replacing them with other (tastier) varietals. **For a chart of coffee varietals turn to p. 104.**

Variedad Colombia: An iteration of the Catimor developed by Colombia's coffee science force at Cenicafe. It is delightfully resistant to leaf rust without tasting terrible.

Roya: Coffee leaf rust. Saying it aloud almost feels like uttering, "Voldemort," because it can send Death Eater-level chills down the spines of caficultores. All Arabica varietals are susceptible to the rust, and when the orange spores of the rust start showing up on the leaves of a few trees in a cafetal, in a matter of days they can spread across the finca, and within a week the majority of the coffee trees will be stripped of their leaves, meaning they can't produce a harvest that year. Caficultores then have to wait one year for the leaves to grow back and another for cherries to appear again. Depending on the age of the trees, growers may have to prune them to stumps and wait three years for the trees to regrow entirely. There are no organic or chem-free ways to tackle roya. There are preventative and curative fungicides, but both are expensive and neither is a guarantee. Roya is always a low blow.

Broca: The broca is usually more annoying than destructive. Broca is the Spanish word for the tiny black coffee berry borer, a winged insect that flits from tree to tree and bores its way into the coffee cherry, right into the seed that'll become the green bean for roasting. The broca burrows its way in and lays lots of eggs. If a broca just "nibbles" the edge of a coffee cherry, there's hardly any damage to the seed/bean. But if the broca has its way, it literally consumes the entire seed, such that when you open the cherry, the contents are just a dead, brown, baby broca filled mush. Caficultores can treat for broca either with pesticides or with a USDA organic-approved fungus called *beauvaria bassiana*, which seals the cherries so the broca can't get in. Broca infested cherries are less dense, because the broca has eaten away at all the mass inside, making them somewhat manageable to sort out during processing.

Ojo de Gallo: Literally means "Rooster's Eye." A fungus that attacks both the leaves and cherries of a coffee tree. Caused by excess moisture in the cafetal; often seen on fincas with too much or poorly managed shade.

Almacigo/almaciguero: Coffee seeds are germinated in a bed of sandy soil, and once they've sprouted their third set of leaves and are several inches tall, they are ready to be transplanted to bags of dirt, where they'll stay for about 6-8 more months until they're hearty enough to be transplanted to the mountainside. These bags of seedlings need a place to live, and that location is called the almacigo or almaciguero. These terms refer to a, "place where all the bags of seedlings are." Some caficultores germinate their own seeds and build their own almacigos, but there are also those who buy them from caficultores who, instead of cultivating acres of full trees, cultivate stretches of bags of seedlings ready for transplant.

La Medida: The Measurement. Coffee pickers are paid by how much they pick. In Costa Rica and Nicaragua by volume, in Panama and Colombia by weight. La Medida happens at the end of every picking day, where every worker's work is measured to determine how much he or she earns. In Costa Rica the volumetric measurement is a *cajuela*, one cubic foot, typically weighing 12-13 kilos (around 27 pounds). 20 *cajuelas* make a *fanega*. In Nicaragua the volumetiric measurement is still one cubic foot, but there it's called a *lata*. In Panama and Colombia workers' daily bounties are weighed by kilo, and the other common metric used is a *quintal*, 100 pounds. A quintal always refers to measurements of dried green coffee beans, whereas a fanega always refers to cherries and is essentially a "wet quintal." Theoretically, a fanega of cherries yields a quintal of dried beans.

Beneficio: The beneficio is the coffee mill, but like cafetal, the existing translation isn't quite on target. In English, a mill belongs to a grain miller; it's dry and dusty and brings to mind things like "stone ground." Coffee beneficios are wet, sticky, and generate fermenting piles of pulp. The beneficio can be a small building on the finca where one man processes the day's harvest, or it can be a massive industrial operation handling hundreds of thousands of pounds of coffee a day. Like finca, beneficio just means, "place where the coffee is processed in some way," regardless of the scope, scale, or degree of care of that processing.

Depulper: The depulper is the main machine in the beneficio; it separates the coffee skin from the seed inside (one day to become roasted bean). It can be a small, tabletop hand crank model, or a mechanized part of the massive industrial operation of larger beneficios. Most are somewhere in between. Some growing regions of the world don't depulp their coffee at all, leaving the skins on and letting the cherry dry as a whole (known as Natural processing). But this takes sun and space, so Latin America is home to washed coffees, and in order to wash coffee, you first have to depulp it to get the skin off, and then you can wash off the slimy layer of sugary goo known as the mucilage. If you have a more industrial operation that uses the appropriate machinery and a steady flow of water, you can sort out the cherries with broca before depulping them, since they float. In Costa Rica depulpers are called *chancadoras*.

Demucilagenator: This is a transliteration of *desmucilaginadora*, which literally means "something that takes off the mucilage," or "de-mucilages" it. You could also call it a "washer," but that could get confusing, because some coffee is "hand washed" by emptying it into long canals filled with water and then stirring it with a big paddle, so in that case the "washer" could refer to the canal or the person holding the paddle. Coffee that is washed in this way is almost always left to ferment, sit in its own slimy, sticky mucilage, for a few hours (usually 12-24) before being

13

actively "washed." But coffee that passes through the demucilagenator is not left to ferment at all; it is demucilagenized immediately. So "washing" coffee can imply some degree of fermentation, but using some invented form of the word "demucilage" clearly indicates that no fermentation at all has taken place. One of the coolest things about coffee production might be that it is totally acceptable to make up very specific words to describe exactly what you want to explain is going on. Demucilagenators are common in Costa Rica and Panama but rare in Colombia, where almost all coffee is fermented and hand washed in the canals described above.

Natural: Coffee doesn't have to be washed in order to be dried, hulled, and roasted. Instead of depulping coffee to remove the skin, the entire cherry can be dried, skin and all, and then dry hulled once, to remove both the skin and the parchment paper at the same time. This yields Natural processed coffee, which requires less water and more sun, making it common in Africa and uncommon in the rainy jungles of Latin America.

Pasilla: All coffee cherries are not created equal. Even if you're a diligent picker, a few underripe cherries will always end up in your basket, and there are always defects, malformed cherries, and other classes of sub par coffee. Pasilla is the Colombian collective term for all these sub par beans. Because most Colombian fincas have their own small beneficios, when Colombian caficultores sell coffee, they're selling depulped, washed, and dried beans, which are still naturally encased in a seed casing known as parchment paper. Growers sort their coffee between export quality defect-free beans and pasilla, which usually ends up being roasted, ground, and sold for national consumption. Producers are paid different prices for export grade beans and for pasilla, and a third rate for *corriente*, a mix between the two. If you have a high infestation of broca you'll end up with a higher percentage of pasilla, and therefore a lower price for a higher percentage of any given harvest.

Casilla: Once coffee has been depulped, it needs to be dried well or it will rot. Some farms have mechanical dryers, but all have some sort of patio/raised bed space to lay the washed beans out to dry. Big estates will have large patios, but houses on small mountain fincas have casillas, which are typically built on top of the roof of the house. The casilla is essentially a cement bed (that can support the weight of a grown man, because someone has to rake the coffee to turn it over so that it doesn't mold on the underside). But because rain comes quickly in the coffee mountains and can instantly undo days of drying, the cement beds are fashioned with removable roofs fitted with wheels that set into tracks, such that the roof can be rolled on and off the drying space as rapidly as the weather changes.

Parchment paper: Coffee cherries are fruit, and coffee beans are seeds. Like all seeds, coffee beans have a layer of protective seed casing. This is known as the parchment paper (*pergamino* in Spanish). The parchment paper only becomes visible in washed coffees once the coffee has been depulped and dried. As it dries it looses humidity, and this loss of water causes the seed to get smaller, separating itself from its seed casing. The parchment paper is the last thing to come off in order to get green (roastable) coffee. Coffee is always stored in parchment paper in order to protect and preserve it, but it is always exported as green coffee sans parchment paper because the parchment paper not only protects coffee, it covers up the defects. (It's illegal to export coffee in parchment). The final pre-export stage of coffee processing is called dry hulling (to differentiate it from depulping, which is also sometimes called "wet hulling"). If you're preparing Naturally processed coffees for export, you'd just dry hull them once, taking the skin and the parchment paper off at the same time to leave just the green exportable bean.

Receiver: In Costa Rica, coffee growers sell their just-picked coffee to large beneficios. These cherries have to make it from the fincas to the beneficios every day, which means that producers either bring them to the mill themselves, the mill sends a big truck up into the mountains to go get them, or the growers bring their coffee to a "receiver," a hut built into hillsides where farmers in the area can drop off their coffee and get a receipt. In the afternoons the beneficio's trucks come around and collect the

15

coffee from the receivers, which are built at a rake such that the truck can just pull up under the back of the building, open a little "doggy door" attached to a chute, and funnel the coffee from the receiver into the back of the truck.

Technify: In Spanish, coffeepeople often use the word *tecnificar,* which means to "make more technical," or, "to technify." They use it in reference to modernizing agricultural models from more traditional subsistence agriculture paired with some cash crop cultivation. When you technify a farm you make it in the image of more industrial models: straight, orderly rows (with no food crops in the way), regular applications of fertilizers, pesticides, fungicides, and herbicides to keep the weeds down, and higher densities, since all those agrochemicals now boost performance. Technified farms won't have many (if any) shade trees, and the coffee plants will be planted as close together as possible, just allowing room for harvesters to harvest.

To Cup: Coffee's complexity rivals, if not surpasses, that of wine. The same way vine has its sommeliers, coffee has its cuppers. Cupping is a sensory science of evaluating the aroma, taste, mouth feel, body, acidity, and a host of other aspects. In order to cup coffee it must be roasted and ground immediately before beginning the process. It's a technical activity that requires a lab-like space, precision, and infallible attention to detail. Coffees are scored on a hundred-point scale, and these scorings determine the price various lots will fetch. Roasters constantly cup sample lots of coffee around the world in order to determine the best components for a blend that meets the requirements of the standardized flavor profiles all roasters develop over time. Dunkin Donuts coffee tastes like Dunkin Donuts and not like Folgers or like Starbucks because people are in the lab, cupping away all day, to make it so. Professional cuppers, known as Q-Graders are the ultimate authorities on Quality.

Barismo: The art of being a *barista*, someone who prepares espresso drinks, originated in Italy, and has since spread across Europe, the U.S. and Australia like wildfire. It's finally making its way into producing countries, where the people who grow the coffee are learning to turn their home grown beans into lattes and beginning to appreciate the craft of a good cappuccino. Barismo takes expensive machinery, good instruction, and a culture of dedication to making good drinks as much as a culture of willing to pay top dollar to drink them. All elements are converging, bringing a swelling surge of barismo to Latin America.

Ground to Grounds: There's nothing wrong with the phrases "seed to cup" or "crop to cup," but I've heard them so much that they're starting to sound stale, and I can't bring myself to use them. "Ground to grounds" implies a similar acknowledgement of the entire coffee production and preparation process. The soil in the ground is where coffee starts, and wet grounds—be they in a filter, at the bottom of a French press, or in a puck in a porta filter—is where coffee ends up. Those grounds can then be returned to the ground as compost. "Ground to grounds" reminds us that coffee is a crop and can be returned to the soil on the other side of the world, in very "full circle of agriculture" style.

Gracias a Dios: The literal translation would be "thanks to God," but this is another case where the transliteration doesn't quite fit. In English, invoking the name of God is usually reserved for sermons, the condensed exclamation of OMG!, or dropped casually, as in, "Thank God I was able to get to the bank before it closed." But *gracias a Dios* carries a little more sincerity, as in, "We recovered from that year of low prices and now all my children are happy and healthy, *gracias a Dios.*" In English, "thank God," would ring a little sarcastically, and in Spanish it's never used sarcastically. In order to avoid misrepresenting or trivializing a phrase that is present in almost all conversations, be they business meetings or gossip, I've chosen to leave it in its original form.

Fairtrade: "Fair trade" is a concept; "Fairtrade" is the legal name of Fairtrade International, a non-profit based in Bonn, Germany that sets the international certification standards that producers and vendors of a host of products must meet in order to be able to put the Fairtrade logo on their packaging. Fairtrade International simply sets the standards; FLO-CERT a third-party auditor, reviews producers, processors, and distributors against those standards. In the case of coffee, roasters must also be certified in order to sell their coffee under the Fairtrade logo. All parties audited by FLO-CERT must pay an auditing fee. For coffee producers to be Fairtrade certified they must be part of a producer organization, be it co-op or association or other organizational structure. Only a random handful of members of organizations are audited every year and the organization pays the auditing cost. At the beginning of 2013 Fair Trade USA split (not so amicably) from Fairtrade in order to certify both larger estates, thus extending benefits to workers and to different types of groups of smallholders. Both Fairtrade and Fair Trade USA guarantee that all producers receive a minimum floor price of the equivalent of $1.40/lb or a premium of $0.20/lb if the market price is above $1.40. During most of the process of researching and writing this book the price has been sliding farther and farther below the floor price, meaning Fairtrade certified farmers are benefiting. But the drawback comes when there's no buyer for Fairtrade certified coffee, and the co-ops have to move their certified stocks as conventional, thus eating the difference and threatening their ability to continue with certification.

Rainforest Alliance: Rainforest is a New York-based non-profit that sets certification standards based on maintaining holistic biodiversity in accordance with the principles of the Sustainable Agriculture Network. Various auditing agencies check farms of all shapes and sizes against these standards. Rainforest is comprehensive in its concern for individuals, communities, and ecosystems. Rainforest is different from organic because organic certification requires the complete absence of agrochemicals and chemical fertilizers, while Rainforest permits the use of those with low toxicity. However, organic certification does not require that farmers manage their waste products responsibly, whereas Rainforest does. There is no guaranteed premium for Rainforest certified coffee, but there is always some small price differential that makes it to producers.

New York

White Plains

New York City →

Silvia

Recorded May 5, 2012, at Silvia's home in White Plains, New York.

My friend Julio's mom was elated when she heard that I was setting out on a Latin American odyssey with the goal of writing a book about coffee, and she immediately called up all her siblings and extended an open-ended invitation on behalf of the entire family for me to visit the family farm in Colombia. She then graciously invited me to her house in White Plains to share some of her memories of growing up on the family finca. She prepared a feast of (absolutely delicious) Colombian food so that I'd be familiar with the standard fare when I eventually arrived in South America.

After devouring several different kinds of thick corn tortillas (*arepas*), fried pork *(chicharrones)*, fried plantains *(tostones)*, a taste of *chorizo* and a giant stew *(sancocho)*, I sat down with Silvia on the couch in her living room. She wears her hair pulled back, a black sweater and glasses.

Silvia: *I remember when I was five or six; I had to get up very early. My father was basically training me to be able to do everything around the house. At this time we all got up early; there wasn't electricity. We went to bed early too, 6pm! I remember that we would get up around four in the morning, and the workers had been up since two, husking the corn.*

At age nine I was able to do the exact same things as any woman of the house. I was able to make breakfast, make sancocho, *kill a chicken and cook it, feed the workers, and make* arepas. *My mom wasn't the best cook, and while my father was training me we had a few women who helped out. I'd get up with them to make forty, fifty* arepas *for the workers. Everyone showed me how to make* arepas *a little bit differently, so I learned a little bit from everyone and came up with my own way.*

A normal day for us was to get up early—we didn't just get out of bed and hop in the shower like everyone does here now. No, the girls had to go make breakfast and the boys would go get the mules. We had to find the chickens and feed them, collect firewood, and cut the grass for the mules. Normal. I remember that when I was nine I'd had so much experience already that I was able to do it, to get up at four am and make the forty or fifty arepas. *I think that's when I started to do things quickly; I wanted to sleep more.*

We'd get up and start getting all the food ready for the day. We used a fogón, *which is a long, narrow oven that you feed firewood into and it burns down to charcoal. There are three burners on it so that you can cook things in pots or grill the* arepas. *Breakfast was an* arepa, *sometimes egg with rice, and after eating the men would go out to work. Then we'd start lunch. It was a lot of the day in the kitchen. Lunch was* sancocho. *Monday, Tuesday, Wednesday. Always the same. It had yucca, plantain, potato, meat. It wasn't like here where everyone eats different things. It was* sancocho.

I went to school, but after school I came home to do my chores. And during vacations my father didn't pay the girls to help, and I had to do everything! I have one younger sister and a younger brother that I had to take care of. My older brothers were already grown. But I'd want to play with them! So I'd be running around after them, dragging my little brother behind me. I had to learn to do everything they did because I wanted to keep up with them.

So. To get to coffee. It was a coffee farm. The finca produced [coffee] the source of income, but my father always said, "The earth produces everything." We always had vegetable gardens with onions, tomatoes. We had yucca, plantains, bananas, oranges, lemons, avocados. My father would go to the market once a week, on Sundays, to buy meat and other things you could only get in town. We didn't have a refrigerator so we'd hang the meat over the fogón *to smoke it. And we didn't drink sodas like you see here now, we'd go pick oranges ourselves and make juice.*

How do you produce coffee? Well, you learn from your parents. We'd make nurseries of coffee trees. I remember that we'd have to help move the pulp [coffee cherry skins left over from depulping coffee]. Everyone would grab a basket and we'd bring it to a designated area of the finca where it would decompose, break down back into dirt. And we'd used that to fill the small black plastic bags used to hold seedlings. We'd make a little indent in the dirt in the bags and put the little coffee plant into the bag when it had just two or three leaves.

Once the plant was taller and had several sets of leaves we called it an "almacigo." When they were ready to plant we'd have to bring them to the lot where they'd be planted. If it was close we'd all just put some in baskets and carry them; if it was far they'd use the mules. The men would dig the holes and the kids' job was to run and place a seedling at each hole. Once the coffee was planted, after about a year and a half it would flower and start to produce.

Because I was a girl, and my dad looked out for me, I wasn't allowed to go out into the cafetal to pick with my brothers and the men. So my dad said, "These trees right by the house—they're yours!" And I would pick the coffee there, and he'd tell me that he was keeping it apart. Of course he mixed it all together with the other coffee when he processed it, but I believed him! He'd weigh it beforehand, and then when he came back from selling it he'd say, "Here! The money from your coffee!" and he'd give me the little bit of money from "my" trees.

We also had to sort the coffee. After depulping it, you have to sort it. If coffee still has the skin attached after it's gone through the depulper it's considered second class. There was a process of fermentation. After depulping it they'd put it in a tank to ferment[in its own sticky mucilage]: good coffee on the bottom, bad coffee on top. After it fermented you'd have to use a rake to separate the good from the bad. And my dad told me that I could have the second class. Because he didn't have time to peel all the dried skins off, but because we were kids we supposedly had more time!

The depulper only takes the skin of cherries of a certain size; ones that are too big or too small won't get depulped when they go through. That was called the pasilla. You can still sell it but just for a much lower price. My father would go all the way down to Bolívar to sell the coffee, and I'd bring my coffee to [the smaller town of] San Gregorio to sell it there. We'd go to San Gregorio for Mass. And I'd sell my coffee and I'd buy a few candies or something.

The biggest event was Christmas. My father, even though he was a farmer, always invited lots of people for Christmas. My mom would sing; lots of people would come to the house. We were like… the richest of the poor! People were always comfortable in our house. At Christmas we'd make natilla and buñuelos. My father was very generous. He liked to share; he'd say, "Giving produces more; if you give you'll always get something back." There were people with a lot more money who didn't share.

Another big event was when they installed electricity. Or when the first car came. That I'll never forget! A car pulled into San Gregorio, and all the kids ran after it! And the teachers at the school told us that we couldn't go running near the cars because we'd get hit, because one man did hit a boy, and after that they prohibited us to play near them. I remember one day—at that point we were living in San Gregorio—a car came. And the teachers had told us that whomever they caught running after the cars would be punished. A bunch of kids were chasing the car, and I was just on my way home, but they took all the kids—including me! And I was never in trouble! That was the one and only time I was punished. My mom asked me, "Why were you chasing after that car?" And I told her, "I was just running home! The car was chasing me!"

Another big event was my first communion. I remember that dress. I didn't take it off! I wanted to look pretty, but I still wanted to climb the trees and keep up with everyone. That day I slipped and I ripped the whole side of the dress—I was so upset! It was like a mix; I wanted to be a beautiful young lady, but I wanted to have someone to play with, which meant keeping up with my brothers.

I remember listening to all the novelas *on the radio. That's one of the things I used to buy with my money from selling coffee—batteries! Because the radio "ate lots of batteries" we used to say. My dad needed the radio to listen to the news. And I'd be listening to the radio all day, in the kitchen, doing what I had to do. I'd take the radio with me all over the house. If I was washing clothes I'd put it there; if I was making lunch I'd put it in the kitchen. I'd be making* arepas *and* sancoho *listening to the* novelas. *I never missed them. I grew up on* novelas.

I also knew how to roast coffee; because we'd make our own coffee from the finca. When the [depulped] coffee is dried, you take off one more little layer [parchment paper], and then you roast it. Just like you buy in the store, ground, we had to grind it. So we'd make coffee for the finca. Everyone drank coffee in the mornings, it's just that we didn't buy it; we did it ourselves right there on the finca. You roast it [in a pan] on the fogón *with* panela *[brick of molassesy sugar made from fresh pressed sugarcane stalks]. You had to keep it constantly turning. If I tried to do it now I might not remember when it got to just the right point without burning it, but I used to know!*

And chocolate! Cacao! We'd roast that too. Cacao is big giant seedpods. Coffee is tiny [makes dime-sized circle with her hands], *and cacao is big* [makes football-sized measurement]. *And cacao seeds are coated with a fleshy white slime that's very sweet. So you dry them and roast them like coffee.*

One time we were out in the mountains and I cut myself; I was carrying a saw. To light the fogón *you need firewood, so we were out gathering firewood. So we were out in the woods; there was one part of the finca where we just let the trees grow so that we could cut them for firewood. I was carrying a saw with big giant teeth, and I tripped but I didn't want to drop the saw—so I cut myself! This was one of those saws with super sharp teeth. I didn't want to drop it because the one thing my father told me was,*

23

"Don't drop the saw or you'll bend the teeth and it won't cut!" There are lots of things one has to do, one learns to do.

Not all women—I had to do all this because I happened to grow up with so many men! I did the same things they did, and I did the things women did. I learned to do what they did because I wanted to be with them.

The other thing I remember are the landslides. When the rains would come the layers of soil would just slide down the mountain! It's not that there are any rivers on the farm; it's just that the water goes into the soil and needs a way out. It rains and it finds little holes and then it all just moves together.

Another event I'll never forget is when we lived in San Gregorio— for a while we lived in San Gregorio, right up on the top of the mountain. The houses there aren't as…solid as the ones here. And the roofs were made of sheets of, how do you call it, not plastic, but like a thick corrugated sheet of plastic. And one night, a storm blew the roof right off! I remember waking up and seeing the sky, rain, and lightning! At least the house was two stories, so we went downstairs to the first floor.

Even though I had to work hard and didn't have a lot of nice things, I love it. I love the finca. I remember when I was a little girl and I would lie on a tree branch and look at the stars, dreaming. And I was dreaming of this [she gestures to her living room]. *I wanted to be rich, have a pretty house with a nice bathroom and a big comfortable bed.*

But now I really want to go back! Yes the coffee harvest was hard, but the rest of the time I was with my family, and we'd go from one finca to another to visit people, or I'd go visit my friends. You could roam! And now, with Facebook, I'm seeing all those people again! I'm dreaming—what I want to do now is go back and see everyone.

For a conversation with Silvia's brother, turn to p. 288

To get ready to head to Latin America, turn to the next page.

When Coffee Speaks: Stories from Caficultores

Everything has a story. Not one of us, and not a moment of anyone's life, fits a template or follows a formula. We are all the amalgamation of nuance. We are inseparable from our stories, and so is everything we consume.

I'll be traveling through Latin America to collect a healthy crop of stories from coffee farmers (*cafetaleros, caficultores,* or *cafeteros,* depending where you go) in an effort to humanize a commodity we all interact with daily (even if you're not a drinker, you see, smell, and experience coffee in some way every day). This project is an open investigation to gather the human stories behind something that seems so familiar. Coffee is an integral part of our lives, but we as North American residents have no point of reference for how our morning pick-me-up arrives in the paper cups of our favorite cafes or filters into the carafe on our countertop; we have no framework for thinking about what happens behind the scenes of our k-cup or latte.

Coffee is an inherently remote commodity because our North American climate simply does not support its cultivation. Currently, people in this country are expressing a renewed desire to flock to farmers' markets to shake the weathered hands that harvested their lettuce and meet the butcher who personally parsed their recently slaughtered, pesticide-free, grass-fed cut of filet mignon. But coffee is simply impossible to localize—to humanly connect with its source—due to the equatorial climatic requirements of the plant.

Coffee may be close at hand in our daily lives, yet it is colonial and distant in its origins. Along with chocolate and fruits like bananas, mangos, pineapples, and kiwis, coffee is a lifetime member of a family of imperial commodities sourced from tropical colonies, commodities that we've adopted (perhaps kidnapped?) and cherished as our own.

Because coffee is sourced from former colonies, the histories of coffee farmers are largely histories of oppression and injustice. In the face of a legacy of exploitation, the grossest injustice we, as consumers and residents of an imperial power, can commit is to speak for people who can speak for themselves. Even with negligible incomes, without access to clean water,

25

education, and healthcare, the one—and arguably the most invaluable—commodity to which every human still has access is his or her own story. By attempting to peel back the distorting lens that all visitors/observers/consumers from imperial nations inadvertently see and write through, we exercise more equitable storytelling through listening to what people have to say for themselves, rather than putting the stories of others into our own continually privileged and historically controlling words.

Every commodity we consume is itself an amalgamation of nuance and particulars. This collection will offer stories to humanize one of the world's most pervasive commodities: coffee.

Posted May 21, 2012 on whencoffeeespeaks.com

Costa Rica

Costa Rica is known as the "Switzerland of Central America" for its peaceful mentality (no army for 50+ years!) as much as for its verdant mountainscapes reminiscent of the Alps. Costa Ricans call themselves "Ticos" and "Ticas," since they refer to everything with the affectionately diminutive suffix *"-ico,"* as in, "I'll take a piece of cake but give me one that's *chiquitico."*

4.5* million Ticos (equivalent to just over half the population of New York City) live in a land area the size of New Hampshire and Vermont. Costa Rica might have Switzerland as a namesake, but the rolling Tico mountains actually do harken to summertime New England. Costa Rica put itself on North American and European travel radar not for its tranquility, but for its concentration of adventure tourism offerings. The country's best international claims to fame are probably cloud forest zip lining and sloth spotting, followed closely by surfing and toucan tracking.

Costa Rica has eight distinct coffee growing regions, but you could easily miss all of them if you follow the tried and true tourist track, flying smack dab in the middle of the country into the capital of San Jose, then heading straight to find sea turtles on the Caribbean coast, white water rafting a raging mountain river, treking past a volcano, looping over to surf the Pacific, and zipping through the San Jose suburbs (maybe stopping at Hooter's or Outback Steakhouse) on the way back to the airport. Costa Rica has a deeply rutted tourist circuit, but it has a lot going on just two steps off the bruised and beaten path.

Costa Rica draws lots of expats because of its foreigner-friendly tax and business laws and abundance of amenities attractive to retirees and people looking to get away, but not *too* far away. You could very easily spend many happy years in Costa Rica without ever realizing that it has 93,000 hectares of mountain land actively producing coffee.

But produce they do, and every year Costa Rica exports over one million 60kg sacks of washed Arabicas. Planting Robusta has been illegal in Costa Rica for over twenty years, as the country continues to push to make a better and better name for itself with the quality of the coffee it exports. Growing coffee used to be a much more common office for Tico families, but so many foreign companies paying North American and European salaries makes it a less and less frequent career choice.

And yet there are still 52,000 families growing coffee, and they know that they are upholding a legacy that built their country, starting with the first sack exported in the early 1800s. Costa Rica might be a small country, but there are still many Costa Ricas within the nation's modest borders. One of the surest indicators that you've arrived in an agricultural—particularly coffee growing—Costa Rica within Costa Rica is the presence of the "Tico bucket hat." All farmers have their sun-protective style of choice, and Costa Rican farmers overwhelmingly favor a tan/beige shade of floppy-brimmed canvas hat. The casual appearance of the hat is indicative of the calm demeanor that characterizes Tico *agricultores* (people who grow stuff) and specifically caficultores. You can spot a bucket hat half a mile away, and it is always a beacon of joviality; the wearer will always have time for a leisurely conversation. But it's a beacon found only in the mountains and is therefore particular to only some of Costa Rica's Costa Ricas.

Several months after leaving Costa Rica I was talking with a backpacker in Panama, and I mentioned that I'd spent close to five months in Costa Rica. He asked, "Really? Which coast did you do?" I told him neither. I said that I had only been to the beach once, to swim in the Caribbean on Christmas day. He replied, "Wow, so like, where did you go? You never saw the Pacific? You're missing out!"

I'm sure the Pacific coast of Costa Rica is incredible, but the last thing I was thinking of during my five months in Costa Rica was the ocean. I spent my time in the mountains, where coffee lands and lives are exploding with stories before their coffee, packed for export, ever makes it to the sea.

*All country and state populations and land areas presented in the following pages gathered from wikipedia.org

All coffee statistics gleaned from numerous conversations with coffeepeople and information available from ICAFE.

Turrialba

Turrialba is one of Costa Rica's eight distinct coffee growing regions, as identified by ICAFE, the country's national coffee office (referred to as an "Institute," but in the sense that it's institutional, not that it's academic).

The town of Turrialba is at the center of Turrialba Canton, in a lush river valley. The small communities extending up into the mountains around Turrialba rear livestock and produce sugarcane and bananas in addition to coffee. Turrialba is a very rural, agrarian part of Costa Rica, its only small tourist draw being river rafting. Its reputation across the rest of the country is mostly for its incessant rain. In the winter it rains all day, in the summer just in the afternoons.

On the surface Turrialba seems to be an unremarkable town, one filled with lots of little gems but nothing particularly flashy or impressive. Its humble appearance is deceiving. Turrialba, quiet farming town that it is, is also home to one of the most important research institutions in Central America.

Just outside of the town center, past the Walmart-owned superstore (that keeps changing names as Walmart attempts to solidify its Tico identity) but before you get to the turn off for the hydroelectric plant and pass the sugarcane mill, is CATIE (*Centro de Agricultura Tropical de Investigacion y Enseñanza* or The Center for Tropical Agriculture Research and Higher Education.).

CATIE (pronounced ka-TEE-ey) offers Masters and Doctorate degrees in everything from Agroforestry to Agronomy, but it is also home to the largest collection of coffee varietals outside of coffee's native Africa. Thousands of coffee trees of all shapes and sizes create a living library of diverse genetic material, much of which seems hardly kin to the few commercially cultivated varietals.

But I didn't come to Turrialba in search of prized collections. I came here to get my hands dirty on a cow farm. Once I had done that successfully, I felt adequately acclimated to the tropics and dove head first into coffee, both family-scale traditional production and the stuff of world-class science.

Gerardo Jimenez

Recorded Sunday, September 16, 2012, on the Jimenez farm near Esperanza de Turrialba.

Gerardo and I walk through his family's coffee and sugarcane finca. He wears a green baseball cap and black rubber boots.

Gerardo: *I don't usually bring people to show them the coffee. You'll have to tell me whether or not I'm a good guide. I do know a lot because I've worked at the beneficio in Atirro and here. I worked there for like two years. I've done the whole process.*

Look. This is the cherry that you pick, the red one. But it starts out like this: tiny and green. As it ripens it gets red. [Gerardo picks a red cherry off the branch. He pops the seed out from the red skin, known as "pulp." He drops the pulp to the ground.] *That you have to throw away, and this [the seed] you have to dry and then peel. Then you have coffee! And then you have to roast it, of course.*

This is all Caturra. There are some where the cherries ripen to yellow instead of red. These trees are about four years old. When the trees get taller—like the size of those over there—we prune them down to a stump and these little shoots start growing out, like the tree's being reborn again. [He shows me a section of trees where several have been chopped down to stumps and have light green shoots sprouting along the base of their remaining trunks.] *But when they get so old that they don't even sprout shoots, we cut them all the way down and plant new seedlings.*

We have Poró trees planted too because it's good for shade and the leaves are like a fertilizer when they fall around the coffee. We just picked this coffee, but you wait two weeks and then it's ripe again. And then another two weeks and you can pick it another time. It's not producing all year long. It has its harvest time. We sell it to Golden Bean [beneficio]. For example, the coffee we picked today, they'll come get tomorrow. They send a truck up here. They write you a receipt for how many cajuelas you had, and then you take your receipt [to the offices] to get paid. Look, these are getting pretty big. They'll be the next ones we prune. Ah, here's some yellow coffee. It's exactly the same inside as the red cherries. Well, not quite. This one has broca. Look at the little hole she made to get in. And when you dry it and hull it you'll be able to see the little bug inside.

At the beneficio they can separate them because they'll float since they're all dried out inside. Look at the little black dot you can see on the cherry where it went in. You can spray to try to control the broca; you mix the pesticide with water and then spray all the plants, because the broca moves around a lot. When the cherries start growing that's when you spray. At the end of the harvest you have to go around and pick all the cherries—big, small, green—doesn't matter. Then [around six months later] the tree produces a little white flower, and you know the harvest is coming.

Next you'll start to see the little green cherries where the flower falls off, and that's when you spray. But the broca jumps. That's how it gets from one country to another! Right now the broca is the biggest problem. It used to be the roya, which makes all the leaves yellow. You have to spray for that too. You spray for everything. You put the pesticides or herbicides in a backpack pump with a sprayer and go around all the cafetales. [We've been walking as we've been talking, and we stop, facing up a hillside covered with little green coffee seedlings.]

This is the almacigo! The baby coffee trees. First you germinate them in a seedbed. Well, first you let the seeds dry, but you don't hull them. You put them in a seedbed and cover them with some soil. Once they've germinated and they're showing their leaves, you can bring them here, where they look like these [points to the seedlings, just under a foot tall], *and then they'll grow into trees once you move them to the lot that's being planted. This hill is always the almacigo. It's like kindergarten. I think the little guys look good. You can take pictures of them if you want!*

These seedlings will be producing a full harvest within three years. They might produce a couple cherries in two years, but if you fertilize them well, in three years you'll have a good, full harvest. Our land goes to that pasture. [Points down the hill.] *The guy who owns the cafetales on the other side of the pasture has people from Nicaragua pick his coffee. But because most of us are here at home, we do it ourselves. But it depends. Because right now we get paid 3,000 colones per cajuela, and if you hire people to pick you have to pay them 1,000 per cajuela. So if we pick it ourselves we end up with more money.*

That's what producers have to decide: what works for them. We all help pick. If we don't have jobs somewhere else, we'll help. If it were just my dad here all by himself then he would have to pay someone. So, this is the process of coffee. It's not really that interesting.

Rachel: *For me it's interesting; we don't grow any coffee in the [continental] United States. You said you sell to Golden Bean. Is that like a co-op?*

Gerardo: *No, we just sell to them. And then they're the ones who depulp it and hull it and sell it to other countries, so they're the ones who end up with all that money! Because when they pay us they pay us for everything, the weight of the pulp [skin] and all, and you can't sell that pulp, you can only sell the seed. And they pay the costs of all the machines for the mill and everything.*

The sugarcane mill next door to the beneficio is a co-op, and my dad is a member of that. You said that people in the U.S. like to hear that their coffee comes from co-ops, so I'm sure there are lots of places that aren't co-ops that are just saying that they are in order to sell coffee. That's just life; people make their livings off each other.

When I worked at the mill I went out and with the truck that went around to this and that finca to buy [producers'] coffee. [To check the quality] I had to drop a scoop full of coffee cherries into a bucket of water to see how many floated. If more than four cherries floated I had to make a deduction. If they were selling twenty cajuelas I'd deduct one cajuela. The same thing if there were lots of green—beecause they should all be red [ripe].

Even though it was hard to make deductions and tell people that they'd be loosing money, I liked working at the mill. It was a good experience for me. We even got to do the process where you roast little bits of coffee and taste them to determine the good from the bad [cupping]. But to me they all tasted the same—like coffee!

Here in the finca there are maybe twenty hectares. All this—from where you saw Felipe on his moto when you first came in—belongs to my uncle, his dad. He bought it from the owner of a beneficio. And then the rest he bought from the pecaristas* *who sold it to him.*

My uncle is practically a pecarista *himself, he's about to get the land's title. Because when you're on the land for long enough you have a right to it. All this was forest, jungle, and he planted it out. My father's [finca] is from the stream that we crossed up the other side of that hill. I don't even remember how many years we've been here. The previous owner of the finca was a gringo, and he was older. He went to the United States, and so my uncle started planting on his land because there was no one there to watch it.*

And the man realized it, but he died shortly after. So the title is still in his name, but he doesn't have a son and didn't name anyone to claim it, so because my uncle's been using it; he has the right to it as long as he pays the taxes owed. If you don't leave your land to someone who can come take care of it, then someone else will come take it.

Gerardo was determined to show me more than just coffee, which he considered painfully boring and quotidian, and lead me on an impromptu excursion up into the jungle in search of a stunning view. On the way I found out just who those land-snatching someones might be like[Pura Montaña p. 346].

Where does Gerardo's coffee go?
Gerardo sells to the Golden Bean mill, which is owned by the Costa Rican company Coricafe and processes and exports coffee to international roasters. It's possible some of Gerardo's coffee ended up in a bag of coffee on your grocery store shelf.

For a conversation with another coffee producing family, turn to p. 135

For a conversation with someone who works with different varieties of coffee, turn to p. 322

For a conversation with someone who has a very different experience with coffee, turn to the next page.

Pecaristas are essentially jungle land squatters. There's a Costa Rican law which states that if you have made "productive improvements" to piece of land (as in planting a crop or building a house) without the owner of that land noticing and kicking you out or putting up signs telling you to get out and thus indicating that the owner actually knows where the boundaries of his property are, then you have a legal right to that land. Mountain law is that if you don't know where your borders are and mark/protect them accordingly, then someone can swipe your land out from under you. Jungle land rule says, "Use it or lose it."

Elias

Recorded Monday, October 1, 2012, in Elias' office at CATIE.

Elias is known, in international coffee politics and science circles as "the coffee study guy," since his work, a long-term comparative study of coffee production systsms, the result of many sleepless years, brings the two circles together. Elias wears a blue and green striped collared shirt.

Elias: *The study, which is now twelve years in, has allowed us to compare twenty different systems of production and understand what's going on in these different systems. The study is important because it supports all the trainings for technicians and producers. It helps us understand things that weren't clear ten, fifteen years ago. For example, there was a major crisis at the end of the '90s, early 2000s, which generated a major impact. People were looking for alternatives to production because people keep drinking coffee and every year the world demands more and more. But, because of market forces, the producers are the ones who end up most impacted by crises of price. Basically, because of distortions in the market.*

When the warehouses are full of coffee, the ones who are commercializing coffee pay lower prices to producers. But they don't lower prices to consumers. There's a distortion in the market that generates a negative impact for the producer, who's always more and more vulnerable. Nevertheless, coffee is very important, from economic and environmental points of view. The idea is to find holistic alternatives for coffee production.

So we're generating information to help different groups, be it politicians, businesses, the public, to understand how to produce coffee more sustainably, sustainable in economic and environmental terms. So the study, which is the only study of its kind in the world—there aren't similar studies anywhere—has the advantage that we're following the full cycle of production, because in general a coffee plantation has a life cycle of fifteen or twenty years. To see what happens to a plantation over fifteen or twenty years, when it's managed in different ways, is fundamental to be able to support anyone.

These long-term studies are very important. But there are only two in the world. This and one in Nicaragua. So we've taken very good care of this study because it can shed a lot of light. On the other hand, we work with co-ops, national coffee offices, universities, and government agencies so that they can implement different strategies using this information to be able to support producers and better understand sustainable coffee production.

We work in almost all of Central America and even in South America. We're a small team with supporting groups in every country, which is how we're able to share information. Our biggest goals are training and development. We have Masters and Doctorate programs to train qualified personnel who can apply information generated by this project. One important aspect of this academic training is that it's integrally linked to practical reality: projects in the field, contact with producers. When students prepare their theses the students are closely connected to reality.

We often see cases where people want to learn about a reality without living it, and that's very difficult. We've made a major effort to connect the study with academics and academics with practical applications. For example, the talk I'm giving today at the University of Costa Rica, who's one of the members of the project, I'll address the connections between coffee and climate change, which is an important theme. It's important for people to consider both the way climate change affects coffee production and ways that coffee can adapt and respond. We've also been doing important work with co-ops, training producers. We've been developing initiatives in training, technical assistance and strategies for co-ops.

I have a background in forestry, and in the past twelve years we've been working on the possibilities of coffee and agroforestry. We've developed a ton of information and strategies on trees and crop cultivation. But you always have to keep in mind the most fundamental part: human beings. In this sense, the key aspect is that this research gets not just to students at CATIE, but to producers and the general public. Because consumers have a determining role. The more conscious consumers we have, the more force we have in changing urgent situations.

Elias tells me that he could talk for hours about coffee and the study that's basically become his life since he's been conducting it for so many years, but he cuts himself off so that we can make it next door to the UCR in time to give the lecture. Elias and I hop into his truck, parked in front of his one-story office building. To get from CATIE to the UCR you could get back on the main road, or you could weave through CATIE's property to get to the back of the campus. Elias chooses to weave, and we pass groves of palm trees, fruit trees, even towering pines. Elias slows to point out the collection of coffee trees. Some look like black berry bushes and some look like giant firs, with trunks so thick a grown man couldn't wrap his arms around it.

Elias tells me that I can have a chance to walk through the collection if I come back to CATIE next week and tag along on a with a co-op from another region who's touring the CATIE facilities to learn about the work CATIE does. I tell him to count me in. We can see some women picking coffee from the trees in the living collection; they have baskets tied around their waists and scarves wrapped around their head to fend off sun and bugs. Elias comments that the coffee picked at CATIE make the most varied, unique cup of coffee in the world.

When we arrive at the UCR campus (totally open-air style, which baffles my New England-born brain a little bit) I sit with the students, also in one of those tiny college desks, while Elias gives a lecture that briefly addresses the CATIE study and mainly focuses on the role of agroforestry systems in responding to climate change and ways that agriculture, particularly coffee, can neutralize negative contributions and make positive ones. He shows dramatic slides of cow pastures after severe rain storms, where landslide erosion leaves jagged scares of exposed red dirt throught the grassy hillsides, next to pictures of cafetales managed according to agroforestry principles in the same area after the same rainstorm, where the roots of the coffee and the interplanted trees held the soil in firmly in place. Elias talks for hours, exceeding the allotted class time, but the professor and the students sit respectfully until he completes his presentation. If Elias lived in Athens he would have been an orator.

At the end of the three-hour lecture a student came up to Elias and said, "Thank you so much for this presentation. I could have listened for many more hours. My brother is just getting started in coffee, and I want him to start out right."

For a conversation with someone else who practices the practical application of agronomic principles, turn to p. 195

For a conversation with a beneficio owner, turn to the next page.

Jose Cruz

Recorded Thursday, October 3, 2012, at the fincas and mill of
Beneficio Santa Rosa in Turrialba and environs.

Beneficio Santa Rosa owns several of its own fincas where
they grow Caturra and graft Catimor into Robusta rootstock. Jose
gives me a tour of the full wet and dry mill parts of the beneficio,
including the water treatment ponds, the last of which is filled
with lilies, which he tells me are a sign that the water comes out
clean and uncontaminated. We climb back in his car to visit
another yet piece of Santa Rosa's land where the almacigo is.

Sound of weed whacker in the background. We stand
under the black mesh "shade fabric" covering the nursery,
surveying the rows of bagged seedlings. Jose wears a red white
and blue checkered collared shirt.

Jose: *These are a Brazilian variety. Very productive. They're for a new
planting. We have a finca that used to be all cattle, so we'll plant these there
and make it a cafetal again. The idea, Raquel, is—we do this every year—is
to select material and transfer it to the producer, so that the producers have
plants that are every year more productive. So that they have a bigger harvest.*
[Weed whacker gets louder as we walk back to Jose's Toyota
HiLux* truck.]

Rachel: *Out of everything you've done in your twenty-eight years of owning
this company, what was the most challenging?*

Jose: *The biggest challenge, Raquel, was that, when I came here... I had
been working for a German company, and Germans are very energetic and
strict. I had gone as high as I could go in that company. I was the General
Manager of the business and had bought shares. I was a partner of the
company. But I started working for the German when I was seventeen. When
I was thirty I still looked to him like a father, and I didn't know if I was
capable of running my own company. So I left there in order to build my own
company to see if was really able to run my own business.*

*So I came here. He was a partner in this company. And what I had
to show him was that I was in fact capable. That, yes, that was a challenge.
To effectively demonstrate to him that I had what it took to manage a
business. That really was a challenge. And it took ten, fifteen years. Because*

the company was small. And I kept growing and growing it, until it got to be the large company it is today.

I was a challenge to prove to him that I could do it. I started with his company when I was seventeen. I was a messenger. I ran errands and swept the floor. I started as just a messenger, and little by little he gave me opportunities to learn and grow. I liked the coffee business, so I involved myself more and more. He gave me the chance to buy shares in the company, and it was a big company. It doesn't exist any more, but it was a large business, the largest in the country at that time. Grupo La Meseta. They processed 500,000 fanegas of café [ten million cajuelas, or 120 million pounds of fresh picked coffee cherries]. But he went back to Germany. He lives in Hamburg. And today this company is mine. I bought the whole thing. He went back to Germany; I bought all his shares. [He pulls the car to a stop. We get out.]

This is a beautiful farm. It has a river; the Rio Aquiares runs throught it. Very good water. This here is a spring— right in the middle of the finca! This finca belonged to family with a long history in coffee growing. But all the coffee growing families of the country are disappearing. They're evolving to do other things. Younger generations don't like coffee and are involved in other activities. [We get back in the car.]

Rachel: *So would you consider your biggest success to be demonstrating that you were capable of managing a large company?*

Jose: *Well, that was one. But there were other circumstances too. There used to be ten beneficios in this area. Now there are only four. There used to be four big co-ops, and they all failed. To stay alive has been a success. And we started out as one of the smallest. Now 1,200 producers send their coffee here, but they're all small producers. In Turrialba the biggest producers have their own beneficios. Aquiares, Juan Viñas. We receive the coffee from all the small producers. We're probably the biggest producer to feed into our mill, with 4,000 quintales. Here in the beneficio we process 38,000 quintales of coffee a year, more or less.*

The HiLux winds all the way back down the snaking roads into the valley of Turrialba's center. Jose drops me at my hostel, which is right next door to the Santa Rosa offices.

For a conversation with a Panamanian beneficio operator, turn to p. 205

For a conversation with someone else who grew from humble beginnings turn to p. 319

For a conversation with a producer who sells to Santa Rosa, turn to the next page.

*Costa Rican coffee production would not be possible today without Toyota vehicles, most notablly Landcruisers and HiLux trucks. In the U.S. Toyota is probably most often associated with the Corolla and with people who work nine to five and drive their sedan to pick up their kids from ballet. Here, "When I grow up, I'm gonna get myself a Toyota," is the ultimate litte boy's dream of getting himself a hardworking, rugged vehicle that can scale vertical, mud slick roads filled with potholes, hair pin turns, and sheer drop offs.

Coffee hauling used to be the work of mules packing sacks and oxen pulling carts, but today it is the work of Toyotas, some that are shiny and new, and many that are at least thirty years old. There are very few "easy access" cafetales in Central America, and Toyotas have proven to caficultores, generation after generation, that they can handle the rugged finca life.

Gerardo Aguilar

Recorded Monday, September 30, 2012, on the Aguilar's front porch in Guayabo, about thirty minutes up the mountain from Turrialba.

Three tourists who just went for a hike wait for the bus on the Aguilar porch out of the rain. One sits on the floor, back against the yellow wooden panels of the house. Another shares the bench with me. The third sits on the edge, legs dangling down to the packed dirt and fuzzy grass. A soggy dog lies curled on the steps. Several of Gerardo's eleven kids run in and out of the house onto the porch to see what we're doing. Teletica, Costa Rica's one (free to all) channel blares in the background. No one's really watching it. Gerardo wears an off-white button-up shirt with the sleeves cut off and the top three buttons open.

Gerardo: *Well, you can work with agrochemicals, right? And depending on what you're going to plant you can just put in the seeds, little by little. But what you do depends on money. Sometimes you have to do it part by part. It's nice because you can do the work with your family. It's really good to work like that; I love it. We're building a house up on the farm now. Little by little we're changing the land.*

My father and uncle worked here, on this land where the house is now. They worked here, and when they died we kept this in the family, and we still work here a little too (he motioned to the two rows of coffee trees next to the flower gardens and grove of guava and orange trees). The land up on the mountain was prepared carefully. You have to see what works best for the land. So we keep changing.

Rachel: *And it's much different working the farm now, than when you first planted the coffee twenty-two years ago?*

Gerardo: *Of course. Now there are many more conveniences. There's a road. Now there's running water. Before there wasn't. And now vehicles can get there.*

Rachel: *When they couldn't did you have to carry everything down by mule? Did you just, like, tie it on?*

Gerardo*: Obviously. It's different now. Everything's different.*

Recorded Thursday, October 4, 2012, on the Aguilar's farm, two miles up the mountain from their house.

We stand under the tin roof of a three-walled shed. Inside the shed are seeds, coffee-picking baskets and belts, changes of clothes, spare machetes, shovels, sticks, two tires, hammers, rope horse halters, spray cans of pesticides, half-filled bags of fertilizer, big clear plastic bags used as *capas* when it rains (more desirable than a rain coat because you don't sweat under them and you still have all your mobility—none of those heavy, soggy raincoat arms), and anything else that could ever come in handy.

I want to pick coffee. Gerardo wants to show off his farm and give a few coffee lessons before he lets anyone do anything. He motions for me to come over a shelf, where several dirty papers are stuffed under a can of nails.

Gerardo: *[The beneficio] pays by the cajuela. After I empty the cherries into their truck, when I later get to the mill, how do they pay me?*

Rachel: *They give you a receipt, right?* [He pulls one of the dirty papers out from under the can of nails].

Gerardo: *This is a receipt. Have you seen one before? For example, it says the name, Gerardo Alvarez, handed in so much, the number, in cajuelas. And here written out in words. Sixteen cajuelas, three* cuartillos *[quarter of a cajuela]. This is the price they pay us per fanega, which is twenty cajuelas. I go into the office with this and they pay me. If I don't turn in the receipt, they can't pay me. The driver fills in everything; he fills in the date, the name, the place where he picked it up, the amount in numbers, the amount in letters, owner of the farm. The truck will be there this afternoon.*

Raquel: *And you can go to the office any day?*

Gerardo: *Mondays, Wednesday, and Fridays. Yeah, Monday, Wednesday, Friday. Well, it's raining; do you mind getting wet?*

[A few minutes later all but the youngest of Gerardo's eleven kids, and one granddaughter, who had been out picking, come running in out of the rain. They pull dry t-shirts off the clotheslines crisscrossing the beams of the shed, peel off their wet clothes, and hang those on the line as they change into dry shirts.

Sonia, one of Gerardo's daughters, is in charge of lunch, so she opens the backpack and pulls out containers wrapped in layers of plastic bags, followed by a stack of plastic bowls. Her niece runs over to help, and the two of them scoop out portions of rice and beans. By the time we've finished eating the rain has stopped].

Gerardo: *We're gonna send Raquel off to pick coffee! To get rid of a ton of green* [chuckling]. *Raquel, do you know what it means to* raspar *coffee? We also call it "stripping" or "the final strip." We pick coffee for five months here in the Turrialba Canton. After the mill closes in January there are always a few last cherries left. What we pick off the trees after the mills have closed, we call "the strip." You pick all the ripe, half-ripe, and green, everything.*

And here we call it the raspa. *There are people who grab the branch and "raaaa!"* [Makes motion of stripping all cherries off branch]. *It really messes up your fingers. It can be pretty rough on them.*

Rachel: *And you do it to control the broca?*

Gerardo: *Yeah, you make sure there's no fruit left lying around so that there won't be a problem with the little buggers, with broca. These next few months, November and December, are the best for picking coffee. Everything's ripe. It's when things are better for the market, and the picker. The picker makes a lot of money because everything's ripe. Those are the best months. And they're almost here.*

And this [grabbing a yard-long stick stuck upright in the dirt] *this is the famous* estaca. *What does the* estaca *do? It marks the rows we're picking. Raquel, in the big estates there's foreman called the* cortero: *the person who assigns the rows to the pickers. So the* cortero *goes with a stick like this and says, "Alright, Guillermo, these rows are yours," and puts the stick there and no one can pick from his rows. They use this a lot on the big fincas, like Aquiares. Ariel, is there a basket for Raquel? Ariel! Throw me that basket with the belt!*

Sonia [in the distance]: *Make sure she doesn't* chucarear! [to Ariel] *Hey, bring me a basket. You know what* chucarear *means? If you're going* *along picking this row and I'm picking that one, I can't just come over and pick from yours because I see some nice ripe cherries in it. That's* chucarear.

Gerardo: *You can't change rows because everyone has his row. And if I come and start picking from your row you can say, "Gerardo! Don't* chucarear *me! That's* chucarear. *Which one's my basket, Ariel?*

In the background Ariel shouts where the basket is. But before answering his sister's question, he shouts, "Oohh." The "oohh" is part of a language particular to fincas and cafetales. What all sounds to me like the same shout yields very different responses. Sometimes "oohh" means, "Identify yourselves," in which case anyone near by shouts back. This is just to see who's where in the fields. Another "oohh" means, "Come here," and the responder will shout back and then walk to the "oohh"-er. Ariel just used an "oohh" that didn't require an immediate response, one that indicated, "I'm about to tell you something." Sonia then called back a fourth kind of "oohh" to show that she'd heard.

Perhaps even more impressive than the variations of "oohhs" is that fact that you can hear everything perfectly in the cafetal. There is no droning traffic, no humming AC unit, not even a rushing river in the background. Other than the birdcalls and insect buzz, it's pretty much silent. The wind rustling the dried banana leaves against the trunks in the grove below makes an occasional background noise, but if you have a lifetime of practice shouting, you can more than make yourself heard across the finca. The volume of the "oohh" also communicates whom it's meant for. Ana was picking way on the other side of the property. To get in touch with her they'd use the loudest "oohh" they could muster. But Sonia is only five or six rows over from Ariel, so he just gets a moderate "oohh." This is off the grid technology. The coolest thing about it is that it works. Well.

Where does Gerardo's coffee go?

Gerardo sells his coffee to the Santa Rosa mill, and then coffee from Santa Rosa is exported all over the world. There are a few Italian roasters who buy coffee under Santa Rosa's own brand, so if you're vacationing in Tuscany or Rome, your espresso just might be brought to you by Gerardo.

For a conversation with other caficultores who value family, turn to p. 275

For a conversation with a Panamanian coffee grower who's also observed changes over the years, turn to p. 202

For a conversation with someone who works in coffee at the genetic level, turn to the next page.

Karole

Recorded Friday, October 5, 2012, in the hallway leading to CATIE's labs.

Earlier that morning members from the Coopedota cooperative of Santa Maria de Dota had followed Elias de Melo around CATIE's sprawling property to see both the long-term study of twenty types of coffee management and the world class collection of coffee tree varietals. The day ended with a lecture about coffee genetics by one of CATIE's researchers.

I tagged along to all parts of the tour. Coopedota's lead agronomist, Daniel, is a leader in the best sense, in that his enthusiasm and desire to learn and apply new things infects the entire group. The assembled Coopedota members include bothers and sisters, fathers and sons, teenagers, middle-aged women, and a few feisty grandpas. Coffee growers are as diverse as coffee.

Karole, the CATIE researcher, stands ready to give us a short bio lecture. She wears black glasses and a blue and white striped t-shirt.

CATIE Host: *I'd like to present to you Karole, who's a biotechnologist. The development of hybrid coffee plants is being promoted for their productivity, resistance to diseases, and cup quality. She'll tell us a little about how these hybrids are developed and how the contents of the collection you saw today are being used to arrive at new varieties of coffee. Unfortunately, we don't have any seats in this area.*

Daniel: *You're talking to farmers! We're on our feet all day!* [The consensus ended up being that sitting on the floor is just as viable an option. Farmers know to roll with it.]

Karole: *Welcome and thanks for coming. I'm an agronomist and I've been working here for seven years. Right now I'll give you a summary of the work of thirty years of research. Today we have the fruits of this labor. The research was a project started in '90. It was a collaboration between CIRAD, a French research institute, PROMECAFE, the center of all the national coffee offices in Central America, and CATIE.*

This investigation started with the basic objective to increase the pool of genetic material, of varieties of coffee, available. The three sources of material were the commercially used varieties: Caturra and Catuai, wild

varieties: what you saw today in the collection, and developed varieties:
Catimors and Sarchimors. With these three broad groups, traditional cross-
pollination was carried out to generate new material, and a log was kept of
what was crossed with what. It was a five-year process. The result was one
hundred hybrids. When I say "hybrid" I mean the first generation resulting
from the cross.

The next stage was to evaluate the material that had been generated;
from that pool twenty were selected. Next began the process of multiplication.
These materials, as hybrids, are genetically very unstable. This is the F1
generation, the first generation. Everything that will come from this
generation—if we multiply them by seed [germinate]—will be completely
different. It's very probable that from one hundred seeds, at least eighty seeds
will become eighty different plants because of the genetic variability that there
is. So the only alternative to be able to multiply these materials is through
grafting the stalks or through tissue cultivation, which is what we'll see now.

In coffee, stalk grafting is a technique that we've mostly stopped
using, not because it's not viable, but because of its low efficiency on the scale
of commercial production. Now we're 100% focused on techniques using plant
tissue. By seed, it would take about eight generations for the F1s to arrive at
genetic stability. If each generation takes four years to produce, that's thirty-
two years we'd have to wait for producers to have that material via seeds. So
that's where the process of education starts in explaining to producers that
from these hybrid plants, you won't be able to save seeds, rather you'll have to
buy the seedlings.

What we do here is clone plants. All the plants that we end up with
at the end of the process are genetically identical to the mother plant. When I
say "mother plant" I'm referring to the [hybrid] plants that were developed as
a result of the research in the '90s. Every three years we graft the material
into new trees to have young material, but it's the same as what was developed
originally.

The process of tissue culture is entirely contained in the lab. Out in
the field you use soil. What we use is a substitute: this gelatin. [Karole
holds up a test tube half filled with clear gel]. *The gelatin is*
synonymous with soil, but we can't use any organic material because it would
contaminate the environment [the test tube], and it's likely we'd loose the
material [leaf cutting]. So we store the grafted parent plants in a greenhouse
where they're much less contaminated by the sun, rain, dust and everything
you see in a cafetal.

This gelatin is almost identical to soil in that it has micro and macro-nutrients, but in the form of concentrated salts. The nitrogen you see in your fertilizers we have in here too, just at a lab grade purity. Which means that the process is very expensive, and losing a tube of this gel is like throwing out $1 or $2. So we focus on maintaining the aseptic environment; I can assure you there isn't a single fungus, virus or bacteria in this tube.

Karole continues her lecture in the form of biology show-and-tell; for every step she describes in the cloning process, she pulls an example of the tissue culture at that stage from a shelf underneath the table she stands in front of. With every test tube of leaf cuttings, Petri dish of grey undifferentiated cells, and jar of tiny plant embryos she produces, the assembled group scoots forward, like a magnet tugging in metal shavings as the members of the group bunch closer. Finally, when she pulls out a tray of shiny green plantlets that look exactly like the seedlings you'd see in the black bags of any almacigo, everyone jumps to their feet and rushes towards Karole to get a better look, camera phones brandished.

For a conversation with another biotechnologist who works with hybrid cloning, turn to p. 99

For a conversation with an agronomy student, turn to p. 312

For a conversation with a caficultor from Coopedota in attendance, turn to p. 143

For a conversation with a caficultor who's benefited from other CATIE coffee research, turn to the next page.

Jose Fuentes Gamboa

Recorded Saturday, October 6, 2012, on Finca Cañaveral, in Tres Equis outside of Turriabla.

Jose and his wife Flory have a small finca that they have managed organically for over ten years. Today they are a success story and love to invite visitors to see what they do, how they do it, and why they do it. They've worked closely with Elias and the team at CATIE to develop agricultural best practices.

I toured the farm with Elias and his wife, as well as a Peruvian agronomist named Jose Manuel, and a Brazilian agronomist named Marco, both of whom were visiting CATIE for an agroforestry conference. Jose led our eclectic group through the carefully marked paths of his finca. He wears a pressed light green collared shirt and a tan Tico bucket hat, typical of farmers from the Pacific to the Atlantic.

Jose: *We planted this coffee back in '98, when we were working with agrochemicals. At that time this area [of the finca] was a* plantanal *[place where plantains are grown]. And there was a tremendous problem with a bird that was eating the plantains because there were no more guavas.*

In the '80s there were seven beneficios in Turrialba and they bought large quantities of firewood [to burn to dry coffee]. So everyone started cutting down their guava trees to sell as firewood because the mills were paying a good price. And the birds that lived off of guavas had to find something else to eat, so they started eating bananas. They ate my entire harvest of plantains. I realized I couldn't continue with plantains, so I planted coffee.

I also planted beans and tomatoes in the cafetal when the trees were little. And in '99, when we decided not to use agrochemicals anywhere on the farm, it was a young cafetal. The big error we committed—I say "we" referring to my family and I—was that we stopped using agrochemicals out of fear of the risks they represented, but we didn't find out what we had to do to ensure that the finca would keep producing. If you could have seen a photo of this cafetal in 2002—oof. Luckily, a friend gave us a hand and the team working with Don Elias gave us lots of advice.

We learned about how to control diseases, how to fertilize, and how to manage the farm. Now I'm not embarrassed to show it off! We planted lots of shade trees, doing some things differently just because we were curious. We see everyone doing the same things and getting the same results all the time, so we tried to do things differently to see if we could get different results. So we

51

decided to plant Poró, which is typically used for shade. But it doesn't bother us to prune it because it serves as food for the cattle. When we prune the trees we don't call it "pruning," we call it "harvesting cattle feed." We started making changes.

Elias: *In three years the production went from three quintales to eighteen quintales [a year]. After just three years of work. I remember he was worried at the beginning about adding shade because he was afraid it would increase the instance of disease. But he came to the workshops to learn. And he left silent, silent because he didn't like the idea of having to climb a ladder to prune the trees. So he invented a tool to prune with his two feet on the ground. He developed his own style of managing shade.*

Jose: *Here's the tool.* [He holds a 6-foot pole with half a metal disk attached to the end]. *You can see that it's semi circular; half moon. The whole perimeter is sharp so it cuts from above and below. [So you can push up under a branch to cut it halfway from below, and pull down on it from above to lop it off.]*

Elias: *The most important is that by winning second place [in the agricultural innovation contest], he won $200 that he invested in a weed whacker!*

Jose: *Because we had been doing everything by hand with machete. And that gets expensive. But I'm happy I won the prize for this invention, because pruning was the first coffee job I had. I used to work on a large farm until in '93 we were lucky enough to be able to buy this finca. I've worked with coffee since I was a kid. When I was ten I worked with my grandfather, and it was my job to strip off the branches when he pruned the trees to stumps [in order to let them regrow].*

That's when I fell in love with coffee; I've always liked working it. Now, working it without agrochemicals, we've learned different ways to manage coffee that support the environment as well as production. It's satisfying to do things not just for yourself, but for the good of everyone.

Jose shows us the beans he plants as ground cover around the coffee to keep the weeds from growing and his complex system for worm composting. We end back at a little pavilion he built a few years ago, where Flory has set out fresh juices, homemade bread, and of course coffee from the farm.

If you came from Arturo and would like to return to Colombia, turn to p. 268

For a conversation with Jose Manuel, the Peruvian agronomist, turn to p. 90

For a conversation with another long-time Turrialba caficultor, turn to the next page.

Roberto Ortiz

Recorded Monday, October 8, 2012, in one of Roberto's cafetales in Esmeralda outside of Turrialba.

Roberto has taken on the whole process of producing coffee. His day job is working as a grounds keeper at the local high school. He has a few acres of land up in the small town of Esmeralda where he grew up and a little beneficio with a depulper and drying beds he built himself behind his cousin's house. He lives with several family members in a small house in the center of Turrialba, and in the tiny garage where he parks his moto, he has a coffee roaster and grinder he also built himself. The propane-fueled roaster is screwed into a graffiti covered desk he pulled from the high school's trash pile. He calls the final artisan product Café Don Beto coffee, after his father, and sells it for 2000 colones, or $4, in stapled brown paper bags with a sticker logo of his father's face.

Roberto points out different types coffee trees and identifies all the hardwoods he's planted. Sounds of scuffling leaves and squawking birds. He wears a navy polo and a Tico bucket hat.

Roberto: *Some of these trees are thirty, forty years old. Obviously the harvests aren't the most optimal, but they still produce coffee. This land used to belong to a family who lived in San Jose. We all worked on the finca; my father was the manager. Eventually we had the opportunity to buy part of the finca. Between two friends and I we bought a piece of the land and then divided it up into three equal parts.* [We get back in his 1977 blue Toyota Landcruiser ("Chola") and drive to his cousin's house where he built his beneficio. Sound of squwaking chickens and the occasional barking dog in the distance. Radio plays low, melodic ballads of wailing woe.]

This is the chancador *[depulper]. You can operate it by hand, but I attach the motor there. Getting this was hard! I finally found it from a man who was selling off all the machinery from his old beneficio. I got it for 80,000 colones [$160], which is much cheaper than it would be buying it new. This is my very "rustic" beneficio, but it has enough capacity for what I need.* [We continue the tour and pass by a lot where some employees are picking. Roberto introduces me to Carlos and Mario, who make small talk without missing a beat in their

54

lightning-quick cherry-from-tree revmoval. Their hands work so deftly I literally can't see how they're managing to pull only red cherries and leave the green ones on the branch. They also introduce me to Mono, the puppy frolicking underfoot.]

I love the whole process. I'm happy. I like that it's all mine. And I really like when someone tells me, "It's delicious!" My idea is to subsist. And if someone likes the final product, that's even better. Personally, I'm proud that I know something about coffee. There are people, the cuppers, who know too much about the flavors of coffee and ways to prepare it. They can taste it and say, "Oh, this is from this side of Costa Rica or that side of Colombia." Someone told me that in France you can buy a cup of coffee for the same price we're paid per fanega. It seems like the coffee business gets better the farther you get from the cafetal! [We climb back in Chola. I'm sufficiently impressed that she's ten years older than I am and going strong.]

I have ten siblings. Seven sisters, three brothers, and me. Only three have moved away, the rest still live around Turrialba. We used to live up in Esmeralda in a big wooden house; it had eleven bedrooms! Like a hotel! We lived there until...my father died in '71. He died in the cafetal from a heart attack. So in '73 we moved down into Turrialba.

I'm the third youngest. We're all getting old! I have three children. Two are already in their thirties, and the third is twenty-five. My dad was the one who managed everything. When he died we were left in a lurch. But my mother is very wise, and she kept us together. She lived until age ninety-three.

Where does Roberto's coffee go?

Roberto sells to the Juan Viñas beneficio, where his coffee could get shipped to the other side of the world or could remain in Costa Rica. But the coffee he processes himself stays close to home, in the coffee makers of Turrialbeños.

For a conversation with another life-long, innovative caficultor, turn to p. 226

For a conversation with someone else who takes on the whole process from production to sale, turn to p. 233

For a conversation with another Turrialba caficultor, turn to the next page.

Marie

Recorded Wednesday, October 10, 2012, in the cafetales at Finca Monte Claro, not far from the hydroelectric plant outside of Turrialba.

Marie moved to Turrialba from France in order to revitalize her grandfather's largely neglected farm. Her family had owned coffee land in Costa Rica since 1830, when they took their earnings from successful wine production and bought land just outside of San Jose to begin cultivating coffee.

There they managed extensive farms and even had a processing mill bearing their name. Over generations her ancestors gambled away tracts of land and drank away most of the family fortune. Marie's grandfather sold the last of their land in San Jose to a real estate developer building apartment complexes.

Her grandfather took the money from the sale of the land in Central Valley and bought sixty hectares outside of Turrialba. There he cultivated coffee and sugar and had pastures for his horses and cows and even built another small benefico. But over the years the property became neglected, essentially left to its own devices.

Marie arrived to literally dig out the farm. Since the farm had already been without chemicals for so long, she decided to continue with organic management, which demands that soils be free of chemicals for at least three years before there's even potential for any certification.

She restarted the mill as the area's only all-organic beneficio and poured labor and love into revitalizing the farm. But corruption in the local organic co-op lead to the closing of the mill and all but dissolution of the organization. For financial reasons, Marie had to turn one of the plots of coffee into a conventionally managed cafetal, meaning using chemicals in order to ensure she'll have enough harvest to at least break even.

Marie and I traverse the farm on horseback, examining the various cafetales and lots of the finca. Marie wears jeans and a black t-shirt. We pause at the edge of one cafetal where a foreman and workers are picking.

Worker: *Organic coffee should earn growers twice as much as it does because it's much harder to manage. You put in a lot more work, but the harvest is*

*much lower. Because there's less harvest per tree, pickers expect to be paid
more when picking on an organic finca. It's a much more expensive process. If
I'm fertilizing a tree with 4oz of chemical fertilizer I have to apply 2kg of
organic! The volume is huge. And it's more of a long-term process because the
tree absorbs the organic fertilizer more slowly.*

Marie: [waving goodbye to workers] *These are the stars of the farm!*
[Clop clop clop of horse hooves on packed dirt as we continue
riding]. *My grandfather was the first one who came to Turrialba, but in
1830 my first family members came to Costa Rica. They grew their holdings,
built a beneficio and everything. In San Jose it's still called, "Barrio
Tournon," where all our cafetales were. But with all the development in San
Jose, there haven't been farms there for years.*

*If we had more workers we could get more done more quickly! It
depends a lot on the money you have to invest. If you go into one of the organic
cafetales and grab a handful of dirt it smells like forest. The ecosystem is self-
made. For example, the only place we have broca is in the conventional
cafetales. When we sprayed the conventional coffee with beauvaria bassiana
[the fungus used to control broca], a week later it had died from being in such
full sun. When you apply it to the [shaded] organic lots, it stays. And in all
the organic cafetales there's no problem with broca. People told me I'd have
problems with ojo de gallo and everything, but there's very little.*

*There's one cafetal that doesn't get any conventional fertilizer or any
organic because one of the problems that I have is that I don't have enough
people to have time to apply as much fertilizers as I should. But in that cafetal
there's Poró trees, which provide a lot of nitrogen. And most of the coffee there
looks half dead, but the twenty plants around the Poró are green and strong.*

*The other big problem we've had has been this whole mess with the
organic certification. They [the auditors] came to check, and they bothered us
about having registrations and paperwork, all that. Never once did they come
to take a soil analysis. Meaning I could have been applying chemical fertilizer
without telling anyone, and they wouldn't have noticed. I asked them, "Are
you at all concerned with things that really matter?" Checking on traceability
is fine and all, but the most important part is that you actually look at the
soil on my farm, or at least some farms in the Association. Or analyze the
leaves. It's expensive, but, out of thirty producers, at least look at 10% every
year—three farms!* [We arrive back at the stable. The workers there
are repairing support beams and singing along to the upbeat song
playing on the radio.]

I was very surprised to find how preoccupied they [the auditors] were with the paperwork. For example, every person who transports coffee has to have a registration that states that they're responsible for the coffee and that their vehicle is clean and all that. Which is absurd because there was one member who didn't know how to write, so I helped him get the paperwork. But if someone is underhanded they can just lie and there's no way to really check, because [the auditors] didn't actually look at the vehicle. Just see if it's covered in burnt oil; if not you can assume he cleans his truck.

When [the auditors] come to check they review a random selection of member farms. And maybe they tell you that you need to change something, like your living fence isn't wide enough or something. The next year they should at least follow up to see that you made those changes. Or at least require proof that our internal system of control went to follow up. But they don't. They just review another set of random farms. So I was very surprised.

Monte Claro is like an accidental coffee experiment, with varying degrees of human intervention and natural circumstances. It's pretty impressive to see that coffee, a tree native to Africa, can hang on for decades in the Costa Rican mountains, totally untended but still producing cherries.

If you came from Ariela and would like to return to Santa Maria de Dota, turn to p. 147

For a conversation with another organic producer in Turrialba, turn to p. 63

For a conversation with a woman with very different roots in Turrialba, turn to the next page.

Lucy

Recorded Saturday, October 12, 2012, at a fancy cafeteria in downtown Turrialba.

    Lucy and I have just ordered coffee milkshakes with lots of whipped cream and chocolate sauce. Lucy had mentioned that she used to work in coffee but didn't think what she'd done was important enough to bother telling me about. I told her that I would take her out for a "girls' afternoon," and that it would be more of an excuse for an outing and less like an interview. She agreed that she would probably be less nervous about being interviwed if there were chocolate involved.

    Lucy wears large silver earnings and a blouse with a colorful floral pattern.

Rachel: *If you could just explain a little more about what you were telling me before, that you used to wrap the seedlings up in—what kind of leaves was it again?*

Lucy: *Sugarcane. It was called "wrapping up the almacigo." This was like forty years ago. There was a group of men who pulled up all the seedlings that were planted in the ground. It was usually in a fairly flat place, but sometimes on a hillside. So the men pulled up the plants with all the soil clustered around the roots. The men, the Uprooters, were standing in a line. And the Wrappers were sitting on the ground in a row. We'd put a pieces of plastic or sacks over our laps. The Uprooters would pass us the plants, but very quickly.*

Rachel: *Like an assembly line?*

Lucy: *Exactly. So we were sitting on the ground with a bale of [long, thin] sugarcane leaves [from the tops of the stalks] in front of us. We were ready with three crossed leaves laid out on our laps to quickly wrap up the seedling's roots. But at high speed. We had to wrap up the roots well and tie it off at the stalk, so that it'd stay put. You had to make sure it was tied nice and tight, or the dirt around the roots would spill all over the place.* [As she's describing the root wrapping, she's making the motion with her hands, over and over again. Tying invisible sugarcane leaves over invisible seedlings. This is what muscle memory looks like.^{If the Suit Fits p. 351}]

59

At that time I also worked planting the seeds. We called them abejones.* *That's what they called the germinated seed once it had a little stalk. So we'd plant those in big beds, huge beds that were prepared. They'd dig drainage ditches so the beds wouldn't get water logged. That's where we'd plant the* abejoncitos. *After a few months they'd be ready to be wrapped and transplanted.*

First, the owners made the seedbeds [for germination]. They'd sprinkle dried coffee seeds [depulped, but still with the parchment on] into the beds, and they'd cover them with a layer of dirt. After a few months the abejoncitos *would be pushing up through the dirt. Then we'd plant them in the beds, wait for them to grow, uproot them, and wrap them up. I did all of that.*

I also went to pick coffee when I was young. Maybe fourteen. I went with my husband, because I was already married. I got married when I was fourteen. And at fifteen I was working, picking coffee and planting it in the almacigos. *Wrapping the roots, picking more coffee. And I'd even help my husband prepare land to plant the coffee.*

We lived here in Turrialba, but the finca we worked on was in El Alto de Las Barras up on the way to Guayabo in the middle of the mountains. And we'd also stay up there to watch the huge almacigos. *Because if no one was there watching, people would come rob; they'd take the* abejoncitos.

Rachel: *You mean come in at night and rip everything up?*

Lucy: *Exactly. Because a sack full of those* abejones *is expensive. My husband's boss, who has since passed away, owned massive* almacigos *in El Alto de las Barras. He put my husband in charge of taking care of the* almacigos. *And I went with him.*

It was pura montaña. *There was nothing there, just a little shack surrounded by* almacigos. *We couldn't even see another building. Nothing, nothing, nothing. The only thing was that at night you could hear the monkeys. I was still a girl. I was scared, and I'd start to cry.*

We didn't have [running] water. We had to bring it from up by the almacigo. *We'd see snakes. I was very afraid; it would make me cry. It was a very narrow trail between one* almacigo *and another, and one time a snake darted across the path, and it scared me so much that I dropped everything!*

The shack [where we stayed] was basically just a room. It had a bed, and a little two-burner cook stove with a tank of gas. We had pots of water stored. We'd spend the weeks up there, uprooting and wrapping the almacigos, planting, and watching them. On the weekends we'd come down to Turrialba with the owner. We'd buy our groceries and everything. And early Monday morning we'd go back up with the owner and all the workers.

And we'd watch the almacigos again. Because people robbed. They'd even go into the cafetales at night and pick coffee to steal it. And then they'd sell it. That didn't happen all the time, but it happened. Luckily no one ever came into the almacigos while we were there. But sometimes we'd have to spend two weeks up there and work on Sundays. If it was a long way to the truck, we'd have to carry all the wrapped seedlings. And they counted them because we were paid per unit. Both the Wrappers and the Uprooters.

I remember that if the Uprooters were getting ahead and there would start to be seedlings sitting next to you they'd say, "Watch out, or you're gonna get buried!" It was like a competition between them, to see who uprooted more. And who wrapped more. If you uprooted the most you had a solid reputation as a good Uprooter. And if you wrapped the most you were known as a good Wrapper. So there was always a competition between everyone to take the title from whoever had it.

We'd do it during the summer. And it was rough because the sugarcane leaves cut your hands. And if it rains, it rains. If it's sunny, you're in the sun. Now they don't use this system. Now they go around with a machete and jab it into the ground to cut the root [so that it stops growing]. Then they wait a couple weeks and just come and grab them all to transplant. They don't wrap them in anything. It's a totally different system.

Years after that, I went back to picking coffee. I separated from my husband, and I'd go pick coffee, bringing my children with me. They'd sit right down under the coffee trees. We'd just barely get up to the cafetal and they'd already be asking for lunch! [Laughs softly and smiles.] *Some would pick coffee and some would just play under the trees. I say "some" like I have a ton of kids! I only have four.*

Instead of wearing baskets they'd tie little buckets around their waists. It's a very beautiful experience. At Christmas the families would buy chickens, clothes, furniture— all with the money from the harvest. I wasn't a very good picker. The most I picked in a day was fourteen cajuelas. But there were people who'd pick much more.

So, Raquel, I don't really know much about coffee.

Rachel: *I'd say that you do. Like I said earlier, I think you have a lot more stories than you realize.*

61

Lucy: *Oh, I have many more stories. But they have nothing to do with coffee. Well, maybe they do, because I drank coffee every day! I've been drinking coffee every day for forty years.*

Long after the waitress had clared our milkshake glasses, Lucy was still telling stories.

For a conversation with another woman who knows more about coffee than she's willing to admit, turn to p. 283

For a conversation with someone else who works alongside his children, turn to p. 125

For a conversation with a producer who has seen other changes in coffee, turn to the next page.

*The word for a germinated coffee seed that has just sprouted its first pair of leaves differs from place to place but is always illustrative. They're known as *abejones* (bumblebees), *mariposas* (butterflies), or *fosforitos* (little sparks).

Fabio

Recorded Monday, October 15, 2012, in the cafetales around Fabio's home in San Juan de Turrialba.

Fabio grows organic coffee, come hell or high water (and it seems both might be on the horizon). He was a member of APOT, the Turriabla Association of Organic Producers, but the organization is struggling to scrape itself back together from the ashes (roots?) of what it once was. Fabio leads me through the coffee planted closest to his house. He wears brown work boots and a tan Tico bucket hat.

Fabio: *We try to combine coffee with other crops and trees; here we have a bunch of orange trees. That's a Sapota tree, and that's Laurel, a hardwood. These things help us diversify, so that we're not just growing coffee. To give us added value and something to eat!*

Here, we grow organic coffee, which means we need a certification that serves at national and international levels. We work with Ecologica, [a third party auditor that checks against USDA standards], which is recognized in the U.S. and Europe. We grow our coffee with a certain degree of shade in order to protect the environment and for the coffee.

We used to be traditional, but we've been organic for over ten years. It's hard. Growing organic coffee is hard. You have to put in more effort, and the compensation isn't much. But, one does it out of love. There are lots of added values to working organically: the elimination of the use of pesticides, of all kinds of agrochemicals. That's an indirect added value; you have better health. You don't suffer from the consequences of using agrochemicals. It extends to you and your family. [Leaves and branches crunching. We traipse between the plants. Fabio pauses and faces the down the mountain to the town of Turrialba below.]

One of the nice things about Turrialba is that it has panoramic views on all sides! [We continue up the hill, crushing through the increasing overgrown undergrowth.]

With organic coffee, you don't clear out all the weeds. You maintain a layer of growth to protect the soil. I like to plant this kind of guava [pats a tree trunk], *because it generates a lot of leaves, which fall to the ground and help the composition of the soil. Guava is also a good tree for this kind of soil because it fixes nitrogen. It's leguminous, like Poró.*

Most of the coffee is Caturra. There's still a little Catimor here and there, but the majority is Caturra. We prune plant by plant every year at the

63

end of the harvest, in January. We also plant bananas; that's another added value. Every three weeks we can harvest some.

We used to sell to APOT, but because they shut down, now we have to sell it to the beneficio. Which is a shame, because our coffee is organic and there they just mix it with everyone else's. We've tried to find other contacts, but the market in Turrialba is non-existent for organic coffee. So we sell to Santa Rosa; their truck comes right through here. It's the only one left near San Juan. There used to be a guy from Heredia, but I haven't seen him this year. [We pause in front of a hillside that's been partially washed out. Coffee trees are inverted in the dirt, leaning precariously with their roots in the air.]

You remember that one day of heavy rain last week? Well, it caused a landslide. And it took all this coffee with it. It costs a lot to produce organic coffee, and in the end the price is the same. Honestly, it wears down your motivation a little bit, to know that we're not getting any economic advantage from it. It also generates frustration because, for all the work we put in, no one can even enjoy it as organic. Even if we aren't making a lot of money, if the person who bought it could at least recognize it as organic, that would be better.

There are some attempts to continue with the organization, so we'll see if we can reactivate it and continue with the project. In this lot, we're just replanting new coffee. We selected the seeds, planted them, made the almacigo, and now we're transplanting them. You can just buy seedlings, but you either have to pay money or put in the work. We put in the work. [We slowly make our way through the cafetales, and eventually finish making a loop up and around the finca. We return to Fabio's house. I sit on the couch and he sits in a chair. His son is at the kitchen table doing math homework. I can tell it's math homework because he has a calculator on the table and a scowl on his face.]

We hope to get APOT going again. We need to be better about doing our part. The people who are leading the organization get tired, so we have to do our work too. Because you have to work together. One producer alone— no one will listen to you or give you any opportunities. But when you have an organization behind you, that's when you can receive help and support from other sources. Hopefully there's something left in the ashes. Or the roots, let's call them.

Organic coffee is hard. It's much easier to spray herbicides and just go do other work and not have to come back for three months. Clearing manually is much more constant.

Rachel: *Why did you choose to change from conventional to organic?*

Jose: *Indirectly, circumstances bring you to these decisions. Because of how expensive agrochemicals are. Because of how much you invest in those chemicals and the actual yield you see in the harvest. The balance was not in our favor. So we decided to eliminate those chemicals, to stop investing in herbicides, fungicides, pesticides, and fertilizers. But we knew we needed to do something to give the plants nutrients, so we contacted APOT. And they helped us with [management] guidance and all the paperwork, and we started our three years [of required chem-free soil before you can even apply for organic certification].*

Right now we're in the middle of a river, and we don't know if it's better to keep crossing or go back where we came from.

In my opinion, the paperwork is the biggest threat to producer organizations. We're farmers, and not all farmers know how to manage all that paperwork. So often people are doing everything right, everything they should be, but because they don't understand all the paperwork they can't see any benefit from it. Even harder than doing the actual work is getting that paper in your hand that says, "You're organic." You need someone more trained to help you deal with that aspect.

But around the world people want to buy more and more organic products because they see how dangerous agrochemicals are to their health. The hard thing is that there's not much compensation in it for the people who are growing these things in our very own land. To think how much a cup of coffee costs in the U.S. or in Europe—"The Europes," my grandparents used to say- it's incredible. And we don't see any of that. You cry out but no one hears. So we're stuck with trying to find someone to help us do paperwork with the hope that that will let us earn a little bit more.

We're not asking for handouts, but the ones who carry most of the load are the ones with the soil, the ones on the bottom. And we're in a bad spot. Because you can have a finca, have the coffee, but not have any way of making money off it. It's hard, but we have hope. You have to keep fighting, to take care of your children.

Wise people say, "In the midst of crisis comes opportunity." We hope for that opportunity, whether it shows up in the short term or the long term. And we can see that international politics are leaning in favor of organics. People are loosing trust in the companies who make agrochemicals. Every day it's more evident that they're harmful. They end up producing cancer, things that affect people's health. The whole agricultural machine that says, "Spray! Apply!" is, little by little, slowing down. Because people are realizing that it's dangerous and that the chemicals are harmful.

Fabio looks tired. He offers me a cup of coffee while I wait for the bus.

If you came from Marie and woul like to visit downtown Turrialba, turn to p. 59

For a conversation with another organic grower, turn to p. 217

For a conversation with someone who sells agrochemicals, turn to p. 330

To continue to another part of Costa Rica, turn to the next page.

Santiago de Puriscal

Puriscal, known locally as "Puris," is even farther off the tourist track than Turrialba. In between San Jose (in Costa Rica all roads lead to San Jose; you can't get from one major city to another without passing through the capital) and the Pacific coast, Puriscal is the perfect small town. Most of its residents either work in the town itself or make the daily hour-ish commute to San Jose (the bus is under $2 each way).

There isn't nearly as much coffee in the area as there used to be, but there are still plenty of small producers tucked into the hills around Puriscal. And Puris is pure hills, but the hills mean pure views and sweeping mountain vistas. Every bend and dip in the road reveals yet another panorama of lush, rolling mountains. Many fincas have cattle, and the green hillsides are dotted with white cows grazing lazily. This is what grass-fed looks like.

For all its lazy cows, Puriscal's most recognized cuisine is its *chicharrones*, fried pork chunks. There is no shortage of roadside restaurants with open-air balconies facing beautiful views and serving up heaping platters of succulent *chicharrones* and stewed yucca.

Puriscal is also one of the best illustrations of Tico family values. I visited several farms in the area, I but never managed to corner anyone with my voice recorder because people were too busy serving me overflowing platters of platanos, thick slices of birthday cake, brimming cups of coffee, and inviting me to swim in the river, feed the parrots, walk the dogs, and color with the grandchildren.

They wanted to hold me in the status of guest and then seamlessly transition me to family friend and then family member, somehow subverting all my plans to ever put on my journalist hat. *Ud. es periodista, pero con nosotros eres familia.*

Puriscal showed me why small two-hectare family coffee farms can in fact be a viable business model, even in the age of extensive estates and exporter-owned beneficios: when people like their family members and respect the importance of family they can actually get work done together. A lot of work. Work that on paper might seem impossible.

Rodolfo

Recorded Thursday, October 18, 2012, at Beneficio Palmichal.

Benefico Palmichal is a wet mill, dry mill, and coffee roaster all in one. It is a standard Costan Rican beneficio, where producers sell their fruit as ripe cherries and the mill churns them through massive mechanized depulpers, sorting machines, and dryers. Rodolfo is the general manager of the mill, which is operated by the Costa Rican company Ceca and owned by the German coffee trading company Neumann Kaffee Gruppe.

I sit across from Rodolfo at the desk in his office. As he starts to talk he gets up to point to what he's describing. He wears a navy windbreaker.

Rodolfo: *This is a reconstruction of what the coffee harvest is like.* [Gestures to the mural covering two walls of his office. The other two walls are glass, one looking out to the receiving area where trucks full of coffee pull up, the other facing the mill's machinery: a maze of gears and conveyer belts that spit out sticky, depulped coffee beans.] *The families go out into the cafetales to harvest, and they're always accompanied by dogs. They bring their lunch to eat there. It's all the culture of picking coffee. Generally, here it's done by families. Mom, dad, and kids. Some are picking, some are carrying sacks of cherries, because you have to haul them to a central point for the medida. Others are sorting, to separate the green cherries. That's what people do here in the cafetales. You start at five years old.*

You asked me how I started in coffee. I'll tell that my whole life is coffee. First, starting at seven years old, I went to the cafetales to pick coffee. I was able to go to school thanks to the coffee harvest. When school was out, I'd spend the two months off, December and January, picking coffee to save money to keep studying. And that's how it is with all the families around here. Coffee is a difficult crop to cultivate, one with many processes. There are lots of hands involved so that you can drink a cup of coffee in the United States. It passes through so many hands!

It starts with the selection of a seed, in order to germinate a coffee tree. After selecting the seed, you make an almacigo. After the almacigo, you plant the tree and let it grow for three years until it starts to produce coffee. Then you have to harvest it and bring it to a point of purchase. Here in Costa Rica there are many; we're one of them. The coffee arrives here in cherries, then it passes through the whole process here. [He gestures to the glass.]

You have to depulp it, you have to dry it, you have to store it, you have to hull it—all to be able to export it.

And once it's passed through that whole process, it goes through the roasting process. And that's the final product, once it's roasted and sold.

I've been working in coffee for twenty-seven years. My life has revolved entirely around coffee since I was nineteen.

You've seen the receiver buildings, right? Do you know about the boletos? *They were like a form of currency that producers were paid in when they delivered coffee to a receiver. Every beneficio has their points of purchase, so every beneficio had their own* boletos. *Now, at the receivers the producers get a receipt when they drop off their coffee. We're regulated; by law we have to do it. In our case, a lot of producers come right to the beneficio, because we're located in a place where a lot of producers live close by. And then we also have our truck that goes around and collects coffee from all the receivers.*

Rachel: *But the coffee can't spend much time in the cherries, right?*

Rodolfo: *Right. The receivers open at noon and close at five in the afternoon every day. And sometimes the trucks will still be arriving here at midnight, 1am, depending on the distance [they have to travel in their collection routes.]*

Rachel: *What was the first job you had in coffee?*

Rodolfo: *I've done everything. From planting coffee onward; I've worked in all parts of the process. The process here in Costa Rica yields very good coffee. Very clean. Palmichal only has one finca of its own, but it's big. It produces 5,000 fanegas. But the majority comes from producers with small fincas.*

Rachel: *Of all the things you've done, what was the biggest challenge you encountered?*

Rodolfo: *Well, to answer that I'll speak as a producer, because I'm also a producer. It's difficult. Very difficult. Because what a producer receives is very little. In the chain of coffee, most of the money is at the top. And the ones who produce are the ones who receive the least. It's very hard. It costs them a lot of money and effort to produce, and the pay is very little. That's the most difficult part.*

I've been on all sides, because I've produced and I've worked. Working has allowed me to have a different quality of life, because I'm here as a part of a [giant transnational] company. But the most difficult is this: in the business of coffee, the most difficult is that the profits stay in a sector that doesn't understand what it takes to produce. That's the cruelest part, I'd say. It's not well distributed. More money should make it to the producers. Because if not, we're going to kill the hen who's laying the golden eggs.

That's the most difficult part. But it's great working with coffee; it's a beautiful thing. Drinking a cup of coffee is such a luxury. It's six in the morning, it's raining, but you go out to the cafetal. You go. You have to earn your living. You go pick the coffee, even though it's raining. That's hard too. The value is poorly distributed.

It'd be interesting to do an analysis to see how much a fanega of coffee is worth in cups of coffee. Because a fanega of coffee [20 cubic meters, roughly 250kg of coffee cherries], yields 36 kilos [79lbs] of ground, roasted coffee. I know because I also roast it.* A cup of coffee needs about 10 grams of grounds. So you could figure it out.**

Right now, we're changing out a bunch of machinery to newer models. We also just got a new oven [to heat air to blow into mechanical coffee dryers], so switching that out in the middle of the harvest has been a little crazy.

Rodolfo explains that it's been so crazy that he really must go check and make sure everything is running smoothly with the transition. He excuses himself.

Where does Rodolfo's coffee go?

Some of it goes into Café Yodito and Café Economico brands to line Costa Rican grocery store shelves. Because Neumann owns the mill, most of the exportable coffee gets traded along with coffee from other origins around the world. Neumann sells significant volumes to Starbucks, and Starbucks loves Costa Rican coffee; maybe some of the beans for your Pumpkin Spice Latte came from Palmichal.

If you came from Orlando and would like to return to Panama, turn to p. 207

For a conversation with a different kind of beneficio operator, turn to p. 129

For a conversation with someone in a place where the system of processing is very different, turn to p. 288

For a conversation with someone else who feels the impact of inadequate price distribution, turn to the next page.

*In addition to wet milling (depulping) and dry milling (hulling) coffee to export as part of the Neumann Kaffee Gruppe international coffee commodity trading behemoth, Palmichal also roasts, grinds, and packages coffee to sell in grocery stores around Costa Rica. They sell pure coffee, but they also sell coffee that comes mixed with sugar. At one point most—if not all—coffee in Costa Rica was sold that way, in order to mask the bitter taste that comes from only using leftover, defect-filled beans that didn't make the grade for export. New domestic brands aimed at improving quality proudly claim, in boldface type, that their coffees are, "100% PURE COFFEE! NO SUGAR ADDED!" But Palmichal is pumping out grocery grade, and there are still plenty of Costa Ricans who want coffee to taste like it always has, burnt sugar and all.

**36kg are 3,600g, or 360 10g cups. If every cup gets sold for $2, that fanega is worth $720. And producers get paid around $100, on a good day, for a fanega of coffee. But, dividing up coffee costs/payout is a little bit trickier than linear calculations like this. See "Worth," p. 393.

Ronulfo

Recorded Friday, October 26, 2012, in the mountains outside Puriscal.

 Ronulfo and I are seated on the porch of one of the houses he's leading construction on. The owners are Canadian. Ronulfo wears a yellow baseball cap.

Ronulfo: *Right now we're in the process of harvesting coffee; which I'd say is the most complicated part. Which is not to say that it's not an involved process during the rest of the year, because you have to work all year long to be able to get to the point where we are now, where you have something to harvest. But I'd still say this part is the most complicated. Why? Because coffee is always harvested at this time of year, in the rainy season. You know, you saw the rain last night. This year, strangely, has been very dry. Although you wouldn't think it! What happens when it rains is that the cherries get very soft. And if it rains for three or four days in a row, which is very common when hurricanes pass through the Caribbean, by Cuba and Haiti, this coffee gets soft and falls off the trees.*

 Why? People in Costa Rica are going to work and going to school; there aren't many coffee pickers. Because picking coffee you get paid for two months of the year and then you don't make money. A finca always has some full-time workers, but not the number you need for the harvest. So people prefer to work and have a stable income all year long rather than wait for one time of year where you might earn more. The same thing is happening with the families. It used to be that families planted coffee and harvested it themselves. But now coffee alone isn't enough to sustain a family, so the kids go to school, high school, college, and get jobs. Or they just go get jobs. So it's hard now for us to find people to pick coffee. Especially when it's raining!

 Right now people are paying 1500 colones ($3) per cajuela. This means- we sell coffee per fanega, a fanega is twenty cajuelas—this means that we, the producers, right now are paying 30,000 per fanega just for harvesting. Right now the mills that buy the coffee are advancing 40,000 colones per fanega. This is how coffee is sold. You turn in the coffee, they pay you part of the money. And during the year they pay you one thousand, five thousand colones more so you can keep working, keep taking care of the coffee.

Rachel: *So this is after they sell it, then they finish paying you once they know the final sale price?*

73

Ronulfo: *Correct. There are laws in Costa Rica—I'm sure you know about ICAFE. There's a certain quantity that they have to pay you. One quantity, by law, has to stay in Costa Rica [1% of export quality coffee must remain in the country for domestic consumption.]*

In the Puriscal area we've had problems with mills that bought coffee from us, because we never had, how do you say it, a co-op or a anything that said, "Ok, we're going to collect all the coffee from the producers in Puriscal; we're going to process it, and we're going to export it." There wasn't this initiative, this union, so mills from outside the area came in to buy the coffee. But these people came and offered to the grower, "You sell me your coffee and I'll give you so much money," but at the end they never did.

The prices were always low, until four years ago, until an association, from here in Piedades, precisely, it was a group of five people, they made an association and asked a co-op, Coopeatenas, to be members. Now in the Puriscal area there are like seven Coopeatenas receivers. And to turn coffee in to them there are two options; you can be a normal seller or a member. From the member, obviously, they'll take a percentage and put it in your account, and you have other benefits. You have the benefits of supermarket, gas station. But the problem is that those are located in Atenas. For us right now it's not very useful because it's far away. But the time will come when they make investments in Puriscal that will benefit us directly.

The best for the growers in the area that's happened with the co-op is that they stabilized the prices of the other outside mills. Because the co-op said, "This is the real price of coffee," not the lies the other mills were telling. So when they stabilized the price, the other mills, to be able to compete with Coopeatenas, they raised their prices too.

The prices are so low because of speculation; they're expecting a huge harvest in Brazil. And if that harvest is like they say it'll be, they'll supply the entire world with coffee! With so much supply the demand will obviously decrease. Which is lucky for them, but right now we're suffering through it.

100,000 colones per fanega would be profitable for us. But because the prices don't stay at that level, I've had to find work elsewhere. I work with foreigners [supervising construction]. I have the ability to speak a little English, and they know me and I seem like a person who can help them. For me it's more profitable to come and work for them than continue to work in coffee. I'm always still involved, because when I have free time I go to the finca, Saturdays—for example, tomorrow I'll be on the farm. But we now have look for other horizons because it just isn't sufficient.

74

The point that we've always wanted to make, and I think it's an important one for your book, is to differentiate* our kind of coffee. We have a very, very, very high quality coffee. The coffee from Coopeatenas goes to Switzerland and Europe mostly. We don't have the blessing to have our best coffee here in the country, but we still have very good coffee.

What do we need in Costa Rica? To be proud of our coffee and get the right price for it. It doesn't' matter to us if there's lots of coffee in Brazil or not. You're buying Costa Rican coffee, not coffee from Brazil.

Right now we have about twenty-five hectares of coffee. About fourteen or fifteen years ago we didn't have that many hectares planted with coffee because we planted tobacco too, but when tobacco disappeared, because it's cheaper to produce in other places because of the cost of labor and all that, we started working with just coffee.

People like to say, "Look, coffee! How nice," but they don't know all the work that went into it. I think what you're doing is important so that people can see what's behind their coffee. Because a coffee plant is beautiful, and you see someone there up in the cafetal picking the cherries and that's beautiful too; it's something really stunning. But to be out there every day doing it is very difficult.

For example, in our property—gracias a Dios there's never been an accident—there's a type of snake called the oropel *that wraps itself around the trunk of the coffee tree. She's very poisonous, but at least she's not aggressive. They're nocturnal, but if you bother her… One time I was picking coffee and I had just gotten all the cherries off a tree. When the tree is full of cherries you just put your basket right in the trees to be able to pick with both hands. So I was right up in the tree, picking coffee. I went onto the next tree, but as I turned I realized I'd missed three little cherries. I went to grab them and there was the snake—ready. So I jumped back! But I had bothered her enough to make her ready to strike.*

But coffee teaches you how to fight, to work for your goals. You're fighting for your dreams, so are we. We're fighting for our families, to be able to move forward. People from Puriscal, or people from any rural places, when we go to work at professional companies we're very successful. Why? Because we've already seen this [he gestures to mountains]. *We've spent our entire lives working at something that's very difficult and doesn't generate much and then we get to a job where we have to do less physical work and just exert a little bit of mental effort, so we're successful. Hopefully we don't loose that ethic.*

75

My sister's husband was asking me the other day, "What's going to happen when your father dies? What's going to happen to the cafetales?" My father is seventy years old. My brother in law is a high school teacher, my other brother in law is an electrician, I work here; what will happen when my father passes? Because it's not profitable to continue with his business of coffee. We all have our other jobs, and we're not going to quit them for coffee because coffee won't give you the same stability.

Ronulfo also mentioned that coffee is his second joy in life, second only to the joy of raising his eight-year old daughter.

Where does Ronulfo's coffee go?

Coopeatenas does sell to Switzerland and Europe, but it also sells to Starbucks, illycafe, and Green Mountain, so Ronulfo's coffee could also be any where in the US from coast to coast. Maybe it's in the Green Mountain coffee at a gas station in Pennsylvania, or maybe it's in the illycafe espresso served at a schmancy restaurant in downtown L.A.

For a conversation with the president of Coopeatenas, the mill Ronulfo sells to, turn to p. 87

For a conversation with another jack of all trades, turn to p. 283

To continue to La Potenciana mountains, turn to the next page.

*Coffee that's traded on the commodity market is subject to regional differentials, so Arabica coffee from Costa Rica and Brazil will not fetch the same price. However, the principle of commodity markets is that they look at supply and demand on a global scale, so the amount of coffee in Brazil directly affects the market price, which then directly affects the base price to which differentials are applied. But producers are paid according to the overall coffee "C" market price at the time of sale, without any regional differentials being factored into their payout. So regardless of what's happening on Ronulfo's farm, in his area, or even in his country, he is always paid according to a price determined by the overall stocks of coffee available worldwide pitted against the overall international demand for coffee by major roasters.

La Potenciana

The Potenciana mountains are vertical tracts of land where something special brews. The communities that live in these mountains are small, even by rural Latin American standards. The closest real town is Puriscal, and it is anything but close. Much of Costa Rica's natural wonders and mystery have been plundered by zip-liners and sloth-spotters. Plundering is not necessarily a physical exercise; the overpresence of people, both local and foreign, can somehow sop up the dripping soul of a place, absorbing the mystery and leaving nothing but the quantifiable.

Potenciana's soul is still wet. The community highest up the mountain, the community of Potenciana itself, is a collection of a few families, but there is still enough mystery left in the red soil and spiraling mists that the sum of the place is greater than its parts. Here, the qualitative still reigns.

I'd read Tim O'Brien's accounts of Vietnam and Gabriel García Márquez's tales of Colombia, but I'd never really understood how a place itself can be as malleable as thought. I don't think it's possible to understand the way tropical mountains can bend reality until you actually stand in the middle of them, trying to catch the clouds in the act of transforming an infinite clear sky into a suffocatingly oppressive rug. Droplets of water somehow become greater than the sum of themselves; their absence can convince you that the Pacific is only a stone's throw away, while their presence can take you underwater to the depths of some humid cave on the ocean floor.

The magic of the place is qualitative, but the coffee the Potenciana offers up is very quantifiable. The one farm I visited in the Potenciana had one-year-old trees bearing full harvest, as though something deep in the bright orange soil had bent time in favor of the young plants. The rows of squat trees seemed to whisper, "There are still some things you don't know." Science lays a heavy hand on coffee production, but when you drop science into places that are still infused with so much of their own natural chemistry, the outcomes are often inexplicable.

There are still a few places left on earth to remind us that everything is not as straightforward as we might want it to be.

Luis Angel

Recorded Tuesday, October 30, 2012, at the Orlich receiver in Potenciana.

Luis Angel works for Potenciana Café, a coffee finca owned by Mike and Bill, two valiant gringos who poured their financial and emotional resources into resurrecting a left-for-dead finca in the middle of the mysterious Potenciana Mountains. Along the way they converted themselves (or the potent Potenciana fog converted them?) into community revitalizers providing employment that is drawing locals back to their roots rather than pushing them into other lines of work in other places.

Sounds of river water. Bird calls. Luis and I are seated in the shade at the intersection of two roads, one dirt and one paved. The dirt one heads over a recently constructed and somewhat scary—even for Costa Rica—bridge and straight up the mountain to Potenciana. The paved road heads through a tiny cluster of buildings then also up the mountain to Potenciana by a slightly less vertical route.

Luis and I had ridden down the mountain with Walter and a truck full of coffee. Walter, one of Potenciana Café's most energetic employees, had dropped the sacks of coffee at the receiver and then continued into a nearby town to go pick up some pickers that he'd been tipped off about through the finca manager grapevine.

The only receiver in the area belongs to FJ Orlich, a formerly Costa Rican company that is currently a subsidiary of ECOM, the Swiss commodity trading giant. The employee manning the receiver knows every farmer who drops coffee there, and he chats with Luis as they measure out the day's fanegas, going through the medida process to generate the official receipt. Once that's done, Luis and I have nothing to do but sit in the shade but wait for Walter to come back with the new employees.

We find a few rocks to sit on. Luis wears a black back support belt around his waist. (Mike and Bill gave them to all the guys who do any sort of lifting. They said it took them a year to get the men to get over their vanity and actually wear them.) It makes me think of the men in the lumber aisle at Home Depot.

Luis: *What is Potenciana? Well, years ago it was just mountain. Forty-seven years ago, which is how old I am, when my dad came, it was just mountain. There was barely the cleared area for the houses and the ranchos [roof-only barns without walls]. And the rest was mountain on all sides.*

They say that there were still [mountain] lions and tigers [cougars] here then. And over time people cleared the land for working, you know, and there were less. Some people say everyone killed them all, some people say they just left.

They say that all this [gestures to the paved and dirt roads we're sitting at the intersection of] *was just oxcart paths back when everyone had oxen. People used to come from Potenciana to San Pedro with their carts full of crops, beans, corn, everything. All the way to San Pedro- to the stream. The train used to pass there, so they loaded everything onto the train to San Jose.*

Sometimes they would go on horseback to San Pedro. Or where we just were, that turn off we passed on the right, that goes to La Palma, Puriscal. I know the way; I've been taking these routes my whole life. Two, three hours on horseback. Then we'd tie up the horses and take the bus to Puriscal. The same thing on the way back. There was a guy who rented space for us to leave the horses, so they'd be there waiting for us, and then we'd take them home.

About six or eight years ago people started using cars here. Because before the bus would just drop you here, and the only way you could only leave or get to La Potenciana was by horse.

So we're all always saving, little by little, making the effort to be able to have our own cars.

And when they [Mike and Bill] came and bought the finca there— well, we've practically all our lives, lived here. I was born in Barbacoas, and then I've lived my whole life here, in La Potenciana.

And we used to work for the guy who just passed away, from the big house. He was the owner of the farm that they have now, of Mike's house; that was his farm. When the former owner had the farm he had it all as pasture. He had cows, so we worked for him, most of the time. Me specifically; I worked for him almost all the time. I would clear the pastures with machete. And then he planted a little bit of coffee, so we helped him with that.

When he didn't have work for us we went and helped other people. Those farms you passed on your way in, where they have the equipment to build their road, we went all the way down there for work.

And when they bought the farm, and planted more coffee, we started working for them all the time. About five years now. Practically since they bought the finca up there, I've been working for them. Like I told you yesterday, that coffee that's just starting to produce its first harvest, we planted that. I think they might have gotten it from Turrialba, but I don't remember.

You saw what we planted this year, and a few years ago we made an almacigo and everything—right by the bodega [storage shed], and then we had to drag it all the way down to where we planted it. And that coffee is now producing and everything. Right where we planted it!

I was telling Barbara [Café Potenciana's legal counsel], when we were in Sarchí and saw they have coffees that are from there, the almacigos are made there and the coffee is planted right there and harvested there, and they call it "café de Sarchí," so I was telling her that this should be called, "café de Potenciana," Potenciana coffee! Germinated right here, grown here; they should put the name Potenciana coffee on it!

Rachel: *I think that's what Mike and Bill want to do; buy the machinery necessary to build a beneficio—*

Luis Angel: *They already have a depulper—you didn't see it in the bodega? I'll show you when we get back up. Next year they might get the depulper up and running to process the coffee right there, themselves.*

They told us, a month or so ago, that they only want us to pick fully ripe coffee. But we told them, "The mill will pay you the same for the ripe coffee and the partially ripe coffee you bring to the receiver. They'll pay you the same price for cherries that are between green and red and ones that are all red. They get the same price."

I turned in the first fanegas of the harvest here [motions to receiver] only ripe red, because that was what they asked us to. And if that's how you want us to sell them, well, that's how we'll sell them. But the second time [Barbara's husband] Alex [master troubleshooter] was here we told him, "Look. If you want, we'll only turn in ripe cherries. But they're going to pay YOU the same for ripe coffee and under ripe coffee." So what profit are you going to get? You're not going to get any more profit.

It's fine when they want to depulp it themselves and make a beneficio up there, because they'll be the ones processing it right there. So then we can only pick ripe coffee, because they'll be processing it themselves. But to bring these guys all ripe coffee, here [at the receiver], for no extra profit, doesn't make any sense.

The profit is when they're processing it right there. I told everyone that I'd talk to them and see what they think. Look; from much experience, if you're just picking fully ripe coffee, a week later the almost ripe coffee is ready to be picked. You have to go back again; the cafetal is big. And there are almost fifty thousand coffee trees. Fifty thousand coffee trees, with the few of us that there are. Today, thankfully, there were a bunch of people picking, but the few workers there are, the six of us who work full time, to be able to pick all that coffee, we can't do it. We'd never be able to just pick ripe coffee.

As soon as we finished one lot it would be ripe all over again. It wouldn't give us time to make it through the whole cafetal. So it's hard. So we told them, that if we pick the almost ripe and the ripe, we'll have more time to cover the whole cafetal, and then the coffee that was completely green will be ready where we started.

But the vision they had was to only sell completely ripe coffee. But we told them that, supposedly, they're being paid 40,000 [$80] a fanega. They'll pay you the same for completely ripe or partially ripe. So we'll see.

Barbara was telling us that we should pick coffee that's only the color of your nails. [My nail are painted bright red, because three days before I had dressed up as Snow White for Halloween. It was true that Mike and Bill had told the guys to pick coffee the color of my nails. When they noticed that I had my nails painted, on a visit to a remote coffee farm, they joked, "What, is that so you don't forget what color cherries to pick?" Then they looked at each other and said, "Hey now, that's not a bad idea. Maybe we should require all the pickers to have a "reference nail" painted on each hand so there's no confusion about what we mean when we say, 'Pick only ripe cherries.' Do you have any more nail polish with you?" I didn't, but my nails were solidified as part of the "pick red cherries" discussion].

She told us, "This is how you have to pick it." And we'll pick it like that, but it will be bad for them. Because if they're going to only turn in ripe cherries and be paid better for it, it's fine. But they'll be paid the same. They won't make any more profit. So we've been telling them, "When you have your chancador in Potenciana, you'll be able to enjoy the advantages of having only ripe cherries." They'll depulp the coffee themselves and it will have a better flavor. And they won't be giving profit to someone else; they'll be the ones with the profit. So maybe next year that's what'll happen. Nunca se sabe. [Pause. Sounds of river water and mountain birds.]

And the story of Potenciana, supposedly, they say there was a couple, recently married, who was on their way up to what is now Potenciana. And the bride was named Ana. They were coming up, but she didn't think she would make it; she was tired. And so he kept telling her, "Potencia, Ana," "strength, Ana." And so that's where the name comes from. Potenciana.

After about forty-five minutes Walter comes back, with two young guys standing up in the bed of the truck, and a mom, dad, and daughter (who was probably my age? Guessing ages is much trickier without any of the identifiers you're used to using in your own culture) squeezed into the back seat of the truck. The daughter's husband sat in the front seat and jumped out to offer it to me. He and Luis hopped in the bed with the boys and we started the vertical ascent up the mountain. I ask Walter more about the area. He's wearing a yellow t-shirt and one of the back support belts.

Walter: *Well here, since '85, '90 there's been coffee. Practically all my life there's been coffee planted from here down the mountain. There's always been fields for cattle too, but definitely since '90 there's been coffee.*

He passes someone he knows and calls "oohh" out the window. I turn around and see the wide-eyed faces of the mother and daughter seated behind me. I tell them not to worry, that even though it's ridiculously steep, Walter's a good driver. The daughter tells me it's totally flat where they come from in Nicaragua.

They're clutching bags on their laps. I think, "Wow, it must be absolutely terrifying to be sitting in a truck with people you don't know, heading up a slick mud road further into nowhere, with no idea who or what is at the end. They probably have a good portion of their belongings with them. It must be really unnerving to have to go that deep into the unknown in order to work to survive."

And then I think about what I did yesterday. I got into a truck with people I didn't know and headed up into the mountains on a vertical road that plunged into nowhere. I had a bag that didn't necessarily contain the majority of my belongings in the world, but did contain the majority of the belongings I had to my name to survive the year. I had done it as a choice, and I wasn't going to live on this mountain for an entire harvest season, but heading face first into the unknown and just hoping/praying/trusting that wherever you're going will be someplace you can survive, and maybe even like, is a feeling that doesn't discriminate.

Where does La Potenciana's coffee go?
  Potenciana Café currently sells to an Orlich operated beneficio, which is owned by ECOM Agroinustrial. ECOM sells to major international roasters (think the scale of Kraft), who produce varying grades of commercial coffee. Soon Potenciana Café will be sending their coffee more places, more directly.

For a conversation with someone else who lives in mountains swirling with mystery, turn to p. 243

For a conversation with a scientist who works for an "arm" of ECOM, the trader buying the coffee Luis Angel helps produce, turn to p. 99

For a conversation with a Colombian finca employee, turn to p. 327

To continue to an industry conference in San Jose, turn to the next page.

24th
International
ASIC
Conference

ASIC is the Association for Science and Information on Coffee, and they represent an academic and investigative catchall for anything you could ever study about coffee. If you only know coffee as the stuff in your cup that you sip as you drag daily spam into the trash folder, then it might not seem like it merits a particular amount of scientific attention. But coffee is a crop and it's a food, and science (quite a lot of science) goes into everything we grow and everything we eat.

For the purpose of the ASIC conference, the golf umbrella of coffee science was divided up into agronomy, biotechnology, physiology, chemistry, processing, sustainability, climate change, coffee quality, pests and diseases, and genomics and genetics. When you study coffee you can study it at the micro scale, looking at ways that our brains perceive different tastes at different temperature, or you can study it at the macro scale, considering coffee's role in global climate change.

Over the four day conference researchers made 83 presentations and displayed over 200 posters in the daily rotating gallery; the compilation of abstracts from the conference totals 385 pages. Study titles range from "Blanching and air drying effect on antioxidant capacity and fiber content of processed coffee pulp for human consumption," to "Impact of crema quantity and appearance on expected and actual coffee perception." I got lost somewhere between "Coffee cysteine proteinases and related inhibitors with high expression during grain maturation and germination" and "Large scale expression of genes related to phytoalexins, phenols, flavonoids and lignin biosynthesis in coffee plants infested with leaf miner."

The ASIC conference, this year in San Jose but taking place every two years in a different corner of the world, came on the coattails of Costa Rica's annual Sintercafe conference focusing on the business side of coffee. Instead of researchers sharing slide after slide of gene sequencing charts and scatterplots of broca instances, there, rockstar traders rubbed elbows with exporting hot shots. Coffee's ubiquity from single-serve packs in every motel room to piping hot air pots at 24 hour gas stations in every town in the country is no accident; it is the product of all this business, all this science, and all the producers and pickers with their hands in the dirt.

Guido

Recorded Monday, November 12, 2012, in the lobby of the San Jose hotel hosting the 24th International ASIC Conference.

Like me, Guido is a conference attendee. On the conference participant list he's listed as a "Local Committee Organizer." I approached him because I overheard him mention Puriscal. Turns out, he's much more than a committee organizer and has influences that extend far beyond one town. He wears a crisp white guayabera shirt and a light tan Tico bucket hat.

Guido: *In agriculture, there's always the need to take care of the family and the farm. When prices fall—international coffee prices—the first impacted is the plant, because first we have to feed ourselves and then comes the plant's needs.*

I'm a member of Coopeatenas. I've held almost all of the administrative roles, and then I was President for seven years. Then I spent four years doing other things, and now I've been President again for the past eight years. I also belong to an association of small and mid-sized agricultural producers, called UPA Nacional. We're a group of more than ten thousand coffee growers, plus other agricultural producers. I'm also the President of FENACAFE, the Federation of Coffee Co-ops in the country. I've been very involved with coffee. Also four years as President of ICAFE [Institute of Coffee, Costa Rica's national coffee office].

I've always been close to coffee production, and I'm still a very, very, very small coffee producer! But very proud to be a caficultor.

We [Coopeatenas] were born out of necessity. The need was the industrialization of coffee. And later, we thought about services. We developed them and now we have a gas station, a supermarket, a hardware store. The profitability of those lets us throw more money in the coffee basket. We now sell to major labels and also have our own brands. We're very satisfied because those larger brands have come to appreciate our beans, and we greatly appreciate the management they do in store to sell our coffee to consumers. So it's very interesting.

We never would have gotten to this point if we weren't part of a co-op. In fact, I never would have gotten to the position on the Board of Directors of the Institute with out the Co-op. A tiny producer. But this is another part. We modified the law about relations between producers, processors, and exporters—the 2762—and we democratized it. So we were elected by a democratic process. So that's the other part.

[I spoke with Guido about a month later in his office at UPA Nacional in Tibas, one of San Jose's suburbs. Recorded Wednesday, December 19, 2012. Guido wears a navy polo.]

Guido: *I don't know if I mentioned before that I'm part of an organization of small and mid sized producers. UPA is an organization of seventeen thousand farmers, and in coffee we're more than ten thousand. We're part of a historical fight for dignity for farmers and for the sons and daughters of rural producers.*

We've worked a lot proposing public laws. Coffee had lot of taxes that we considered excessive. We said that we were completely in agreement with a contribution towards the development of the country, and that this wasn't about trying to not pay taxes, rather that the taxes were excessive. Because there were taxes as high as the value of production and of the value of exportation. One was 15% and the other was 18%. If those had been 25%, it would have meant that for every four hectares of coffee, one belonged to the state.

But the state didn't plant it, didn't fertilize it, didn't prune the shade trees on it—I say that because you have to keep pruning shade trees so that they create a natural screen—didn't prune it, didn't harvest it, and didn't bring it to the point of sale. We did that. So we started changing the way the taxes were determined. We proposed that the tax calculation take into account when the price of coffee was below the cost of production.

The other work was to change a property tax law with the understanding that agriculture is different than other human activities. And we were successful: they introduced a new variable to the appraisal criteria. Because for the appraisal they looked at nearby services, topography- there were ten elements. And we said one was missing: land use. Because to us it doesn't matter if the land is worth $10,000, $100,000 or $1,000,000; one hectare of coffee—for as much as the land is worth on paper- doesn't produce any more fanegas of coffee[Trampa p.350]. Or tons of sugarcane. Or fatten any more cows. When the land use changes they can appraise it differently, but we were successful in changing the way they calculated that tax.

We [small producers] have a good track record, especially coffee growers. Our balance sheet is very clean. We can say with pride that we've honored our obligations.

The other thing we've been noticing in the past few weeks, maybe even months, is a terrible attack of roya. It's like a new race that we're not

88

battling well. There are many, many concentrations [of the rust] where trees are loosing their leaves. This has us very concerned. Even the [two ornamental coffee] trees planted out in front [of this suburban office building] have rust. I've never seen that before.

Another problem the fall of international coffee prices. In Costa Rica, to produce a fanega of coffee costs us 50-55,000 colones, so that'd be $100-110. The advances are at maximum $80. And from that we have to pay the harvesting, the transportation, and we have to pay the people who financed us to be able to maintain the farm during the year. We see that the problem for farmers—it's the same all over the world—as developed as the country may be, as the directly or indirectly subsidized as they are, it's always the same problems of high costs of production, of chemical and fertilizer inputs, of fuel. That and changes in climate. Because we don't produce, we induce nature to produce for us.

We believe that if the prices stay low it will impact [coffee] producers around the world. The trees won't be well fed. And we'll go back to having yellowed trees with short branches and tiny cherries. So that's what has us most preoccupied, but understand that we're survivors. Survivors of so many crises. And we hope to survive again, that the wave doesn't wash us away.

Guido pulls out his phone to show me a few pictures of his finca, of the leafy green coffee trees and the recently pruned Poró trees and hardwoods towering overhead.

On the way out Guido shows me the two ornamental coffee trees planted in big pots outside of the UPA office building. He turns up the undersides of several leaves to show me the dusty orange leaf rust spores mottling the green.

If you came from Ronulfo and would like to continue to La Potenciana, turn to p. 77

If you came from Froilan and would like to return to Cedral, turn to p. 129

If you came from Arturo and would like to return to Colombia, turn to p. 268

For a conversation with another ASIC attendee, turn to the next page.

Jose Manuel

Recorded November 14, 2012, over lunch in the converted ballroom of the hotel hosting the 24th International ASIC Conference.

Jose and I are finishing our plates of catered lunch. We both look quite different from the time we met at Jose Fuentes Gamboa's farm in Tres Equis. This time I'm wearing a pencil skirt and heels. Jose wears a light yellow long-sleeved collared shirt. The presentation immediately before lunch had been about "Identifying the vulnerability of coffee farmers' livelihoods and development of adaptation strategies to climate change in Mesoamerica," and everyone was already buzzing about the presentation that would immediately follow lunch; the outspoken Peter Baker would be addressing "The changing climate for sustainable coffee." The intersections of coffee and climate changes were on everyone's minds.

Jose: *Yes, there are evidences* [of climate changes]. *For example, we recorded broca at 1000 meters above sea level, and now we're seeing it at 1400. These new infestations are lowering production. Higher temperatures present greater opportunities for damage. When the temperatures are higher [the broca] have more opportunities to move from one place to another, more pheromones.* [Man at table behind us takes a very loud phone call in Portuguese.]

It's maybe a period of six or eight years that we've been seeing this. It shows up on every grower's farms. They'd never reported broca before, and now they're seeing it at high levels. I think the need will be for us to start work on looking for new varieties to plant.

In the case of Peru, 26% of production is located between 800 and 1100 meters above sea level. And just with a temperature increase of one degree, it makes things very complicated. Because people live from this. What's going to happen to this number of producers who are affected? If we don't take measures to find [new] varieties, we're going to have many problems. Social problems.

Rachel: *Like they just said in the presentation, there are possibilities that come from diversification, whether it's within coffee, such as planting more varieties, or diversification with hardwoods or other crops.*

90

Jose: *I want to get started already! And work hard at it! There's no other option. If the temperature rises but I have good shade, it'll be in my favor.*

Rachel: *Do most of the fincas in Peru have their own beneficios? Do most people sell to co-ops?*

Jose: *The co-ops have become…politicized. The management—there's a group of people always looking to be in charge. Eh, it's not pretty.*

Rachel: *But you don't work for a co-op.*

Jose: *No, no. I work* for the monster; Louis Dreyfus Commodities. They're a trader like ECOM, and they sell to roasters all over the world. Big guys like Kraft. They buy from growers all over Peru— organic and conventional. But they don't have as much social responsibility as ECOM has implemented. And Olam, which is certifying organic.*

Rachel: *I've been seeing significant erosion in some parts of Costa Rica. Is that a problem in Peru?*

Jose: *Not particularly. But all over there are people planting on lands that aren't apt for agriculture. And poor soil means poor farmers. There's a direct correlation.*

I work with producers. From December to March, we run a land diagnostic. We evaluate fincas to see what the production looks like, looking to see what their volume is to see if it's worth investing in supporting them. It's open. They don't have to sell to us. But for producers who do we offer technical assistance in how to prune, how to fertilize, systems of agroforestry too, what species they can plant— hardwood or not. That's what we do from December to March. Then from March to September it's time when the company just focuses on buying coffee. The harvest starts in March and goes until the middle of August.

In March it starts at elevations around 700-900 meters above sea level, and goes until May. For farms that are at 1000-1600 meters above sea level, it starts in April and goes until September. There are no centralized beneficios, like here, so producers bring coffee of varying humidities. 20%, 25%, 28%, 15%, 14%. It's a mix. So we take it all to the dry mill and dry it until 12% [legal export level for green coffee is 10-12% humidity]. Then we hull it and pack it for the ports, where it goes to Europe, all over.

Rachel: *So the producers don't have any contracts to sell to LDC?*

Jose: *They can look for other options. They can go to the co-op and see if the price is better. The competition is very strong. There are lots of companies.*

The fincas can be one, two, up to three hours away— between the purchasing points and the fincas. There are fincas that don't have good access roads, and it can take four or five hours to get to them.

People own their land, but they don't necessarily live there year round. They might go live there during the harvest, but live mostly in a more central city the rest of the year. But if we're talking percentages, only about 25% actually have a title for their land. The other 75% doesn't have titles, which makes it very difficult to extend them lines of credit, because the bank doesn't have a guarantee.

But the producers follow the market. Because most are members of co-ops, they see the prices through there, and many have children who are in high school and know how to use the internet and all that. It's rare to find a producer who doesn't follow the price.

I have a finca up in the north part of Peru. I'm planning to expand, plant about another ten hectares. In the district where I'm working we have some twenty thousand hectares of coffee. But the soils are getting tired. And that's when you see nematodes and other plagues.

But all the problems have to do with climate change. We're trying to make changes now, proactively, before it's too late. We see things changing so we're trying to act.

If you came from Jose Fuentes and would like to return to Turrialba, turn to p. 54

If you came from David and Albello and would like to return to Colombia, turn to p. 319

For a conversation with a Costa Rican caficultor who practices sustainable finca management, turn to p. 151

For another conversation with someone who works for a branch of ECOM trading, turn to the next page.

Jose Manuel no longer works for LDC.

Nicaragua

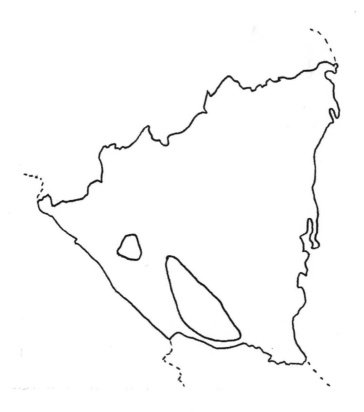

Sébaco
Jose Navarro..............Laboratory manager *99*
La Virgen
Henry Hueck.................Caficultor *107*
El Roblar
Maria Rizo................Caficultor *115*
Matagalpa
Santiago Dolumus........Central Co-op administrator *118*

Nicaragua is Costa Rica's neighbor to the north, and it is worlds away. Costa Rica is filled with plenty of Ticos who have two cars, three TVs, and comfortable pensions. Nicaragua is Central America's poorest country, and it supplies Costa Rica with a significant portion of its manual labor work force.

The country is socialist, with a rocky and fairly violent political history. Today, tourists and backpackers are trickling down Nicaragua's coasts, largely avoiding the capital of Managua, which was destroyed by an earthquake in the 1970s and never quite recovered. One of the main tourist draws is Lake Nicaragua, the largest lake in Central America. Nicaragua is more than twice the size of Costa Rica and home to around six million Nicaraguans (still less than the population of New York City) in a land area about the size of Alabama.

Nicaraguan coffee is receiving more and more attention of late; the country's cafetales grow mostly the same handful of varietals that are seen elsewhere in Central America in similar volcanic soils at similar elevations, but Nicaraguans are working hard to differentiate their products. Due to the country's tumultuous history, landholding of coffee growing hectares is divided between giant, organized estates that employ upwards of five hundred people at harvest time and clusters of small producers working one or two hectares of land with little external input or guidance.

The process of processing looks quite different than in Costa Rica; here there are no large communal beneficios where producers sell fresh picked cherries. Depulping is the responsibility of every grower, large or small. The coffee growing regions of the country are concentrated in the mountains to the north, where clouds hover continuously and allow little or no sun to aid in drying coffee. Many farms truck thousand-pound loads of still wet, just-depulped-and-washed coffee down from the mountains to the hot, dry, sun baked expanse that stretches between the coffee mountains and Managua. The section of the Pan American highway that passes through is lined on both sides by massive coffee drying patios, with men and women covered in head wraps shielding them from the sun as they rake the drying coffee, walking back and forth through the stretches of beans to dry them as quickly and as evenly as possible.

This collection is filled with stories, but it is also filled with voids. I did not interview anyone who works raking coffee on the patios, and I did not formally interview any workers on the large haciendas employing hundreds of people. These voids are important because they're not voids generated by negligence or laziness or disinterest, rather voids generated by the realities of circumstance.

One reality is that is it difficult, often to the point of being impossible, to speak with some people. Many people who work as pickers on large estates communicate with each other and with other predominately with hand gestures. For one reason or another, they don't speak. And when they are spoken to, it is usually in the form of directions. Conversations involving questions are not a typical exchange. They get told what to do, but not in an emotionally abusive way, just in a practical one.

No one asks them what they want to do on the finca today; someone tells them which lot to pick. No one asks them what they want for lunch; everyone lines up and gets the same thing. This is not because workers aren't valued as independent human beings; it's because in their line of work, asking questions and making decisions based on personal wants and preferences just isn't part of the deal. Being given instructions is.

For me, as a foreign woman, to approach a worker and ask him or her a direct question, the inevitable response I'll receive is silence. Direct questions, even phrased as friendly and as harmlessly as possible, can still make people feel interrogated. Asking to record the conversation also makes many people feel like I might have an alterior motive, since most people don't walk around asking to forever document your words.

Many hacienda workers are single men who spend their lives as migrant laborers. They live their lives in housing provided by their employers, float from place to place as they please, and have patterns of communication that are simply too far removed from my own to make an interview possible. A recorded interview involves a level of trust that can't always be established in day, a week, or even months. In between the stories told here are many silences, but those silences are not necessarily indicative of marginalization; they remind us that we don't all tell our stories in the same ways.

Sébaco

Sébaco is in the heart of the hot, dry, sunbaked expanse along the Pan-American highway between Managua and the beginnings of the coffee mountains in Matagalpa. One of the biggest coffee drying facilities in Sébaco is ECOM's Nicaraguan subsidiary, Exportadora Atlantic. The Exportadora Atlantic dry mill receives coffee in various forms from producers of various sizes. Coffee might arrive still sopping wet from washing and need to spend days on the sunny patios or hours in a mechanical dryer, or it might arrive half dried after spending some time on a producer's own drying patios. Whatever state it shows up in, it gets dried to within the 10-12% humidity range, then eventually hulled and packed for export to roasters.

On the same property as Exportadora Atlantic is ECOM's division of Sustainability Management Services' (SMS) regional lab for studying and propagating new genetic material. In the middle of ranks of illiterate Nicaraguans who've survived the several generations of political turmoil and now work raking miles coffee spread out to dry on blue tarps and sheets of black plastic, lies a lab on the forefront of coffee genetics. In this small facility a small team of scientists works to carve out the future of coffee production via hybrid plants, integrated management, other alternatives.

Coffee science in the midst of coffee production regions is rare. French and Portuguese research institutes are responsible for conducting good portions of the world's coffee research. Brazil by far leads producing nations in scientific efforts, as the country is massive and can justify amply funding coffee research, since Brazilian production accounts for 40% of all the coffee produced annually on earth. Holding pace with more glamorous operations, this innovative lab is in a one story building under the shade of some old trees in the dust of the Panamerican Highway, right in the thumping heart of Nicaragua's raw coffee production.

Jose Navarro

Recorded Monday, November 26, 2012, inside the laboratory facilities of ECOM SMS in Sébaco.

Jose and I stand under the florescent lights of the "shake table room," where constantly vibrating shelves hold hundreds of flasks with leaf tissue suspended in a clear gel. Jose wears a white lab coat. We both wear disposable white booties over our shoes.

Jose: *The parent plant [of these H3 hybrids] is Caturra, crossed with an Ethiopia, one of the trees brought from Africa that's at CATIE and is used for crossing. The H3 is Caturra, the H1 is Sarchimor, which is a Catimor crossed with other material.*

In the process of somatic embryogenesis there are three stages [the genetic material] has to pass through. We call them, "globular, "heart-shaped," and "torpedo." It takes us a year and a half to get to the third stage. Because it takes so long, it's very hard to change from cloning one hybrid to cloning another.

And the electricity can't go out on us. Ever. Not even for half an hour. We work twenty-four hours a day, 365 days a year. There always has to be someone here.

Rachel: *And does every one of these containers yield [plantlet] embryos?*

Jose: *Not always. Because this liquid in this container is different from the one in the previous stage. And this one is our "industry secret." With all the nutrients. You can ask me what's in it, but I can't tell you!* [laughs] *CATIE doesn't know it. We know what they do, and we don't do it! Because CATIE conducted their investigations with CIRAD, who we also work with now, so we know what CATIE does, but they don't know what we do. You know how these things go.*

More or less, every two months we produce 500,000 [plantlet] embryos. Which means that here we have a capacity for 3 million embryos a year. Look, I'll show you what it looks like at the beginning of this stage and at the end. First we put the embryos from the previous stage in this container [which looks like a jumbo-sized clear plastic Slurpee to-go cup, complete with a ventilating "straw"]. *These are embryos that already have their first pair of leaves, which we'll next transfer to the greenhouse.*

But, the problem is that when they go from [these containers], it's like moving from a hotel, with climate control and all the amenities, to being out in the real world. So a fair amount die. The biggest loss is in this transition. The idea is that we do it better than CATIE [laughs]. But working with cloning is hard. We principally sell these seedlings to larger companies, because of the price, which I'll explain later. [We walk out of the humming lab of shaking shelves and to-go cups brimming with tiny coffee clones and into a greenhouse.]

These are the mother plants, where we get the material [leaf cuttings] to use for the embryogenesis. These are the original hybrids, brought from CATIE in 2003. So we take the smallest leaves, the youngest and most malleable like this one [he turns up a soft, light green pair of leaves at the tip of a branch] *and from there we cut the little pieces and then take them to the lab.*

Right now we're renewing [the hybrids] because these trees are already ten years old. The producers ask us, "What's the productive life of these trees?" and truth is, we don't know! Because the oldest ones are these, which are ten. But even in this amount of time hybrids have many advantages.

There are five main advantages to hybrid trees. One is that they produce more, 40% more than Caturra, which is the standard used to measure productivity because it's the most commonly cultivated variety in Latin America. Second, they produce more quickly. In their second year they're already producing because of their hybrid vigor, as a cross. The third advantage is that they were chosen for their final quality in the cup. There are varieties, for example Catimors, that produce a good volume, but the final product has a bad flavor. These have an attractive one. The fourth is that, because of their hybrid qualities, they're more tolerant to disease. For example, the H1 is very tolerant of roya. Right now in Nicaragua there's a very serious problem with roya. And the fifth characteristic is that these hybrids were developed by CIRAD to produce optimally in shade conditions, meaning on fincas with trees.

Because Catuai, for example, which is a brother to Caturra, is designed to produce in full sun, as a monoculture. It produces more but only when it's alone in the sun. The advantage is that it produces more, but the drawback is that there aren't other trees. It's not as sustainable. So our platform is to sell these to producers, telling them that they have to have shade. Because if you have shade you have trees, and if you have trees you can sell them. I mean, it's not like we're going to save the world, we know that, but these are the five positive characteristics that our hybrids have. I know this from memory because I've told it to producers like a hundred times!

Rachel: *How are the hybrids first crossed to get the parent plants?*

Jose: *They first developed the hybrids in CATIE; they brought pure varieties from Africa. Big, tall trees, monstrous ones. They take the pollen from those trees and put it in the flowers of a Caturra tree. From the seeds they produced there were thousand of trees, thousands! Thousands of offspring from the seeds that they planted. They let them grow, and when they're producing, they evaluate if it's a good hybrid.* [And if it does make the cut as a "good hybrid," it then becomes the source of the leaf cuttings that undergo somatic embryogenesis to produce clones. This cloning process is needed because these hybrids are not necessarily true breeding. If you germinated the seeds from one of those very productive trees (out of the thousands that came from the initial cross pollination), there's a good chance the resulting tree will no longer make the cut as a "good hybrid," that it won't have the same desirable qualities as its parents.]

The other thing we're doing is an experiment that we just started, but we're very hopeful because somatic embryogenesis in a lab is very expensive. We sell the seedlings, ready to plant in the field, for $0.60 each. Which is around 15 Cordobas [Nicaraguan currency]. And a producer can buy a seedling of traditional Caturra for 3 Cordobas. So if you tell him, "15," he'll tell you, "No." It doesn't matter that you say, "But it produces more and this and that." That doesn't matter if he can't pay for it now. So medium and large producers can buy them, and do, but we also want to look for new clients.

The idea of the company, because we [ECOM SMS] belong to Atlantic, and Don Eric [Exportadora Atlantic's CEO], and he's looking to differentiate ECOM as a company that offers technology, that supports the producer. Not just one that collects the coffee and doesn't care if you died, if you couldn't produce one year to the next. One that offers services more than anything. So we're selling tubing, a type of fertilizer— that one's from Mexico, systems for controlling weeds and disease. Every new technology that comes out, that no one has tried, we try.

Things already on the market we don't bother with, because producers can get commercial fertilizer anywhere. We don't want to become the big export houses that also have agrochemical warehouses. They don't deal with new technology. We want to be about technology, how we can improve what's out there. Innovation. [We turn away from the piles of tubing and stacks of sacks of fertilizer.]

This here is a storage room where we store seeds. We have many varieties, but most importantly the Starmaiyer and Marseillesa. The Marseillesa is a pure variety of Sarchimor, which was selected by CIRAD over the course of many years. We're already selling it. For producers who can't afford hybrid [seedlings], we sell them Marseillesa. It's a pure line, and it's slightly more productive than Caturra, but not much.

Our new research is on the Starmaiyer, a hybrid of Marseillesa with semi-sterile material from an African variety. We're working on developing it. It would be a hybrid seed, but it would be much more affordable.

The other big advantage is that we have this room. In all of Central America we're the only ones who have this room. It seems like a lie, right? But we're the only ones in Central America who have a room designed for proper seed storage. [We walk out of the main room and back towards the lab.]

Rachel: *I'm sure I'll see when I go up to the farms, but is the system for selling coffee here similar to Costa Rica?*

Jose: *No, because here every producer has to sell their coffee in parchment paper. Every little co-op can provide its members with a beneficio to depulp. Costa Rica is very institutionalized in its coffee production. It has ICAFE, CATIE, the Ministry of Agriculture. Very socialist, actually. Here in Nicaragua it's really the opposite of how it's painted around the world; it's a free market. If you do it well, you do it well. If you don't do it well, you're out. There's no one to support you. The government doesn't have money to subsidize you. Whereas in Costa Rica, even if you're a small producer, there's lots of support. There are incentives and programs; they give you a hand.*

Here it seems like a lie, because Nicaragua is socialist like Venezuela. But in reality it's the complete opposite. For example, co-ops bring their coffee to Atlantic. They can just sell it to Atlantic, or, they can use Atlantic and pay for the service of drying, hulling, and sorting. But it's still their coffee. The producer, or the co-op, makes their own contact with a buyer in the US, or Ireland— Henry Hüeck has a buyer in Ireland— or in Austria or where ever. So it's their coffee. Atlantic just offers the services of preparation and export.

In Costa Rica it's different. The producers just sell the coffee and now it's [the mill's coffee]! In Costa Rica producers sell their coffee and that's it, and they sell it right to the exporters, like Volcafe, Neumann, the co-ops, like Coopedota. I have family in the Los Santos area, in Coopedota, all over, and they have no idea what the market price is- they just know the price per fanega. Here, everyone knows exactly what the New York market is doing.

Rachel: *There are lots of ways to work with coffee. Out of everything you've seen, from your family in Los Santos to the labs here, what would you consider the biggest challenge?*

Jose: *Well, look. What I know is that the world is the way it is, even though everyone says you should try to change it. I've seen—I've harvested coffee. And I know that agriculture is difficult, very dirty, and very poorly paid. Coffee is part of that. And in Costa Rica, if it weren't for immigrants, they wouldn't be able to produce coffee. Or at least much less than what they do.*

    For me, the biggest challenge with coffee is—when I heard about this job I came up here immediately; I was so excited. I wanted to work with coffee; I'd seen the hybrids and I knew that they were the bomb. I guess they must have sensed my excitement because they offered me a job right away, gracias a Dios. But the challenge with coffee, as with many other sectors of agriculture is that it's hard for small producers to get ahead. Society is not developing towards agriculture. Because I grew up with coffee I consider it very important. And the application of biotechnology might be the way to move agriculture, and small producers, forward.

If you came from Karole and would like to return to Turrialba, turn to p. 51

If you came from Luis Angel and would like to attend a coffee science conference, turn to p. 85

For a conversation with someone just entering the fields of coffee science, turn to p. 312

To continue up into the moutains around Matagalpa for a conversation with someone who has lots of ECOM hybrids on his farm, turn to the next page.

Tree of Coffee Tree Varietals

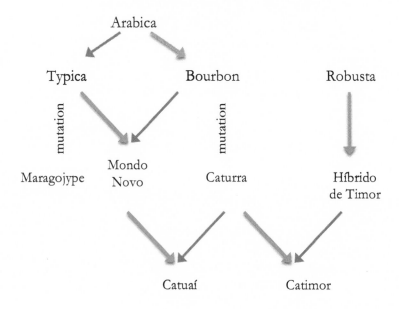

There are hundreds of coffee tree varietals, but these are the most common varieties grown in Costa Rica, Nicaragua, and Panama.

For descriptions of coffee varietals, turn to p. 10

Ramacafe
Finca La Virgen

Finca La Virgen lies outside of Matagalpa up in those coffee mountains where the clouds hover day in and day out. The trek up is as steep and muddy as the trek up to any Latin American coffee farm. Finca La Virgen is filled with trees, birds, and people. The scale of coffee operations in Nicaragua is massive compared to that of Costa Rica simply because the country has over 126,000 hectares of coffee versus the Tico 93,000.

Land ownership is distributed differently; here running a productive coffee farm is not just a matter of working with your family, it takes all the management of running a sizeable business with hundreds on the payroll, or like running a school filled with hundreds of children who need schedules and meals and guidance, or like leading an army of hundreds of infantry who have been enlisted to battle the elements and take on mother nature. Or all of the above.

Finca La Virgen is part of Ramacafe, which is a coffee producing business, but with so many hundreds of employees and then all of their families to manage, the on-the-ground execution of coffee production- from planting to harvesting to processing to loading the trucks with sacks of wet just-washed coffee to bring to the Exportadora Atlantic dry mill- starts to look like a base camp or a summer camp as much as world class company.

La Virgen lies at the end of the road to itself in the Nicaraguan coffee region of Matagalpa, but the coffee from La Virgen's loins is only the beginning of a much more complex journey to somewhere else.

Henry

Recorded Friday, November 27, 2012, in the living room/office of Henry's house on Finca La Virgen. Interview recorded mostly in English.

He wears a blue turtleneck and a khaki vest with many pockets and many more Ramacafe badges, each boldly emblazoned with the omnipresent slogan *"Dios Te Ama"* ("God Loves You").

Henry: *I have four fincas, so we don't buy coffee from anyone. We don't have our own dry mill; we send it to ECOM Atlantic. Because there are roasters all over the world who know me, I'm able to sell some of my coffee— not all of it, but some of it- through direct channels at differentiated prices. It's a family business. We live coffee 24/7.*

The story is this: I was born in 1959 to a family who was, politically, Liberal Samozistas. From the time of the Samoza government. There was an earthquake in 1972 [that leveled much of the country]. My father was a lawyer, and my mother worked in social work. I don't know how far back you want to go, but to go all the way back to the beginning, I was born in '59. I come from two families who had fincas, but for cattle ranching. Then, in '72, there was the earthquake. At thirteen I left to learn English; I went to live with a family in Alexandria, Virginia. An Irish family, Irish. The Butlers. This was in '72, '73. I was there for like five months, and then I came back to Nicaragua. But classes had already started. So I had to go to the American Nicaraguan School because of the schedule. But my father didn't like that school, and I didn't either.

I had several friends who'd gone to a military academy in Indiana, and they were asking me if I wanted to go. Some of my best friends were there, so I went too, to a military school in Indiana called Howe. I graduated from high school in '76, with honors! Instead of fighting, I went along with it. I was good. I shined my shoes; I did everything that I was supposed to do. I was seventeen when I graduated. My father didn't want me to go to a big school, so I went to a junior college in Indiana, Vincennes University. After Vincennes University, I transferred to Tulane. And there, I partied. I was going wild, you know? I almost got thrown out. But I graduated, finally.

I went to Tulane in '77. In '78 there was a revolution here in Nicaragua; there was war and everything. So my parents told me to stay. So I stayed doing summer school in New Orleans. Finally, in '79, there was the revolution, and my whole family had to leave. So I had to get a scholarship to

*finish my school and work and study. I finished school in December '79. I
went to my graduation in June of 1980. I graduated with a degree in
Economics. Then I went to Miami, where we lived twenty-three people in one
house, three families. Because we had to leave the country.*

*The took everything away from us. We were in exile. Which is
another part that's important to remember, that the Sandinistas kicked us
out. And they killed my grandfather, also in 1979, because he was the
president of the congress. My grandfather is well known here. I have his name,
Cornelius Heinrich Hüeck; I'm the oldest grandson. And my son now is the
fifth Cornelio Henry. I was the fourth.*

*We lived in Miami from 1980 until 1995. And I didn't do
anything that had to do with economics! I graduated with a BA in economics,
and ended up selling clothes. Well, first I worked Friday's washing dishes, but
I was the best dish washer— that was to be able to get money to go to my
graduation. And then I sold clothes, and I became the best salesman within
six months. I beat this Jewish old man; he just about died the day that I
beat him in December, by about $2,000. He sold about $110; I sold
$2,100. Selling clothes in a men's clothing store in Miami. It was a chain.
But they sold very nice clothing for gentlemen. I was twenty years old and I
worked every day, every hour that I could. I didn't mind; I didn't get tired. I
hustle, hustle, hustled. And, unfortunately, I made too much money doing
that. I made $29,000 that first year. And that was in 1980! I was supposed
to go back for my master's degree, but that never happened. Long story short,
I made a career out of that.*

*I was a manager. A friend of mine from Italy, who had married a
Nicaraguan girl, his sister had a store in Coconut Grove, but she decided to
quit. So she left the store and he told me, "Come run this for me, because if
not I'm going to lose all the money!" It was a boutique! I was there two years.
I was in the U.S. until 1995, and then I came back here. I was married
then, and I had two daughters. I came back in 1995, and I came to take two
fincas without knowing anything about coffee. They were both abandoned
farms, La Virgen and San Martin, and this is what they are now.*

*Ramacafe is named for the [first letters of] the last names of my ex-
wife. I made the fincas what they were. I got divorced in '97, but I stayed
working for my ex-wife's family. Now I remarried in 2005, once my
daughters, Grace and Tatiana, were older. In 2005 I met my wife Gabby.
Everybody likes Gabby because she always has a smile. They might not like
me, but everyone likes her. I met her at the Ramacafe conference, and [snaps*

fingers] *right away we knew we liked each other. It was love at first sight. We got married in 2005. Within a year Cornelio Henry was born.*

But, this was a hard time to be in coffee. My ex-wife's brother [who at that point still owned Ramacafe], had a lot of money. He had fertilizer companies, banks. He was used to having companies that brought a lot of profit. And back in 1997 when we started, the cash flow looked good because the prices were high. But in 2000 we went through the low price coffee crisis that lasted five years: the longest crisis in history. And he didn't like it. He told me, in 2007, that he was trying to sell the company.

But for me it was different, because I'd made it. I made it from scratch. And I made it as though it were mine. Because it was mine at the beginning. It wasn't mine after I got divorced, but it was still my daughters'. I was doing it to leave them something. I was just an employee. But I did it for my kids. Part of my salary went to my daughters.

In 2008, my good friend Eric came from New York to open ECOM. He graduated from Cornell. He'd married a woman from Costa Rica, and they came here because the owner of ECOM wanted to open here; they saw opportunity. And [the owner] knew Eric's father, who became the partner here in Nicaragua. He said, "Ok, I'll do it. But only if you have my son run it. Because I want my son here!"

And I needed to find a partner in order to buy [Ramacafe]. It's very difficult to find someone for a business like this; it had to be 50/50. So when we decided to buy the company, Ramacafe, it was just two farms. But before we actually purchased it, Eric's father, Don Clemente, had been pushing me to have my own farm, saying, "You have a family now! You need your own!" So he financed the purchase of Finca San Francisco in 2008. We purchased land in Jinotega that was abandoned. He wanted to do leather leaves on part of it. So he told me, "You find the financing to do whatever you need to do in order to do the rest in coffee."

But before this, I was the godfather to Eric's son, and Don Clemente is the godfather to my son. So I called the company Cafetalero Los Compadres.* That's part of the story. Whey Cafetalero los Compadres? Because I'm the godfather of Andres, Eric's son, and Don Clemente, the one who pushed us to do this, is the godfather of my son.

But then my ex-wife's brother found out. And he didn't like it. He said, "You cannot be working for me on my farm and have your own farm." He pushed me to finally get financing to purchase Ramacafe. But this was 2008. September 2008, the world finance crisis. So it was very difficult. We had already put down a deposit. If we didn't come up with the financing we would loose the deposit; that was in the initial contract.

I didn't have that money to loose! Finally, we got the financing, and we ended up buying the company. By 2008 it was ours. Look, we already went from '59 to 2008— that was pretty quick! In 2008 Eric was the head of ECOM in Nicaragua and Costa Rica, and his father owns the largest single estate in Nicaragua. So we're coffeepeople. The other thing we have in common is— I have a big heart; not because I say so but because other people say so— the social aspect.

Now you see this big, organized estate, but if you'd have come in 2004, 2005... I didn't have a house. I slept in my car when I came here. The money was all going into fixing the farm. Eric is also like that. If you see that award [from Rainforest Alliance], that's very special for him to win it as an individual. All the other honorees were companies. And he's the other 50% of this company. He's not money hungry. His father is one of the biggest advocates for reforestation in Nicaragua; they've planted over two million trees.

But, to go back to 2008, when we bought the company we were up to here [gestures to eyeballs] in debt. The prices were down because the economy, worldwide, went down. Fortunately, I came here and decided to engage very heavily. I'm a coffeeperson. I had made a team that I'd been building since 2001. Everyone here who knows how to use a computer learned with a teacher that I brought in 2002. And I brought internet in 2004. And it's been a certified farm since 2004. We're the second Rainforest Alliance farm [in Nicaragua]. Then we became the first farm with three certifications, Rainforest, UTZ, and [Starbucks] C.A.F.E. Practices. And we were the first strategic supplier for Starbucks for C.A.F.E. Practices; they divided suppliers by score: less than 60, 60-90, and 90-100 meant strategic supplier.

But in 2010 I had a surgery, and it didn't go well. In Nicaragua, when you have complications, the doctors are good...but you don't have the tools. I went into the surgery March 18, 2010, and on April 21 I ended up going on an ambulance plane to Miami. And they saved my life over there. Three weeks in intensive care. I didn't come back to Nicaragua until September 21st. And this didn't sink. Eric was in Costa Rica; I was in Miami, but because of the team that I had built over the years, and the way that we are— everything still ran smoothly. I had beautiful letters that the children wrote for my birthday and for me to be safe.

The reason that I have "Dios Te Ama" written on everything** is because I made a promise. I know that I was saved because of the prayers.

110

I've always been a Catholic; I believe in God, but I never say it. And I told my mother one day, "I want to have the feeling- I know that God is all over, but I want to have the presence felt more intensely on the farms. I know that I'm here for a reason, I don't know why, but he left me here for a reason. So I'm going to have his name everywhere." I even put it on the big banners I make for the Ramacafe conference.

And some people think that I'm an evangelical, or part of a sect or something. I don't care. It's just a promise that I made. And everyone here feels it. For me, I feel great! Only good things have happened. I go to board meetings and I go like this. [Gestures to what he's wearing, the blue turtleneck and khaki vest with Ramacafe badges proclaiming *"Dios Te Ama."*]

And now, people here are buying their own [they sell *"Dios Te Ama"* tees at the commissary.] *You know how people buy Yankees shirts? Well, my employees and workers want to be part of the team. And the commissary is a revolving door; it goes to offset the costs of paying teachers and the psychologist. When the prices go down, like they're doing now, it puts all this in danger. But you can't tell just by looking, because we've invested the money to maintain it all. Eric and I took out a $2 million dollar loan to renovate San Francisco. Improve the fincas.*

They were already good. Since 2003 they've been calling us model farms. Seven years later they're still saying that. We've done a lot of work in the social part. Like my buyers say, "Happy people make happy coffee." And it's part of our corporate social responsibility. We're working to educate people. When my son comes here he plays soccer with the children. They come and knock on the door, "Can Cornelio come out?" They'll probably all be working together when I've passed away.

Coffee is generational. And all my children love the farm. They've been here since they were three months old. Part of the crisis that [coffee growers] have all over the world— in Africa, Vietnam— is that the youth don't want to be farmers. So that's why were working with technology. I'm a technology freak. I want everyone to have access to it. Here, everything you see has been done with our money. No NGO. No help from anybody. It's a nice place to be. A nice place to work.

The positive environment here has helped me ask for and receive quality work from my employees. You see on the bags it says, "Quality Ensures Our Future." People are understanding these things. There's an internal revolution happening towards quality, order. There's no trash here. We have five hundred people right now on the farm. There are other farms

111

that sell liquor to people. Here no. I like order, I like discipline, I like the presence of God.

> ### Where does coffee from Ramacafe and Cafetalera Los Compadres go?
>
> Some of it goes to Bewleys in Ireland via a direct trade model, where Bewleys people come to the fincas and check things out and then pay a premium for quality lots. Some of it goes to Starbucks, strategically, and even makes it into their Nicaragua Black Diamond Reserve collection. Some of it gets sold to ECOM Atlantic, part of the massive Swiss commodity trader ECOM, which sells to roasters worldwide.

For a conversation with another family who feels the presence of God in their cafetales, turn to p. 275

For a conversation with someone else who runs the production chain- and then some- turn to p. 300

For a conversation with a very different Nicaraguan Producer in another community in the moutains around Matagalpa, turn to the next page.

*In Spanish, the word "compadre" describes the relationship between a father and a godfather. For example, "Don Clemente is the godfather of my son, so Don Clemente and I are *compadres.*"

**literally everything. The best city taggers would be proud. The phrase is in the bottom corner of every signpost, painted on every wall, printed on every coffee sack, and even woven into the hammocks hanging on the porch. It's in the header of the stationary, in the email signatures, and on the badges the agronomists have sown to their vests.

El Roblar

El Roblar is also in the mountains of the Matagalpa region but is the antithesis of La Virgen on the spectrum of Nicaraguan coffee production. El Roblar is also at the end of a long road extending up into the mountains of the Matagalpa region, but this time the road doesn't end at a cluster of buildings housing and feeding estate workers and processing the coffee they produce, it ends at a cluster of small family homes and buildings, including a few small stores and parking spots for the brightly painted school buses that serve as public transportation between Matagalpa and El Roblar. The land here is owned by families who grow coffee as well as some subsistence crops. Kids run around in knots, teenage boys gallop past on horseback, and dogs trot in packs.

This is what rural Nicaraguan coffee looks like. The men wear wide brim cowboy hats and walk slow. The women wear their long black hair in slick pony tails. At night everyone walks with flashlights, because between the houses with a few bare bulbs and glowing TVs, there's no source of light to illuminate the muddy road when the clouds cover the moon. Small family homes sit along the road and tucked farther between densely packed trees. There are a few brick beneficios scattered around. People who have coffee but no beneficio can pay to use their neighbors'.

At night El Roblar sounds like mountain: humming insects, creaking branches, and murmuring leaves only occasionally interrupted by human shouts and dog yelps. By day it smells like thick forest and burning firewood cooking tortillas and pots of beans on the heat of the *fogón*.

Maria

Recorded Thursday, November 29, 2012, at the kitchen in Maria's house in El Roblar.

Maria is a widow, but her home is filled with her children, children-in-law, and grandchildren. She also has one room set aside for guests of the rural tourism program she's a part of. The coffee on Maria's property is planted almost all the way up to the house. She owns another little plot of land down the road and has her hands in much of the community's forward motion. She wears a navy blue sweater and a teal skirt.

Maria: *We had the idea to organize ourselves into a co-operative. What happened? There were five women who wanted to organize. So we decided to join the co-op Daniel Taylor, which was a co-op of men. They accepted us. We went to the meetings, we paid the dues, but we realized that they weren't taking us into account; we were just there to be there. What happened?*

People from CECOCAFEN approached us and proposed to us that we organize ourselves as our own group. We started saving up. When we had 100 cordobas ($4) together, we had the right to a loan of 1,000 Cordobas ($40). We started talking with the people at the UCA (Union of Agricultural Co-ops). The group that was saving up included thirty women. So the people from the UCA suggested that we consider organizing as our own co-op, and we said yes, that we liked that idea.

And this group needed a name. So we called ourselves "El Privilegio," *The Privilege. The people from the UCA were still telling us that we could form a co-op if we wanted to, to separate ourselves from the men. All the people at the UCA supported us so much, with the forms and the paperwork to be legally constituted as a co-op.*

In 2010 we made the business plan to start a roaster [to sell roasted coffee]. We went to trainings, five women went to Honduras to be trained in roasting. After a year of trainings we asked ourselves if there were enough women ready to build the roaster. And there were. Last year we started building. We were hauling sand, bricks. Just about a year now since we started construction. The goal was to take initiative and move ourselves forward, to have access to loans to build the roaster. Now we receive guests [as part of their rural tourism project].

It's been a beautiful experience for me. At first we were a little worried about having foreigners, people from other countries, as guests. Because sometimes you can be embarrassed to talk with people from other places. But now we're used to it. People from Denmark have come here! Gracias a Dios, we'll continue to move forward. We don't get too much coffee out of the finca, just around three quintales, but now we won't be selling it [in parchment] any more; we'll be selling it processed: roasted, ground and packed. The coffee will be called "El Privilegio." [Sound of kids laughing and the TV playing in the other room.]

Rachel: *So you've worked in coffee your whole life?*

Maria: *Yes. Since I was a very little girl.*

Rachel: *And your family has a farm or...?*

Maria: *No. We all worked at a big estate. A big* hacienda.

Rachel: *So that's wonderful that now you have your own property.*

Maria: *Um hm.* Gracias a Dios.

Rachel: *Did you all live on the estate during the harvest?*

Maria: *Yes. Some people came from other places to pick. Us, when we picked at the* hacienda *we lived there permanently. We worked in the off-season. We picked during the harvest and then maintained the land or planted. Or filled bags for the almacigos. This was near Jinotega, where I'm from.*

Rachel: *And do you have brothers and sisters?*

Maria: *Yes, I have— with all my brothers and sisters and I there's 13 of us. There are 6 men. Yup, thirteen of us in all. But one lives in Managua, another in Jinotega, and four of my brothers live here.*

Rachel: *And you came here because this lot of land was available?*

Maria: *It's...when we came here one guy had a house- where we went earlier* [to a neighbor's wet mill]*, he and my husband worked together in the mountains. And when he offered us this land, it turned out that we didn't have enough money together to buy it. But he told us, 'I don't have all the*

116

money I need to buy another piece land I want. If you're interested, at least give me something for it so that I have the money to buy the land I'm looking at." He had one female cow. So he told us, "Look, since you have part of the money we can work something out." We had two cows, a male and a calf. So he told us that if we gave him the two cows then we could pay the rest bit by bit.

And then we worked on the land together. But when we first got here it was ugly. Ugly ugly! There was nothing here. We planted all the coffee. The house wasn't here. Light either. We got the light three years ago.

The next day Maria shows me the roaster, a brick building with a 10kg roaster, a grinder, and a press for sealing the plastic bags of coffee. I helped four women portion coffee into 12oz bags. They all wore aprons monogramed with the Café El Privilegio logo.

Where does Maria's coffee go?
What she doesn't sell roasted, ground, and packed to community members, Maria sells via the women's co-op El Privilegio to Cecocafen, who then sells it to clients all over the world, including the wholesale roasters Equal Exchange and Café Campesino, who has an online store where you can not only order Cecocafen's coffee but also track specific containers of coffee exported from Nicaragua to New Jersey. Who knows; Maria's coffee might be in your cup at your church's coffee hour next Sunday.

If you came from Rocío and would like to return to Colombia, turn to p. 288

For a conversation with another woman who went from coffee picker to caficultor, turn to p. 135

For a conversation with another woman runs her farm, turn to p. 249

For a conversation with someone who helps sell Maria's coffee, turn to the next page.

Santiago Dolmus

Recorded Friday, November 30, 2012, in Cecocafen's offices in Matagalpa.

CECOCAFEN is the "Central de Cooperativas del Norte," the umbrella co-op to which many smaller co-ops belong. The main office building for Cecocafen is in the bustling little town of Matagalpa, the portal to the fertile surrounding mountains that produce beans, corn, and cacao as well as coffee. We're sitting in the basement conference rooms, away from the administrative chatter of the upstairs offices and reception. We drink cups of hot black coffee. Santiago wears a maroon Cecocafen polo.

Santiago: *We think that Cecocafen has the potential to be a…particular case in Nicaragua. Nicaragua has about forty years of movements towards forming co-ops. In the '80's there was a boom of forming co-ops, especially in rural areas, because of agrarian reform laws that were passed.*

Cecocafen was born in 1997, in the '90s, after the fever of co-operativism had passed. After the boom in the '80s, there was a change in governments in 1990. The Sandinistas lost the elections. So there was a change in power. And it started a backpedaling in the co-op movement. The first reform had been to give people land, and now the land was going back to big landowners.

There was a group of co-ops that were determined to survive. But the common problem was the sale of coffee. The families produced coffee but then had no way to sell it. So they had to turn to middlemen and large transnationals that had been here for years.

So Cecocafen was born. Principally, in order to commercialize coffees from co-ops. I say it's a particular case because it's an inverted phenomenon. It's not like when there's a large company that forms branches; Cecocafen is the inverse. There were people in their communities, there were co-ops, and from that we formed a unit, the unit as a commercializer. Cecocafen came from the bottom up. In order to comply with Nicaraguan law, the legal entity was the centralized body. It's a grouping of co-ops.

When it started there were five co-ops; now there are twelve. It's been around for fifteen years. As it has grown, Cecocafen has taken on new roles. First, it was commercialization. Then we added financial management, extension of lines of credit so producers can maintain the production, and, accompanying that— out of necessity— trainings and technical assistance.

118

But, in order to live up to our roots as a co-op [with members' best interests at heart], we also focus on environmental management. And we expect co-ops to follow social justice principles with all their members. When I say environmental management, I mean working to bring new technologies. For example, organic coffee and natural production. Carrying out a series of actions to conserve soil, water, biodiversity. And social justice meaning integrating women and young people as active members of the co-op.

To do that, you have to work on education, education for the entire family. All this can be interpreted as acting in new ways and not just following the traditional. When Cecocafen was created there was a serious market situation: the price crash. We had to look for market options, and one of those was to involve ourselves in Fairtrade. On a global level we know it applies to many things: fruit, honey, cacao, coffee, and crafts in many countries. Cecocafen successfully entered this system of fair trade.

This was the context into which the Co-operative El Privilegio was integrated. The Co-op El Privilegio was the legal way that these families, in this small area, could take on other activities. The women weren't just waiting for men to come home with money or bring them to work at a coffee farm. Rather, they have their own work. Which is why they have local businesses of small stores, selling food, raising chickens, and running their rural tourism project. And the coffee roaster is new, because they were looking for work they could do that would complement growing coffee.

They identified roasting as an option, did a market study, looked for financing, and right now are coordinating the funding so that next year they can open the roaster. Looking at Ceocafen this way, you can see it's an integration of people that came from one need but then grew to address many more.

Rachel: *So all the members of Cecocafen have Fairtrade certification?*

Santiago: *Every one. But, not all the coffee can be sold as Fairtrade. That's the other condition. If there are consumers, the vendors in those countries will be able to sell this coffee under this label. But if there isn't a market for it all…[then it will be sold as conventional coffee, without any premium or floor price]. We've done a lot— a lot! — of work to comply with the requirements of Fairtrade.*

Rachel: *Is coffee sold as coffee from Cecocafen? For example, when Doña Maria sells her coffee to the co-op in El Roblar, where does that coffee go?*

119

Santiago: *That's where Cecocafen's role as a hub comes in. All the co-ops have their points of purchase. But we have a central dry mill, Solcafe. So all the coffee from all the [twelve member] co-ops comes to Solcafe. That's where all the coffee from all the members is collected, from all 2,500 member producers. All smallholders like Doña Maria. There are some that are a little bit larger and some that are even smaller!*

Once the coffee's at Solcafe we do everything else: dry it, hull it, sort it, eliminate all the defects. We've had to educate members as to the quality of the coffee we're looking for. The transnationals will take anything; and they don't ask anything about what's going on on the fincas. We ask for a different behavior from the co-ops. Why? Because we want to be very respectful of the consumers. Because if Fairtrade is paying a better price, it should be for good coffee.

We understand it like this: like a pact between the producer and the consumer. Because now the big companies also want to be part of Fairtrade. There's no way to avoid the fact that Fairtrade is contaminated by purely monetary interests. The big companies and estates want to enter into Fairtrade. If someone were to ask them, "What's the reason?" I'm sure they wouldn't have an answer. It's because Fairtrade pays more for coffee. I'm sure some people would mention, "It's because it helps people! Look they built a nice little school in Nicaragua." But maybe a school isn't what's needed. What's needed is to change the relationship. Respect for the consumers over there, respect for the producers here, respect for the law, respect for the environment.

When we talk about quality of life we often relate it to the quality of the food, whether or not someone knows how to read, things like that. But it's about emotional quality. The peace of someone who wakes up in the morning— however early— but knows that when she wakes up, opens the kitchen, starts the fire, and makes coffee, she's not waiting for someone to tell her what to do.

The big producers, the big businesses say coffee is only for them. They say that the small producers should just be providers of raw material, that we don't know how to do what they're experts at. We're showing them that that's not the case.

For a conversation with someone else involved in Fairtrade, turn to p. 339

To return to Costa Rica, turn to the next page.

Back to
Costa Rica

Cedral *123*

Los Santos *141*

Monteverde *175*

Alajuela *175*

Cedral

Cedral is a tiny mountain community up, up, up from the small town of Cajon outside the city of Perez Zeledon (also called San Isidro) in the southwestern part of the country. Costa Rica doesn't have addresses per se; they use descriptions to, well, describe where places are. If I were telling someone in Costa Rica about Cedral I'd say, "*Estuve en Cedral, arriba de Cajón de Pérez Zeldon,*" which means, "I was in Cedral up from the Cajon area outside of Perez Zeledon." The system for giving directions and discussing places might not be quite as formal or as standardized as North Americans are used to, but it works.

The city of Perez Zeledon and its environs, including Cedral, are considered part of the Brunca coffee growing region. A giant Volcafe beneficio right on the main road through Perez is an illustrative indicator that this the land of yet another foreign processor and exporter. Volcafe is the coffee division of ED&F Man, the British commodity merchant with roots all the way back to imperial go-getters. (Think scoring the sole contract to supply rum to the British Navy. This is what original entrepreneurialism looked like). The next largest regional buyer is Coopeagri, a co-op with roots in the co-operative collectivism that means all coffee cherries, gorgeous and carefully grown or otherwise, get pooled at the same receivers and depulped as one.

Cedral might be a tiny mountain community, but its residents know a good idea (and a bad one) when they see it. The bad idea was subjecting their high grown, potential-packed coffee to commodity price fluctuations reflected in the price paid by the massive local mills. The good idea was certainly much better, but it was anything but easy. This is what today's grassroots entrepreneurialism looks like. (It actually includes grass, roots, and a few teams of hardworking oxen).

Froilan

Recorded Monday, December 3, 2012, in Froilan's home in Cedral.

Froilan, his brother Donald, Froilan's wife Aña, and their son Carlos picked me up from the bus station in bustling Perez Zeledon. We bounced our way up to Cedral, which was not quite as vertical a trek as the trip to Potenciana, but close, and there was one river-crossing that made me think, "Wow, if that bridge goes out Cedral will be my new home."

Froilan and I sit at the kitchen table. Aña is making tea and their sons Alejandro and Carlos play in the background. Froilan wears a white t-shirt and a plaid button-up.

Froilan: *We're an association that's not just dedicated to coffee. The association was born in '96; it's called Association of Producers of Cedral. But in 2006 we wanted to start a project, because as an association all we did was manage money [from small government incentives for producer organizations]. We wanted to start a project that would give some more structure to the group.*

So we started a tourism project, but we found it was very difficult. Instead, we decided to focus on coffee. Because we ourselves could form a tourist attraction. So we started, two years ago, building the small coffee beneficio. And up until now it's been pretty hard, because the prices of coffee are low. The market is very volatile. It's been pretty costly. But the most difficult part, which is to have the beneficio built, with all the machinery, we've already accomplished. Now we just have to focus on growing quality coffee. And make ourselves attractive to direct trade buyers who demand quality.

That's what we're working on now: improving quality. Communicating with producers about what are the best ways to grow coffee, such that we can produce a cup of coffee for demanding buyers.

Most of the producers who sell to our beneficio have been selling coffee to big companies their whole lives. So the idea was to improve the prices for producers. There are few producers who aren't from here, who live down at the bottom of the mountain, but have their fincas up here, and they produce a little coffee. They're the new ones who want to join us this year. Because they see it as an attractive way of selling their coffee.

It's just harder to explain to them the importance of picking high quality coffee. Because in the lower areas they're used to selling large volumes of coffee to large companies. It's a struggle we have with them. The producers here are more conscientious about picking only the ripest coffee, but we understand that it's a process of several years to really have a high quality coffee.

We know that at the end of the day the coffee is in the hands of the ones who harvest it. Because if they harvest underripe cherries, that's affecting our overall quality. So our business is also in their hands. It's a cultural struggle. Because people are accustomed to pick all the coffee they can see, even if it isn't all ripe. It's a struggle for the wellbeing of the whole group. Some producers are giving an incentive to harvesters who pick quality coffee, so that there's something in it for them. The pickers live a little better, the producers live a little better, and we sell our best coffee.

Really, I've always been a dairy farmer, not a coffee farmer. When we started with the beneficio I wanted to plant myself a plot of coffee, but my brother Donald has more coffee; he's grown coffee all his life. Our cafetales are at 1500 meters above sea level. We think we have, no, we know we have the optimal conditions for growing coffee. You have to take advantage of what's in your favor.

Rachel: *Is your family from Cedral?*

Froilan: *My father, and most of the people here, came from Santa Maria de Dota [one of the "Santos" of "Los Santos"]. But we're talking about in the '40s or '50s. My dad is from an area called Copey de Dota. They first went to Rivas, but my dad said they went there when he was eight. At that time everyone still traveled on foot; they walked from San Jose to San Isidro. There weren't roads. It was hard.*

They lived in an area called Buena Vista de Rivas starting when he was eight. And then they came up here, but he was already grown. And he liked it. He met his wife here, so he stayed. We were born here and we stayed here.

I tell Aña, my wife, that to leave here, you would have to practically [makes throat slitting gesture]. *Because to leave here— we feel like our roots are here. It's our community.*

Sometimes it's hard because the governments [Canton and National] want to impose things. Regulatory plans. They think that people can't live in this area. I think they're crazy. They say these are dangerous locations; but there's nothing dangerous here.

Rachel: *Dangerous how?*

126

Froilan: *Natural disasters. But in our community people live in flatter places; there aren't houses in dangerous locations. So it's hard to hear. But because of it, some people from here are leaving, one by one. And it shouldn't be that way. Because this is a place that produces a lot and where you can live in peace. It's a very peaceful place; there aren't thieves or anything. I always leave my car and house open and no one does anything to them. Maybe there's not much money, but there's a lot of peace. That's the most important. The kids are happy. They may not have all the technology in the world, but they have freedom. To leave here would be very difficult.*

The government also tries to tell us that these are freshwater producing areas. But we take good care of our water. Maybe we're not all organic, but there are reasons why [we still use some agrochemical products]. If you want to have a high quality coffee it can't be organic. We know beneficios that produce organic coffee, and it sells well, but because it's organic, not because it's good quality. We've tasted organic coffees and they taste very different from ours. So we can't sell quality coffee if we're organic. And if I'm organic I have to be certified, and to be certified they charge me $2,000 a year to certify my coffee. So other people are making a business out of adding costs to mine.

I can sell my coffee directly, and in that case the certification [the vendors are] giving is to come and see for themselves. What we're trying to do is have producers not use herbicides. And recycle agrochemical packaging. And we've started worm composting with cow patties and other organic material. We're trying to broaden people's environmental consciousness. So even though it's not organic, it's still environmentally friendly. We plant fruit trees so the birds will come and eat. Not like the big companies that plant pineapple, where all you see is yellow, yellow ground, and the only green things are the pineapples, where the rain falls and washes all the herbicides and pesticides into the rivers. It's disastrous.

So we've tried for our production and our producers to be conscious of what they do. And we've achieved a lot. We've really been focused on the water, that all the water that comes through our community leaves clean. We're only about a kilometer from the border of the Chirripó National Park. Because we're part of that protected area, we received money from PNUD Costa Rica (United Nations Program for Development) to be able to focus on points of contamination. They approved a $20,000 project to work on that, to improve the worm compost and build biodigestors to take advantage of waste products. Because people can compost the cow dung, but when they wash the *floors of the dairies, those contaminated waters can go into a biodigestor to create gas [that can be used for cooking].*

Those are the current focuses, but we'd also love to have a small lab to be able to reproduce microorganisms that can help rebuild the soil. We've realized that, over time, we've killed the helpful microorganisms in the soil, so we want to reincorporate them. And if we improve the soil we don't have to use as much chemical fertilizer.

We also hope to find money to buy a small roaster and a grinder for the beneficio, to be able to sell our coffee here in the Canton, and maybe even on the coast. So we can promote our coffee, and maybe then link back to tourism. Because we've talked to people at the hotels on the coast, and a lot of people, once they've gone surfing and all that, want to come up to the mountains. But that means we have to work hard on the environmental aspect, so that when the tourist comes he won't see something ugly.

And we'd love to do something that would be affordable for national tourists. Because there are lots of people right here in Perez Zeledon who don't know anything about coffee. Maybe they'd like to come to the mountains and see too. Rather than have someone who just comes once, we would make it affordable so that Costa Ricans would want to come back again and again.

If you came from Lucy and would like to return to Turrialba, turn to p. 63

For a conversation with another coffee grower active in organizing producers, turn to p. 87

For a conversation with another family who works together to grow and process coffee, turn to p. 193

For a conversation with Froilan's brother Donald, turn to the next page.

Donald

Recorded Wednesday, December 5, 2012, at Cedral's new micromill, Los Jilgueros.

Donald and I stand under the edge of the tin roof covering the coffee washing machinery. The weather oscillates in and out of drizzle but always staying all the way in the fog. Donald's horse, Chile, is tied to a nearby Poró tree. She chomps on the leaves. Donald comments that she's hungry after a hard day of work. She hauled two loads of coffee sacks down the mountain from the cafetal where we'd been picking that morning. The second load had four sacks of roughly 30 kilos each. She still wears her wooden "sack rack." Donald wears black rubber boots and a beige Costa Rican bucket hat.

Donald: *We really like, and are really happy, with the new type of work we've been doing. Well, last year Froilan and I did everything [processed all the coffee] by ourselves, but this year we were able to hire two employees for the beneficio. Because it's difficult for us, growing in quantity; we can't take care of our own things [fincas and cattle] and be dedicated to all the paperwork. But that's the point of the project— to keep growing so that we can provide employment to the community.*

For example she [one of beneficio employees, currently climbing up the side of the depulper to make sure the coffee is flowing smoothly] has three kids and is a single mom. So we taught her all the basics of operations and she learned really quickly and has been working really hard. And he [the other employee, a wiry eighteen year old currently filling sacks with washed coffee and loading them into a wheel barrow to bring to the drying beds] has really dedicated himself to all things coffee. The hope is that he can keep learning about the whole process of coffee and maybe in a few years study even more so that he can learn how to cup. Which would help us a ton. They're part of the association [of agricultural producers], which is a good thing.

Yes, the beneficio certainly has offered a lot of opportunities. And with the roaster, the idea is that the women, within the association there's a group of twenty women, the idea is that some of them can learn to roast coffee, and then we can keep growing by selling roasted coffee too——at the national level. So that will create jobs for the women who roast and pack and get the coffee ready to sell. Another hope is that for the women- because a group of them also grows flowers to sell— we can provide organic fertilizer from the coffee cherry skins, because flowers are hard to grow, so we do lots of work with worm compost. Because overall it's important to take advantage of the waste.

> *We're going to lay this [load of coffee the wiry eighteen year old just walked past carrying] in the beds up the hill so that it doesn't get wet. It's just that we don't have a lot of space left for the beds, and if we get a lot of coffee, we'll need to make more, I don't know, somewhere up there. For next year. Globalworks* offered us a group in March, so we'll keep working with them building more drying beds. It's a lot of fun to teach them every year, the kids.*

Rachel: *And do the same ones come every year?*

Donald: *No, they're different ones. After a few days they know how to do all the jobs, and they like it a lot. It's work they've never done before. The first year, when we started with this construction, literally started digging, it was just a hole in the ground; that was hard! And it was raining! And the students were all having fun,; they were starting mud fights!*

Rachel: *And before you built the micromill, everyone just turned in their coffee to Volcafe down there [at the receiver about a kilometer down the hill]?*

Donald: *Yes, Volcafe, and Coopeagri. Coopeagri is a co-op from Perez Zeledon that had a lot of strength in coffee, but they started…I don't know, their prices were really low and people started to look for other options—small depulpers, micromills. And now, people saw that the quality [in this area] was really good, and what [the larger mills] did was mix it all together; they didn't separate it. There was this opportunity to separate it, knowing that [the higher elevation] coffee has, has a different value. Higher quality."*

Rachel: *Where we were [picking coffee that morning] up the mountain, that land was always yours or your family's?*

Donald: *Yes…the first person to come to Cedral was my grandfather. So he started working. More or less fifty years ago, Cedral was founded. And people have always lived from the same things: coffee, dairy, cattle, garden vegetables, edible crops; they planted corn.* [Sound of coffee dryer churning in the background. Coffee parchment paper being burned to dry another batch of coffee. Rolling over and over in cylinder. Whir. Hum. Buzz. Mild industrial white noise.]

And we realized that we were at a good height to plant coffee, so we wanted to take advantage of that.

Coffee's always been more valuable in the Los Santos region. And in the Central Highlands. And the Brunca region, here, the cuppers always said that it was bad coffee— but we realized that there was a high part of the Brunca region that did produce good quality coffee. So, upon separating it, the cups did turn out well. So that's the importance of the project. [Another grower who just turned in his coffee comes over to talk to Donald. They discuss how they both have kids who will be starting secondary school (seventh grade) and that they will have to take a bus "down" to the next town instead of just walking 1km to the primary school.

Sound of rain plopping on tin roof. Sudden start. Quick ascension to high volume but not quite the deafening sound of a real mountain downpour.]

Rachel: *There wasn't anything here when your grandfather arrived?*

Donald: *No, only mountain. And there's a tree called cedar, sweet cedar. There was a lot here when they arrived, so they gave [the town] the name, they said, "We've come to cedar grove [cedral], with so many cedar trees." But they learned that it was a really good hardwood, and people were exploiting them, selling the wood. So they started to move farther up into the mountains. All the way up there are trees that grow really quickly, that are a meter in diameter. But then they eliminated most of them. So we've been trying to bring seeds to plant, to have cedar in the cafetales. Because it was a* cedral, *but then there were no cedars.*

And my grandparents...there were very difficult times. They talked about— here it rains a lot, but it used to rain even more. It was just forest. So as it's been getting a little warmer [every year]... Then there was a time when people, when the town was growing, and people carved out farms way up the mountain. And when they passed the law about protecting national parks, when they defined the border of the Chirripó National Park, a lot of farms were within the boundary, and so they had to move out. But, thanks to [the park], now we have a large quantity of protected water, and, well, they're working on the aqueduct [to bring water] to the whole Cajón district. And it's one of the three best waters in the country. And so we've learned, through programs and trainings- environmental ones, to take care of what we have and to live- to be able to take advantage while still taking care of nature. The way of working with cattle- of not cutting trees near the streams to protect water sources from the waste from the herd- we've been making small biological corridors along the streams so that people can keep producing, taking the same advantage, but at the same time protecting. That's the idea. [Dryer drying. Depulper depulping. Washer washing. Beneficio cranking out coffee. Low drone].

With coffee, the goal is that it's not just coffee but that there's also more variety of crops, trees, so that there's diversity. More than anything so that we maintain a green cover for the majority of the year so there's no erosion. And not use as many herbicides. To make the change from working conventionally to doing things organically, one has to go little by little. And the crops feel— eh, they don't produce a harvest. The plants are accustomed to one way of being treated, and if you want to turn organic from one year to the next there won't be a harvest. The idea isn't to work suddenly organically, but to go changing little by little. Every year we can move forward until we get to at least a point of equilibrium* with nature and man. That we use the land, but we also take care of it.

Rachel: *So you also hope to be totally organic?*

Donald: *At least some producers have that idea. Everyone is working on some small organic lots, but starting everything from the beginning, from the almacigo and the soil used for that.*

Rachel: *Then it's a little easier. Because the soil has to have three years without…without anything. And to make the change can be a challenge, but if the soil never had any chemicals, it's better.*

Donald: *Yeah, it's easier. What I say about coffee, to get good cuppings, is that it's hard for organic coffee to offer that. There are some finer elements [of cupping flavor notes] that organic coffee doesn't give.*

Rachel: *Here at the micromill can you keep them separate, like if one producer has organic coffee and others no?*

Donald: *Yes, of course. We can keep them apart and processes them separately.*

Rachel: *Yeah, because [organic certification] auditors are always looking for that, to see that the beneficio can ensure that it's been processed separately.*

Donald: *Yes, here we can process it apart. If there were coffee like that, we could process it apart. Organic coffee sells for a good price, and quickly. But organic coffee doesn't give the same cup. So it brings down the quality a little bit. But it does have another advantage because it doesn't have chemicals. We do hope to have some certification, that's true.*

Our buyer this year, he's British, is asking that we keep logs of everything we do to the coffee on the finca, before it gets to the mill. What processes we've applied, so that when it gets to the beneficio, we keep another log— from up at the basins where it's unloaded to when it's packed in storage. And then it leaves storage with the log. And so they, over there [in England] also have to keep a type of log to say, "Ok, we did this or that roasting." Light roast, dark roast, whatever roast, so that— totally— the client knows what the process was for the coffee right up until it arrives at the table. So that he knows with certainty that he's drinking the coffee that has all this information behind it. Because maybe he says, "I really liked this coffee, what did they do to this coffee to make it taste like this?" And we can show him, from the finca, what the process was, that we're here for a long time, picking out the under ripe cherries by hand.

This is the traceability of coffee: what was the entire process? This is so that the coffee will have added value. We can say that the producer is dedicating some time to maintaining these logs, and we can show the cuppers what was going on on the farms. We can tell them we did such and such with the coffee to help improve the cup; we regulated the shade. All these things that coffee really feels. Coffee…changes. The cup changes between coffee with shade and coffee in full sun. There are variables.

Rachel: *Yeah, and coffee also responds to weather changes. Even if it's just one degree, or shade, or something different in the soil, the type of fertilizer, herbicide. Whatever thing it is, the plant responds. And its response carries through all the way to the cup. It's pretty impressive.*

Donald: *At the end you can see it reflected in the cup. Everything you did to the coffee back there, every change, ends up in the cup. We, as producers, three years ago, didn't have this understanding. Nothing more than— maybe that one variety was easier to roast than another, so when one was burning the other was just barely toasted. But with this* [gestures to the beneficio around him], *we've had to start to do other kinds of work. We've had to learn about more than just different varieties to find ways to improve the cup. And, at the end, we can use this to help producers. That's the idea.*

Rain continues to plop on the tin roof.

If you came from Rodolfo and would like to return to Puriscal, turn to p. 73

*For a conversation with someone else who values equilibrium, turn to p. 162

For stories of another town founder, carver out of pure mountain, turn to p. 249

For a conversation with the man who exports Cedral's coffee to Direct Trade clients all over the world, turn to p. 181

*Globalworks coordinates community service travel for groups of students. Donald explained that the first group of Globalworks students to visit Cedral was studying "pre business" at Harvard and came to learn about the source of coffee and jumpstart an entrepreneurial community project, which turned out to be helping lay the literal foundation for the beneficio and the structural foundation for the micromill business.

Aña

Recorded Thursday December 6, 2012, at Aña's home in Cedral.

Aña and I sit on the couch drinking tea. (It's cold but too late in the evening to drink coffee. Finca life means early nights and early mornings). Carlos has gone down to the little cluster of buildings by the school and Alejandro plays with a few racecars on the floor in front of us. Aña wears a navy sweatshirt.

Rachel: *Froilan and Donald's grandparents were some of the first people here, right?*

Aña: *Yes. Froilan's mom's parents. They were some of the first people to arrive here. His dad's parents came from the Los Santos area. They went first to Perez Zeledon. There was nothing here; you had to cross Death Ridge on foot. It was very difficult, that's why it's called Death Ridge, because lots of people died trying to cross it. They arrived at Buena Vista de Rivas and from there, people had told them about a place up here, so they came.*

When Froilan's dad's parents came, his mom's parents had already been here a little while, and they had cleared out some of the mountain a little bit. They had something done. And all their children continued to develop it.

Rachel: *Were you also born here?*

Aña: *No, I was born in Santa Teresa. Until I was thirteen I lived down there, by the highway [through Perez Zeledon]. I was born there, and my dad had a small finca, tiny, tiny- like one or two hectares. Later he'd turned it into five [hectares], and he planted a little bit of coffee, had a pasture for the cow. He liked coffee, and he liked cattle, but there wasn't space for all that.*

At that time it was very common for families from this area [Perez Zeledon] to go and pick coffee in Los Santos, where they made good money, and they lived the rest of the year off that money. We went away several times. That's what we called it "going away." "Going away" meant going to Los Santos. And one time when we went, in '94, when we came back from going away, my uncle- he had a finca in Cedral, but he'd had various personal and family disputes- so my uncle said, "I want to get out of here." And that was when he proposed to my dad that they switch farms.

But ours was five hectares and my uncle's was forty-five. Very big! So they negotiated. For me it was incredible. I was thirteen, almost fourteen. When I was twelve my family had come here [to Cedral] to pick coffee on a

135

man's farm. I dreamed- we came up here to pick coffee, and I could hear the cows and the calves and everything, because there used to be more dairies. And I dreamed of one day coming back, to be able to hear the cows, to come back here to live. I wanted to live here. I prayed to God that I could live here!

And I barely knew the place. Really, I just was dreaming of listening to cows and wanted to one day live here. My friends told me not to be stupid, that it would only occur to me to think that it was pretty here! And I told them, "But one day I want to live way up there." I was only twelve or thirteen.

When my father came up here to buy the finca, I was beside myself. I was so happy! Thrilled! I wanted to get going already and move up here right away. When they made the deal, our finca was worth 5,000,000 colones [$9,750, at today's conversion rate] and my uncle's was worth 10,000,000 [$19,500]. So we still owed him 5,000,000 colones. We paid him back by picking coffee and growing stuff on the finca. But the finca is big, so my dad had coffee, and dairy cows. And we started working.

That was in '94. We got to work. But we had to work very hard, because we had to make an annual payment on the farm. We had to pick coffee. A lot of coffee. And my siblings were little. Just my older brother, Andrei, who's two years older than me, and the other three were in school, and then another little one was born. It was very difficult because Andrei and I were the two oldest, and we had to work with my father. It was just us: Andrei, me, and my father. To work. And it was a big finca.

We managed to pick around 260 fanegas a year [5,200 cajuelas]. Just the three of us with two workers. It was incredible. We'd pick coffee from five in the morning until five thirty in the afternoon. You have to do what you have to do. We'd milk the cows in the morning, and at six we headed off for the cafetal.

But I loved it. As hard as it was, I was giddy to be living here. The finca's still there. My father's still there, working it. Just that now he works alone because my siblings aren't there. Just my older brother is left here, who also works with coffee. And the youngest, who's in high school. The rest left to work, make their lives elsewhere. And I came to Cedral!

And I got married and stayed. Even better! And I still want to live farther up in the mountains! [Laughs] Because I'd love to have free range animals: pigs, geese. But for now we'll just stick with the cows and the oxen.

Froilan and I always say it's not about "having;" it's about how you live. To live peacefully and have what you have. I don't know; it seems like we don't have to complicate things so much. I think we can be happy without having to have so many things. And showing your children how to take care of what they have. To be happy with what you have, whether it's a lot or a little.

And to help others. That's important. Because in a community like this, if we didn't live that way, we wouldn't have anything. Only working together can you improve things. In reality, coffee has been one of the most important things for us because it helps develop the community. Here, when the coffee's ripe, everyone picks coffee and everyone gets paid. It might be little by little, but things are developing, and we'll all come out ahead.

The kids go pick coffee to buy their things for school, like Jairo and those guys.* They learn the value of things because they have to work hard. That's how it is.

Rachel: *Before you built the beneficio, did everyone used to sell to that receiver?*

Aña: *Yes. But back then we picked coffee very badly. Like I was telling you up in the cafetal this morning, we would just strip the whole branch of everything all at once, ripe, half-ripe, green, everything. We'd pick quickly in order to pick a lot. I was especially quick, which is why it's so hard for me to pick coffee like this [only the ripest of the ripe], because I spent so many years stripping the branches, in the culture of "the best worker is whoever picks the most cajuelas, doesn't matter of what." It was about quantity not quality. And now it's quality, not quantity.*

It was even more drastic if you went to pick in Los Santos. Two parents with two kids could pick eighty or ninety cajuelas in a day. It was pretty incredible the amount of coffee. And it's a place with wind and sun, very beautiful. But because of the climate the coffee ripened all at once- the whole entire tree! You wouldn't see a single green cherry! That was then; I don't know about now. But that was a place where you could strip every branch.

The last time we went away to pick coffee, it was my mother, my father, Andrei and me, the little kids didn't do anything but play in the cafetal- like Alejandro now. The four of us earned enough money to come up here- because my dad didn't pay for the finca [he'd traded and owed the rest], he used the money from selling his land to buy cows, oxen, horses, pigs. He bought everything. With that money we bought all the animals, and the animals started to reproduce.

And there was even a sugarcane mill where we'd make sweets. We also made cheese. And there was coffee, a lot of coffee. It was good because we didn't have to go away and pick coffee in Los Santos anymore. It was a different way of life. It was something we'd never experienced, being able to flourish on our own finca. And work for ourselves and grow our own things. My father also planted beans, corn, yucca, even oranges. He always maintained a milpa [plot with many integrated crops]. It was all there. It was awesome.

So that was the last time we went away to pick coffee in Los Santos because it was no longer necessary. We had everything. Gracias a Dios. Because going away to pick coffee is very difficult, exhausting. Terribly exhausting. You have to start early, and sometimes they were measuring the coffee with just the light from the truck's headlights because it was dark. From the morning to night picking, and then the medida by headlights.

But that's life. It's beautiful. As long as you have your health and are able to work. When we came up here, my sister didn't want to come. She said it was too far from where we'd lived before. Andrei didn't want to either. Just my father and I wanted to come up here. And I was so happy that we did! And we had pigs, cows, horses, so many animals. Now my kids are growing up here, and I hope they stay and continue to move the community forward. Work in the microbeneficio one day. And be able to sell our coffee to the world.

Carlos walks in and starts giving us an update of the men working on the aqueducts that are being installed through Cedral to bring fresh mountain water from a spring to the city of Perez Zeledon below. Alejandro jumps to his feet, a racecar in each hand. This is what the future looks like.

Where does Froilan's, Donald's, Aña's, and the rest of Cedral's coffee go?
Via the boutique exporter Exclusive Coffees, some of it goes to Union Hand Roasters in England. Some of it might go to Exclusive's other clients, and some of it stays right in Cedral, where the Diaz family drinks it every morning.

If you came from Gerardo and would like to return to Turrialba, turn to p. 33

If you came from Maria and would like to return to Nicaragua, turn to p. 118

For a conversation with another coffee grower who really loves what he does, turn to p. 229

To sidestep to San Jose and then continue to Los Santos, turn to the next page.

*Jairo is a neighborhood teenager who'd picked coffee with us up in Donald's cafetales that morning. School had just closed for the summer (in Costa Rica Christmas coincides with the middle of school-free summer, and no one can fathom that people in the U.S. go to work and school immediately before and after Christmas, as though the holiday itself needs ample padding of free time to actually be enjoyed.) Because school was out Jairo was eager to get to work because he wanted to earn some money. As we were picking he was trying to decide what he would use his earnings for: a new pair of sneakers, a better cellphone, maybe a backpack.

As we all ate lunch together, seated on the leafy ground of the cafetal, right next to brimming sacks of picked cherries, Jairo pulled out his phone saying, "At least there's no 3G up here. At one of the other farms I was at last week there was. And if you can be on Facebook in the middle of a cafetal, what is the world coming to?!"

Highspeed
Earlymidnight
Before the opening closes
Faster
It's getting dark
What can you see when there's no light?
Lies.
Brown eyes
Rushing bodies
Streetdirt caked and smeared in creases
Folds of faces
Backs of necks
Pantleg wrinkles
Invisible curls of cigarette smoke
Hawk
Repeat
Hawk
It's getting dark.

San Jose, January, 2013.

Los Santos

Los Santos is yet another of Costa Rica's eight coffee producing regions. On international packaging and coffee menus it is often referred to as "Tarrazú," but internally it's "Los Santos," named as such for its concentration of towns with "San" or "Santa" in their names. The internal and external consensus is that Los Santos is home to Costa Rica's "best" coffees, and Cup of Excellence ^{Huila p. 337} winners do tend to come from this zone. It was the first region to capitalize on the success of the good reputation of Costa Rican coffee and market itself as having single origin coffees exclusively from Tarrazú Zona de Los Santos that were even better than the Costa Rican average.

Because Los Santos coffee has been marketed so well for so long, Ticos from the zone have a tendency to automatically market themselves as part of the collective Los Santos narrative ^{Collective Regurgitation p. 402.} They know what sells, and they'll keep selling it. Many of the farms in Los Santos are relatively close to the beneficios, meaning doable logistics for all parties involved.

The emotional heart of Los Santos is easily Santa Maria de Dota, a small Costa Rican mountain town that is everything you'd want a small Costa Rican mountain town to be. On the main square (it has a main square!) are a church, a few shops and some hole-in-the-wall eateries. A soccer ball's kick away is the soccer field. Along one side of the field is the Coopedota complex, which includes a large wet and dry mill, coffee pulp composting facilities, giant storage silos, the hardware store, and a sizeable roasting and packing facility which preps everything from the Quetzal brand grocery store blend to the $13/12oz Dota Fresh, which is on the short list of the best coffees I've ever tasted. The roaster also roasts coffee for Café Privilegios, the adjacent coffee shop, which serves everything from black drip coffee to giant macchiatos. This is what ground to grounds looks like.

Dota is a moderate tourist attraction and certainly a coffee buyer's dream source trip. Everyone in town knows everyone, and everyone seems genuinely happy to meet foreigners, and not in the slimy, "How can I take your money?" sort of way. There is a bright, optimistic energy here, one that seems to be infusing some new soul back into a place that might have been wrung dry in the overpresence of the recent past.

Ariela

Recorded Monday, December 10, 2012, in the Coopedota
Cupping Lab.

    The cupping lab, with its sample roasters and stacks of
handleless ceramic cupping mugs, is inside the Coopedota
complex (under the coffee shop and next to the storage silos). Co-
op members mingle and slowly exit the lab, in high spirits after
finishing their comprehensive course on coffee agronomy, ground
to grounds. This is the same crew I met at CATIE, and I make a
round of hellos. I remember Ariela because both times she wears
blue eye shadow.

Rachel: *I'm interested in the lives of the people who produce coffee. Where
do they live, what kind of work is involved in being a producer, how did they
start being coffee growers? The histories of your farm— is it family property?*

Ariela: *In my case it was passed down. My parents gave it to me. And since
then I've been trying to put lots of love— more than anything— into it. Little
by little, effort. They showed me how to work, and by seeing them work I
learned how to relate to the plants.*

Rachel: *Do you live on the farm?*

Ariela: *No, I live in downtown, and the farm's 2km away. So I go back
and forth every day by car. Or by foot. I like walking more. It's highgrown,*
café de altura.

Rachel: *And it's you who's in charge of the farm?*

Ariela: *Yup, just me. All the work. I take care of the farm by clearing
weeds manually with a machete.*

Rachel: *What are some of the challenges you have to face?*

Ariela: *Well…the rain. It's a humid place so…*

Rachel: *How have you seen things change? Since you've been working with
coffee since you were a kid; what's different now?*

Ariela: *I tried to work organically. So the quality is getting much better.*

Rachel: *So working organically means using less herbicides and things?*

Ariela: *Less chemicals. The soil itself makes a good fertilizer. And hardly any fumigants.*

Rachel: *Do you use microorganisms to control pests and plagues? Do you have shade trees?*

Ariela: *Yes, we do, and we have a little bit of shade.*

Rachel: *Do you have lots of types of coffee or…*

Ariela: *We do but everything we're replanting is Caturra. There are lots of plants that are older so we're switching them out with new ones.*

Rachel: *So the cupping course is finished? What types of things did the course include?*

Ariela: *We learned to cup coffee.*

Rachel: *And have you tried yours?*

Ariela: *Yes, today yes! That was something I've always wanted to do; I wanted to know what my coffee tastes like. And it was good— really!*

Rachel: *I'm learning to cup too.*

Ariela: *You have to go a little bit at a time. It's hard. You can tell that they're different, but you don't know what they taste like.*

Rachel: *So you were cupping coffee from…*

Ariela: *From various producers. And international ones too.*

Rachel: *And did you have to explain the differences between them?*

Ariela: *Um hm, we had to find different flavors. And even from the same variety, if it grows here downtown or mine from up in the mountains we noted different flavors. It goes back to how you manage it. If you use a lot of pesticides, lots of chemicals, it'll also alter the flavor.*

Rachel: *That's true. Because if it's in the soil it's in the roots…*

Ariela: *Yes. And also in the fruit. If we spray now then in the* recolección *[final harvest] you'll be able to taste a little.*

Rachel: *And by working more organically, this means more workers, to maintain it?*

Ariela: *Yes, and lots of compost. And clearing with machete, to keep the weeds down.*

Rachel: *Why did you decide to make the change to organic, to a more sustainable management?*

Ariela: *For our health. To not be putting people in danger. If it's something we're going to drink it should be healthy, right?*

Rachel: *But here can you sell organic coffee to the co-op? Do they have a separate place to process it as per organic certification requirements?*

Ariela: *They do. But it gives low production, so one can't manage it purely organically; you have to boost it with some fertilizer and compost.*

Rachel: *Well, I always say that even if it's not perfectly organic, the less chemicals the better.*

Ariela: *Yes. And it was exciting to finally try it. Because here they mix my coffee with everyone else's, and to try it [separately] one never knows if it might taste ugly, terrible! But it was good!*

Rachel: *That's great! Anything else you want the people who drink your coffee to know?*

Ariela: *Nothing other than I was very proud to try it because it's made with a lot of love, produced with lots of love; and it's the most natural possible.*

If you came from Karole and would like to return to Turrialba, turn to p. 51

For a conversation with a woman who runs an organic farm in Turrialba, turn to p. 56

For a conversation with a Panamanian who has also tasted the coffee he grows, turn to p. 189

For words from the **CEO** the co-operative Ariela belongs to, turn to the next page.

Roberto Mata

Recorded Tuesday, December 11, 2012, in the dry mill/storage section of Coopedota beneficioShapes of Coffeespace p. 354.

Roberto is Coopedota's CEO and is opening the opening ceremony for the barista competition that is the final assessment of the fiteen high school students who've completed a two-year integrated course on coffee, ground to grounds. In Costa Rica December is the season for graduations and wrappings up. This is also not your average assessment; the Dota high school students will be observing the strict rules of the World Barista Championships.

Two high stainless steel tables are set up with fully operating espresso machinery. Two dining tables are set with four colorful place settings each. Family and friends of students are dressed in collared shirts and dresses, seated in rows of wooden chairs. Roberto wears a black apron monogrammed with the Dota Fresh logo.

Roberto: *We're going to get started. A very good morning to Mr. Adrián Cordero of the high school, to the members of the school board, to family and friends, champions, students from the high school. I'm going to present the judges we have with us: Mr. Jose Solís, part of the barista team representing Coopedota, also Ms. Paula Chauverria. Jose and Paula come from Specialty Coffee Association of Costa Rica. We remember that Jose, right now, is part of the team in charge of barismo at the national level, along with Paula Chauverria. Audrey is a French barista who is working in Norway and right now is visiting Costa Rica. I'm Roberto Mata, for those of you who don't know me well. The four of us will be the sensory judges. Sensory judges look for the visual component and judge the taste of the coffee prepared by the presenters. Remember that each participant will try to make, in fifteen minutes, four espressos, four cappuccinos, and four original drinks. We are going to judge how the process looks and how the coffees taste.*

We also have William Roja; William is the technical judge. The technical judge is in charge of watching how [the participants] manage the machine and how they leave it. It has to be clean. This has its techniques, which maybe they've explained to their parents and families; you have to manage quite a few steps and closely controlled situations.

Very good. Allow me to inform you that we have, on behalf of the Co-op, an extremely important message for everyone. The Co-op, over the last

147

two years, has been working with these students for an average of three hundred to four hundred hours that they've dedicated. And they've studied from the agronomic part, through the processing part, to roasting, and finally barismo. For us it is extremely important that these youths understand what goes into the local coffee industry. We work very hard at this here at the Co-op because the different phases that we're showing them are the different activities of the Co-op. Beyond the requirements of any job description, everyone has his or her responsibility to dedicate time to these students. It's extremely important and we do it for two reasons: the first is so that they feel the passion for coffee, that 85% of the income of the Canton comes from coffee. So, the better we carry out all the phases of the coffee producing chain, we are going to prepare better coffee growers, and we are going to visualize better business endeavors and better lives.

The second reason that we do this is to show much-deserved respect to Co-opedota's coffee producers. These people spend all year, they're starting the nice [harvest] part right now, but there are many parts behind it, the times when it's raining and still necessary to be in the cafetales, when everything's expensive and the prices might not be that good, and this is an homage to all the coffee producers. We always want to show this great respect that all the coffee growers of the Santos region deserve, particularly those from the Co-op.

Students about to participate: relax, take a deep breath, concentrate, apply what you've learned. The judges will try to evaluate the work you do very objectively. And you're going to come out ahead! We hope that in the future you, students, will be the people who improve the coffee industry and the work of the Co-op. That is why we want you to carry, written on your heart, everything you've learned about coffee and also some lessons of ethics, of how to be better students, better citizens, to be happier every day. And— accompanied by a good cup of coffee— we will be happier even more easily.

For another conversation in the shadow of stored coffee, turn to p. 268

For a conversation with a growers' association president, turn to p. 339

For a conversation with a participating student, turn to the next page.

Fernanda

Recorded Tuesday, December 11, 2012, in the dry/mill storage area of the Coopedota beneficio.

Fernanda has just successfully completed the barista evaluation, expertly making her twelve drinks in under fiteen minutes. She wears an embroidered yellow blouse and a matching ribbon around her ponytail.

Rachel: *At the beginning of the course what goals did you have? What did you hope to accomplish as a result of being a part of it?*

Fernanda: *Honestly, I didn't really even want to be a part of the course. Because the beginning part, the agriculture, is pretty tiring, with all the diseases, certain kinds of coffee and certain kinds of plagues. Then, the part about processing is pretty cool, where you can see the types of drying: mechanical, patios in the sun. All the different kinds of coffee, and how whether they're dried in the sun or not makes a difference in the roast.*

Then, when we got to barismo, that's the most important part of the course. Because that's where you get to apply everything you learned. I've worked a little in the café, so I knew how to do some things. People are really becoming open to everything barismo is. People are happy, super satisfied with what you make them.

Rachel: *Would you like to keep working with coffee?*

Fernanda: *Yes, I want to be a barista! And I made it! Because I made all my drinks within the time limit, so now I have my title.*

Rachel: *Of everything you did in the course, what was the most challenging, and in what were you most successful?*

Fernanda: *With barismo it's tough to learn to control so many things. Because you have your time very calculated: you have to pull every espresso in a certain number of seconds, and make the foam, keeping the milk texture consistent and the right temperature. It was very interesting. Barismo was the most challenging. But getting my title was a huge success.*

Rachel: *Congratulations! Best of luck.*

Roberto announces the next participant. Applause.

For a conversation with someone else who values careful drink preparation, turn to p. 240

For a conversation with someone who has worked in a very different kind of coffee making, turn to p. 307

For a conversation with a lifetime coffee producing family in Santa Maria de Dota, who maybe even produced some of the coffee Fernanda used to practice making the perfect cappuccino, turn to the next page.

Miguel

Recorded Tuesday, December 11, 2012, on Miguel's finca.

It's a sunny and clear afternoon. Miguel's finca is just a short drive from downtown Dota. Dry leaves crunch underfoot. His wide yellow pickup is parked behind us. Miguel wears a green baseball hat.

Miguel: *I'm trying to see if it will work, giving the same fertilizer to the avocado trees. That's more or less what the idea of the avocado trees is. Along all the paths— all of them— they all have avocado trees along the edges. I didn't want to see avocado trees in the middle of the cafetal. They seemed like they'd work best along the paths.*

This year's harvest is looking good. The last twenty-five years of my life [gestures behind and around him] *this here. From the river all the way up here. The river is like 200, 250 meters down there. The property ends there at the river. More or less 900 meters wide. Coffee, all of it. Coffee and avocado, trying to create the best conditions, give it the best conditions for production. So it can produce in the best way. So, what it is you want to know?*

Rachel: *Like you said, this is the last twenty-five years of your life. What went into making it? Did you have to plant all this or was there already coffee here?*

Miguel: *No, this was pasture twenty-five years ago. Twenty-five, twenty-seven years ago this was all pasture. My family also had a dairy. And there came a time when they closed the dairy. And life being life, my parents arrived at a point when they decided to pass down what they had to their sons— the two of us. So they gave this to me. I had, at the beginning, two* manzanas, *as we say. It was more or less a hectare and a half. And from there, I started to plant. Just with the help of my wife, from the point of physical work we started the fight together. We got married, and we decided to plant more, and there we went! There we went and here we are, way up here. We have those newest cafetales up there. We keep going; there are two or three new plantings up there, and now we're trying to plant even more.*

It's a story, how do I say it, it's not a question of— I'm not going to paint it like that, not all black as black, but also not all clean and white. There's been some of everything; there's been some of everything. Gracias a Dios, I think that the majority of it is very beautiful, very good, because

151

apart from all that one has to do to fight for what one wants, the education of my children has come from here; the health of my children has come from here. Their food, ours too. Now, an extremely important and fundamental part of this fight is the Co-op. A lot of the economic part that we used to do this has come from them. And not just to this, also to recover from a ton of, from a series of events that was truly difficult, to do with my oldest daughter's health- the one you know, that you met yesterday there [working in the cafeteria]. She had a very serious health problem. She had a transplant. Thanks, thanks first to God, and second to the, to Coopedota. We could carry out all the treatments necessary to still have her with us.

And so, this is the finca. There are some parts that are steeper, some parts, like this, flatter. This part where we are now is the flattest. This, agriculture, is a difficult profession. Difficult in the sense that you live on illusions. The illusions are affected by a ton of variables that often are out of your control, in most cases. In most occasions one doesn't get the price they should get for the work put in. On the other hand, we're exposed to a series of events, also at the economic level, that in other crops you don't see. The good part: you have the chance to be a landowner, to be your own boss, to...make your own decisions in all areas of your life; you're not depending on someone else to see if you have a job or not.

You have *to work, you* should *work, you* can *work. And in my case I'm truly grateful to God. I'm very proud that I have someplace and I can keep going. I can fight, and I can, also, give other people jobs. We're in a field, Raquel, where, I think at least, that is the most democratic in the sense of wages for society. Like I said yesterday, from this plant, a picker who's five years old makes the same as one who's eighty. For me, that's the most satisfied I can feel. A Saturday at noon, when I sit in any corner [of two paths through the cafetal], with cash in my hand, and people come with their, what do you call it, their, their proof of how much they've picked that week, their "timesheets." They give them to me, and I start to say, "You earned so much, here you go." That— that is— I wouldn't change it for anything. I wouldn't change it for anything. It gives me enormous satisfaction.*

Now, there are also things that are helpful. Yes, they've been helpful, but they're, how do I say it; there are things that aren't as...clear. There are seals [of certification] that are important and that are real, that are more sincere, Rainforest, for example. For me, that's the most, the most...real seal there is. The most real and most... certain, Rainforest. The others, damn, it's just all twisted. It's twisted to give them so much credibility or to manage so

152

much… which has led me to look closely at the work they do and the truth is I hate it.

Rachel: *But all of Co-opedota has Rainforest?*

Miguel: *Yes. Right now they pay us, per year, 2,500 colones [$5] more than market price [per fanega]. For the ones who have Rainforest because, you know, you have to be enrolled, you have to meet the set of requirements and all that, and Co-opedota gives us those 2,500 colones per fanega per year for 100% of the harvest, for those of us in the group certified by Rainforest.*

Rachel: *So each farm has to be certified?*

Miguel: *Yes, that's right. Every farm— and Coopedota [as a mill] is certified— and we as producers also are; they come to us to do audits. They've come to me several times. People contracted directly with Rainforest [third party auditors].*

Rachel: *But do you have to pay for that, for the certification?*

Miguel: *No. The Co-op pays for it.*

Rachel: *So they pay the certification fee, and then they pay you for producing certified coffee?*

Miguel: *Yes, that's right. It's pretty good. It's easier. For the size. Nationally there are smaller producers, more medium like us, and some a little bigger, because here the distribution of land is very fair. Very fair…maybe that's not quite the word…but everyone has something. Everybody has his little piece. With this type of [land] distribution, for everyone to pay for the Rainforest certification…not everyone would be able to pay. So the Co-op assumes this cost. Part of the excellent…I believe strongly in the Co-op. And in co-operatives in general. For me it's the most…most…it's the optimal type of organization to bring small producers together and bring them to the market with a product- too bad it's not more consistent and homogeneous in quality- but at the end of the day the Co-op tries to have everything be equal, or at least similar, and that the earnings it brings are shared in a fair way.* [We continue walking. More dry leaves underfoot.]

And here, too, we have avocados! Here, over there. The paths were really wide here, so we planted avocados, for variety. So we'll see how it goes. This year I have the possibility to harvest.

All of this is Catuai. The majority are red, but there's a few yellow trees over there. All of this is pure Catuai. There's one little bit of Caturra, but we've been replacing it. Renovating. Trees that are dead we cut and what we plant is Catuai. They're around, more or less, these cafetales are around twenty-four years or less. There are some are eighteen, some that are twelve, others that are ten. And the newest ones are three, two, and one. Those lots are all the way up at the top of the property.

Rachel: *So you've done a lot of replanting over the years.*

Miguel: *That's the idea. Also, within the lots, we replant one by one. If one plant dies and we rip it out then we refill that spot. There's one there, over there there's another one, and another one.*

Now, the shade [gesturing up to the trees], *the shade I use, a lot of people don't like. Because the trees get big, and it's expensive to manage, to pay people to prune. But I love it because of this* [kicks pile of leaves].

Rachel: *Free organic fertilizer that distributes itself!*

Miguel: *All by itself. And furthermore, the weed and fungus control that I have with this— it drastically reduces the cost of herbicides. I only use herbicide on the paths once a year, to get ride of the grass. Just once.*

Rachel: *And what are the shade trees?*

Miguel: *Poró; it's all Poró Copey. Every single shade tree is Poró. There are one or two native trees, trees from Costa Rica, in this part there's a few of a tree called, "Dama," another called, "Tite." This is part of the certifications too. The certifications ask for native trees to preserve the species. They also ask that the trees be edible; trees that generate food for birds. There's another one called Anona.*

Rachel: *Your one daughter works down at the cafe, but does the rest of your family work on the finca? Do you need to hire a lot of people to run it?*

154

Miguel: *Nomally, we work, my family...I have three kids: two sons and a daughter. The oldest works at the Co-op cafe, the youngest is studying technology- construction, and the other studied in the INAN; he studied automotive mechanics and works at the Toyota agency. And here, really, I work with two other people. We work the three of us, two other guys and me. The rest of the family, no. They don't work here.*

Rachel: *I see. And, well, obviously to harvest you need more.*

Miguel: *Oh of course. Yes, yes. Pickers, we usually need around seventeen or eighteen.*

Rachel: *Wow. But to manage the shade with just three people...*

Miguel: *Yeah...Generally we have to work really hard. And sometimes we do have to bring on another person. We try to do it as simply as possible but...* [Miguel takes a phone call. I pick, what looks to me, the ripest avocado hanging on the tree next to us.]
    You have to do this [he takes out his pocket knife and cuts off the stem at a diagonal] *so that it finishes ripening faster. Put it in the bottom drawer of the refrigerator so it matures little by little. Let's go up to the top of the hill.* [We climb in the yellow pickup. Sound of slamming doors and diesel engine.]
    Right now, Raquel, in the coffee business, we're going through a very grave situation; the price is very bad, very low. This is a hurdle we've seen in coffee all our lives. I read in a book a few years ago, called The History of Coffee in Costa Rica. *It said that the profession of coffee cultivation, from various points of view, starting with the social part, with the part that influences the history of the country, that the problems experienced on the producer's level, the exporter's level, in two hundred years, the problems are exactly the same: a market that goes up and down all the time. A form of payment that, really, doesn't favor the producer.*
    That there aren't any employees [to pick coffee]...that's a very relative hurdle. The fact that there's no one to do the work is very relative. I don't think that's the case. Right now, it's not such a big problem on national scale because coffee production has gone down so much. But during one time coffee was extremely important, extremely powerful. Extremely powerful in the economic interests of the country. Coffee contributed hugely to the construction of the highway to Puntarenas [on the Pacific]; it had a big influence on the

construction of the highway to the Atlantic. The construction of the National Theater, which is completely and totally built from coffee. Coffee was one of the products most exported, to the point that an ex-president of the country said, "The best national administration is a good coffee harvest."

And so…now we're finding ourselves very affected. One tries to keep growing, not just growing in production, but growing in terms of one's life. Buying new things, fixing your house, getting a new car that works. This implies, this is a question of credit, really. It takes a lot to get to that point that one is even thinking of selling. Because, either we sell a little piece, or we loose it all. And that's the part you have to work out. It's interesting. I don't know if you know if you've seen the same thing in other types of agriculture, but in agriculture it's almost all like this. [Truck makes a hairpin turn around a switchback as we continue to climb.]

Here's one of the new lots with coffee. And over there too. Working with shade, we're adding it from here up. I like it better when it's taller. For the type of, for the quality of the shade, for the quality of the air circulation in the cafetal. With taller shade the air low is better. These are, this is the agronomic part. Now, this is another situation, Raquel. This finca is my grandparents;' they gave it to my parents, who then gave it to me. And, one, over years, goes making changes. This was a dairy farm that produced milk, then it was a cattle ranch for a time, then, after, when my brothers and I came, it was a cafetal, and now we're adding avocados.

There was a time when there were people with huge properties, what, like 150 manzanas. Or something like that. But then came the generations that have been making small properties passed down by families. This is a pattern that has influenced the type of land ownership a lot. [Truck grinds around another corner.]

That's how it is. Something else you want to know?

Rachel: *Well, just, of all the things you've done here in the last twenty-five years here, what's been the biggest challenge?*

Miguel: *The biggest challenge? To do with coffee? The biggest challenge I've had, on a personal level, but related to coffee, was my daughter's illness. That was the most difficult, not just for me but for my family. It's been the hardest thing we've had to overcome. And, the most successful, the biggest success, today, is that we've grown the way we've grown. And to have a farm of the quality we do. For me that's the best part. My family is the most difficult*

156

business I have, the business that brings me the most satisfaction. That's how I see it. That's how I see it.

Rachel: *Um hm...did you join the co-op right away when you started planting coffee, or later?*

Miguel: *When I joined, I joined because I picked my first harvest. The first harvest I picked ten fanegas. From two* manzanas *I picked ten fanegas. I joined the Co-op so I could sell it there. And to this day, I've never sold a cherry of coffee to anyone else.*

Here are the new plantings, but the lot looks a little unkempt because I don't like to use a lot of herbicides when the plants are so young. So we maintain this with machete. It gets cleared with machete and we leave it. So now it'll be cleared for the summer. There are more new plants there, over there, on the other side.

I believe in this a lot. I believe deeply in growing coffee. Especially in our case. We have a level of quality pretty recognized in the international market. Now, we're creating options, developing options—for example, the cafeteria—we're developing the roasting side, we're creating different ways to sell coffee too. This is very important. For me it's very important and very valuable, and it gives you hope that we can keep growing coffee. I strongly believe, too, in the Co-op as a business, as a way of organizing; I strongly believe in the Co-op as a solution for my needs. I believe in that a lot. And, overall, I have strong faith that God doesn't know how to abandon us in any situation. And taking in account, remembering, that we are, that we should be, the ones who sustain the community. As producers, as citizens, as parents, as spouses, as brothers, as everything. [Truck engine cuts out].

Vamos, *come this way so you can take pictures, so you can see all the way down into town. Look, you can see the whole neighborhood.* [All of Santa Maria is laid out below. I usually find the word "hamlet" an idealistic overreach, but once Santa Maria must have been a hamlet. The valley is illuminated in full sun and I can make out the football field, the main road through the center, and the two largest structures in town: the church and the beneficio].

Rachel: *With all the changes in the market, does the co-op do anything to stabilize prices? Do they do anything to keep the price they pay you per fanega more stable?*

157

Miguel: *There was— there is— a mechanism that we've implemented, through, through the initiative of the administration. For example, you're a buyer, and I'm a producer. You and I decide that during the next three years, you're going to pay me X amount of money per sack for three years. We reserve a margin of a certain amount, in case the price goes up or down, so you can defend yourself and so that I can defend myself, that existed. But, a group of members thought that someone was robbing them or— I don't know. So they abandoned that method.*

That [system], for us, helped us a lot. Because at this moment, when you're about to start picking the coffee, you knew what they were going to pay you. Which is one of the things that affects us drastically. We make a prediction of costs, but income no! We have half the picture, but the other half we don't know until the end.

[Gestures up the hill]. *From here on up, from here on up is the part I'm trying to keep planting new. This was all pasture. Yes there were trees growing, and my idea is to not touch the majority of those trees. Just plant the coffee under them. I have cafetales like this* [motions to land to his left and right, filled with healthy Poró]. *So I think the stupidest thing I could do would be to cut everything down to just have to replant it. That doesn't make any sense* [We climb back in the truck. Doors slam].

Now, too, there was a time when we also tried to produce something to eat. We planted beans over there. Every year we plant beans. Right now they're ready. In this part, we've been trying to clean it out, to go along getting the ground ready to replant. These beans here are asking to be picked, as we say. That's the good thing about it. You can use the land in a cafetal also as a food garden, for the family. Because something like beans also works well because it fixes nitrogen, and they're not as much competition as another big tree would be. [We go around another hairpin turn. The property on the left turns into a cafetal with banana trees interplanted between the coffee].

Rachel: *For all the new plantings did you have an almacigo?*

Miguel: *Every year I buy one.*

Rachel: *Normally, how many fanegas do you harvest a year?*

Miguel: *More or less four hundred or five hunred. At the end of the day it's between four-fifty and five hundred. The harvest lasts more or less three months.*

Rachel: *So that would be ten thousand* cajuelas?

Miguel: *Yup, ten thousand cajuelas. Ten thousand times to say, "One!...Two!..." and throw the cajuela of cherries into the truck. Every day we're turning in around 100, 150 cajuelas, more or less. There are days of more, days of less... It's always very satisfying at the medida.*

All that part over there, Rachel, that high part, all that was pastures, for cattle. And, like a told you a little while ago, the grandfather died, so he left it to his sons, and the sons opted to leave cattle and to start to plant coffee. One time I told a friend of mine, "Los Santos has become one big cafetal with lights! Just a big coffee farm with electricity."

Rachel: *Since your parents weren't coffee farmers, when you started, did you just have to try things to see what worked, or did you ask for help from, like, friends or neighbors, other people? How did you come to your understandings of how to grow coffee?*

Miguel: *Well, my parents, my father, when he was younger, he worked on coffee farms, so he still had that background. In his younger years he worked on coffee farms and then did other things, but he still kept that knowledge. At the beginning we just had a little piece of land. So there, my dad showed us how to plant, how to apply herbicides, he showed us how to control weeds, how to manage shade. Then came the time when I had the chance to plant my own cafetal, and, more than anything, I was influenced by his knowledge, that he gave me but also for the technical assistance of the Co-op. In my case, that has been one of the resources I've used the most, the technical assistance. Also, having friends who have coffee too. We get talking and we start telling each other what we're dealing with it, what each other's doing about it. So we go exchanging information. For example, there are things they tell me, that don't work for me. Just like there are things I tell them that don't work. So we maintain the conversation and just have to see where something works for one person and where it works for another. The different understandings you have get stored through experience.*

Rachel: *Very true. And have you had a lot of problems with ojo de gallo, la roya?*

Miguel: *Ojo de gallo, yes. That creates a lot of problems, but la roya, no. Not that. Right now, like twenty-two days ago, we did a test of broca here, and there was very, very little. And still no roya. Ojo de gallo, if you leave the farm without taking care to catch it, it'll be everywhere.*

There's something else that's interesting, something else that always draws my attention. Something we talked about yesterday. It's the fact that there are people who know— people who've never seen a coffee plant, and know more about coffee than I do. Because, it's just that, how do you say it, we've never been interested, really, to know, the finished product.

Like I said yesterday, I live at the gate to heaven. I've had the opportunity, gracias a Dios to travel a few times; I went to the United States, to Mexico. And within Costa Rica I've been around to lots of places, and I still haven't found a place better than this. Not yet. It's part of what keeps one tied to this. Apart from the profession of growing coffee, there's also the fact that the families have strong roots. In my family, we're, let's see, there's… [mumbles various names as he counts on his fingers]. *I'm the fifth generation to live here. So it's really interesting. So much legacy. But yeah…anything else Raquel?"*

Rachel: *Is there is anything you want to share with the people in New York who drink Coopedota coffee?*

Miguel: *It's the most beautiful work there is, to suffer as we do in agriculture. But it's the most beautiful work there is. The best thing that can happen to a human being is produce coffee. And with the added value created by knowing that there is a person who is enjoying my work at the moment of drinking a* good *cup of coffee. It's too bad that the economic compensation isn't that fair, but that doesn't negate, doesn't impact the pride that I feel to know that my- that a cup of my coffee, is served in New York, in Germany, in Italy, in France, in…all over the world, there are so many places. Even in Australia! There they're serving a cup of my coffee. So its…there's nothing that can take that away. Now, my, my final reflection…is… coffee is my life.*

The more people that know us…that's why I believe— I think what you're doing is very important. Why? Because it's a way of giving people a chance to know us from another point of view. With other eyes. Not just with the eyes of the exporter, or with the eyes of the roaster, or even with the eyes of whomever's drinking the coffee, rather with the eyes of a person who wants *to see the situation.*

Rachel: *Exactly. When people talk about coffee they talk about it in numbers, in prices, in terms of flavors, they use lots of words to describe flavor and to explain the market price peaks, but I want to put together a book that talks about coffee in human terms-*

Miguel: *In terms of people.*

We've parked the yellow truck in front of the Co-op. Daniel sees us sitting in the truck and waves.

Where does Ariela's, Minor's, Miguel's, Susy's and the rest of Coopedota's coffee go?
Coopedota's coffee reaches around the world, to clients in Costa Rica, the United States and beyond. Some micro lots go to direct trade roasters like Intelligentsia. In Costa Rica, Coopedota sells to McCafe and roasted, ground, and packaged coffee to local grocery stores.

If you came from Jose Manuel and would like to continue to Nicaragua, turn to p. 93

If you came from Guillermo and would like to return to Colombia, turn to p. 300.

For a conversation with a Coopedota member who has a different view of coffee, continue to the next page.

Minor

Recorded Tuesday, December 11, 2012, at Coopedota's Café Privilegios.

Coopedota's lead agronomist and champion people person, Daniel, sits with Minor, Minor's wife Lucidia and I at a table in the café facing the street. Daniel wears his teal Coopedota polo, Lucidia wears a black sweatshirt, and Minor wears a maroon polo.

Minor: *Bueno, Rachel, I see it as...something very important for me. It's important there are people from your country who can bring back a reality of how things work in other places. In my case, well it's my family. My family's here. Here's my wife, and my parents... we're all family in this area. We maintain a connected chain. Parents, children. We have a very, well not paternalistic culture, but something like that. People always help their parents.*

In my family's case, with coffee, we reached a point where we practically disappeared. Because we were ignorant of [effective] herbicide use. There are proper ways to use them, but we didn't know. Gracias a Dios, one looks for answers, reasons. And so we've realized that the relationship between the plants and the soil's health is very important. Investments in regeneration have their price. And this has forced us to work with borrowed money. In my family's case, we'll be out [of debt] this year. And then we'll be working free.

Daniel: *But farm management also has to do with prices. Prices are always elastic for the producer and stable for the consumer.*

Minor: *I don't know, maybe I'm wrong, someone correct me if I am, but it seems like the New York Stock Exchange price favors the people who come to buy our coffee [from the Co-op]. Because they ignore, or tend to ignore, our costs of production. They're just interested in a cheap product. Around here, people have access to health care and basic necessities. But in other parts of the world, people work to not starve to death. And that's wrong. It's like saying the only thing that matters is making money. But it's important to create a social balance among human beings.* [Daniel excuses himself as he jumps up to greets a group of people who just walked into the café.]

Right now, the advance is 40,000 colones ($80). And from that we have to pay the pickers [at 1,000 per cajuela, of which there are twenty in a fanega], so that's 20,000. And with the other 20,000 we have to pay fuel for transport, pay the electricity. And since my wife and I have decided to eradicate herbicide use on our fincas, we now have to pay workers to clear with machetes. And I'm out checking the cafetales. And repairing cars, because I have to make sure the cars for my finca and my father's are in good shape, or they won't be able to haul [people and coffee]. And with this money-

Lucidia: *You just can't make ends meet.*

Minor: *You can't make them meet. The crisis of this year will be that those of us who've been paying our debts won't be able to any more. So we have to make a plan. In our case, the loan we have is with the Co-op. So, we've spoken with the head, Roberto, because we can't just leave it unpaid. We can't be in bad standing with the Co-op because they lent us a hand. And we also can't leave the coffee untended, because then next year we'll have nothing. We can't falter on fertilization and things. There's no space for more unemployed. We have to maintain the coffee to maintain jobs for people.*

My friend Fernando, who's from around here too, told me, "People talk about the word 'sustainability,' but the word can be defined many ways. For example, the lamp is screwed to the wall. It's not going anywhere, so it's sustainable. A human being can be a walking skeleton, but as long as he's walking, he's sustainable." So we're using the word "sustainable" as a word that's obstructing reality. Fernando told me, "The word we're looking for is 'balance.' If you have balance, things are good for both sides." But if only one side looks good and the other is deteriorating... ^{Ingenuity is Sustainable p.396}

I have another friend, Juan Carlos, an agronomic engineer, who built a fertilizer plant with his family. He studied at a university in Brazil and another in Honduras. I got in touch with him, because what I'm trying to do on my finca is give life to the soil. If I adjust the composition of the soil with microorganisms and minerals, if I can find this balance, the coffee, and the checkbook, will automatically respond.

He's coming on the 21st to give a workshop, to show us this product. So I got together a group of producers who understand the importance of adjusting the soil. [Juan Carlos] will show us how to perform soil analyses without needing to go to a lab. I have to try it to see if it works, because my parents depend on this coffee farm, as do the rest of my family and my wife and I. And if I apply something that causes us to lose an entire harvest, it *will be a problem. But, if this fertilizer is as I expect it'll be, it will give us an advantage.*

We're also working on this tourism project called "Heart of Gold" with people from the University of Vancouver. The tourists wouldn't come here just to pay for a tour, rather, they'd feel part of a family. They'll have the freedom to go talk with and meet other people in the community. They'll get to know a lot about different things. Like I said, there are people who live from coffee, others who work with intensive organic farms, like my friend Felicia who even does yoga; they have more things than I offer. There are people who produce honey, and can offer a tour of their bees— with protective gear of course! [Laughs]

For us, for the producers, the most important is that people can come and experience coffee as directly as possible.

Our coffee cups are empty. We exchange phone numbers and make tentative plans to meet up in San Marcos the following week, so I can see Minor and Lucidia's farm. As it turned out, not only did I see their farm, I rode in the back of a pick up truck with around 10 cousins, nieces, nephews, and neighbors, about an hour up the winding windblown mountain roads to the most remote lot Minor owns.

He parked the truck on the one flat stretch of the road, and we unloaded the plastic laundry baskets to start picking. The coffee was planted on a steep "fold of the mountain's skirt," and from where we were we could gaze out at other folds and almost see to the Pacific, but there was not a single building in sight, just coffee and lots of pure mountain.

If you came from Donald and would like to return to Cedral, turn to p. 135

For a conversation for a producer who's successfully integrated coffee and tourism, turn to p. 226

For a conversation with other producers who value balance, turn to p. 275

For a conversation with another producer who sells to Coopedota, turn to the next page.

Susy

Recorded Wednesday, December 12, 2012, in Susy's cafetal.

    Daniel had a scheduled visit to Susy's finca in order to perform a sort of agronomic diagnostic of the overall growing conditions. He invited me to join, and I eagerly donned my black rubber boots for the agronomy ride-along. Up in the cafetal of Susy's finca it's a gorgeous sun drenched day, and from our mountaintop vantage point we can see far across to the cafetales of Santa Maria and San Marcos. Susy wears a brown t-shirt and a white baseball cap. Her brother, who joined us at the top of the finca, wears a grey t-shirt and baseball cap.

Susy: *A little bit of the history? Well, my grandparents were here…right?*

Brother: *Um hm. This was my grandfather's. But up here he had cows, a few little ones for milk for the house. Down where we passed earlier, that's where he started with coffee, just a little. Just a hectare or two. And from there the family grew with coffee, buying more little pieces of land. In El Vapor there have always been like six or seven houses. First our grandparents, and then they moved to the center, to Santa Maria. And the people left there now are workers.*

Susy: *And we lived there for a little while too. Our father died some, what's it now, twenty-five years ago. When he died we moved to Santa Maria. We would go back and forth and check on things. But he was the one who worked the most with coffee. But his kidneys failed, and he was sick for 3 years. I was young when he died. Seventeen.*

Brother: *So the coffee suffered. There was less to harvest because it hadn't been tended to. And now—*

Susy: *—we've started to really get going again. Our families our getting bigger—we have a lot of siblings, and we've been buying land. So we're trying to see if we can improve what we have. Like Daniel said, we have good amount. So now what we have to do is stop, slow down, and start to take better care of it so that it produces more. Like I was telling you before, we've depended on coffee our whole lives. There are crises, but, like you always hear coffee farmers talk about, there are two good years, one where the price is low,* *and then two good years again. And it's the same thing with the harvest. Because if this year the tree gives a lot, the next year it'll give a little less.*

Brother: *But this area here, El Vapor, is always very stable. If production goes down, it's by very little. The harvest is pretty stable.*

Susy: *Practically since childhood we've been working with coffee. We all had to go pick coffee in order to buy the basics, to buy school supplies; our university studies were half coffee and half scholarship. Also, my some of my brothers went to the US to work, so that helped too. There's a lot of emigration here. They go to be able to buy themselves a piece of land here.*

Brother: *They work a year there, and then come back and work for themselves, mainly in coffee. And then they stay here.*

Susy: *One of the big advantages we have that you don't see a lot in other countries is that we're small producers. The Co-op helps us a lot in commercializing the coffee. But it's an advantage that we have over other countries, where the [landowners] are big companies. They manage everything and everyone else in an employee. Here, everyone has their own little pieces of coffee, and they work them how they want to, maybe with other sources of income, administering them how they choose. Really, I think all the stories around here are very similar. Because Santa Maria is a cafetal! So we have a lot to thank coffee for. You have to work it very diligently, but everything we have we owe to coffee. We have what it wants to leave us with. It surprises us when we learn what a cup of coffee costs in other countries; we have it right here!* [Gestures to the coffee growing on all sides of us]. *You, who's visiting all around here, with the chance to share with the world what we do; it's reminding us to love what we have, because it's ours. And around here, it's pretty much all coffee, right? There's hardly anything else.*

Daniel: *This is a pure* cultura cafetalera. *The economy here revolves 90% around coffee; the rest is services and other crops.* [Daniel walks away to look at some low growing plants on the side of the road.]

Susy: *I think we'll stick with coffee! This is our history. We depend on coffee. Some nights, when it's raining really hard for example, my mom and I will stay up all night, worrying about the coffee. You have to be very vigilant.*

166

Some people are becoming independent, building their own micromills so that they can sell directly. Right now it works like this: the buyer gives us a price. We want to produce higher quality coffee, one that tastes good but also has less chemicals, so that we can tell the buyer, "We have a quality cafetal. We cannot accept that price." So that we're setting the price. Obviously not mistreating anyone, because if we put it too high no one will buy, but we want to turn the situation around. That the vendors set the price. In reality, that's how it should be. Just that with coffee we're doing it backwards! The buyer says, "I'll give you this much— "

Brother: *—and we can't say no because we can't look for another option. Because all the buyers agree together to pay the same price, and so we don't have another option.*

Susy: *So a lot of people have become independent. We'll see how it goes. I think we all need to be united in producing a better product. The buyer needs the product. He doesn't know that we have to come up here and take care of the coffee—all the risks associated with working in a cafetal—that's what we want the buyers to know. That it's not easy. It's a long, difficult process. Of course, it's ours and we like doing it, but it also costs us. So we want them to give us a fair price, and for them to know everything that we went through to put up good coffee to sell.*

Brother: *A fair price—not an exorbitant one—just one that pays for the work done. And leaves us with a little something. To be able to eat tamales at Christmas!*

Susy and I both laugh. I comment that I've been hearing about these Christmas tamales from all sides and am eager to try them.

For a conversation with another grower who talks price, turn to p. 207

For a conversation with a member of an association, not a co-op, turn to p. 339

For a conversation with a grower, and independent micromill owner, in the next valley over, turn to the next page.

Esteban

Recorded Monday, December 17, 2012, in the cafetal at La Candelilla.

La Candelilla is in the next "Santo" over from Santa Maria: San Marcos. The local co-op is Coopetarrazu. Coopetarrazu sells to Starbucks and has worked with them in several collaborative environmental programs. Coopetarrazu has a grocery store and gas station as well as a hardware store adjacent to its offices. But it doesn't have a cafeteria, and it just doesn't have the same spirit as Coopedota. This absence of spirit leads people with spirit to strike out on their own.

Esteban's niece is seated on a fertilizer sack and I on a log in a clearing in the cafetal. Esteban's brother Marvin picks coffee nearby. It's a warm day, but the large trees cast a comfortable shade. Esteban wears a blue, green, and orange striped polo and a typical Tico bucket hat.

Esteban: *Raquel, this finca, if we go all the way back to the beginning, has roots back to my paternal grandmother, named Lucia Mora. She married Rafael Sanchez, son of Angel Sanchez. Don Angel came from Spain, leaving the war, from the Canary Islands. He arrived here with his small son; he married my paternal grandmother, Lucia Mora. And so she inherited this property. So it's been worked by my grandmother, my uncles, and my father. For a while they practiced subsistence agriculture. My dad and an uncle, the oldest sons, worked as laborers on nearby farms. My grandfather planted garden crops to eat. Ñampi, chayote, yucca, all that. And from there they got the money to buy what he couldn't produce— with the wages my dad and my uncle earned. When it came time, my grandfather and grandmother split up the property between their children. There were seven men, so they split the farm up into seven pieces. And over time, my father rented this piece of land. My father died thirty-two years ago. We stayed on the finca, and my uncles were selling off pieces of it. So we've bought back a lot.*

This is the main, central, part of the finca. We've acquired new land, too. For example in Napoles, San Guillermo... And, also, when we were older and we started getting married, we also had land from our wives' families. For example, that little piece right over there [points to a hill on the other side of the valley] *belongs to Marvin's wife. We now have a new finca in San Guillermo, which belongs to my wife. We have, also, a finca called Monte Canet, that belongs to the wife of another one of my brothers.*

168

We have another that's two years, old called Finca Los Compadres, that belongs to my sister's husband.

This way we've been able to have the opportunity to have around sixty hectares of coffee planted. They're not all in one place; here in Tarrazú the land is very evenly distributed. There aren't big plantations or estates. Maybe you'll find two or three fincas that are bigger than fifty hectares, but in reality the land is very well split up. So we have two hectares in one region, two in another, two in another. That's how we accumulated our sixty hectares.

Furthermore, in the case of La Candelilla, so that you understand the concept, our main mission and vision is to know the client— tell us what you want and we'll do it. It's that simple. To do this, we have an enormous range of conditions that let us produce coffee that satisfies the preferences of any client. Why? We're in a zone where we produce facing into the wind and away from it— the conditions of the mountain with respect to air currents. We have conditions facing the sun and facing away from it. We have conditions from 1200 meters above sea level to those over 1800. All these conditions permit that, in every small finca, by producing under different conditions, every finca yields a different coffee.

Some fincas give us acidity. Others give us volume of production. Others give us large sized cherries. In addition to all these agroecological conditions, we've been developing a process of selecting coffee varietals. You know that there are thousands or varietals of coffee. So all these agroecological conditions, with all these different coffee varietals that we plant in our various fincas, allow us to have an enormous array of coffee flavors. From acidity to chocolaty, to fruity, to floral flavors, sweet flavors, astringent flavors. By also varying the production process we can form a very specific product. The quality of our coffee is intrinsic. Coffee quality is not made at the mill. Coffee quality comes from here, in the finca.

La Candelilla is much more than just cafetales. The brothers process all the coffee they grow right there in their own micro beneficio. They have large drying patios, a mechanical dryer, and large storerooms. Esteban proudly tells me that, "No one else touches this coffee until it arrives at the roaster."

La Candelilla practices exclusively direct trade. Esteban also proudly tells me that, "If I want to contact a buyer in Japan I just send an email or—look [he pulls out his phone] people in Japan can just text me!" His coffee shelf^{The Coffee Shelf p. 398} is lined with shiny bags from Japan, Korea, and Starbucks reserve collection.

One of Esteban's favorite factoids to impart is that a well-processed coffee bean will still germinate post-processing, provided that it's been processed correctly. Meaning, theoretically, that a 60kg sack of coffee in parchment could be converted back to a bunch of almacigos. It is cool to think that a coffee seed is alive, sleeping, until you cook it in a roaster.

Where does Esteban's coffee go?
    La Candelilla's coffee goes as far as Japan, Korea, and Starbucks in various countries. La Candelilla has many direct trade clients, including Irving Farm roasters in New York.

For a conversation with someone else who recognizes the importance of agroecological conditions, turn to p. 217

For a conversation with another direct trade vendor, turn to p. 238

For a conversation with another microbeneficio owner, turn to the next page.

Javier

Recorded Thursday December 20, 2012, at micro beneficio La Cabaña en San Pablo de Leon Cortes.

Still another valley over in the next "Santo," San Pablo, agronomist Gabriel excitedly explains to me the ways micromills can mean positive community impacts in many areas. He cites one of the biggest benefits of the movement towards micromills to be that it has prompted producers to think critically about what they do, why they do it, and the impacts of their actions on quality of their immediate environments as much as quality of the final product.

Gabriel wears glasses and a beige polo.

Gabriel Umaña: *One of the principal reasons that the micromills started was for a question of price. Very low prices with very good coffee. So, small producers started thinking of how they could improve their income. And it's good coffee, fully ripe. They wanted to move beyond just being primary producers, so they said, "Ok, let's see what machines we need, what we need to know, what kind of space we have to have, what's the necessary paperwork—" because for many people that's the hardest part, because [the fees] are also expensive.*

It yielded a pretty good result, because globally there are lots of roasters interested in quality coffee. So they were heading for that niche in the market. These coffees go to Europe, Japan. You can see that we're in the first two weeks of harvest; look at the trees. Some cherries are still green, half ripe. They just started up the beneficio last week. What they're picking now is for national consumption. The beginning and the end of the harvest is coffee that stays for national consumption, and the ripe coffee, the 100% ripe coffee is what gets exported.

There are lots of different types and styles of microbeneficios. Just because you have enough money to buy lots of machines doesn't mean you'll be successful. Anyone who thinks that is wrong. It's a question of concept. [We pull up to the mill and get out of the car. A dog immediately runs up and starts jumping on me. Muddy paws on jeans. His name is Rosco. Javier greets us with a smile and firm handshakes. He wears a blue and white baseball cap.]

Javier: *This is our sixth year. We're three families; my wife, my children, my parents, and my brother. It's a very small business that processes around* *three hundred fanegas- or three hundred quintales- per harvest. This year, because the coffee prices are so bad, I'm buying a little bit from my neighbors and one of my cousins, so that I can make a little more money and so that they can too, because I'm paying a little bit more than what the big companies are paying.*

So, this is our project. This part is the wet mill. Here we depulp it and we wash some. This year we started working with Honey coffee. And then the store room and the mechanical dryer. We almost always sun dry on beds or patios. Today we had to cover them up because it rained. But, tomorrow's the end of the world, so we don't have to worry about anything! [Laughs.] Gabriel said you're writing a book?

Rachel: *Yes. People in the U.S. right now are interested in where their food comes from. There are lots of markets where producers bring trucks full of their products right to the consumers. So I'm collecting stories from the people and places behind a cup of coffee, so that people knows what's going on behind what they drink.*

Javier: *Well, I can't speak for the big companies, but we small companies can guarantee 100% traceability. We have the finca, the beneficio, a space to dry hull it, and we're even now selling it roasted and ground as the final product. Come look at the Honey coffee! It's darker than washed coffee because some of the* miel [Spanish word for the sticky mucilage, which, when transliterated to English becomes "honey," thus generating the term for coffee that is depulped but not washed] *is left on. It's harder to get this result. This is Caturra and Catuai; those are the two varieties we have. This takes a long time; so we'll probably have to use the mechanical dryer some because we're running out of space. This year people are asking for a lot of this coffee.*

Rachel: *So you already know where this coffee is going?*

Javier: *It already has an owner, yes. This is going to Japan. Well, probably not this exact coffee, since this is still early harvest, and it won't have all the characteristics. So I'll probably [have this roasted and] sell it ground.*

Rachel: *What motivated you to start all this? Because this is a big undertaking, not an easy thing to do.*

Javier: *It wasn't easy, and it's still not easy. We started six years ago because the coffee prices—like this year—were very low. To grow coffee and be just a producer wasn't a business; it wasn't profitable. We were loosing. So we made the decision to start. I started with my family, with a loan we're still paying off. But it's been going pretty well; every year we earn more than we would if we didn't have the beneficio.*

It's more work. More responsibility. We've had to learn to do lots of things—things we didn't know at all about the coffee process. Even though we'd all spent our lives working in coffee, there were lots of things we didn't know about. We had to learn and train ourselves—we're still training.

Now, we don't just process it. We're trying to work on selling a finished, final product. With the logo of the benefico, La Cabaña. It's a small project with my family. We process a small amount of coffee to not loose control of it, so that at the end it's good coffee.

Rachel: *And you export the majority through Exclusive?*

Javier: *The majority. There's the law that says that 1%* has to stay for national consumption, but other than that we export it to the world. I also sell to Deli Café. And my lower grade goes to one of the big companies. It's been to lots of different places; Canada, Japan, Germany, Greece, the US.*

Rachel: *Of the whole process of making this change— or even before— what has been the biggest challenge to overcome and the biggest success you've achieved?*

Javier: *The biggest success? It would be that we were able to do it. Because when we started we didn't think we'd get here. We started with a lot of fear; we had to find the money to do it. In terms of success, the biggest is to see this all done and to be selling coffee. Nevertheless, the biggest challenge was to sell our coffee. Because we didn't have the slightest idea how to do it— or who would buy it. Or how to get it ready to sell. So the most difficult part was to commercialize it.*

And there are still complicated issues around selling it. But it's not as hard as it was. The first year when we started to work my warehouse was filled with coffee! And I didn't have the slightest idea who would buy it. I didn't know the international prices of coffee, nothing. A company appeared, one of the big ones, and thankfully, I sold it that year.

But we started like that— blind. That was the hardest. And nevertheless, yeah, the success is to see it all. More so because it's my family that made it happen, my children, my father who works just in the fields, my wife- in the summer, because she's a teacher so when she has time she helps- but for me that's the success. Unite the family in working to make this possible.

In my case, I'm the third generation working with coffee. My grandfather started, and my father still does, all his life he's worked in coffee. When I left high school, in '83, coffee was a very good business. So I didn't want to study more. I thought it would stay that way all my life. So I dedicated myself to coffee, and now I've spent thirty years working in coffee. So yes, a long time.

Javier explains the work the micromill has done to earn their good reputation in the neighborhood: compost coffee cherry skins and treat the water post-washing in order not to contaminate rivers and generate stinking piles of pulp. He also tells me about the new project of a biodigestor that uses sheep dung to generate fuel, and the sheep creating the dung are hard at work eating weeds. There is always space to move onward.

For a conversation with the man who exports Javier's coffee to the world, turn to p. 181

For a conversation with someone in another part of Costa Rica who boldly ventured into uncharted coffee territory, turn to the next page.

*1% of export quality coffee must stay in Costa Rica for domestic consumption. Costa Rica is the only producing country to have legislation that guarantees that its citizens have a right to drink their nation's best coffee.

Monteverde
and
Alejuela

Monteverde is another point of convergence between coffee and tourism. Monteverde is right along the most deeply rutted tract of Costa Rica's tourist loop and for most travelers is synonymous with "cloud forest" or "bird watching." Monteverde was founded by a group of Alabama Quakers looking to find a peaceful place to live their lives. They ended up developing the area as a dairy farming community, and today Monteverde still produces sought after milks and cheeses. But, milk is not all the area does. Monteverde is one of those places where you can grow all the ingredients for your *café con leche* all on the same finca. Sugarcane and coffee production follow dairy, and Monteverde's green mountains, for which it's named, are as productive as they are pretty.

Monteverde is everything you see on postcards brought to life: lush jungles, suspended bridges through cloud forests, lounging sloths, and happy birds perched on the branches of coffee trees. But, for all its picturesque convention, some unconventional ideas are afoot in Monteverde.

Alajuela, a suburb of San Jose, is everything you don't see on the postcards, but is every bit as Costa Rican as waterfalls and jungle. Here you'll find office parks, shopping complexes, condo developments, and restaurant chains. The majority of Costa Rica's population lives in suburban areas like these and would consider a trip to Monteverde as much of a vacation as would any North American.

Alajuela is not on anyone's tourist itinerary, but that doesn't make it any less filled with cool things. Funky little family-run restaurants are tucked into ugly strip malls and game-changing businesses are hiding in unassuming warehouse spaces.

Alejandro

Recorded Friday, December 28, 2012, at Thr!ve's Café Colibrí on the edge of Monteverde's cloud forest reserve.

Bags of Thrive coffee don't look any different than any other one pound bags of whole bean or ground roasted coffee. Their artwork is pretty but typical, and the packaging material is standard. The coffee itself is above average tasting Latin American coffee. But even though this coffee seems like it might be comparable to other coffees, it is fundamentally different not in form, but in ownership. This coffee belongs to the growers until it belongs to the final consumer. And that simple shift just might be a way to change coffee commercialization forever. Alejandro wears black square-framed glasses.

Alejandro: *Really, Thrive is a relatively new project, about two and a half years. I'm a fourth generation coffee grower. My family's produced coffee for many years. The story has been, well, it was the same, until 2006. We were traditional producers here in Monteverde. The finca is nine kilometers from the center of town.*

For all those years we basically just grew cherries to sell to the co-op, Coopedos. From 2005 to 2006 I had the opportunity to live in the United States, to work. I saved a bit of money with the intention to improve the finca, and that's what we did. We reinvested in coffee, my older brother Lexis and I.

And in 2006, during the off-season I worked with the University of Washington, who runs a ten-week program of study about coffee. And in reality, that's when I realized the complexity of the business. So, working with the University of Washington, I went on many tours of Tarrazú, Dota, Naranjo, Doka Estate. We met with people from Starbucks. And I arrived at the conclusion that the problem with the coffee business is the misalignment that exists in the value chain.

There are so many players for just one product. All of the processors, the broker who buys at origin, the broker who buys in consuming countries, the roaster, the wholesaler, the retailer, and the client. At the end of the day, for everyone to make something, the cash for the producer is very low, mainly. And furthermore, many players add value, some make less than others, but, really, the ones working the hardest are the producers. And for them there's only 2 or 3% left of the total earnings.

My family converted the farm, what's called vertically integrating. We invested in a wet mill, a dry mill, a roaster, and, later, with my wife, we

177

opened this café. It was a more than a three-year project until we opened the café. In 2008 we opened the cafeteria on February 7, 2008. We opened the café and…and from there things got much more interesting.

Because the way a project like Thrive was received by consumers was very good. The real truth is that the consumer wants to know where his or her money is going. We have a business that is completely transparent, that is family run, that's vertically integrated. After we opened the cafeteria the demand for our coffee increased. We started to build a network of clients.

So, in 2009, at the end of the year, with Ken Lander, we created something much larger, called the Consortium of Sustainable Producers of San Rafael. It wasn't just my family, but my family's families and other families in the community. And so at the end of 2009, beginning of 2010, we opened the project on a larger scale. And now we're around six hundred producers between Costa Rica, Honduras, and Guatemala. And all the coffee is processed in each of the countries, in each community separately. And then it's all exported to the U.S. It all goes through Atlanta, where there's a distribution center. To the clients, to the roasters. Sometimes we roast for supermarkets or churches. The logistical center where everything is managed is Atlanta.

Rachel: *I read on your website that the growers are the owners of the coffee.*

Alejandro: *Yes, that's the big difference. That's the biggest difference between our coffee and any other coffee. It belongs to the producer until the moment the final consumer buys it.*

Rachel: *So you don't sell to the mill, you use the mill like a service?*

Alejandro: *Exactly. The coffee belongs to the producers. The coffee is exported under the mill's license, but it belongs to the producer. Once the coffee arrives in Atlanta it's the responsibility of Thrive as a business to take care of marketing and sales and all. The producer is a business partner up to 50%.*

Rachel: *Do people who are partners sell their entire harvest to Thrive?*

Alejandro: *No. The process, to start, the first year it's 10% of their harvest. And for that 10% we'll pay them four, five, or six times more, so 10% will produce [monetarily] like 50%. The second year, they put in 20%. And that will earn them the same or more than the other 80%. And the* *third year, it's 30%. And then, later, we don't usually let people put in 100% of their crop. We like it to be 30% or 40% at most so that they can also have the chance to sell some coffee in the local market.*

Rachel: *And do you then sell the coffee according to New York commodity market prices?*

Alejandro: *We use the market price as a placeholder. Then there's a clause that says that the producer is a partner up to 50% of the value of roasted coffee or up to 75% of the value of green coffee. So from there comes what would be, in Costa Rica, like a bonus.*

Rachel: *How do people get involved?*

Alejandro: *First friends of the family. Then friends of friends. It's very organic. Everyone who's part of Thrive ends up recommending it to someone.*

Rachel: *So there aren't any requirements to join?*

Alejandro: *Well, there are requirements. Once you're part of Thrive, part of the sustainability aspect is to reduce the use of Round Up. When you get to [selling] 30% [of your harvest to Thrive], you have to have zero use of Round Up. We can't obligate zero use starting the first year, but once their income is higher, they have to have zero use of Round Up and chemical fungicides.*

Rachel: *Round Up is a glyphosate, right? What are some of the negative effects you've seen from using glyphosates?*

Alejandro: *The biggest effect is the deterioration of the soil. Because being completely exposed during the rainy season washes away layers. It exhausts soils very quickly, which will obligate caficultores to use higher quantities of fertilizers because the nutritional demand will be higher when there are less layers of nutrients available naturally.*

Rachel: *Do you work with any certifications?*

Alejandro: *We don't. We do have some certified organic coffee, because we have clients who buy certified organic, but we really don't want to be part of that system because the producer has to pay for all the certifications.*

Traceability and transparency are important— and that the producer remembers that it's his coffee! If he's tricking someone he's only tricking himself; we're not tricking Starbucks or a broker. It's the producer's own coffee, so we do follow-ups and offer lots of assistance, but we don't have the outside requirements of a certification, except for the organic.

Rachel: *And what differentiates Thrive from a co-op or direct trade model?*

Alejandro: *Well, we're not a co-operative system because we're not democratic. We see the business as a business, and as a business we started with the intention to make money. The co-ops have lots of good things, but they don't have a business mentality. And, at the end of the day, they ended up floundering in the market because they couldn't maintain themselves. We've taken the best of the co-ops and implemented that in a business. It's a 100% sustainable business; environmentally sustainable, socio-culturally sustainable, and economically sustainable for the main partner in Thrive: the producer.*

We're different than anything that calls itself Direct Trade because those are companies that buy from someone; we don't buy coffee. Thrive sells coffee because the coffee belongs to us. The goal of Thrive is to change the way coffee is commercialized, directly and indirectly, because once the producer sees that there are other ways of doing things, he will be able to demand more.

Alejandro offers me a coffee. I sip a cappuccino as I watch the rain fall on the jungle.

Where does Alejandro's coffee go?
First, all Thr!ve coffee gets shipped to Atlanta. Some of it is then roasted and sold in one pound bags to distributors. Some of it is sold wholesale to roasters like Eote coffee in Chandler, OK.

If you came from Pedro and would like to return to Colombia, turn to p. 305

For a conversation with someone who commercializes coffee in a more conventional way, turn to p. 268

For a conversation with someone else who's changing the ownership patterns and the path of coffee commercialization, ground to grounds, turn to the next page.

Francisco

Recorded Wednesday, January 16, 2013, at Exclusive Coffee in San Juan de Alejuela.

We stand in the lobby of Exclusive. Through a set of frosted glass doors bearing the Exclusive logo is the dry mill section of the facility, with women hand selecting defects from a conveyer belt of coffee, a *trilladora* dry hulling machine peeling the layer of parchment paper of dried coffee, and vacuum packing machines sealing up extra special micro lots of coffee for export.

The prep and packing room opens onto a docking area where trucks, including ones towing full size shipping containers, can pull up to load. Exclusive's "boutique dry mill" is in a facility called *Ofibodegas del Este*. An *ofibodgea* is an invented word that fuses "office" and "bodega," which here does not mean a corner deli, but rather a storage space for dry goods. Exclusive is every bit an *ofibodega*, but it is also something else. It is an organized, detail oriented exporter with immaculate understandings of international markets, an exporter that lets determined families move their coffee in ways that compensate them for outstanding individual effort.

Francisco: *This is Exclusive Coffees; it's a company that started in August of 2008, August 1ˢᵗ 2008. It's a company that was created with the proposition of accompanying Costa Rica's micromills with new knowledge and information, so that that information could be implemented on fincas and at mills.*

My partner, Juan Ramon is an agronomist; he's also a micromill owner and operator, his coffee is called Brumas de Zurqui, and together with him, we started to develop strong work on the farms. We're not coffee traders; we're coffee creators, together with the coffee growers.

Four years ago we started in a garage. We didn't have a car, an office; we were a truly small business. We went through a very steep learning curve. And two years ago we had the great opportunity, and the blessing, to move ourselves to our own space to process. Because microlots from micromills need microcare, right? So we needed to rent our own space because of the growth— both together with producers and internationally— so we moved to our own processing plant.

This is our logo [gesturing to frosted glass wall between lobby and dry mill floor] *this is Don Tuto Gamboa, a producer and micromill owner, a pioneer of the micromill revolution. His mill is called "Montes de Oro;" it's in San Pablo de Leon Cortes, Tarrazú [right across from Javier at La Cabaña].*

Our logo says "Coffees with Identity," because that's what we do. Create coffees with the identity of the producer.

Where does the coffee that Fransciso creates and exports go?

Exclusive sells a host of Costa Rican coffees to many well known direct trade roasters the world over, including Portland's Stumptown and Seattle's Caffe Vita.

If you came from **Cedral** and would like to return to the finca, turn to p. 135

If you came from **Javier** and would like to continue to Monteverde, turn to p. 177

For a conversation with a **Panamanian caficultor** who exports directly to roasters, turn to p. 233

For a conversation with a **Colombian direct trade grower**, processor, and exporter, turn to p. 300

To continue to Panama, turn to the next page.

Panama

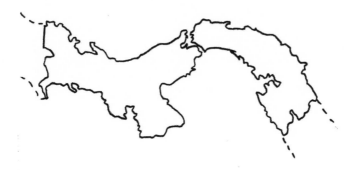

Panama is a country of pockets. It's the narrowest point on the Central American isthmus and is best known for its Canal. The Canal tends to be people's single association with country, but this skinny place concentrates the allure of two continents and packs a raw diversity of people and place into a land area the size of South Carolina, with a population of roughly 3.6 million.

Most of the capital of Panama City looks like Miami, save one crumbling old neighborhood built by waves of French and Spanish explorers, which looks like a cross between New Orleans and Barcelona. Because the US controlled the Panama Canal from when they started building it in 1904 until Panama gained control in 2000, Panama uses the US dollar, lots of people speak English, and chains like Hard Rock Café abound.

The building of the Canal drew people from all over the world, and descendants of immigrants from China to Eastern Europe weave Panama's textured ethnic fabric. Indigenous histories are very different between Central American nations, and Panama's is unexpected. For all this international diversity, by far the greatest in the region, Panama is also home to three very different, very distinct indigenous groups, each of which owns a large area of land, collectively comprising a significant part of the country.

Apart from Costa Rica, Panama boasts the only other place in the world where you can see the Pacific and Atlantic oceans at the same time, from the top of Volcán Barú. In one pocket Panama has soaring mountains, in another soggy forests, in another baking desert, in another droves of drunk backpackers littering Caribbean beaches, and in another expanses of roadless jungle controlled by native Americans. In one small pocket there's some coffee, but most of it is the specialist of specialty coffee; Panama's export volumes don't make international trade waves.[The Significance of Being Statistically Insignificant p. 371] This specialist of specialty coffee is the Geisha varietal, a variety of coffee that made its own tsunami when it accidentally inundated the specialty scene.

Panama is the bottleneck of the Americas, and Panama City is the bottleneck of the bottleneck. All wildlife and humanlife in transit between points north and south must traverse Panama City. And all cargo in transit between the Pacific and Atlantic

185

must bisect it. Quietly, Panama is the gatekeeper of voyages, land and sea.

Panama is the single pulsing vein through which all the energy that defines the Americas must hotly course.

Because of its history of prolonged interaction with the United States, and because of the United State's profound determination to set up schools and teach the locals English wherever it goes, English crops up in Panamanian Spanish in ways that are uniquely Panamanian.

Common Panamisims:

Estamos todo full
Está en el closet
Pongalo en el locker
Se puso muy crazy
Fijalo con el tape
Es muy pritty
Te doy un ride
Está marcado con un esticker
No worry, todo cool.

Comarca Ngöbe-Bugle

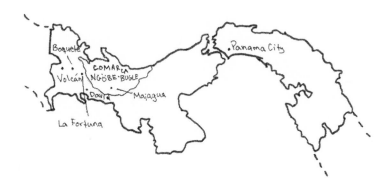

In the northwest quadrant of Panama the Ngöbe-Bugle owned land (Comarca) extends from the Caribbean—almost the border with Costa Rica—to the dry, dusty, hot interior of the country in the Chiriquí Province. The Ngöbe have their own language that is entirely unrelated to Spanish. Most families subsistence farm, and some also grow coffee and cacao, some have cattle, and almost all are characterized by stoic facial expressions. Most families who own land in the Comarca will also spend time working in cities, and the women in their vibrant dresses are a common sight in surrounding urban areas.

Farther east in the Caribbean is the Guna Yala, a group who owns thousands of pristine, white-sand-beach-drenched islands. They make their money predominately from tourism, charging chartered boats a docking fee and selling jewelry, sandals, and anything they can to the waves of tourists licking their shores. But no one else is allowed to build on their islands, so they get the income without the corporate takeovers. The Guna Yala women don very different, but even more vibrant, attire can be see all over Panama City.

The Embra are by far the least visible of Panama's indigenous groups, living deep in the Darien jungle that divides Panama from Colombia. They're known for the dyed tattoo patterns that cover their faces, necks, and arms.

Peace Corps Panama has an active presence in the Ngöbe Comarca, with volunteers working in areas of small business development, environmental health, and sustainable agricultural systems. In a few pockets where Ngöbe are growing coffee, there are a few Peace Corps volunteers working to help make coffee cultivation more viable and sustainable, sustainable in that it's something that people will be able to continue doing for a long time. But this is no small task, as within the Comarca there are many more pockets, some where coffee farmers plant Robusta deep in the mangroves, on fincas accessible only by boat; some where Arabica varieties of Typica and Bourbon are planted at 700 meters above sea level on bald sun-cooked, windblown hilltops.

People from all cultures can all appreciate that drinking a cup of coffee just makes life a little better, but ways of growing it are cultural[Agriculture p. 372] and look quite different in the diverse coffeepockets of the world.

Federico

Recorded Saturday, February 2, 2012, in front of the school building in Majagua, a community in the Ngöbe-Bugle Comarca.

Incessant chainsaw in the background. Federico and I stand side by side drinking coffee from plastic mugs. It's the lunch break of a Peace Corps "in-the-field" practical workshop about general coffee agronomy and the importance of tree pruning. Federico wears a crisp new red and green Chiriquí Province baseball hat.

Rachel: *How did you start growing coffee here?*

Federico: *We started because, before, we didn't know what coffee was. But from information gained elsewhere, people were buying coffee. And we thought it might be easier if we grew our own plants. That's where we started from.*

We planted the first trees of our own in order to not have to buy coffee. We thought it would be easier to have coffee if we planted our own; that's why we started to plant it. Starting around 1994.

Rachel: *Was there one person who planted it first and then—*

Federico: *Other people started to do it too. We started growing it individually. But, because the seeds aren't from here, we had to get them from Boquete. But there the soil is moist, and [the trees] produce well, like the technician* was saying. Here the land is dry.*

Here, bananas give the best production. And coffee, but a good variety that produces here. The seeds from Boquete were Catimor. People know about coffee from being in Boquete, and that's where we brought the seeds from. Because there they have coffee that's well-tended, well-managed, that produces every year. Here no. We don't fertilize at all. That's where the failure is.

Rachel: *Do people here go to the harvest to pick coffee in Costa Rica or other parts of Panama?*

Federico: *Mm hmm. They go to Costa Rica, Boquete, Cerro Punta, Volcán, Rio Sereno. [Pause.] You're still recording? [I nod.] Our main failure was lack of knowledge of how to fertilize coffee. That's something else*

189

we didn't know about. Like I was telling the technician, it hurts me to prune this coffee down to stumps, but... I guess we have to.

Dog yelps and barks as it runs over to us. We rejoin the rest of the group for the second half of the workshop.

If you came from Ariela and would like to return to Costa Rica, turn to p. 147

For a conversation with a coffee grower in Boquete, turn to p. 243

To continue to Panama's mountains, turn to the next page.

*Peace Corps Panama Sustainable Agriculture Volunteer Matt Tansey. Matt was my Comarca connection. He invited me to spend ten days at his Peace Corps site in the Ngöbe community of Bahía Ballena (Whale Bay). I stayed with Natalia and her twelve-year-old daughter Kati. Natalia and Kati don't grow coffee, but they were gracious hosts who taught me how to peel green bananas with a machete and say quite a few phrases in the Ngöbe language of Ngobere. All visitors to Ngöbe communities, whether they stay for a day or a year, are given a Ngöbe name. Because I was staying with Natalia, she had the privilege of naming me. Twenty-four hours after my arrival she'd dubbed me Mechigo, which Matt said translates to something like "sweetheart."

Bahía Ballena is accessible only by boat, and during my stay I did visit Natalia's neighbor's (also named Federico) finca deep in the mangroves, where we macheted away the jungle to make room for the Robusta seedlings. While Matt, Federico, and I worked with the coffee, Federico's wife and daughter dug up various kinds of root vegetables similar to taro.

In the evenings Natalia, Kati, and I would listen to the radio by flashlight (most of the Comarca doesn't have electricity) and go over my Ngobere notes as I entertained them by trying to say phrases like, "It's raining out and the food is good."

Volcán

The town of Volcán is not named haphazardly; it sits right at the base of the Barú Volcano, in the "skirt folds" as the Spanish imagery goes. The volcanic soil makes for great coffee growing, and the high elevations allow for the slow development of sugars that yield the most sought after Arabicas. But coffee is not the only thing that grows well in Volcán and its environs; *agricultores* plant potatoes and onions and there is no shortage of cattle ranches and dairy farms lining the roadsides.

Volcán (and its twin sister Boquete) are fairly close to the Costa Rican border and seem very Costa Rican indeed in their climate and topography. It's pretty much eternal spring in the shadow of the volcano, with none of the unpleasantries of malaria and aggressive-fauna filled jungles or discomfort of bone-dry deserts. Volcán still has a small town feel, the pros and cons of which reminded me of the pros and cons of the small town in New Hampshire where I grew up. The pro is that everyone knows everyone. The con is that everyone knows everyone.

I was only in Volcán for a week, and already people were beeping and waving at me out of friendly recognition as I walked through town (and not out of gringa novelty.)

Panamanian coffee has only recently made a name for itself in global specialty niche markets, but prior to finding itself as a frontrunner of the coffee growing elite, Panama produced a bunch of coffee. It just didn't export much; the majority remained in house for domestic consumption. And this domestic coffee is anything but elite. It often comes sold in little single serve "envelopes" which people then prepare as cowboy coffee— just mixing it into a pot of boiling water and holding back the grounds with a spoon when they pour it into your cup. Rumor has it Panama grown, Panama consumed coffee is mixed with ground rice and beans, because there is definitely some kind of filler in there, evident even through the musky Robusta taste.

I love this coffee. It's dark and dirty and gritty and just like a fresh, local version of the dollar deli coffee I drink in New York. What I don't love about this coffee is that I know it was picked by Ngöbe families living in less-than-savory facilities on the large plantations owned by the domestic coffee mills. But the entire Panamanian coffee scene is changing, and as consumers expect better coffee, workers expect better pay and perks.

Alan

Recorded Wednesday, February 6, 2013, at the Hartmann family estate in Santa Clara de Volcán.

 The Hartmann family estate is part of the new Panamanian coffee growing elite. Alan handles the processing link of the coffee chain. We bounce around in the pickup truck as he shows me the newest lot planted with baby Geisha and points out all the primary forests surrounding the cafetals. He wears a tan baseball hat and a red t-shirt.

Rachel: *And it was your father who came here for the first time?*

Alan: *Yes. My grandfather arrived in Volcán for the first time in 1912, when he started farming here in Chiriquí. 1912, when he started in Las Lagunas de Volcán. And little by little he migrated up here, to Santa Clara. He always liked planting coffee, and his sons basically all did the same thing. It was a pretty attractive thing to do in this area. They'd harvest the coffee and carry it out on horseback. There wasn't a road then, but it wasn't bad. It wasn't work where you had to move a product every day, like milk or something. It was pretty comfortable for this part of the country.*

 From there, my father— at that time you could pretty much mark your own land, because everything was open. My father chose this finca [Ojo de Agua], and then the one below [Santa Clara]. My father's been growing coffee since '60, when he dedicated himself completely to coffee. He used to live in the capital, in Panama City. And we've followed him, incorporating ourselves into the work of producing coffee.

For a conversation with Alan's father, turn to the next page.

Don Ratibor

Recorded Monday February 11, 2013, at the main house on the Hartmann family estate.

Alan's father Ratibor sits in a rocking chair on the front porch of the main house. He wears a navy blue sweater.

Rachel: *That buoy is from the Canal?* [I point to a giant round bouy suspended from a tree that's probably three stories tall.]

Ratibor. *Yes, from the Canal. I got if for $20! My brother helped me get it up there, with a winch from a car! Iron! It was pretty heavy.*

Rachel: *And did you work on the Canal?*

Ratibor: *No, not directly with the Canal. I worked in a lab, as a technician. As an entomologist. Through all of Central America up to Mexico. We worked on malaria and yellow fever. And when I retired I came here. And here I am! When I came here there were monkeys. There aren't monkeys now. They left. They got afraid and they left.*

But it's still beautiful here, with the rainforest. All the primary forest.

Rachel: *Were you the first person to plant coffee on this property?*

Ratibor: *Yes, I planted coffee. It was the only thing that would grow up here. It was coffee. Nothing else worked. I tried coffee and stuck with coffee. And here I am, still.*

Have you met my children? Alex? Alan? Ratibor? Kelly isn't here right now; he's the youngest. And then my daughter, she was born a year after Kelly. They all work together. Would you like to work here? [Laughs, and his face crinkles into a smile.] *But you're traveling.*

Earlier Don Ratibor had told me that the reason he planted coffee in first place was because, "sheep and goats walk away. Because I couldn't be here all the time, I needed something that wouldn't walk away."

For a conversation with another of Don Ratibor's sons, turn to the next page.

Alex

Recorded Monday, February 11, 2013 outside the cupping lab at the Hartmann family estate.

Alex and I are seated on the picnic table on the porch outside the building housing the cupping lab and a little museum of cool things found on the finca, including way too many snakes preserved in jars for my liking. Jute coffee sacks, stamped and painted with logos and names of coffee farms all over Latin America, are attached to the ceiling of the porch, making a sort of international coffee tent. Alex wears a maroon polo.

Rachel: *I'm interested in the stories of people who work in coffee, told by the people who work in coffee. Because there are lots of people from the U.S. and Europe who come and write lots of things, but maybe we're writing about stuff that doesn't really matter. Maybe we're missing the important stuff.*

Your brother told me that you're a family business, that all the siblings are—

Alex: *Involved. Yes. Really, this is what it is. I'm guessing he told you about how the business started. My father started it years ago; we continued it. Today it's divided by roles. Every one of us has a responsibility. Mine is the fields. Everything that has to do with planting, maintaining the fincas, everything up until we put the cherries in the beneficio. So, what would you like to know?*

Rachel: *I saw the Ojo de Agua lot, where all the new Geisha is planted. What I'm curious about is how you decide what to plant when, and where? How do you make those decisions?*

Alex: *Ok. All this starts—well, you know that the coffee growing region of Panama is small. Many people must have told you that, and I'm sure you've seen it for yourself. Compared to our neighbor Costa Rica, we're very small, and if we compare ourselves to Colombia to the south, we're extremely small, both in overall land area and land area for producing coffee.*

We're all small businesses, small farms of ten, twenty, thirty hectares. Small beneficios, small companies. And this has obligated us to look for a more direct niche in the market. Not working so much with brokers but with micro roasters in the U.S., Europe, wherever. Working directly with these roasters, they're the ones who tell us what they want, or what the public is asking for, as much as in varieties as in processes [washed, Honey, Natural.]

And that is what directs us on the course we take. We decided some time ago to start replanting part of the farm that had been overgrown with coffee. So what tells us what varieties to plant is really the consuming public. And how do we know that? Through our contact with our buyers, who are the owners of foreign roasteries.

On the other hand, when I change a lot, from old plants to new ones, the plants themselves tell me when. I keep a logbook of what I planted when. So when the plants get to a certain age, I start to evaluate if I'm going to just replant within the lot, or if I change it completely. If I have a variety that isn't very profitable, I might change it completely. This is what tells me when and how to renovate different lots.

Another thing is, if I have, for some reason, some type of problem, whether it's weather related or a plague, I might change it sooner. Because we're working with specialty coffee and fulfilling a bunch of expectations, we can't apply products that are too strong, or the final product won't serve. So here we don't use any of these toxic products, but by not using the strongest products, the plants become worn down more quickly, so we have to renovate. This is basically what tells me when and how: the plants' physical state, age, variety, what people are asking for.

For example, a few years ago, it was the famous Geisha. Geisha is still popular, but there are other varieties that are trending. So that's what we go with. It's like a style. Because we're a small farm, we have to follow that. We can't be traditionalists, rather, we have to be innovators. To think, "what do people need? Want?" And that's what we deliver. And we're completely committed to keeping a balanced ecosystem. Not affecting the wild flora and fauna we have; we have quite a bit of protected area. We maintain an environmentally friendly farm.

We live from the production of coffee and the sale of coffee. But we work with a conscience. In protection of the environment. Because we want to leave this to our children. Our parents left it to us, and we want to leave it to our children, so you have to work in environmentally friendly ways, in the most sustainable ways possible.

Rachel: *Of all the work you've done with coffee, what would you consider the biggest challenge and the biggest success?*

Alex: *Well, the biggest challenge that one encounters in growing coffee is to be able to produce every year. Because we're faced with inclemencies in weather, with changes in the climate. Right now, things are changing very quickly. The biggest challenge is mother nature herself. To be able to produce. Because across Central America agriculture is suffering many blows. Really, we don't find ourselves with much support from the government, from laboratories. Panama is an orphan in this sense. We have a Ministry of Agriculture, but there's no one office that has to do with just coffee, that helps us with problems we encounter in the field. With plagues and all that. So we're practically orphans in that sense. And our challenge is to face all these obstacles that we find ourselves with daily. With the prices of inputs; the prices are very high.*

People think that our products—be they coffee or other vegetables—are expensive because we make them expensive. No. The reason they cost what they do is because of the costs of everything needed to produce them. So that's the most difficult. To stand up to nature, with all the problems she brings, and the ones people have brought on themselves, with all these climate changes. To be able to continue to produce. That is the biggest challenge. To not disappear as a caficultor. Because every day another coffee grower is disappearing. Today Panama isn't producing half of what it was producing even ten years ago. We're disappearing. So the biggest challenge is not to disappear.

And the biggest achievement, is to have been able to keep going! In spite of all these things, to be able to pass this business on to our children. And continue as a coffee farm, with good products. To continue offering quality coffee to the consuming public, free of any traces of chemicals. Something truly good. That's the biggest desire, to continue in our work successfully.

Rachel: *Lastly, what is one thing you'd like people who drink your coffee to know?*

Alex: *What we need is that you keep drinking coffee! Really, it's important that we have the support of younger generations. Because we need the new generation, seventeen, eighteen year old kids, to be coffee drinkers for many years! We need young people to try something that has existed for years, an excellent drink, the beverage of conversations, meetings, of closing business deals! Good business ends with a good cup of coffee—or a good glass of whiskey!*

Rachel: *Or, they start with a cup of coffee—*

Alex: *—and end with the good whiskey! But really, we need the support of all you New Yorkers drinking our coffee.*

Rachel: *Well, I drink lots of coffee, and I have lots of friends who do too!*

Alex: *Good! I'm happy to hear that!*

Rachel: *Thank you so much for sharing all this.*

Alex: *No, thank you. Really, these are interesting topics, especially how you framed it. To come and talk, and take notes- or record- the conversation with the producers themselves. For the reason you said; you can come and take lots of notes and share your opinion, but they way someone feels who's actually* involved *will be very different.*

I say this as a joke but also seriously; the business of coffee is in the hands of new consumers, the ones we can introduce into this. Not to mention that it's a delightful drink that enlivens you, motivates you, that gives you energy! Again, thank you.

Where does the Hartmann family's coffee go?
The Hartmanns sell to Blue Bottle, Phil and Sebastian, and other roasters who buy directly from farms with whom they have relationships.

If you came from Elias and would like to return to Turrialba, turn to p. 40

If you came from Froilan and would like to return to Cedral, turn to p. 129

For a conversation with a Colombian coffee growing family, turn to p. 319

For a conversation with a former coffee buyer and roaster, turn to the next page.

Sipke

Recorded Wednesday, February 6, 2013, on the Hartmann family farm. Interview recorded in English.

Sipke is a retired coffee roaster and former buyer for several major European grocery brands. He's one of those brilliant, energetic, and brilliantly energetic people who does not sit idly in retirement, but rather volunteers with an organization that places retired European experts in developing countries to act as pro bono consultants in order to help accelerate local businesses.

Sipke and I are seated at the picnic table outside the cupping lab. He wears glasses and a white polo shirt.

Sipke: *After being retired I didn't do anything with coffee, except for the museum. Part of the company relocated and had to move all the materials and everything. So I said, "What are you going to do with this old roaster?" They said they were moving it too," and I said, "No! It should stay in the museum." But they asked, "But who's going to roast? We'll have problems with the quality!" And I said, "No. Because I'm going to roast."*

So then we donated the thing to the museum. And now I roast from time to time, when there's no more [coffee for sale] in the museum shop. They call me and I roast. I have a trainee. He's five years older than me! [Laughs] A trainee! But I also have another one, so we're three. So I can still go do my projects.

Rachel: *I've always wondered if there's any general difference in taste between organic coffee and coffee treated with chemicals. I know most people who buy organic coffee usually buy it because they want something organic, not because they think that coffee tastes amazing.*

Sipke: *I think that if you put coffee from a tree treated with chemicals and coffee from an organic tree side by side, they'd probably taste different. But I've never been able to do that. There are so many other factors that affect taste. You could say that organic coffees will come from countries where certification is possible.*

You can't to go Cameroon, for example, where there are five trees on one farm and ten trees on the next; that doesn't work. You have to go to a serious plantation. If you go to Mexico you can find one with 1500 hectares, *which is 3000 acres; that's a good one. So you can ask Rainforest Alliance** *to go there and check. I say, I don't even trust it.*

[Years ago] I was at a farm in Mexico, and, well, a lot of things happened, but we were going through a stock of green coffee, that was when the prices were a little lower than they are now. And he said, "If you want to buy— " "I had to buy for Hills Brothers, and for El Marino, in Mexico. You know El Marino? It's the second biggest brand in Mexico, and it's roasted in the Netherlands. So we were buying for them, in Tapachula, that's in the south of Mexico, near the border with Guatemala. They showed me the coffee and said, "Well, you can buy that as well." And I said, "But it says Fairtrade certified." He said, "Yeah. Same price." So I said, "Why is that?" He said, "They want me to certify, they want certified coffee, but they don't buy." So the farmer has paid for everything, but they don't take the green coffee, so I could buy for the same price.

So usually organic and fair trade coffees come from larger farms, not from the smaller ones that really would need it. That's my feeling a little bit. Then there's also corruption. The guy doing the certification says, "I'll give you the certification for maybe, so much." And he will put, "ok, ok, ok, ok." But that's fraud. It's not fair. So the fair trade's not fair. I have my doubts about that. Especially if you need to buy these big volumes like we did. You can't find it.

You go to a co-operative. I go to, what's his name, Cooxupé, the largest co-op in Brazil, four million bags. The biggest in the world. I had a meeting there and I told them, "I'm thinking of becoming a farmer, and I would like to join your co-operative," because I had some questions a farmer would also have. But there were some they couldn't answer very well. Especially, "If I have this fantastic coffee that I've put all my efforts into it and then some ass comes by with mold in his beans, they would go into the same hole?" "Yeah." I don't like that. So they didn't have, really, answers to all my questions. They were too big.

Rachel: *I've seen similar things. Farmer's who were co-op members who did something like this [Hartmann family estate] with their families and started their own mill because they realized that their coffee was different than their neighbors, and they were getting paid the same price.*

Sipke: *And they were proud of it.*

Rachel: *And they wanted to put their own names on it instead of watching somebody else's name go on it.*

Sipke asks me if my book will be the best book about coffee that's ever been written. I tell him I don't know if it will be quite that grand. He tells me, "If you're going to write a book about coffee then shouldn't you want it to be the best book about coffee that has ever been written?" I tell him that that is indeed a good way to approach it. I put that goal at the top of my to do list.

He excuses himself to go bird watching. He's keen on spotting an elusive quetzal before going back to the Netherlands.

For a conversation with an artisan coffee roaster, turn to p. 229

For a conversation with a caficultor from Volcán who has a different background from the Hartmanns, turn to the next page.

*Rainforest Alliance is not responsible for certifying farms as organic. Farms Rainforest Alliance certified must meet standards relating to biodiversity as well as responsible management of the human and natural environment. Farms certified as organic must meet standards regarding chemical use set by the USDA. Third party auditors check to see if farms meet these sets of standards. If you want to be Rainforest Alliance certified in Mexico, Productos y Procesos Sostenibles, SA would be your "certification body." If you want to be certified organic you could hire one of twenty plus accredited** auditing agencies operating in Mexico.

**Third-party auditing agencies are accredited by the IOAS (International Organic Accreditation Service), itself a member of the ISEAL Alliance, the "global membership association for sustainability standards."

Don Villa

Recorded Thursday, February 7, 2013, on Don Villa's various fincas in Rio Sereno and Renaciamiento, right on the Costa Rican border, about an hour from Volcán.

Like most of the fincas in the area, Don Villa's properties incorporate tall hardwoods and many other species of trees of varying sizes. Don Villa wears a white baseball cap and a short-sleeved white collared shirt.

Rachel: *And all these fincas are from your family?*

Don Villa: *Yes, from my family. I started here—I'm not from this area; I'm from an area in the valley called San Andres. I studied agriculture. I came first here with the government, with the National Coffee Program. And after being here, I really liked it. I didn't like it that much down in [San Andres]; it was too hot.*

I bought this farm in 1976. Seventeen hectares. Then I bought a little more, and now I have almost twenty-six hectares. I've also worked with coffee in cherries at the mill, for a big coffee company. I was there for eighteen years. I'm retired now, but when I retired I already had this. I like being here.

Rachel: *You worked for a Panamanian National Coffee Program?*

Don Villa: *Yes. I was in Costa Rica at IICA [Interamerican Institute for Co-operation in Agriculture] for six months in a coffee course. In Turrialba.*

Rachel: *I know Costa Rica has ICAFE; does Panama have a similar office?*

Don Villa: *No, which makes us worse off. There isn't a plan. There isn't an office that's dedicated to coffee and nothing else. Colombia has one. All of Central America does.*

Rachel: *The government program you worked for was to help producers?*

Don Villa: *There was a coffee program in this area, and a lot coffee was planted here. I made nurseries. People here didn't know how to make them. So I'd sell them seedlings to plant. But the National Bank of Development* *paid for the seeds. I was producing seeds for at least five years. We improved the densities of planting and made everything more organized.*

But, when it came time to prune, which was three years later, the government abandoned the program. And so people never learned to prune! And it was disastrous for them. That's why we need a program, one that will last years. Right? Like there is in Colombia and Costa Rica. [As we walk through the finca, Don Villa points out recently pruned plants, beans growing below the coffee, and lots of bananas. We get back in the car.]

I have a daughter who lives in Atlanta. I was in New York, but just in the airport. I went to Italy. And with my daughter we were in Orlando, New Jersey, and Washington. I have five daughters and one son. [He stops the car and we pull up in the shade of a large tree.]

This tree, this eucalyptus, was the first tree I planted. In 1986. There was just this and all the wild trees. There wasn't anything here. There wasn't coffee. It was all abandoned pastures.

Rachel: *And the beneficio you sell to now [Association of Producers of Renacimiento- APRE] is pretty new, right?*

Don Villa: *About four years old. Before that we used to sell to the big buyers around here. You just dropped off your coffee and that was it.* [I snap some pictures and we get back in the car to head to the area where Don Villa has his almacigos.]

Rachel: *So you worked for this National Coffee Program before you had your own farm?*

Don Villa: *No no, I already had it. I went to the Agricultural High School, in a town between Panama City and David. And then when I came here I worked with Interamerican Co-operative Agricultural Service, an agency of the U.S. government. They helped me get the scholarship to go to Turrialba. I was there at IICA for six months. We studied coffee, out in the fields, too. I've been working in coffee my whole life.*

Rachel: *Of all the work you've done with coffee, what has been the biggest challenge to overcome, and what has been the biggest success?*

Don Villa: *To overcome? That would be...in the Association there are different people with different mentalities. And it's hard to encourage people to change. That was the biggest challenge to overcome. I think our biggest success would be to have the mill. Because then you have added value. We want to go all the way to roasting! We're still missing that step. But we've made it to green coffee. We've gotten better prices. We have the coffee pulp [to use for other things].*

I think the most important thing that's happened to us here has been developing the mill. We did it little by little; we didn't have the capacity to do it all at once. Some financing from the government helped. But we're still paying it back.

Rachel: *And you were one of the first members?*

Don Villa: *I was, I guess you could say, one of the founders. I've been working for ten years to do this! But it was the only way to get ahead.*

On the way back from the alamacigos Don Villa shows me his house, where he has hundreds of pounds of red and black beans sitting in sacks on his porch waiting to be sold. He grows the beans in between the rows of young coffee in newly planted lots.

Where does Don Villa and APRE's coffee go?
Don Villa sells his coffee cherries to the APRE beneficio. APRE sells its coffee to a few European clients, including illycafe, but around sixty percent of their coffee goes to the U.S., and much of that goes to Pan American coffee, a private label roaster that works with many national grocery store chains. Don Villa's coffee might already be in you cup.

If you came from Gerardo and would like to return to Costa Rica, turn to p. 48

For a conversation with an APRE employee, turn to the next page.

Orlando

Recorded Thursday, February 7, 2013, at the APRE beneficio.

Orlando, the APRE beneficio manager, starts the beneficio walk-through at the receiving station, where producers bring truckloads of ripe cherries. Everything looks pretty similar to the Costa Rican mills, but here the fanega-sized containers are attached to scales because producers are paid by weight and not by volume. Orlando comments that this change was made during a particularly bad period of broca, when a volumetrically full unit could be half broca devoured floater cherries that don't actually yield any coffee. The physical measuring buckets and bins are still the same sizes, and here a container that in Costa Rica would be a cajuela becomes a lata. Orlando wears a green polo.

Orlando: *We have between ninety and a hundred members. APRE, as a business, is responsible for processing the coffee and looking for— guaranteeing—buyers who will pay a better dividend per lata. The beneficio consists of three depulpers. One that depulps 5,000 kilos an hour, one that does 2,500, and another one that does 5,000 but guarantees a better classification and sorting of the coffee. So we have a, you could call it, "semi-ecological" system. We recirculate the water and have a dry depulper that has a high water pressure to use less water. All coffee is machine washed because of the volume we have.*

The coffee is depulped, washed, and pre dried. We have one dryer that holds 120 quintales [12,000 lbs] and two that hold 60 [6,000 lbs]. Right now, we're pretty much done with the harvest. We're just processing underripe coffee that they pick to control for broca. We work with a system of firewood and hulled parchment paper [to fuel the drying ovens]. Our ovens have a siphon system, so the smoke doesn't contaminate the beans.

Through here, we have the storerooms. All this is in parchment. We just filled three [shipping] containers, so we've moved a lot of what was in here. Yesterday we sent out three containers, one to New Orleans, one to New Jersey, and one to Spain. This is the storage. Over here we have the preparation [for export].

This dry huller processes 40 quintales [4,000 lbs] an hour. It allows us to prepare a container's worth in reasonable time, and it gives us the parchment, which we use in the ovens. We have a machine that classifies by size, which lets us send coffee to Europe, where they ask for them by screen size, 20-15. We also have machine that classifies by weight. [The shake table. Dense beans to the right, light beans to the left.] *With these machines we can also divide our lower grade coffee by quality.* [We walk out of the dusty and deafening hulling, classification, and preparation room—which is the step in coffee production that most feels like an industrial activity and is most similar to processing grains— into a quiet hallway and through a door into a clean, white kitchen-type room.]

This is our cupping lab. We have a huller for samples, a little roaster. Here are all the samples from all the lots we processed this harvest. [He points to a shelf full of Ziploc sandwich bags containing grey-green unroasted beans. He picks up two small white mugs. Sound of clinking.] *Want some coffee?* [We drink.]

This is the third harvest we're processing here at this beneficio. It's pretty new. And this is only the third year that we're doing everything from receiving coffee [in cherries] all the way to filling containers to send to the ports. Before we processed at a rented beneficio. That was when we were working more with illycafe. One of their representatives came to make sure that we were processing at a quality level that they could guarantee to purchase a certain amount.

Come upstairs; I'll show you the view! [We climb the stairs.] *This is the office. We're still working on it. Just think, this all used to be pasture...*

Don Villa walks up the stairs and starts talking to Orlando. I look out the window at pastures, cafetales, mountains and clouds. I wonder if I can see across the border into Costa Rica.

If you came from Jose Cruz and would like to return to Turrialba, turn to p. 43

If you came from Jaime and would like to return to Colombia, turn to p. 312

For a conversation with another beneficio operator, turn to p. 69

For a conversation with someone who works with a direct trade model, turn to the next page.

Haydee

Recorded Friday, February 8, 2013, at the Janson family estate just past the abandoned airstrip outside of downtown Volcán.

Haydee and I are seated at the picnic table on the porch of the finca's small café on a hill overlooking the benefico and drying patio. The café is closed for the day because the barista was being trained. She makes us two espressos. Haydee wears a black blouse.

Haydee: *I've been here for twenty-three years, but [my husband] Calle knows a lot more. Well, to start, his father was a Swedish immigrant. He arrived in the early '20s. And like lots of people who came from Europe at different points in the history of Central America he came to make a future for himself. And so he ended up, by chance, in Panama. He started working in the Darien with a Swedish company, counting bananas, and little by little he was progressing, he established a system for transporting bananas. He ended up in the shipping industry.*

He bought this farm; I think it was in the '40s. There were colonists here from Austria. And so there was an Austrian who was good friends with my father-in-law. And he had a whole lot of land in this area, which had been used for harvesting trees for export. He was the owner of this farm. And, because he was good friends with Calle Janson, my husband has the same name as his father, he invited him to buy this finca, which has a few lakes. And that's how the Swedes arrived here.

Calle Sr. got married, and all his kids were born here. This farm had coffee, originally. But at this time coffee was not a good business to be in. But he was more visionary; he wasn't a farmer. He lived off his shipping business. Agriculture, for him, was a pastime. He started—he had a mechanized dairy, which I think was the first in Central America, he brought Angus cattle from the United States, but he didn't develop the coffee at all because it wasn't his principle focus.

What happened? Years passed, and then came the years of the dictatorship. When the invasion* came, the year right before the invasion, he and his brother were thinking of ways to launch a business from the finca, because everything [at the ports] was on hold. And they came up with the idea to plant coffee—again. In the forests of the finca you could still find original coffee trees from what they'd planted before. So they started twenty-four years ago.

When they started in the coffee business, replanting, Calle wasn't happy with the idea that the coffee was just—he wanted the coffee from the farm to be of a better quality than the coffee that people normally drank. And there weren't any beneficios that could separate coffee by qualities. Or that could process coffee from individuals. Because, at that point, we had to bring our coffee to a beneficio where they mixed all the coffees, because that was the system. Until we built our mill.

The big mills mixed all the coffees and produced "coffee." So, our beneficio was originally designed to have the capacity to separate coffees. Calle's business was in shipping too. He'd started his own company; he had other businesses outside of Panama. When the invasion happened, many Panamanians returned to Panama to reestablish themselves and propel the country forward.

Calle had a different vision; so did I. I work with children; I'm a child psychologist. So we had the vision to start a business—because we'd withdrawn from what we'd been doing before—that would be sustainable, because we'd be living on the finca, that improved the quality of life for the people who worked with us, and, of course, that we could make money with! All these factors had to be there.

We live here. We work with our employees. We educate their children. We're in contact with each other every day. We work as a team. Year after year we've been improving, in many aspects. From the finca to the beneficio, moving vertically. We saw that there were times when coffee didn't pay well internationally, that it was subject to whims of people who told you what you should be doing, but at the same time didn't want to pay you for your efforts. So we started to sell roasted coffee, especially the varieties we have now, which are superior varieties. We're also concerned with the quality of the roast, with better coffee, basically. That was the idea.

We also have children like Ingrid [ten-year-old girl I'd met earlier], who are children of employees, who have scholarships to private schools because they're children with particular academic potential. We even have some clients who award scholarships to schoolchildren. We have a certified adult education teacher who gives literacy classes to adults who never attended school. We have a daycare center—today's the last day; they're packing up if you want to go see it later—the instructor is in charge of creating a safe environment so that the children don't have to go to the cafetales with their parents. You see? We provide the kids breakfast, lunch, and a snack. The teacher gives them activities, and during the school year she gives classes. We have many indigenous children who don't speak Spanish. We've seen over the years that every year their language skills improve.

That's my part. We work like a family; they need us and we need them. We always try to maintain that mentality, of a team. The seasonal harvesters who come are pretty much the same people every year. It doesn't change much. These are people who come back. We have facilities for them to stay in. They're humble; they're not luxurious, but we offer basic facilities so that they can live with their families and go work with the peace of mind that their children are safe.

One of the other things that we do is that we don't sell coffee to people we don't know. We decided not to run an impersonal business. Gracias a Dios, we have the ability, the mobility, to go and visit our clients. We've formed long-term friendships. Sometimes we see them once a year, sometimes twice. But we don't sell coffee to anyone that we don't know. The personal aspect is important. We don't want to be an impersonal company who just throws a product out there and doesn't care. We're also interested that the people who buy our coffee understand the human component that is the quantity of labor that goes into the cafetales. The responsibility you have when you buy a product, whatever it is. To know how it got to you.

To know that when you drink a cup of coffee, there are many lives behind it. It's a process, a slow process. Quality coffee can take four months to prepare, from the time of harvest, the fermentation, the time [drying] on the patio, resting in storage, until it's toasted and you drink it. It passes through many hands here on the finca, such that you can never say, "This coffee is too expensive!" Look at the quantity of people who earn a living at various points of the process so that you can drink a good cup of coffee.

And that's what we developed into our business philosophy: not selling to people we don't know and who don't know us. We're a little different in that. It's one of the things that sets us apart, because there are many producers who are also very responsible with their employees. What else would you like to know?

Rachel: *Well, out of all the work you've done, what has been the biggest challenge and what has been the biggest success?*

Haydee: *The biggest success is to produce cups of coffee that right now can be found in some of the most prestigious places in the world. It brings us enormous pride and satisfaction.*

The biggest failure is...to realize that you're not all-powerful. I'm the daughter of a farmer. But Calle, he was used to working in businesses where he had total control. And when you're a producer, one year you have the rain, one year you have the droughts. And at one point I told Calle, "Look, you can't change nature! You have to accept things." We'll see how we work it out with all the climate changes.

Another frustration in certain moments was having- encountering people who simply thought that- I don't want to criticize- but you find a lot of people who treat producers like...like...not condescending, but with a note of arrogance, thinking that, well, they're working with ignorant people. And so you have—it's easy to be in your business, in, Chicago, what have you, California, Los Angeles, what have you, and say, "Well, these kind of people are like this or like that and I don't like it, and this it has a flavor of—it has a—"There are naturally variations in coffee. The products aren't- and people are also human. If you're very demanding you have to be ready to pay the cost of the product. There were—we encountered people who were very demanding, but at the same time didn't want to pay the price. Entiende? This, yes, was very frustrating.

Because they wanted you to have all these certifications for your coffee- which for us is totally humiliating—because it comes across to us that asking for certifications means that you don't trust the person producing. And people like us, the people who buy from us come here; they know how we work. So we realized that paying for certification—what it entails is one more middleman who's getting a whole lot of money, because we have to pay for the certification ourselves, and when you go to sell that coffee, no one wants to pay you for it. That's the difference. It's like one more burden on the producer.

But that's my point of view. Another producer might have a different one. But I found it frustrating. For a while we had Rainforest Alliance— Calle researched which certification was really was the best for us, because we also have a forest reserve—and so, well, we were certified by them. They're extremely demanding and we worked very well with them. But we realized that the amount of money we were paying them we simply couldn't transfer to the consumer. You see? So that was a frustration. You find people who want certifications to ease their consciences, but at the same time they couldn't care that the producer had to pay more.

So...we realized that, really, doing business like we do, that we have a direct contact with our clients. Our clients come; we're open. Right now we have a barista from one of the clients we sell to, and she's here. She's helping us in the coffee shop; she wanted to pick coffee, well, go for it! Every year people come who really care about where their coffee comes from, or they send their employees. So they see how we work. And this history, and this human contact passes by word of mouth, and they can say, "I know where this coffee comes from," when the person about to buy the cup asks them. "Because I went, and I know the owners, and I know the employees, and I saw, and they do this that I like and that that I don't like as much, but overall I know where this coffee comes from." See? So for us this is the most honest way of doing things.

It was frustrating, at the beginning, to organize a good group of workers. The workers arrived with a mentality that was completely different from the attitude that we wanted to achieve here. They thought, "You're the boss and I'm the employee; the company is one thing and we're another." It's taken us years to change this mentality that comes with the culture. To explain that all the work that's done here is equally important. By some stroke of the universe we're the ones directing things; it's not to say that the guy who's sweeping the patio—that's an extremely important job!

Extremely important. And the people working the finca. And Yofo who's roasting. Everyone here is equally important. If not, it doesn't work. We've done cuppings with the employees too, so that they see why it's important that they do certain things. You don't have to be a great cupper to notice the difference between coffee that's been picked up from the ground and coffee that's been picked as it should be. When they taste it they realize the importance.

We're proud to have people from all over the world come here to see our coffee, to drink our coffee. And we're just as proud when we go to other places and we see our coffee, or any coffee from Panama. We were in Taiwan and there was coffee from the Peterson's, who are good friends of ours. It was right there on the menu! The more Panama becomes known for specialty coffee, the more it benefits all of us.

What else would you like to know?

Rachel: *Do you just process your own coffee at the beneficio, or other people's too?*

Haydee: *We do process coffee for other people, but we keep everything separate. Some people bring us their coffee in cherries, and we do the entire process for them. And we keep it apart. We sometime separate our own coffees by lot, by selection. Right now we're still harvesting, so you'd only be able to see the wet process. All of our coffees sit for at least three months of aging in*

211

the warehouse before we [dry hull them] and prepare them to export. Some of our clients have their own sacks they use.

Because we have a good reputation as a mill, one of the most organized—various times we've won awards for the cleanest benefico—we use all the waste products we generate. All the pulp gets broken down by enzymes and microorganisms that help break down the sugars more quickly, and we use it in the fincas as organic fertilizer. All the water from fermentation, which is highly contaminated with sugars, goes to ponds, where the same microorganisms create sediment, which we also use as compost, and then the water is cleaned. We were the first ones here to use this system.

We live here. We test the water every year. We have springs on the farm, which we use to process the coffee and for drinking water. More than 70% of the property is forest. We conserve the land and use it to generate a little bit more money through agrotourism; we're not too organized in that respect right now. When tourists come they can ride horses, hike, birdwatch.

We also have nurseries, with coffee seedlings to sell to other farms. We select the best seeds we have, plant the seeds, and transplant the seedlings. Replanting or trying new varieties. Right now we have Catuai and Geisha, and we sell some to other fincas. But also, a large part of the nursery is trees. So we also sell trees of various sizes to people who want to reforest. [A young woman walks up the stairs to where we're sitting.]

Ahh, Marike! This is Marike! She's staying with us; she's a coffee nut! A barista; she works with one of the clients we sell to in the Netherlands. And she's also a trainer with Bagels and Beans, a company in the Netherlands. We started working with them when they opened their first shop. About ten or eleven years ago. Going back to, "We don't sell coffee to people we don't know," they were starting the business, and I remember they approached us. We had friends in common, and they came to the farm, thinking about the concept that they were going to establish. They were interested in setting up something with coffee; they were in the restaurant business before. They wanted to buy very little coffee.

Calle told them, "We'll sell you what ever quantity of coffee you need." So we started selling them, I think it was a bag of coffee. A year! Now they're buying a container full of coffee every month. We've grown together. We have a very, very good relationship. Marike can be a witness that we go the Netherlands twice a year, and we visit every shop that is open. And we're talking about a franchise that has already fifty stores.

We've followed through, in terms of the human contact, with everyone who buys our coffee.

Haydee invites me to eat lunch with Marike at the lake house After lunch Marike and I head up into one of the lots where people are picking Geisha. To read a post about the intricacies of being a barista, inspired by the conversation we had en route, turn to "Barista's Burden," p. 359.

Where does Haydee's coffee go?

The Janson's coffee is exported to direct trade roasters, all of whom Calle and Haydee know personally, in the Netherlands, other European destinations, and places around the world. The Jansons do roast some for domestic sale, and the bags marked with the iconic Guna Yala *mola* style bird logo can be found on the shelves of grocery stores from Volcán to Panama City.

If you came from Susy and would like to return to Costa Rica, turn to p. 168

For another conversation with another woman who is actively involved in managing a Panamanian farm, turn to p. 249

For a conversation with a Colombian woman who's experience with coffee is very disparate, turn to p. 283

To continue to the coffee town on the other side of the Barú Volcano, turn to the next page.

*Invasion. "Did you know that the U.S. invaded Panama? I ask everyone I meet from the United States that. I'm still waiting for someone to say, 'yes.' Did you know?"

I was sitting at a divey roadside half tourist trap, half local watering hole on the outskirts of San Jose, dinking an Imperial and eating tortilla soup when Saul asked me that. I'd lucked out to have Saul as my Couchsurfing host because his apartment was a convenient ten-minute bus ride away from the hotel where the ASIC conference was taking place. He happened to be Panamanian, not Tico.

He proceeded to tell me that he was surprised when he first learned that most United States of Americans don't know about the U.S.'s invasion of Panama in 1989. He told me, "Google it! It's not a secret. But most Americans don't know it happened."

He told me that he remembered being two years old, hearing the explosions and hitting the floor, crouching in the dust with his mother and brother as the invasion happened right outside their home. It was something he'd never forget, and he was always waiting to meet to meet some American his age who at least knew it had happened.

I didn't know. But now I do. And whenever I mention to people in the US that I was in Panama, that I went to the Canal (twice!) to watch boats pass through the locks, I try to mention that Panama now controls its own Canal. But it didn't used to. Because the U.S. did. And the U.S. also invaded Panama.

Most people are surprised. It is surprising, but it's also a good reason to travel. Because you can learn things about your home that you never would have learned if you'd stayed at home.

Boquete

Boquete is land of the Geisha, coffee buzzword/ trend/ fad if ever there was one. But for the caficultores of Boquete, Geisha is a way of life. There is an entire book devoted to the evolution of the obsession with the Geisha varietal, *God in a Cup* by Michaele Weissman, which is certainly an epic in itself. The coffeepeople who speak in the coming pages touch on their roles in and opinions of that epic, but the highlights boil down to a few indisputable facts: Geisha is the first coffee to earn a perfect 100 point cupping score and auction lots regularly sell for over $100/lb. It's that good.

To some people. It's a coffee that kind of doesn't taste like coffee and tastes more like an herbal tea. It's definitely cool, but true to my New York deli roots I'd just as happily drink a cup of domestic rice 'n' beans robusta as a cup of Geisha. My humble evaluation is that it's important to appreciate the good stuff but not lose sight of the fact that all coffee is coffee, and true to its actual roots, it all grows on trees that are tended by people.

Boquete is an interesting place in that a few serendipitous things happened simultaneously to turn this agricultural community on its head. A magazine named Boquete the world's number one place to retire, and in spontaneous exodus a bunch of North Americans moved down here to test that claim. Not too long after that, Geisha was "discovered" and launched Panamanian coffee, and the tiny town of Boquete, out of oblivion and into the specialty coffee spotlight.

The convergence of these two phenomenon resulted in the rapid transformation of the town from a rugged, cowboy-style hub at the end of the road to nowhere into a flourishing tourist destination. No one does coffee and tourism quite like Boquete. Here, you can order a $7 cup of Geisha, grab a local version of a Frappuccino to go, and then go zip lining over a cafetal. You can see coffee being roasted, participate in public (watered-down versions of) cuppings, and even wander along birdwatching trails, flanked all the while by the coffee diligently growing on the hillsides in the distance.

Only in Boquete can you see a Ngöbe family in their formal wear, a middle-class family on vacation, and a group of retirees from Georgia all having lunch at the same restaurant. Coffee really does bring people together.

216

Ricardo

Recorded Friday, February 15, 2013, in the Café Kotowa coffee house in downtown Boquete.

Ricardo brings two cups of coffee to the table. He wears a light yellow guayabera shirt.

Ricardo: *So. Boquete is a town that was founded at the end of the 1800s, 1895, beginning of the 1900s. It was colonized by Canadians, North Americans, and Europeans who liked the cooler climate, different from the rest of Panama. Since the beginning, Boquete has been dedicated to coffee, mainly. Every finca, apart from coffee, had her parcel of agriculture, cows, chickens; people were very self-sufficient.*

Boquete has the shape of a "U." When you arrive in Boquete, in the far end is a mountain, a mountain range, which is part of the Central Range. If you were to go up then go down the other side you'd end up at the Atlantic.

When you arrive in Boquete you're coming from David, from the South [via the only road], heading towards the north. On the right, you'll see another mountain, and to the left still others. On the right is Cerro Azul, and to the left is the Barú Volcano. This forms the Boquete Valley.

The Boquete Valley has different microclimates. Why? Because Panama, as such a narrow country—like 85 kilometers [53 miles] between one ocean and the other—we have influences from the Atlantic as much as from the Pacific. What does this mean? There are times of the year when we receive rains from the Atlantic and others when we receive rains from the Pacific.

The rain from the Atlantic is concentrated more in the Central Range, in the northern area. But, depending where you are in the Boquete Valley, you'll receive more wind from one side or another, and this causes different climates. What does this mean? In some parts of Boquete you have four meters of rainfall. Or even six. Extreme quantities of water. It's very difficult to grow coffee in these areas. There are other areas where the least that falls is two. So between two and six meters. You can see the difference in vegetation.

There are some places where it rains ten months a year, and others where it rains seven—just by moving from one side of Boquete to another! And you can see the difference in the color of the soil. Where it rains months a year is not necessarily where there's the most rainfall. It can be that the total rainfall is low, but that it's always raining a little bit. This has created a variety of microclimates, which permit us to grow different types of coffee.

217

Different flavors, different profiles. This is one of the most special features of Boquete. You can find very different things within a very small area.

Boquete is curious because it's missing a generation. Here, you'll find people over seventy or under fifty. The generation in between didn't stay in Boquete. The one's who stayed are the one's fifty and below. What happened? Thirty years ago, agriculture—the people who lived in the mountains educated their children to be lawyers, doctors, but not to stay on the farms. In the last twenty years, yes, a new generation has returned to work on the fincas. This new generation, in the case of Boquete, brought many changes, which are the ones that make Boquete the way it is today.

I graduated from university in 1970. When I returned to Boquete, coffee, in reality, wasn't a good business. I'm here through my family. My grandfather arrived in Boquete in the early 1900s. He was Canadian; he was the mayor of a small town near Vancouver and had businesses there. He saw a letter that someone from Boquete wrote and had published in Canada. He was interested, and he wrote this person and they became friends. He came and saw Boquete and said, "I'm going to live here." And he bought a farm, returned to Canada, and several years later came back to Boquete and started to produce coffee here.

Like many others, he put down roots. After my grandfather it was my mother, and then I followed. I have two sisters, but they live in Panama City. So I stayed working on the finca. I'm an agronomical engineer, and I have a degree in business administration. When I came back here, in 1990, we started working with coffee, but the price was extremely low. The international market was at around $0.60 per pound.

$0.60 per pound! There was no way to produce coffee at $0.60 per pound. So, along with me, many of my friends—who maybe you'll meet too— were returning to Boquete. The new generation. We started thinking, "What do we do? Either we change crops or we do something with coffee."

It was a little difficult at the beginning, because that older generation was very closed. If you asked them, "Hey, why do you ferment the coffee that way?" They'd say, "Because that's how we ferment it!" "Why do you harvest like—" "Because that's how we harvest!" "But why?" "Because!" It was all tradition. It was the way my grandparents had done it, the way my dad did it, and that was how I had to do it.

So we started to think- that was the time the specialty coffee movement was starting in the United States. We went to a few fairs, and we saw there was a trend towards higher quality coffee. And we started to see that we had to better understand this market.

Panama had a very bad reputation. It had a bad name, because during the time of the dictator—the military, under Noriega, which was during the time of the quotas—Panama bought low quality coffee from other countries and then exported it—the military did. So, what was known internationally as Panamanian coffee was very bad.

When we started to sell Panamanian coffee- I remember when I sold my first pound of coffee to a roaster, he looked at me and said, "Panama? But that's a canal. Panama doesn't produce any coffee." The guy thought it was all flat, just a canal. So we thought, "We have to figure out how we can change this [perception]."

We understood that we had to learn more. It was a little difficult, very difficult at the beginning—very difficult to break the tradition. We formed an association of specialty coffee and the goal was twofold: one, try to get more information to better understand the market, because if we better understood the market, we could better decide what to do differently. And two, to try to better understand Panama.

We started to do lots of experiments, with fermentations, with sun drying, machine drying. And we started seeing differences; we started to learn to cup. The change happened when we learned to cup in Panama.

Because when someone tells you something it's not the same as when you experience it for yourself. We started to cup, to understand the differences, to improve techniques of cultivation, of processing. And we started having better coffee. This awakened an interest from buyers; more people started coming, we started holding competitions, we started having events.

One thing led to another and we were improving quality. And in one of these competitions a family, the Petersons—they had bought a farm. It was from a brother of a priest, the head of the Church of Panama. But, in reality, what this guy did was throw parties there. He wasn't interested in growing coffee. So he just left the farm for years and years. With the much older varieties that were there. He never changed to newer varieties.

So when the Petersons bought the farm and were cupping the different coffees on the property for the competition, and there were old coffees there that they just found, Geisha was "rediscovered." And it was a big job to start to market it, and they did a very good job. So other farms started looking, and they too found Geisha plants on their farms because a lot of people had old varieties.

At one time people had been planting Typica, then around the '60s people brought some new varieties from CATIE in Costa Rica, because Geisha was a little bit more productive than Typica, but a few years after, like four years, they brought the Caturra variety, which was much, much more productive than Typcia.

Because this variety produced more, people replaced what they had. But on a few farms there were some Geisha plants left. People were selecting their Geisha, reproducing it, improving the ways they processed it. First just washed, then Honeys, and now we're doing Naturals. Amplifying what we're doing.

Boquete offers a spectrum of varieties and a spectrum of processes, which reach many markets. We've held competitions every year, and lots of interested people come.

In my case, I'm here because my grandfather came here, started growing coffee, my mom continued, and then I followed. When I returned from the university, we only had one finca, which was where my mom lived. And, they'd stopped processing coffee there in 1970. There had been flood that destroyed the water source, so they'd been selling cherries to the big local buyers.

When I returned, I wanted to start processing again, so I put together a small beneficio because I didn't have the resources to do anything else. I just had $3,000, and with that I bought an old machine that was discarded from an old beneficio, and I started depulping. I rented patio space to dry the coffee. Little by little, I added another depulper, then two dryers, and I started opening a few local coffee shops, and exporting some specialty coffee.

I bought a few more pieces of land, before Boquete had its tourism boom, which put land at unrivaled prices. Now you'd never buy land to plant coffee, just to plant houses. And sell them. If not, you'll never pay back the land. So, I started working with coffee, and from there I grew.

Today, I don't know if you've seen, I have farms in various areas of Boquete. Some produce certain varieties, others produce others. I have a central beneficio where we take all the coffee to process it, and we bring the coffee to patios to dry, which aren't right on the farm because it's so humid there. We send coffee to the U.S., to Japan, to Taiwan, to Australia, Europe, England, Holland, Norway. To different countries.

The market I'm looking for is the market of roasters who are able to value to the final cup, less for what I say, and more for what the cup says for itself. The market can ask for anything, but if the cup doesn't have it, they won't pay you. So, I'm interested in—and I always look for—roasters and businesses who are going to keep the name of the coffee until it's served. They roast it as Kotowa coffee, with the name of the finca it came from, and that's how they serve it to their clients.

This is important because it creates loyalty. Loyalty in two senses. The longer the relationship I have with someone, the more they're inclined to promote my coffee. So people want my coffee. I'm making myself irreplaceable. And this is very important because this means that that the roaster then has to buy my coffee. If my costs go up and I have to tell him, "I have to raise my prices because my costs have gone up," he already has a market for my coffee, so it's easier for him to pay more.

This is a little bit of the logistics behind what we do. It's a general summary of what I do.

Rachel: *So you roast all the coffee you serve in your Kotowa Coffee Shops?*

Ricardo: *Yes. Right at the beneficio where we process it we also roast it. There are sixteen locations in the country right now. David, Boquete, the beaches, and Panama City. So that absorbs about a quarter of my production. I export the other three-quarters to different clients.*

Rachel: *When you export, are people buying full container loads?*

Ricardo: *A few people buy full containers. But it's not very common, because these are coffees that cost a lot of money. For example, when you're paying $5, $6, $7 for a pound of green coffee, it's hard to buy a full container's worth. But the people who do buy a full container are buying a hundred sacks from one finca, a hundred from another, and a hundred from another. So together it's a full container, but really they're buying three different coffees.*

It's hard. The company that buys the most full containers is probably Stumptown, in the U.S. They've bought the biggest quantity of one coffee, which was actually from the organic finca. This finca produces almost two containers worth of coffee a year.

Traditionally, when you talk to people they tend to think that "organic" is a system of production by nature, almost through abandonment. "If I don't do anything, it's organic." If I just clear out the weeds and collect the harvest, yes it's organic. But this will decrease the production enormously.

An organic farm should be managed the same as a conventional one. You have to prune, you have to fertilize, but just fertilize with organic fertilizer. Maybe you have to spray against a couple diseases, but you spray with products certified as organic. So the management doesn't change. But traditionally, organic coffees come from indigenous areas, where people basically just go and collect the cherries. There is very little management involved in the production.

But this is wrong; organics shouldn't be approached this way. In reality, a coffee plant has a capacity for production. Generally, a Caturra plant should produce around a pound of green coffee [per harvest], more or less. In general terms, that's what it should be producing. To achieve this production, I need a certain quantity of chemical fertilizer. If I need ten sacks of chemical fertilizer, I'll need one hundred organic. It's almost ten times the amount, to be able to maintain those high levels of productivity.

What you want is for the plant to reach its potential. Why do you want it to reach its potential? Because a plant can only offer its best qualities when it has all the nutrients to feed what it's producing. When you give it more food, it will produce more cherries until it reaches its max capacity. But you have to give it food for this. And obviously this costs money.

The other thing is that you should only produce organically where the climate is correct. Here in Boquete—later we'll go see the farm—if you go to the places where it rains more, the instance of diseases will be very high. It doesn't make sense to grow organically in a place that isn't appropriate for organics. Sometimes people say, "But I want to be organic!" But you can't grow organically if it isn't the right place. [I like to think of the ideal climate for organics as comparable to the top shelf of a refrigerator; cool and dry. Growing good coffee, and growing it successfully, is about realizing the reality of what you have and making informed decisions accordingly.]

What I do with people [who want to know why I'm making money and they're stuck selling their coffee for peanuts] is do a cupping. I put out a bad conventional coffee, a coffee that's moldy, and a coffee that was carried on horseback and tastes like sweat. Literally. We pick coffee, put the bag of cherries on a horse, run the horse around, and we have coffee that tastes like horse sweat! People don't think about that; if you pack coffee directly on a horse, and that horse is sweating, the coffee absorbs the sweat and that taste of sweat is super strong!

Very strong! So when people taste it they say, "Hmm, it tastes like horse." It tastes like horse. Because you carried it on a sweaty horse, and the sweat sticks! Or they'll say, "This tastes like old clothes." Yes! Because it's moldy. And they go, "Ahhhh." If you don't show people, it doesn't matter what you say. They can't imagine it until you tell them. [Moral of the story. Get your mule a backpack. (Which is actually a thing. They make cool wooden frames that hold the coffee stable and sweat free as you pack it on your mule down the mountain.) Moral of the larger story. There is always a solution. There is always something you can do.]

Rachel: *It's true. I was cupping [in Volcán with the Hartmanns], and there was one coffee on the table that, as soon as I smelled it I said, "I don't even want to taste this! It smells like cigarette ash." I did taste it, and it tasted like cigarette ash. I wouldn't have believed that defective coffee could taste like that if I hadn't tried it myself.*

Ricardo: *The most important thing you can do is educate. One of the things Panama has done well is that it's had lots of contact with the market. And we've been receptive to what the market says. We started doing Naturals about three years ago. Last year was the first year that Naturals were officially part of the [annual cupping] competition.*

Four years ago we first presented them and asked people to try them; their conclusion was that, "Panama is not a country for producing Naturals. Please forget it." That's what they told us. "Forget it. Panama does not lend itself to producing Natural coffees. The microclimates and the environment don't permit the production of good Naturals."

We thought, "Maybe the coffees were processed wrong." So we started trying different processes, different lots of the fincas, different varietals. We understood the message: it wasn't that we were crazy; it was just that we were doing a bad job. Now we have a separate part of the competition for Naturals, and my coffee's won several times [and been auctioned for lots of money per pound.] If we had listened to what they said, we never would have never done it. But we were stubborn enough.

You know who you should meet? He's poor, he works with his hands, he makes his own machines, he wraps a chain around a bike wheel and—it's—he's genius! He doesn't talk much, but he's always listening, learning. His name is Hector Vargas.

Rachel: *Yeah! Someone from the Peace Corps also recommended that I talk with him.*

Ricardo: *You want me to call him?*

Rachel: *I have his number, I was going to call him when I had-*

Ricardo: *Here, let me call him.* [Ricardo pulls out his phone and dials.] *What's up Hector, how are you? I'm waiting for that shot of whiskey you were supposed to invite me for!* [laughs] *Listen, I have here a person that I think you should meet. She's a writer from the US, and she's writing a book about coffee...*

Ricardo tells my story, and by the end of a two-minute conversation has given Mr. Vargas my number, promising him I'd call that afternoon.

He also confirms that I can catch the 1pm trolley up to the Kotowa finca with Geisha growing on it, which is also home to the"Boquete Tree Trek" zipline canopy tour. (Ricardo knows how to run a diversified business.) He assures me I can also tag along on one of the guided tours of the various lots of Geisha plants, an alterative option for visitors who prefer to keep their feet firmly planted on solid ground.

Since we've been sitting and talking in Café Kotowa for nearly two hours, watching Boquete go by, Ricardo excuses himself. He has a mini coffee empire to run.

I squeeze into the next day's 1pm trolley filled with tourists ready for zip-lining. Not only did I tour the Geisha plants under the zip line with a nice retired couple from Canada, a few days later Ricardo also showed me Kotowa's organic finca and the central beneficio. Adjacent to the beneficio is the roaster and the packing room for all the roasted coffee needed for the sixteen Kotowa coffee house locations across Panama and the bags of beans and grounds they sell in the stores.

Adjacent to the roasting room is the former beneficio, now converted into a museum. Ricardo's office is tucked into one corner, surrounded by artifacts from coffee processing past. Among the artifacts Ricardo pointed out a frame hanging on the wall filled with what looked to me like old New York City Subway tokens.

He explained that his grandfather issued them as currency to his employees. While waiting to sell the coffee he had in silos, he had to pay people. He had a good enough reputation in town that his homemade currency held water, enough water for people to buy essentials at local vendors. Later, when he'd sold the coffee, he went back and paid the bills that had accumulated everywhere his coins had been amassing, collecting them to issue the next year when the money ran out.

Ricardo said, "He had to be careful not to give out more money than the coffee he had was worth! And he never did; he always paid what he owed."

Where does Ricardo's coffee go?

Coffee from the Kotowa fincas goes to Stumptown, to Sweet Maria's (an online hub for ordering small quantities of green coffee for home roasting), to Willoughby's Coffee & Tea in New Haven, CT, to Kotowa coffee houses all over Panama, and into the suitcases of many tourists who pass through Boquete.

If you came from Fabio and would like to return to Costa Rica, turn to p. 67

If you came from Julio Cesar and would like to return to Colombia, turn to p. 330

If you came from Esteban and would like to return to Costa Rica, turn to p. 171

For a conversation with another man who grows, processes, and sells his own coffee, turn to p. 54

For a conversation with Mr. Vargas, turn to the next page.

Don Tito

Recorded Monday, February 18, 2013, on Finca La Milagrosa.

Don Tito is a known personality in Boquete, a small species of local celebrity. A visit to his farm and hand-built artisan processing/roasting "plant" was suggested and recommended on all sides. He was eager to tell me how Café Royal—named for his parents, **Ro**sa **y Al**fredo—all started. He wears a blue windbreaker and a tan safari hat.

Don Tito: *I had the opportunity, I had the luck, the craziness to buy land, property. In this way I bought what is now Finca La Milagrosa. It was a cow farm, for herding. It was all pasture, so I started to cultivate coffee. And, well, it's been a long time. Right now it's about thirty years I've been doing this. I've tried different varieties of coffee, the most resistant, the most productive— I've worked a long time. But this is how we started trying different varieties: Geisha, Borboun, Caturra, Catuai, Typica. Right now on the farm we have about ten different kinds of coffee. It's a mixed production, more or less.*

And after a certain time, eight, ten years I'd been trying to grow coffee, I decided to start processing it however I could. Very, very artisan. Little by little I started building a few machines. I built the majority of the machinery we have now. Without any knowledge- with just necessity. Well, I always say it was like a hobby. I was occupied, entertained. But it was difficult for us. I didn't have the experience of processing, of production, I didn't know anything about machinery—or coffee either! But, well, trying and trying and trying, right now we have the end result.

The next step was commercializing the coffee, which was also very difficult. It is difficult, still. We've dedicated ourselves to producing quality coffee. And this has brought us to a few clients and markets that are rather attractive. Japan, Taiwan, the United States, France. We've been the most focused on quality.

Because we built our machines by trial and error, there wasn't financing or a way of getting adequate machinery. But, well, that's why the farm is called "The Miraculous," it was all a miracle. But now I have more work than ever! Before I could get up late, now I have to get up at four in the morning. And work doesn't end until nine or ten at night.

Rachel: *When you started, why did you decide to convert the cow pastures into cafetales?*

226

Don Tito: *One, because I like coffee. I like to drink coffee. Further, because I don't like to raise cattle, I'm afraid of them. I don't think I'd be any good at it. I also don't think I'd be any good at raising animals just to kill them. So, it started as a hobby.*

At the beginning, my parents didn't agree with it. They didn't want me to be growing coffee; I was young—I should be studying. But... I was always very rebellious. I never wanted to study. That was the problem. I didn't want to study. And I also didn't want to leave Boquete; Boquete is a very special place, very beautiful. I think that was the main motivation. For me it was like a pretext, an excuse, to look for a type of work that was fixed, like coffee. That way I had a reason so stay here. So that's how it started.

I don't exactly know why. Really, when I started to plant coffee, it was crazy to plant coffee. It didn't make sense. The prices in the national and international markets were very low, so it was crazy. That's why my family didn't support me—because what I was doing didn't make any sense. But after two or three years, my father realized that it was a very serious decision. And they started to support me.

Rachel: *And at this point you were just selling the coffee in cherry form?*

Don Tito: *Exactly. The first years we sold it in cherries to the big companies in Boquete. I think we were one of the first ones who tried to be independent and try to process our own coffee. I think. You'll have to see what information the big companies have. But I think we inspired a lot of people. For some people it went well, but some people ended up leaving coffee.*

Growing coffee isn't for everyone. Coffee is a business, well for us it's a way of life, but for many people, they think of it as a business. But it's not just a business; it's something you can enjoy, or share, or move forward. But there are years that you don't see anything for your work. There are hard years. That's why coffee growing, in Boquete at least, is disappearing a little. In other countries foreigners have invested a lot of money in coffee. Why? Because the locals have realized it's not a great business. For us in Boquete right now, it's more lucrative to sell the land than to produce on it. We're in an activity like this not because it makes us a lot of money, but because we like it.

Right now a finca like this could sell for a million dollars, because people need land to build houses on. So we're crazy to keep growing coffee.

Rachel: *Well, the world needs a few "crazy" people.*

Don Tito: *Yes, but we're going extinct, little by little. That's the other problem. I couldn't do anything else other than be on the farm. I can't imagine myself anywhere else. Giving conferences, being in an office— I couldn't do it. This is something one lives, enjoys.*

After showing me his property and telling me more stories (this is a ten minute excerpt from a ninety minute interview), Don Tito invited me to lunch. I told him it wasn't necessary; I had food at my hostel I could cook. He looked at me and said, "That maybe so. But it's better to eat together." I can't argue that. I also believe it is better to drink coffee together. And having the chance to drink coffee with the person who *made* it—who planted and harvested and processed and roasted it—is probably the coolest thing in the world.

Where does Don Tito's coffee go?

Royal coffee goes to buyers around the world. It also goes into the hands of people who visit Boquete and take the tour of La Milagrosa. As Don Tito was showing me the finca, we stopped and "sat in" on a few minutes of the tour his neighbor, the official tour guide, was giving. A touree asked if Café Royal was certified fair trade. The guide answered, "If you buy a bag of coffee here right now the money goes directly into Don Tito's hand. That's fair trade."

If you came from Roberto and wold like to return to Turrialba, turn to p. 56

If you came from Minor and would like to return to Los Santos, turn to p. 165

For a conversation with another long time Boquete coffee grower, turn to p. 254

For a conversation with someone else who's doing things that his neighbors consider crazy, turn to the next page.

Don Cune

Recorded Monday, March 4, 2013, at Don Cune's finca.

Sidestep to La Fortuna. Boquete, like Volcán, experiences pretty much eternal spring. But the mountains that make Boquete an end of the road town are the same mountains that separate the Caribbean from the Pacific and generate all those microclimates. Boquete is not the only place with unique climatic qualities. Right along the cusp of the Continental Divide, just off the road that connects the Caribbean to the sweltering city of David, en route to the Pacific coast, is the community of La Fortuna.

In La Fortuna is the animated and inspirational caficultor Don Cune. ^{Personalidades de la Taza p. 361} Don Cune's farm is in the breathtaking Hornitos valley, another place still dripping with earthy soul. Don Cune and I sit at a table under his stilt-supported house. He wears a light green button up-shirt, a white baseball cap, and black rubber boots.

Don Cune: *We started growing coffee here in the '80s. We were living here in the '70s, but it took us ten years to get started planting coffee. We had tomatoes, cabbage, vegetables: things to eat. The soils were getting a little worn out, so we decided to change out what we were planting, change to coffee.*

And from the '70s to the '80s, '90s, we continued producing things, producing coffee and some vegetables. But in the '90s was when the price of coffee fell. When the prices fell, when they were oscillating between $28 and $40 dollars a quintal—imagine!—the pickers were getting paid a dollar a lata, and it takes twenty latas of red cherries to get a quintal, 100 pounds, of [dried parchment] coffee. So that represents $20, so with the other $20 we had to sustain ourselves and the finca.

So it was a hard year. So we started roasting in order to find a way to sell our coffee to clients. And it wasn't easy, but it also wasn't impossible. We started packing it in bags, like this one [he picks up a plastic bag full off ground coffee]. *But with just this kind of bags it was hard. Look, since we were new at this—one time we were in Panama City, in '97 or around then, and a guy was going to sell us a better kind of bag. A paper bag, but he wanted us to bring the coffee there for him to pack it. And from Hornitos to Panama City is a long way.*

But I have a way of getting things done. There's a Colombian saying, "If you're going to eat dirt, carry it in a bag." What does that mean? If you grow something, you should always have some of it with you. If you grow coffee, you should always have some with you to sell.

I always tell people that; they should have a little bit of their coffee ready to sell, just in case someone comes. But, some people don't want to be merchants, they just want to be producers.

But God gave me both qualities. You really need both. What else would you like to know? We have here roasted coffee, already ground. We have roasted in whole bean; we have washed green coffee.

We have some beans from the very end of the harvest, the last cherries off the trees. We do that for two reasons: one, not to lose a single cherry. Two, to avoid problems with the broca.

Rachel: *How do you process it? Natural? Depulped and sun dried?*

Don Cune: *All sun dried. We have a little greenhouse-style area with drying beds covered in plastic. We dry it little by little.*

Rachel: *Does your family work with you to help you do all this?*

Don Cune: *Well, one of the reasons I'm in charge is because I have daughters. It's my wife and I and our four daughters. One lives in Colón, one in Panama City, and two nearby. At least my grandchildren are close; I have two here. Felix and Isa, whose name is on the coffee. People who know me ask, "Why isn't it called 'Café Don Cune?'" The first time we made packaging we took a vote, I was the only man and so my vote counted more! Ha! Ha! So that's why it's called "Café Isa." In the morning you can drink a cup of Café Isa, delicious.*

Rachel: *And your grandchildren live here?*

Don Cune: *Yes; I have five. But two live here with us—they're in school! One in second grade, the other in fifth grade. So they're the future; they help us with picking; they do little jobs with tending the beehives, with the vegetable gardens. And we do the tours [to the occasional guest from the nearby mountain hostel, the one and only accommodation for miles and miles], so we sell some coffee directly to people.*

Rachel: *With the roya, do you have to change the way you do things?*

230

Don Cune: *Right now with the roya, we have to try to—well, we're innovators at the local level. In this neighborhood [valley] there are some 130 small producers. Very small. These people aren't always motivated, really, because they don't have any money to work with. Very little money. But, I motivate people. I talk to them about the biodiversity associated with coffee.*

Because coffee is one of the few crops that traps carbon dioxide, which is good. So I have good ideas that could help us, but people are very conformist. The problem is that everything requires organization. Most small producers don't have big visions. Many organizations have come here, one built a community house, a Spanish organization built us two ecological beneficios, one in Fortuna and one here. But we're not taking full advantage of them.

Most people here sell their coffee in cherries. The only crazy person—who washes it, dries it, saves it just in case someone like you comes along—is me! So that we can drink a cup of coffee from Hornitos.

Rachel: *How do you hull it [to take the parchment off]?*

Don Cune: *We have a* pilón *[basin-sized mortar and pestle]. We do it manually. And we have a small grinder to grind it. And then the packer. Gracias a dios, the hotel helped me with that. They helped me buy the first equipment to pack it. Here we have some roasted, and some hulled that's ready to be roasted. We've been doing this for over ten years.*

Through the tours, we've sent our coffee to Europe: to Germany, Switzerland, little bag by little bag, but it's made it there. A little bit of our flavor. The Australians also love the taste of our coffee. And the Americans, and Canadians too. [Bird chirps and trills.]

Rachel: *So you'd call this "ecological coffee," because you're working to maintain biodiversity?*

Don Cune: *Well, we plant it along the curve of the mountainsides to avoid erosion. Our soil here is not that deep; we have to take good care of it. It can wash away in a few severe rainstorms, and we're left with few layers. We also take care of the birds, fruit trees. We've also invented some homemade wines. And sometimes the birds come and eat all the fruit and don't let us make any wine—the poor guys are hungry!*

Right now, the tomatoes are ready, so we have to harvest them. Every morning I have to get up and harvest something. Here, there are some people who abandon their tomatoes and let the birds eat everything.

Right now, we're trying a new coffee that an American brought. We're germinating some new seedlings to replant the farm, because, honestly, a lot of the finca is getting old. We have about two thousand plants of Geisha; in three years we'll be harvesting the first cherries. But, the roya's getting to them. The roya's such a strong disease that it's affecting all of Central America.

I've heard that small producers are striking in Colombia. Asking the government to extend some kind of help to coffee producers.

Rachel: *I've heard that too. You said you have some new Geisha. What other kinds of coffee do you have?*

Don Cune: *Criollos [Typicas], Caturras. Right now I'll introduce you to a plant; this is the coffee that the American brought me. He said it might be a Mundo Novo; I don't know. A Bourbon. But very good looking. We're about to make almacigos! We already have the bags, the seeds. Sometimes it's just me. Sometimes a guy will show up and say he wants to work...*

Rachel: *Of all the things you've done with coffee, what has been the biggest challenge to overcome, and what has been the biggest success?*

Don Cune: *Well. The biggest challenge is right now with this roya plague. At least the broca didn't affect us here too badly. Because it hit so hard other places that the buyers started weighing the coffee. Because a lata should weigh thirty pounds, and if there's too much broca it will weigh less. Everyone is always trying to take advantage of the weakest guy.*

The biggest achievement is that God gave me the opportunity to meet you, and to know that he helps during important moments in life, to be able to keep fighting.

If you came from **Aña** and would like to return to **Costa Rica**, turn to p. 141

If you would like to return to **Volcán**, turn to p. 202

For a conversation with a coffeeman who took on the entire production chain in a different way, turn to the next page.

Wilford

Recorded Friday, March 10, 2013, at Bajareque Coffee House in Panama City's Casco Viejo. Interview recorded in English.

Sidestep to Panama City. Bottleneck of bottlenecks. Painted school buses being replaced by shiny white ones with plastic MetroPasses you dip to pay. Fish market ceviche and Guna Yala women wrapped in rainbows of chiffon, mola, and printed cotton. Nighclubs, taxis, bike paths, hospitals, hotels, highrises, highways, runways, train tracks, and stacks and stacks of shipping containers. Monuments to Chinese, French, Spanish, and United States figures. Policemen dressed in all black stormtrooper suits riding two to a motorcycle carrying automatic weapons. Rooftop terraces and cold Balboas for fifty cents. Crumbling colonialism and dusty children in doorways. Balconies and heat. A charming coffee shop with a shiny red roaster and an owner with a story to tell.

Wilford and I sit at a table in the little vestibule between the room with the roaster and the front of the café. He wears a black golf shirt.

Wilford: *The farm started in 1915 when my grandfather, Robert, was working at the Canal. He had been working at the Canal for a maybe twenty years because I've seen letters that came out now before 1900, late 1800s. When he finished his duty at the Canal in 1900 he went to Boquete. He saw the coffee farm, he liked it, and bought it. He married my grandmother, a lady from Boquete. And then he started the farm in 1915, Finca Elida.*

Elida is the name of the farm. Why? Because my grandmother's name was Elida. So what happened is they married, they stayed at the farm, and they had five kids, one of them is my father. He kept the farm. He was born on the farm, like all his brothers and sisters. Everybody stayed except for a sister who lives in the United States. My father kept the farm and he has been working the farm ever since.

I also help him run the farm with another brother that I have. I was doing it full time until I opened this coffee shop six months ago. I'm in charge more or less of sales, quality, some advising, and [my father] runs the day-to-day operations of everything that is needed. He's eighty-one years old, and he does everything that he has done his whole life, more or less like me. Everything I have done in my life is coffee. The farm has been running for almost a hundred years.

233

Rachel: *And was there coffee there when your grandfather came to buy it?*

Wilford: *No, he started planting coffee, and he bought the whole sixty-nine hectares of the farm. And he got the title- the deed- under his name. Later, like in the 1970's, the Barú Volcano National Park was founded, so out of the 69 hectares, about twenty-five fell inside the National Park. Part of that was planted with coffee, and even farther up—because the Park is above 2000 meters above sea level—he had planted potatoes, because coffee only grows until 1800 in that part of Boquete.*

But part of the Park was open and planted with coffee. Now, if you want to plant coffee inside the Park you couldn't, but we do have about five hectares planted with coffee. Very high grown: a very, very distinguished coffee because of the elevation. It's very difficult to grow this type of coffee. It yields very little. But the farm starts between 1600-1700 meters and coffee's planted all the way to 1900.

Of the twenty hectares of coffee, twenty are producing, and five are not producing because they're planted with [young] Geisha. We have another five hectares of Geisha that is producing.

Rachel: *So you select certain lots to plant Geisha in?*

Wilford: *When the Geisha boom started eight years ago by one of our friends, the Peterson family- Daniel Peterson discovered it. How was it discovered? Because he—like we cupped today—[we had just cupped a table of Geishas, Naturals and conventionals], he had been cupping. For sixteen, seventeen years we'd been cupping and cupping; we'd bring in different processes to try. So Daniel put one coffee, blind, on the table, and it was very, very different, distinguished with all the flavors. All the bergamonts, all the jasmine flavors, all the touches of different refined fruits, very well defined, elegant, sweet, clean cup. So we said, "Wow, what is this?"*

That year it won the Best of Panama competition. And from there on we started collecting seeds from all over, because Geisha was one of the varieties that was brought to Panama in the 1960s together with many other varieties, but quality was not important back then. And Geisha is more difficult to produce, it dies quicker, and it does not produce as much, so everyone eliminated it from their estates. And many of the farms in Boquete had Geisha from back then. Some had more, some had less, some replanted.

234

So that's how Geisha started. So we planted more and more Geisha, cutting it down, planting more, year by year.

Rachel: *So you export everything, except for what you use for here [Bajareque Coffee House]?*

Wilford: *It used to be we exported one hundred percent, now everything but what we need for just this here, and this is only this year.*

Rachel: *And the name "Bajareque," what does that mean?*

Wilford: *The bajareque is the mist, the rain that you get in Boquete, from the coast. Like what I was saying, you have a lot of rain from the mountains. So what happens, when you get a cold front from the United States, that cold air moves down and mixes with the warm air from the Pacific, right at the mountain range. So when it mixes, you have the cold air and the warm air, and that generates a low pressure system, and the rain falls with wind that carries it down through the mountains. But only about five kilometers. It will make it to downtown Boquete, but not to Palmira where the Petersons are.*

The lot where I have the Esmeralda Geisha, it falls there some. It falls a lot in the canopy where Ricardo is because he's right up in the mountain range. So that's what Bajareque means. I named it that so when Panamanians read, "Bajareque," they go, "Wow, Boquete."

Rachel: *And you export mostly to small roasters in the United States, because the lot sizes you sell are small?*

Wilford: *Yes, but everybody keeps asking for more coffee. It's difficult. More coffee, more coffee. Let's see,* [rifles through papers on the table] *I have eighteen different buyers. Taiwan, two. Two from Japan. San Limas California, Klatch. Santa Cruz, Verve. Willoughby's New Haven. PT's Topeka, Kansas. Comma Coffee, Seattle. Suma's Mountain Coffee, Canada. Mega Coffee, Australia. Equator Coffee, San Raphael, California. Coffee Ambassadors, Chicago, Illinois. Germany, Sweden. Kaffa Coffee, Norway. Kopi Coffee—he wants coffee but I—from Sweden too—but he's not on the list yet.*

Rachel: *So it's all, quote unquote, "direct trade?"*

Wilford: *A roaster from Kaffa was here not long ago; he comes here all the time. Jim Taylor, from Chicago from Coffee Ambassadors, he's been here twice. Equator Coffee, they've come a couple of times. So, we do the direct trade with all of them. And then you find an importer in the United States that brings the coffee for the different buyers; the roasters get together five, ten, fifteen, twenty-five bags until they have a container, and the importer distributes the coffee to the different roasters. Café Imports is one of them. A trader from Atlantic USA, Zephyr Coffee also, Royal too. Guys like that import it from here and ship it to different roasters.*

For example, one guy had coffee from Francisco [Don Pachi's son] and said,"Wilford, can you be in charge of the export of the coffee? Because I'm gonna buy it from Don Pepe, Don Pachi, yourself, and one more." He bought sixty-five from me, and you can put three hundred bags in one container. He gets the quantity [from everyone]. We got it together put it in one container; he's in charge of paying for everything, and he says, "Thank you Francisco. Here's your check."

The way it works is [the buyer] talks to the shipping company and then tells me, "Ok your container number is so and so." And then I send the truck driver- anyone can be a truck driver—to the shipping yard to pick up the container. He comes over to Boquete, we load it, he brings it back and brings it to the port, with all the documents he gives to customs, and that's the only thing the shipping line does. They don't care if it's good coffee, bad coffee, if it's under my name—in this case I would be the shipper—I send it to Taiwan, Japan.

The importer is the one who tells me, "Ok, I have a contract with Evergreen or Maersk [shipping lines]." And they ask the shipping line, "When is your next shipment going to Oakland? Ok I want one container," and they tell them it's container such and such. And the freight is paid by the importer. We don't pay the freight. We only pay from Boquete to Panama City.

The shippers charge by commodity. If you tell them it's coffee they'll charge you so much per container. They don't care if you put in one bag or 300 bags, Naturals or Honey, whatever. Putting Things in Boxes p. 366

Did you know that it's more expensive to haul the container from Boquete to here [Panama City] than to ship it? Because here's what you have to do. Go to Boquete, fill it up, and bring it back to Panama City. They charge you for the round trip. You go there and come back. They charge $1200. And shipping from here to California is like $1000, $1200, $800.

At this point it occurs to Wilford that his friend, and fellow coffee producer, is coming into town that evening. He pulls out his phone and calls Carlos Aguilar of Carmen Estate in Volcán. After a sixty-second conversation, Wilford has coordinated that Carlos will call me around seven that evening so that I can talk with him over dinner. Wilford adds my number to WhatsApp as a Beyoncé song plays in the background.

Where does Wilford's coffee go?
    Klatch Coffee, Verve Coffee Roasters, Willoughby's, PT's Comma Coffee, Suma's Mountain Coffee, Mega Coffee, Equator Coffee, Coffee Ambassadors, Kaffa Coffee, importers Royal Coffee New York of New Jersey, Zephyr Green Coffee of New Orleans, Café Imports of Minneapolis, and more small roasters around the world.

If you came from Roberto and would like to return to Turrialba, turn to p. 56

If you came from Francisco and would like to explore Panama, turn to p. 183

For a conversation with another powerhouse who singlehandedly manages the chain from ground to grounds, turn to p. 300

For a conversation with one of Wilford's employees on Finca Elida, turn to p. 246

For a conversation with Wilford's friend and fellow entrepreneurial Boquete caficultor, turn to the next page.

Graciano

Recorded Tuesday, February 9, 2013, in the room behind the roaster at Bajareque Coffee House in Panama City.

Graciano is in town in between running his company HiU Coffee in El Salvador, starting projects in Ethiopia, and growing Geisha at his farm Finca Los Lajones in Boquete. He wears a fitted black t-shirt.

Graciano: *There are a lot of roasters and baristas who want to become coffee buyers. "Back to origin."*

Here, everyone used to just throw the cherries all together. In Ethiopia it's like that, but there no one ever gets to put their name on their own coffee. That's what we're starting to do. I'll never sell my land, so I'll die being a caficultor. My father was more involved in produce. But he eventually started working in coffee too, so he helps me a lot with my fincas. Here [in Pamama].

In 2003, 2004 we started cupping. Before that all the coffee in Boquete was sold as cherries. I was working in other businesses at that time—organics. I certified the first organic farm in Panama.

I went to California to sell coffee directly. But at that point I didn't have a beneficio. So at eleven, twelve at night when Wilford was done processing his coffee, I went and processed mine.

Wilford: *I remember that!* [Laughs] *That was crazy. Do I remember that.*

Graciano: *How could you forget! So from there, I decided to get involved in the coffee business. I went to Ethiopia, I fell in love with coffee. I'd spent so long working with fertilizers [I was ready for something new]. Ethiopia has volcanic soils. It's super interesting. I was always interested in where things come from, how they're made.*

I see fair trade as a big marketing tool. It's supposed to be all for social good, but I see a lot of fat asses. You have Fairtrade Germany fighting with Fair Trade USA. It wasn't a nice split, and it still isn't nice. And the producers down here are still getting their few cents per pound. It's a corrupt system.

And the market is not paying the price it costs to be organic. It costs much more than the $0.20, $0.25 they're giving you. Which is why we're working on the quality of the final cup, on differentiation. Like wine. Everything is based in the quality. In cupping.

Prices should be based on the quality of the coffee, and the quality of the coffee in the quality of the process, and the quality of the process in the quality of the harvest, of the product.

And you have trends like Honey. And Naturals. We had the best natural coffee from Panama, and everyone was like, "What are you talking about, naturals from Latin America?" People were saying that Pulped Natural is the same as Honey. For Pulped Natural you depulp it and dry it on the ground; you don't use any water at all. It's not the same as Honey. Basically, the Honey process is this: depulp the coffee and leave it for some time to let the sugars set in. If you handle it right it won't ferment. [Pulls up a few pictures on his phone.]

These are four teas made with coffee pulp [skin]. They're mixed with other fruits. A food writer, really a food designer, who works with the most famous chefs in Europe, spent six months preparing these blends. They have a low caffeine content and a ton of natural sugars.

The final product is called Cascara (the Spanish word for "shell"). It's available online through Verve Coffee Roasters.

Where does Graciano's coffee go?

Some of Graciano's coffee goes to Verve Coffee Roasters of Santa Cruz, CA to become their "one and one" espresso plus macciatto super serving, among other drinks. Some of the Coffee from Finca Los Lajones goes to Bohdi Leaf Coffee Traders in Placentia, CA, where it's sold to small, local roasters.

If you came from Esteban and would like to return to Costa Rica, turn to p. 171

For a conversation with Colombian growers also inspired to pursue quality, turn to p. 275

For a conversation with someone who looks at quality from the coffee preparation standpoint, turn to the next page.

Lucas

Recorded Wednesday, March 20, 2013, at TéCafé in downtown Panama City.

Lucas and I are seated at a table in the TéCafé dining room. The paper placemats on the tables are printed with facts and figures about coffee and tea. Lucas wears a light green and yellow striped button-up shirt.

Lucas: *No one in my family has any idea about coffee. It all started because I was studying in Boston at Bentley University. I studied business, marketing and management. And I got used to drinking decent coffee there. I used to drink coffee in Panama, I don't want to name names, but... domestic coffee. And I thought it was good coffee, as many people think, until I went to the U.S. and realized that it wasn't actually that good.*

I came back [to Panama], and it seemed like the coffee had gotten worse! How can it be that Panama produces the best coffee in the world, but we were drinking the worst coffee in the world!

This was my sister's idea. I used to be a banker, I worked at Tower Bank, but I didn't like the shut-in office life, that style, having to wear a suit and tie. My sister wanted to start a business because she'd just gotten married and was looking for a way to make money. And she thought, "Well, let's open up a tea shop. Because I'm a tea drinker." And she'd asked me to bring her teas from New York, because you can't get good tea here. Loose leaf teas don't exist in Panama. So she said, "Let's open a tea shop!" And I said, "Well if we're doing tea, we'll include coffee because you can't get good coffee here either." So Ana and I went for it.

I learned on my own; I'm completely self taught in coffee. I'd stay up until five in the morning reading articles. Since I was a friend of Wilford Lamastus' son, I met his father, who's very respected here in the world of Panamanian coffee. And he was teaching me. I went with him up to Boquete to see the farms; I met other coffee growers. Then I took a few courses in Seattle with the SCAA about how to roast and cup.

And I bought a little roaster for my house and started ordering samples of coffee from all over the world, experimenting. I was doing that for about a year, and then we started building the store. I realized that at that point I could sit down at a table with someone experienced in coffee and hold my own in a debate.

Basically, we're in the niche market of specialty coffee and specialty tea. So we planned at first on opening a tea and coffee shop. But then we said,

240

"If we're going to have a tea and coffee shop, we should serve some snacks. And if we're serving snacks why not sandwiches?" One thing led to another, and that's how the concept of TéCafé was born. Which is basically trying to bring together the best of Teavana, Starbucks, and a restaurant, to put it all together.

Here we focus heavily on coffee quality. We're not just a commercial establishment; we're a microroaster. And I'm always experimenting with different profiles for different coffees. Because for every coffee I can affect the final flavor. For example, the espresso here is a blend of coffees from Panama, Brazil, Ethiopia, and one other special coffee that I can't tell you—that's our secret! If you try it, it's a really great espresso. It has a good body, really nice notes.

Rachel: *So this was the first place to sell loose leaf tea in Panama? And also one of the first places with such a wide selection of coffees?*

Lucas: *We're the only ones who serve coffees from other parts of the world.*

Rachel: *Yeah, I haven't seen anywhere else that does. I was thinking about that; in producing countries there isn't coffee from other coffee countries because there's already enough here.*

Lucas: *Panamanians need to be educated. Lots of people tell me, "I love you, and I hate you. I love you because you showed me what good coffee is. I hate you because now I can't drink the coffee in my office!" I've realized that there's a trend; people are starting to drink coffee for the flavor. It's not like it used to be, "blackwater." Blackwater with caffeine, because it didn't taste like coffee. You had to add like five spoonfuls of creamer.*

But the joy of coffee isn't that. The joy is the world of complexity, so many factors that influence the final cup. It's the process of understanding coffee, the process of the roast, the preparation. Because if you make a mistake in just one of those steps, you ruin the final cup. ^{Barista's Burden p.359}

Much more complex than wine in terms of tasting. All this really interested me. I didn't understand how Panamanians—here in Panama, you'll see women asking for loans at the bank to buy a Louis Vuitton wallet. I don't know how they do it, but they do it. They always want to see themselves better; they want the best cars, everything "the best." They want to eat at fine restaurants. So I don't know how they were ok with such bad coffee! That was what I saw, so we said, "Well, we'll offer the best coffee possible!"

There are people who only drink coffee from here; we see them a lot. And it's a shame because there is only one other coffee shop in all of Panama where I can recommend the coffee and that's Wilford's, El Bajareque. In Panama there are just two specialty coffee shops. And in other parts of the world there are two on every block. You can't even make the comparison. In Russia, in South Korea, those are places where the economy is growing.

Rachel: *New markets are opening. Of all this work—from the moment you first had the idea up until now, what was the biggest challenge to overcome and what was the biggest success?*

Lucas: *Wow! Well, in Panama we have a personnel problem. I don't want to speak badly of Panamanians because I'm Panamanian, but it's unreliable. Panamanians don't want to work. To have a team of people who really like coffee—to make coffee well, you have to learn—you have to like it. People won't learn if they don't like what they're doing; they'll do it halfheartedly, and therefore poorly.*

I think one of the most difficult things was to get together a team of employees who are hard workers, but who like what they're doing. Not to mention that this store took almost a year to build. There were a lot of errors along the way; the workers didn't show up, they worked slow. But at the end it was all worth it.

The biggest success is seeing people's faces when they drink a good cup of coffee! Sometimes people will tell me, "This is pure!" I don't know what they were drinking before, but yes. This is pure coffee.

Lucas leads me behind the bar where a barista makes me my first ever cup of coffee prepared with a siphon (which looks like something from a chemistry lab, complete with Bunson burner style flame and all), using Naturally processed beans from Carlos Aguilera's Carmen Estate in Volcán.

If you came from Fernanda and would like to return to Costa Rica, turn to p. 151

For a conversation with a unique caficultor in Boquete, turn to the next page.

Noble

Recorded Sunday, March 24, 2013, at Noble's finca in El Salto de Boquete.

Back to the mountains swirling with *bajareque*. Noble's German Shepard Zeus stands guard at the gate at the entrance to the finca. Before we finally get to the coffee on his property, Noble shows me a giant dried alligator skin hanging on a hook outside the goat pen, a towering avocado tree, and a jar full of scorpions soaking in an amber fluid that he presents to me under the title of "ointment for all that ails you." Noble wears a hunter green baseball cap and an army green jacket.

Noble: *Did you know that bees pollinate plants? And birds, hummingbirds, big birds. I don't know if you know that every animal has its own knowledge, its own wisdom. Look! Raspberries! Try some. Yesterday they picked a whole bunch. If you eat them it'll be like lipstick! They're great with yogurt in the morning. They don't have any fertilizer, no fungicides, nothing. Maybe if I did all that they'd be all big and pretty, but the flavor would change.*

Everything's in the pH of the soil, the weeds. Everything, everything, everything. I'm going to plant more beans because I'm selling a bunch! Where we are here is 6130 feet [1868 meters] above sea level. We're higher than Cerro Punta. But over there it's colder. There, you hear a clap of thunder and five minutes later it's raining. Here, it thunders and never rains. All this is for onions. [Gestures to fields in different directions.] *And that for potatoes. And over there for corn. Eighteen to twenty hectares. You could say it's a lot, but people with cattle will have sixty!*

Rachel: *And you planted all this coffee?*

Noble: *About eight years ago. All those felled trunks over there we'll use for firewood. To roast chicken, meat. Food never tastes better than when it's roasted over firewood! The edge of the finca is over there, at that cliff. All this coffee that's left is just for drinking at home. This is the end of the harvest.*

And you can see, it's just been pruned, severely pruned [down to stumps]. When the rain comes this will start growing shoots. And in two years it'll be a tree again. There's always something to harvest. We do this for quality, quality, quality.

243

The best view on the farm is over there. I brought you down here because you said you wanted to see the coffee. But over there is a big rock. You sit there and you feel a complete peace. There's a point of energy. Did you notice that at the ranch house? That there's a concentration of energy; a tranquility. [Crunching leaves. Munching underfoot. I snap pictures of the coffee. Noble mumbles something about lightning strikes.]

Let me tell you something. I'm sure you can see right away that here there are around seven or eight varieties. So something has happened here. The insects are pollinating here, and here, and here and here. So you can't guarantee that a variety is actually that variety. But the important thing is that it's good.

Rachel: *Do you process it right here?*

Noble: *No, no. I don't have the equipment to process. Look—a bee! Maybe he's pollinating something! I also don't have just one buyer. Look! You can see Palmira from here! Ooof it's like a desert there. Dry. You have to maintain a balance between sun and shade.*

Rachel: *You don't use any fertilizers or agrochemicals?*

Noble: *No, no. Last year, we had so much work and could only do so much. They're paying $0.75 a lata; the real money's in processing it. We sell to, what's his name, the guy with the trout. We sold it all to him. He said that maybe next year he can process ours separately so that we can try it. He sells exclusively to the United States.*

Rachel: *So you didn't sell to a big mill like Sitton [domestic coffee brand]?*

Noble: *No, Sitton's about to go bust. For poor management. That's what always happens. The parents work, and the kids… The family gets too big and just has to sell. We're doing things wrong. For example, coffee doesn't give much. I've thought about abandoning coffee all together and planting papaya, other things that give you more with less problems.*

For example, goats. You have ten goats producing milk. They can each give you twelve liters of milk a day. That's 120 liters a day. You don't need more than that. You just take care of them. It will take about a year to get there. And there's a new kind of banana, the R72, that gives you 100 bananas per tree- per hand. It's $12 per 100. This year the price is around

$6-7. But you have to bring them into town. Last year it was $9. It's because of the commodity market. Whoever invented that is a—a—

The other day a woman was here from a bank, and we were talking about that stuff. Sometimes lawyers and engineers come too. You can always learn something. I like talking to people. And learning. They teach me something, and I teach them something. If someone is sick or falls and hurts their back or something, you take them to the doctor. But you have to have faith in God, because he's the only one who can perform miracles. But if you want, people can help too. [More crunching leaves. We've arrived at another coffee island.]

This is another cafetal. Ah—another thing I wanted to tell you. Nature is temperamental. The harvest ended here a little while ago and now there isn't a single cherry. Coffee takes its time. There are people who are adding two, three rounds of fertilizer and stuff and their cherries are still really tiny. When they go to cup my coffee they'll realize that it doesn't have anything.

That big coffee tree you see there is wild. The day I was planting it the owner [of the adjacent property] was here so I went over to talk to him and he told me, "That's on the other side of the boundary line!" So we worked it out. I ripped up everything that I had supposedly planted on his land, but I told him, "Let me leave that one tree so that we remember where the boundary is, that we have an agreement!"

From the house down to here is a one-hundred-foot elevation change. I took some cherries from these trees here to germinate seedlings, and that's what I planted. This is why I don't get fat. I'm going back and forth and up and down and carrying and pushing and bwah!

Zeus comes bounding up. Sounds of panting German Shepard.

If you came from Luis Angel and would like to return to Costa Rica, turn to p. 85

If you came from Federico and would like to continue on to Volcán, turn to p. 191

For a conversation on another *bajareque* riddled farm, turn to the next page.

Felipe

Recorded Monday, March 25, 2013, at Wilford's farm Finca Elida in Boquete.

Felipe is seated in the benefico on a tree stump stool at a table made by laying a door across two sawhorses. He has a pile of green coffee spread out on the door, from which he is pulling out defective beans and sliding the good beans into a bucket under the table through the hole in the door that would have been used for the knob. He wears a blue and red plaid shirt.

Rachel: *You're in charge of all the processing, or just washing or...*

Felipe: *Everything. When Wilford gets here we can show everything we do.* [Wilford is en route to the finca with two direct trade buyers here on a sourcing trip.] *Come see the machine. We depulp it in the other machine and then dry it here.* [He walks over to coffee spread out on raised drying beds.]

This is the natural coffee. It's marked with lot numbers. And over here is the depulper, and the demucilagenator. The Honey coffee comes out over there. We put a sack here to catch it before it gets washed. Watch out for that guy! [He points to a massive old hand crank depulper.]

Rachel: *Wow! Do you still use that thing ever?*

Felipe: *No, we used to. At the beginning. And for samples. Or for Geishas. And all the pulp goes over here. Once the [washed] coffee is somewhat dried, we put it in the mechanical dryer. Only the lower grade washed coffee gets [fully] mechanically dried. This is the Geisha that we depulped by hand.*

Rachel: *So now you have to go through and sort out the bad beans because with the hand crank they don't pass through the system of sorting out floaters?*

Felipe: *Exactly. This mechanical dryer can dry 500 lbs. You throw it in up there. And it comes out dry. And this is the huller, to get green coffee. And you can throw the chaff back as compost. They're building a storage room below so they can store all the chaff. And up here's they'll put the equipment to sort coffee and make a better space to hand select.*

Rachel: *And you manage the entire process?*

Felipe: *Yes, yes.*

Rachel: *Are you from Boquete?*

Felipe: *No, from Tolé.* [We have a detailed conversation about Tolé and its environs, since I spent the night there in a Peace Corps house en route to the Peace Corps coffee site Majagua where I interviewed Federico.]
The coffee goes through these [shaking] trays, and comes out as first, second, and third grade.

Rachel: *Do the [empty shipping] containers come all the way up here?*

Felipe: *No, just to the [warehouse] in Naranja. They bring the coffee down there. Here we just process it.*

Rachel: *How many quintales have you processed this harvest?*

Felipe: *So far, maybe 300, 350. [30,000-35,000 lbs]. And of Geisha just three quintales. The lot that's planted way at the top. [Just above the] few lots of Catuai.*

Rachel: *Do you also do the planting?*

Felipe: *Um hm. And the germinating, filling the bags, transplanting seedlings, planting, everything! And spraying, clearing. The seedlings are in a separate lot in Naranja. Right now we have Catuai and Geisha. Like 15,000 Catuai and 4,000 Geisha. We'll plant them in May.*

Rachel: *You know a lot about all the steps! Have you always worked with coffee?*

Felipe: *Yes. I've been here for eight years, doing all the processing for five.*

Rachel: *So you were here when the Geisha craze started!*

Felipe: *Yes I was.*

About half an hour after the interview Wilford pulled up in front of the beneficio with Mike from Klatch Coffee in Upland, CA and Jeff from Portola Coffee Lab in Costa Mesa, CA. I piled into Wilford's SUV with them, and we drove up through the same cafetales where I had spent the morning walking and picking. We all got out of the car, walked through the cafetales, sampled wild blackberries and tree tomatoes, and back at the beneficio sunk our hands into sacks of sun dried Honey coffee to savor the aroma you can only appreciate when the crispy parchment paper is still intact pre-hulling.

The next day Jeff and I were talking coffee over a meal of tasty Panamanian grilled fish. He asked me whom else I'd visited in Boquete, and I mentioned that I'd been to the Petersons a few weeks before. He said he'd spent the morning there cupping, and I asked him if he'd had lunch with them. He nodded, and I asked, "Did they offer you a glass of sherry right before lunch? And did you serve yourself from the giant lazy susan in the middle of the table?" He burst out laughing, "Yes! That's exactly what they did!"

A few months later, once I'd gotten on the Instagram bandwagon, I saw a post from Verve Coffee Roasters of Santa Cruz, CA of a juicy cross-section of a tree tomato tagged #panama #fincaelida #farmlevel #directtrade.

Tree tomatoes are why I'm writing this book and why Direct Trade roasters get on the plane to get to know the personalities of the people they buy from. Because when you eat lunch at the Peterson's you get a glass of sherry; and when you visit Wilford's finca he will pick fresh tree tomatoes and slice them for you with his pocketknife.

If you came from Wilford and would like to return to Panama City, turn to p. 238

For a conversation with another farm manager, turn to p. 322

For a conversation with a Boquete woman, turn to the next page.

Milvia

Recorded Tuesday, March 26, 2013, at the Samburg finca just outside of Boquete.

Milvia, her goddaughter Melissa, and I are seated on the wicker couch on the screen porch of her house. The wall of the porch is covered with various birdhouse frames and decorations. Outside in the front yard are three giant birdhouses on tall poles. Melissa wears a black and silver scarf, and Milvia wears a black and white striped blouse.

Milvia: *When did we start? My husband took charge of the finca in 1946. His father died that year. He was eighteen. And he was in charge of the farm. His family was from Sweden. His mother and his father. He was born in David.*

Here, we have cafetales and some animals. That's the business today. We have various hectares of coffee. We cultivate them and sell in cherries, as red fruit. We started harvesting in September, and we're pretty much done now in April. Right now we're still collecting coffee.

Rachel: *There used to be a train, right? That came from David?*

Milvia: *Ah yes, it came from David right up into town. You're making me remember a lot! I was born in '40. And the train was here until '46. I think.*

Rachel: *So it was your husband's father who planted everything here?*

Milvia: *And my husband too. He also planted coffee. [His father] did first when he came in 1911.*

Melissa: *He was one of the founders of Boquete.*

Milvia: *He lived in the Canal Zone and worked there. And when the work changed [because the Canal was done] some people went one way and some people went others. And he came here*.*

Rachel: *And I suppose at that point it was pure mountain.*

Milvia: *Pure mountain. There weren't cafetales. They went around on horseback. And he used to process it all right here too, until 1972. Then he started bringing it to the central beneficio in Cochea.*

Rachel: *Melissa was telling me you also have Christmas tress planted?*

Milvia: *Ah the Christmas trees! Yes, yes, to sell at Christmas time.*

Rachel: *But you have quite a lot of coffee. Forty hectares?*

Milvia: *Correct, correct. Maybe you can see a man way up there?* [She points out up to the mountainside where I can see a tiny dot among the green and grey.] *He's picking. Very high up.*

Rachel: *Is there a part that was affected by roya?*

Milvia: *Yes. It will be a big pain to fumigate it all. They were spraying before to protect it, but I guess we'll have to do it again.*

Rachel: *Those birdhouses are pretty cool; I haven't seen anything like that before.*

Milvia: *We have more than two hundred doves! And there are some goats roaming the cafetal.*

Rachel: *So you must have a bunch of employees to be able to take care of all of this?*

Milvia: *We have twenty. During the main harvest time there are many more. And they finished harvesting the oranges early this year. You want to see? We can walk around.*

Rachel: *In all this time what has been the biggest change you've seen in the coffee business?*

Milvia: *Well, there have been so many changes! Maybe Melissa can explain more than I can.*

Melissa: *Well, starting with the price. It changes a lot, depending on quality too. There are a few differences in the harvest…and there are climate changes as well. But, more than anything, the change is in the price. Because it's varied so much. There were years where it was at $12 and they were telling me there were years it was at $2 a lata.*

Milvia: *And they paid the harvesters $0.70.*

Melissa: *At that time, the harvester, at $0.70, things weren't as expensive. Now, they're paying $0.75. Per lata. And a lata is thirty pounds. And now they're weighing it; they used to measure by [volume]. I think that it's a little fairer for the harvester and the farms. Because sometimes the lata fits more if they're stuffing the cherries in, and then the picker looses more. But if they're weighing it they're paying for every gram.*

Because thirty pounds, cherry by cherry, when it's raining out or hot and sunny, is pretty hard. Here, my Godmother is very conscientious with the workers. They have their nice rooms over there, they have electricity. Their children go to the doctor if they need to. We pay them social security. Most places don't pay that for harvesters, but we do. Also because most of our employees are permanent.

Milvia: *More than twenty years. We have various generations.*

Melissa: *During the harvest, the children, the parents, grandparents, grandchildren all come and pick together.*

Milvia: *One thing that's tough now is that before, a boy of nine or ten could go work with his family. Now he can't. They passed a law that boys can't do anything. So the kids are now just hanging around because they have nothing to do.*

Rachel: *Yeah, I don't understand why they can't work during the summers. School is out. They have nothing to do.*

Milvia: *It used to be that the youngest ones would be with their parents, picking up all the cherries that fell to the ground. Now no.*

Rachel: *It seems like they might be better off if they're with their families.*

251

Melissa: *There kids ages twelve or sixteen can work, but they have to go to an office at the Department of Labor with a parent and fill out a bunch of forms that state that they're working with their parents. Then they're allowed in the cafetal without any problems.*

Rachel: *I understand that children should be in school, but the harvest coincides with summer. It always has.*

Melissa: *There are families that bring in twenty-five latas during the peak harvest. Here, there are three varieties of coffee: Geisha, Catuai, and Caturro. The finca is divided into twenty-eight lots, with different numbers for every lot.*

Rachel: *To be able to track where you're harvesting. And when the harvest is over you have to start pruning?*

Milvia: *And spraying and fertilizing. There's always work to be done. All our workers are indigenous, not Latinos. The Latinos pretty much don't even want to go to the cafetal, just to the office.*

Melissa: *I've seen kids who were born here and now are working. And the elderly who spend the days with their families. And this shows that this is a good place to work, because if not they wouldn't have stayed for so many generations.*

We walk through the old beneficio next to the house (which now has turtles living in the old fermentation tanks and doves roosting in under the old casillas), through the cafetales, past the Christmas trees to be, through patches of cala lilies (which they sell to the upscale hotels in Boquete), and past the workers' houses, which are painted blue with bright yellow trim.

Where does Milvia's coffee go?
Milvia sells to the Sitton beneficio, a company that produces coffee for domestic consumption in Panama.

If you came from Maria and would like to return to Nicaragua, turn to p. 118

If you came from Donald and would like to return to Cedral, turn to p. 135

If you came from Haydee and would like to learn more about Boquete, turn to p. 215

To hear from another long time Boquetino, turn to the next page.

*Milvia's husband's father is not the only one who came to Boquete after working on the Canal. The construction of the Canal drew immigrants from all over the world, and during construction workers lived in the Canal zone. But once the project was completed, all these new immigrants had wads of cash in their pockets and no roots in the country. Many headed for the hills of Boquete in order to escape the oppressive heat and jungle humidity of Panama City. Boquete, Volcán, and areas in the mountains near the Costa Rican border were attractive because immigrants could set themselves up with enough land to raise families off subsistence crops and never need to return to the malaria filled mangroves between oceans.

Don Pachi

Recorded Wednesday, March 27, 2013, in the Boquete Real Estate offices on the main road through Boquete.

Don Pachi wears a short-sleeved white collared shirt.

Rachel: *Everyone here is obviously talking about Geisha. And [your son] told me you brought it from CATIE. So that's what I'm interested in; anything you can tell me about your work at CATIE and how you started growing coffee here.*

Don Pachi: *The Geisha had been tried out in Costa Rica. In a study to decide what to plant on the farms they recommended not to plant it because it tasted bad. They had a very bad impression of the Geisha. Probably because they were planting it at 1500 meters [above sea level]. So the Geisha couldn't flower properly to develop all the flavors we see in it here. No. There, Geisha meant something else; it meant protection against the roya.*

That was the reason; no other reason. Because the Geisha was tolerant to a strand of roya that existed at that time in the Americas. So, the reason for bringing Geisha to Panama was because it's a tall plant that tolerates roya.

Why do I bother mentioning that it's tall? Because Panama, mostly Boquete—had a lot of Caturra—which is a small plant—at that time. And I was interested in what I'd seen, which was taller coffee. For us, taking on Geisha was for roya. It could withstand the rains a little better. We didn't bring it because it tasted great. No, no. The opposite. We knew that it tasted "bad," but it was tolerant to the roya.

I want to confess that I was always afraid of the roya. When ojo de gallo attacks it almost makes noise; you can tell it's coming. But not the roya. It starts with just one leaf here and there, and then three leaves fall off, and then from one day to the next the entire finca is infested. We never brought it for taste, just because it resisted roya. Other than that it had a bad reputation. [Mac truck roars past.]

Rachel: *And when you went to Costa Rica, was it to look for varieties that were more resistant to the roya? Did you already have your farm in Boquete?*

Don Pachi: *We're—let me go back a few generations. We've always had coffee. That a plant was tolerant to roya was not enough reason to bring it. The other reason was that it was a plant that could adapt to our traditional* *ways of farming coffee, which included tall trees. Really, it turned out that it was not just resistant to roya, which really wasn't too much of a problem, but that it also held up better against ojo de gallo, making it more cost effective. So that was another reason.*

There's Geisha planted everywhere now. I think that we're not doing enough work around roya. We don't know if it's mutated. Because if it mutates, it attacks new places. With so many years of having it in the Americas, they'll have to do a study to see if it's mutated. It's surprised us in a big way how quickly it attacked this time.

Rachel: *You're right. When I was in Costa Rica everything was normal; the trees were full of leaves and people were harvesting. And then three weeks later I'm here [in Panama] hearing that Costa Rica declared a national emergency.*

Don Pachi: *It's because we've changed our habits. We all had Catimor, which we changed to because of roya, but which isn't any good against broca. So we started applying pesticides. But because the roya disappeared [since Catimor is resistant to it], we got careless. And we got out of the habit of spraying fungicides correctly.* [Another truck roars past.] *We just had to watch out for ojo de gallo, which you control attack by attack, by centers of infection. All this contributes to the problem we have with roya.*

The broca worries me a lot. Because we have pretty good equilibrium in the cafetales. To apply an insecticide could start a disaster. I don't know how far these things will go.

Coffee has meant a lot for the development of our town. When my father's grandparents started with coffee, it was because coffee was the only way of earning cash; everything else you had to get though bartering. I'll give you a hat, you give me a roast chicken, you know? But coffee meant money. And the certainty of having it, because you could store coffee in the warehouse.

But it's always meant a lot of work on the farms. And now with this world of specialty coffee. Not only can we sell Geishas, but Typicas too. In our case, we've evolved. We planted Geishas and Typicas instead of Caturras and Catuais. We saw this as a form of evolving. We've always known that we had good quality. And we thought that to stand out we should have a superior quality. To have a different flavor. And it turned out that we did!

But we producers didn't actually know that. But the buyers did. We have such a small number of coffee growers that we don't have our own

255

cuppers. When we discovered that we do have a special quality; that was when we started having cuppers. And if it hadn't been for this group of young people who showed us what we had, we would have been much more delayed in improving the economic situation for coffee growers.

Look how all the coffee farms have been sold to build houses here in Boquete. Sold out of necessity. The old land is a heavy burden for us to bear. We've been victim to a ferocious market that doesn't permit coffee producers to grow. A lot of coffee farms have been sold.

It's a shame; it's hard to grow horizontally. If you have twenty hectares of land and you say, "Ok, let me buy five more," no one is saying that. There's not enough money in coffee for people to be saying that. We're small coffee growers; we're farmers. Which means that there's also our pride in our children for being coffee growers. We want to be able to divide our land between our children who also want to be coffee growers, give them their piece of land. [Two more tractor trailers roar past in succession.]

Rachel: *It is a shame. Because the land here is so suited for growing coffee. And people are just planting houses.*

Don Pachi: *And we said, "Look at our geography. Look at where Panama is located." The magnetic north of the country is in the Caribbean. And the south is the Pacific Ocean. This is not the case in other coffee growing countries. All the fincas in Panama are never more than fifty kilometers from the ocean. From the Atlantic or the Pacific. In Boquete, for example, we have the Bajareque; the condensation from Caribbean trade winds has also been a blessing.*

If we look at our growing conditions, there's no reason we shouldn't have a future in growing coffee. We have the trade winds, but also the soil. These volcanic soils are very young. It's about 600 years since the last eruption of the Barú Volcano. So these young soils are very rich, with a very good internal drainage, which allows us to negotiate with some illnesses. We have precipitation and temperature appropriate for growing coffee. In my opinion, the future of our coffee growing culture is in the hands of what we've started in the past years. Maybe this will be what sets us apart in the future, maybe.

If you came from Don Tito and would like to continue to La Fortuna, turn to p. 229

For more on coffee's complexity, turn to p. 312

To continue to Colombia, turn to the next page.

Image by MUERTO. Chinchiná, Colombia, 2012.

Artesanía Cafetera por Moskerman. Chinchiná. Agosto, 2011

Busco una tarde soleada
En medio de una triste mañana
Donde una nube dibuja una ballena,
El eco del gavilán pollero
Y la estela del barranquillo
Por toda la finca me acompañan
Me cargan las barrigas de la montaña
El sudor mis ojos empaña
El café en bruto rojo como llamas.
¡Maldición! Casi no hay partes llanas…
El campesino entrenó su tobillo
También evolucionó su fuerte rodilla
Y trepan por donde baja la lluvia
O el rocío de la noche con luna llena,
Por donde bajaron azules y rojas lágrimas.
Empieza el periplo de la artesanía
El continúo toc toc de granos el coco llena
Cae la tarde y el sudor sus espaldas raya
Cansancio, la uña, el uñero, el gusano de pollo
Y a la máquina fría peladora
Ahora y nunca nada la calla,
Arranca la piel mientras flota la pasilla
El pergamino en agua se hunde y con su viaje sueña
Ambos reciben del cielo el sol, sus rayos
Algunos esperan un beso de ella
Mientras el sancocho en la olla ebulle
Mientras por la gallina el gallo llora y canta
Y por allí viene el jeep para llevar la carga
La carga que visitará los hornos que no conoces
Se tostará el origen de la bebida de los dioses.
Sombrero en el parque y en su vainilla la peinilla
Recrean la vista para empezar otra semana,
Yo escribo y rayo y borro y bebo la octava maravilla
Con mercado y una misa al hombro regresan a la montaña
Trabajando de enero a enero con botas, carriel y sombrero
Esta es la artesanía del corazón de mi eje cafetero.

Colombia

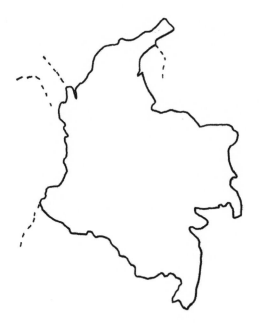

Antioquia *263*

Caldas *305*

Huila *337*

Colombia is geographically separated from Panama by what is known as the Darien Gap. The gap is not in fact a gap in land, but rather one in passable transportation routes. There are no roads through the Darien, which constitutes some of the world's most treacherous mountain jungle. The treachery of the Darien comes not just from the inherent wildness of its jungle mountains but from its history as a drug trafficking route prone to violent encounters. Due to the Darien's impassibility, you can only enter Colombia by air or by sea, and once you're in Colombia you're worlds apart from Central America, and the scale of everything has exploded.

Colombia's population of 47 million is almost one sixth of the population of the United States, and the country's 440,00 square mile land area is equivalent to that of Texas, Oklahoma, Arizona, and Louisiana combined.

The only way to really experience Colombian coffee country is from the back of a motorcycle winding its way through the dusty roads that weave down mountainsides sown with blankets of shiny green coffee trees. Bouncing over holes and bumps, white knuckling the driver or the little bar on the back of the bike, you can maybe get a sense of what coffee cherries feel like, stuffed in an old fertilizer sack and strapped to the roof of a retrofitted jeep, careening down the mountain to be sold.

Standing in the forests of Costa Rica and the jungles of Panama I wouldn't have believed that there could be anything more impressive. But Colombia's mountains are in a class all their own. Standing on one of the endless roads that traces the ridge along the spine of the mountains, you can look around fully 360 degrees and see nothing but more mountains. Even on a clear and cloudless day the layers of mountains fade into the distance. In Central America mountains are framed by sky; in Colombia's coffee lands, mountains are framed by more mountains, and those mountains still by more mountains.

You can stand on the backbone of one mountain, peer into two valleys, and squint across the valleys to small towns clustered on the spines of other mountains. At night, as your moto's single headlight cuts through the blackness, you can peer down into these valleys and see dots of light indicating fincas and homes. Colombia as a whole is more developed than most of

Central America, and even in pretty remote places there is electricity and running water. Where there is coffee there is the National Federation of Coffee Growers (FNC), and where there is the Federation there is work done to improve infrastructure. FNC logos are found on buildings tucked in the farthest corners of nowhere.

With respect to coffee, Colombia is organized. The country is still licking its wounds from decades of rural violence stemming from guerilla drug trafficking and political instability; today that violence hasn't so much disappeared as been displaced farther into the jungles bordering Ecuador and Brazil, deep into the wilds of uncharted, unregulated land, where men flock by the thousands to work in gold and copper mines. The risk is great but the pay is high; Colombia's top exports are by far mineral, earning the country much more than any consumable products.

Why pick coffee when you can mine gold? Mining is the greatest threat to Colombian coffee cultivation because it usurps the labor force needed to plant, tend, pick, process, and transport coffee. Working in coffee is safe and stable but is much lower paid than mining, particularly when the international price of coffee remains so low. Mining could cost you your life, from unsafe work conditions, inherent perils of jungle pests and plagues, or from conflicts with other parties carrying out their own import/export business in the shadow of deep jungle cover. But if you come out with your life you'll also come out with a lot of money, enough to buy a house for your family and take a year or two off from work.

Like all Latin American countries, Colombia has its disparate extremes: a Hollywood-level TV industry in Bogota filming glamorous *telenovelas* that entertain the Spanish speaking world from Guadalajara to Madrid, powerful mining companies funneling young men into dark holes in the ground, and humble coffee farmers feeding their mules, macheteing away the weeds, and cleaning their beneficios to keep producing the smooth, mild coffee that put Colombia on the map for North American consumers.

For more information on the systems behind Colombian coffee growing, turn to p. 380 Juan's World Part 2: Organization of a Coffee Country.

Antioquia

Antioquia is one of Colombia's thirty-two Departments, which are the equivalents of US states. *Departmentos* are divided into *municipios* (counties), *municipios* into *corrigimientos* (towns), and *corrigimientos* into *veredas* (neighborhoods). Antioquia is home to countless *veredas* full of finca-owning families who grow coffee and haul it into the centers of their respective *municipios* to sell. In Colombia coffee is processed on the finca in modest beneficios and then sold in dried parchment paper to co-ops or middlemen.

I was lucky enough to become an active part of the process of processing, hauling, and selling Colombian coffee; because my gracious hosts in Antioquia were Silvia's family, and every Saturday of the month I spent at Silvia's brother Guillermo's finca in the Municipio of Ciudad Bolívar I accompanied Guillermo's son Luis into Ciudad Bolívar to sell the coffee and help run other errands. Luis was also my guide to other *municipios*, *corrigimientos* and *veredas* where I visited finca after finca and met coffeeperson after coffeeperson, arriving at all those meetings on the back of Luis's moto, having watched miles and miles of Colombian coffee land melt by along the way.

Antioquia's urban hub is Medellín, home to the infamous artist Fernando Botero and no shortage of paintings and sculptures depicting his iconic corpulent figures. Botero has explained his work saying, "My figures are not fat; they're full of life." Like his figures, Botero's homeland is bursting with life. The city of Medellín sizzles with activity, and the mountains of Antioquia are themselves alive with wild plants and animals as much as domesticated crops and herds. But most Antioquians have seen violence firsthand and can also name friends and family they've lost. This proximity to tragedy seems to make the place as a whole collectively appreciative of life.

Coffee cultivation is both recognized and promoted as a peaceful activity, and Colombian cafeteros (caficultores) are proud people, but they are also worried that their peaceful livelihoods are being increasingly threatened by complicated factors beyond their control. The effort now becomes to do everything they can to control what they can, never going down without a fight.

Arturo

Recorded Friday, April 5, 2013, in the Co-opeandes conference rooms in downtown Ciudad Bolívar.

Because Luis had worked for the FNC as part of a program taking care of coffee tree seedlings, he's fairly plugged in to the network of coffee education offered by the FNC and the agencies it partners with. The Spanish nonprofit Solidaridad was giving monthly coffee education workshops to anyone who signed up for the "Improvements in Coffee Production" course. One workshop fell about a week after I arrived, so Luis and I headed off the finca and into the center of Ciudad Bolívar for the workshop, which was held in a white-walled conference space in the office suite above the local coffee buying co-op, Co-opeandes.

Arturo sits on a table with his arms crossed, holding a marker. An easel with chart paper stands to his left. He wears glasses and a navy polo.

Arturo: *Today we're focusing on the administrative aspect. Every single one of you has a coffee growing company. It's a company. It requires resources, employees. It requires chemical inputs, which are worth money. And it all goes into the production of a product which you sell, products for export at that.*

It's a business! Yes or no? It's simply a business. For example, we're about to enter the season for fertilizing. We know that we have to fertilize. We have it in our heads that this is something we have to do. But we're also thinking that we might not have the money.

Our business of producing products for export requires administration. And administration requires—what does administration require? First—what's the first thing?

A woman among attendees: *Responsibility.*

Arturo: *Responsibility. What else? We get up at six in the morning and what's the first thing we do? We think, "Today I'm going to get out of bed, wash, drink a cup of coffee, get down to Ciudad Bolívar, get to the meeting, have lunch." Every single one of you thought this morning: "I'm going to Ciudad Bolívar. I have to either go on my moto, take a jeep, or get on the bus. I'll get there a few minutes early, have a cup of coffee. Then I'll be in the meeting, and afterwards I'll stop at the supermarket and then I'll go home."*

You planned. And in coffee, which is our business, we're not planning. Here's a way to look at it. Out of every 100 pesos I spend on my finca, twenty-five are spent on fertilizers. This is a big blow. But the most expensive activity on the finca is the harvest. Out of every 100 pesos I invest in the finca, I spend thirty-seven pesos on paying people to harvest.

Both are costs we have to pay every year. But the fertilizers are all at once; you pay for the harvest drop by drop. And it's the most expensive cost of our business. And then we think about how much it costs to pay people to apply fertilizers and agrochemicals; manual labor becomes almost 70% of our costs.

So we can't be paying people to do jobs that are ill-timed that we then have to redo. If people applied Alto 100 [fungicide for leaf rust] to a lot, but did it at too low a concentration, you have to apply it again. But you've already paid five people do the job.

So what we're going to do now is plan out the entire next year on the finca. What happens when. We're talking about administering. And the most fundamental part of administering any project is planning. More than anything in our business. We're involved in a business that has two faces: the finca as a business and the finca as the family home.

It's more difficult for you because the business without the family doesn't survive. And the family without the business doesn't survive either. They're completely connected. So we have to be even savvier than producers of other things.

Because sometimes these family sentiments cause us to make poor decisions about the business. So we have to try to separate what's the business and what's the family. Yes or no?

In this business it is extremely important that we can make decisions thinking about how one affects the other. Sometimes, we have to tighten the belt and make sacrifices. There are times where we, maybe, for example, were planning on buying a new refrigerator. Because the one we have is fifteen years old. But if at that time we also realize we need to make other investments in the finca, why are we buying a new fridge if the one we have works? We had planned to make a purchase of 600-700,000 pesos [$300-350]. But if we do that, buy that one thing now, that same amount won't be spent on fertilizers and other inputs that could significantly help the farm in the long run.

So that's a moment that we should probably tighten the belt. Because it won't really impact our quality of life. We have to plan what we're doing with our resources. The more we're tightening our belt when there isn't much, the more productive we have to be. The more coffee we have to produce.

Arturo then hands out poster paper marked with twelve columns, cutouts of coffee cherries and flowers, and arrow stickers. We push the chairs out of the way to spread our materials out on the floor. We label the months of the year, and I proceed to attach the appropriate cutouts where Luis indicates, creating a visual timeline of annual flowerings, harvesting, fertilizations, prunings, and equipment maintenance.

If you came from Elias and would like to return to Turrialba, turn to p. 40

For a conversation with someone who recognizes coffee as a complex business, turn to p. 51

For a conversation with someone else who works to help coffee producers make the most of their land, turn to p. 87

For a conversation with the man in charge of buying coffee from producers at the co-op purchasing point (right below where this workshop took place), turn to the next page.

Leon

Recorded Friday, April 5, 2013, in the Coopeandes coffee buying office in downtown Ciudad Bolívar.

Leon buys coffee for one of the large co-ops in Antioquia and the only co-op with a presence in Ciudad Bolívar: Coopeandes. He sits at his desk in the Co-op warehouse. To his right is the loading dock platform where trucks (etcetera) come to drop off coffee and others come to pick up. To his left is a large warehouse space filled with stacks of burlap coffee sacks all bearing the red and green stripes that are the international symbol for Colombian coffee. In front of him is a large scale and above it a mounted flatscreen displaying Forex futures charts of the current New York market price for coffee. Leon closes out a few open screens on the computer at his desk. He wears a brown t-shirt.

Leon: *Basically, what we do here is buy coffee. Coffee in dry parchment paper that meets standards of humidity and number of defects regulated by the Federation of Coffee Growers. We're working according to the standards set by the Federation. And, the Co-op [their buying jurisdiction and practical reach] includes a large area: all of Jardin, Hispania, Carmen de Atrato, Farallon, San Gregorio, which are corrigimientos and municipios around here, near Ciudad Bolívar.*

In the [Co-op] system of purchasing, basically we receive coffee through different modes of transportation: on horseback, in cars. [Producers] bring from 1 to 30,000 kilos at a time of coffee in dry parchment. They bring it here, to the scales, and we unload the trucks, put the coffee on the scales, count the sacks, and weigh it. [Leon's cell phone rings.] *Excuse me.* [He quickly takes the call while I peer out to the street and watch the traffic, which includes mostly cars and trucks of varying ages and conditions of repair but also one or two mules and mule-drawn carts.]

In our system of purchasing, once the scale is loaded and we've counted the sacks and taken the weight- on the electronic scales- we start the processes of sampling. We take a sample sack by sack. If the producer brought one sack, we sample one. If he brought a hundred, we sample a hundred. If he brought five hundred, we sample five hundred. Sack by sack. We take that collective sample, homogenize it—in that machine—[he gestures towards a bronze urn that looks like something you

268

might see in a hookah bar, or perhaps Dumbledore's study] *and we mix the sample so that it's a trustworthy representation.*

After homogenizing the sample, we take the humidity. Here, we work with 400g to do that. The humidity has to be between 10-12%. [More water equals more weight. A man walks up the steps and into the office. He asks the price of coffee today.] *535,000 pesos [roughly $260, per 125 kilos]. After taking the humidity, which should be between 10-12%- which is also a regulation set by the Federation, to conserve the bean. Whatever characteristics a coffee comes in with we have to conserve by means of maintaining the level of humidity. If someone brings in a coffee with pasilla, that will be removed during the physical analysis.*

We then weigh out 200 grams, hull them [to take off the parchment paper and be left with just the green bean] to be able to determine the percentage of healthy beans there are, and thus the yield factor. ^{Juan's World Part 3:} ^{Factor 90 p.384} *That also gives us the percentage of waste: the weight of the parchment paper.*

Because for every 100 kilos, there's an average of 18-20% weight in parchment paper. So with 100 kilos of coffee in parchment paper, you'll get around 80 kilos of green coffee. Once we have the green coffee [after hulling off the parchment] we sort out the defects; defects are all types of irregularities. You can see them all here on the defect chart. There are fourteen defects. All beans that don't have the appropriate characteristics of green coffee are considered defects. They're categorized by group: beans damaged by machinery-flattened or split, also those bitten by insects, under ripe beans- all that- is sorted out as defects. And then we're left with good beans. Which determines the percentage of acceptable beans; also known as the yield factor.

The yield factor is the number of kilos of coffee in parchment necessary to yield 70 kilos of exportable grade green coffee. A "carga" of coffee consists of 125 kilos of coffee in dry parchment.

After the physical analysis [of the coffee producers sell to the Co-op], we store the coffee. Here, we work with various types of coffee. Standard and certified. Within standard we divide them into various types of coffee: Superior and Types 1, 2, 3, 4, and 5. Pasillas and corrientes. And, here in Bolivar, we work with UTZ and Rainforest certifications, and a verification program called 4C. So, depending on the amount of defects—if it's within the level permissible by the certifiers—and the producer complies with the certification regulations and has been certified, which the [computer] system will show us, we store the coffee in the appropriate section of the warehouse. We store it, label it- because all the lots have to be labeled as the type of coffee we purchased them as. The same when we sell it; it has to be labeled.

Rachel: *So you determine the factor once you've taken out all the defects?*

Leon: *Want to do an example? Of how we determine the factor, the humidity, sort the defects and all that, so that you can actually see?*

Rachel: *Ok, sure!* [We stand up, and Leon points to the sign board outside the office.]

Leon: *Look, those are the prices.*

Rachel: *And do they change during the day?*

Leon: *Depends. Every day, we get a message via Skype from the Co-op [main office]. And* [he pulls up a few windows on the computer screen] *535,000. And we see the prices for the certifications our Co-op works with. UTZ, Rainforest, Nespresso, 4C. These are the premiums. UTZ, 10,000 [$5], right now. Rainforest, 12,000 [$6]. Nespresso, which is just in the Jardin area is 50,000 [$25)], because they're looking for certain characteristics. And the premium for 4C, which is the education project of the Federation,* 8,000 pesos [$4] per carga of 125 kilos.*

Rachel: *And this base price of 535,000, does this change various times throughout the day?*

Leon: *If the market is moving a lot, we might have to change it three or four times, or however many times they tell us. The base price is according to a Factor of 93.3. There is [a base price accourding to Factor] 92.8 also, which is for 75% exportable green coffee [think 20% chaff, 5% defects]. We use Factor 90.*

Rachel: *Because that's the most common Factor?*

Leon: *Because it's a more attractive price to put on the signboard.*

Rachel: *So, for example, a Co-op in Chinchiná*[Gloria p. 319] *or Huila*[Miller p.339] *would have the same base price?*

Leon: *It depends on the distance [from the Co-op's dry mill, where the coffee is hulled from its parchment paper to become green coffee ready for export]. They factor in the cost of transport. On the Federation's website it shows the prices they use for every region of the country.* [A few men walk in and ask Leon a few questions. Once he answers them he leads me down the stairs from the platform where the desk and all the scales and sample testing equipment are to the floor of the warehouse, where stacks of sacks of coffee are piled below hanging signboards labeled with their grade or certification. Leon carries with him a long, hollow metal tube that is tapered to a point at one end. This is known as "the sticker," used to "stick" sacks, literally punch a hole in the jute or plastic sacks in order to extract a representative sample of the coffee inside.]

So, this is how we take the sample. Imagine that we've weighed this coffee on the electronic scales. There are twenty-six sacks. The idea is to take the same volume sample from each sack, so that the sample is accurate and uniform. So we don't have more from one sack than another. So that it's really a sample of what they're selling us. [He jabs a sack. And then another and another. He empties each jab-ful into a plastic bowl].

After taking the samples, we homogenize them in order to test the humidity. [We walk back up the stairs and over to the Dumbledore hookah homogenizer. He pours the coffee in and the machine begins to churn.] *If there are only a few sacks we can just mix it by hand.* [The machine shoots out a homogenized pile of coffee at the bottom.] *From here, we take 400g to test the humidity.* [He empties the sample into the much less mystical looking grey plastic humidity testing machine.] *So is this pretty similar to how they buy coffee in other places?*

Rachel: *Well, actually, in all of Costa Rica the producers sell it in cherries, not parchment. So they take samples—like [at the Nespresso-operated collective wet mill] in Jardín—of cherries and then measure the number that float, green ones, all that. They can't measure humidity or anything. And then the dry mill is the one who sorts for defects before export.*

Leon: *Look, the humidity here is 11.86%. Since it's within the acceptable range, we can now measure out 200g to determine the percent of defects. So now we run it through the sample huller in order to find the percent of weight*

271

from parchment paper. [The coffee goes through yet another small machine, this one black and silver metal and the only one that produces a fine dust of chaff. The parchment paper is removed to yield a bowl full of green beans.

Just as Leon walks away with the bowl, one of the shirtless employees who helps unload sacks from trucks/cars/ mules bounds up the steps and into the office. He is all of five feet tall, tanned, and incredibly buff. He sings a deep, throaty tune, runs up to the ledge where coffee is piled when it's loaded off the scales, leaps onto the ledge, and does a backflip over the low wall, landing on the piles of sacks stacked on the other side. I can't see him, but I can still hear him singing the song (which sounds like what pirate shanties probably sounded like) without missing a note.]

So we just take the difference to find the weight of the parchment, so that gives us 38.5, and we divide it by two for 19.15%. For every 100 kilos of this coffee that the producer is selling, 19.5 kilos are parchment. And 81.5 kilos are green coffee. Now, let's determine the defects—beans eaten by bugs, chewed by the machine, flattened—anything on the list of defects. Ok, let's see what you got! [He motions to his desk chair, indicating that I should take a seat. I like this guy; we're clearly on the same page of understanding-by-doing. I sit down in the sunken swivel chair, pile of hulled coffee in front of me on the black countertop. Countertops at coffee buying places are always black so that the grey-green coffee beans are easier to distinguish. The black countertop, whether at the middleman's or the co-op, is as an unassuming Formica slab indicative of serious power. Whatever Factor is determined as a result of the sorted sample in turn determines the final money a producer receives for his 1-30,000 kilos.

Leon bends the squeaky elbow desk lamp (think old Pixar skit) over the pile of coffee and switches it on. My heap of coffee is illuminated, and I start to sort. Most of the idle, shirtless sack stackers come over to watch me and giggle. I try to imitate the way I've seen coffee buyers slide the beans to the left and right of the pile, indicating acceptable or inacceptable. Defective or exportable.

While I'm sitting there sorting, a jovial red-faced man walks in. He plops himself on the chair on the other side of the black desktop. He asks Leon who the new coffee buyer is, then comments on my sorting skills, telling me that I'm putting all the good ones in the bad pile and the bad ones in the good pile.]

Producer: *And what's the price today?*

Leon: *Right now it's at 535,000, Factor 90. It's adjusted 4,000 pesos ($2) per point, depending on the parchment percentage too.*

Producer: *You said 535,000? And yesterday it was 525,000? Let me call my wife. Can I use your phone?* [Leon hands him the phone.] *Sonny boy! Put your mom on. Today it's at 535…* [He carries on a conversation with his wife about whether or not he should sell the coffee today. Leon comes to review my work. He swaps a few beans between the piles, but overall my evaluation passes his evaluation. The producer hangs up the phone and must have decided the price was good enough, because the shirtless sack stackers are loading his coffee onto the scales.]

Producer: *Have you visited a farm?*

Rachel: *I've visited lots of farms.*

Producer: *But you haven't visited mine! Caturro, pure Caturro.*

Rachel: *And you don't have roya?*

Producer: *Nope. Because I spray.*

Rachel: *Hardly anyone around here has Caturra!*

Producer: *Well I do! 136,000 trees of it.*

Leon: *You see, Raquel. This is a real example. He brought the coffee; we weighed it: 693 kilos and counted the sacks: fourteen. And now they'll sample the sacks. First, let's see what percentage of defects your practice sample has.* [He weighs my "acceptable" pile and punches in numbers on the calculator.] *18.7% defects. So this coffee that you sorted has 148.7g of exportable green coffee. Which means 74.35%. We divided*

148.7 by two because it was a 200g sample. So if we want to find the yield factor, because we started with 200g and we want to end up with 70 kilos of exportable coffee, we do 200 times 70 kilos, 14,000, divided by 148.7, giving us 94.15.

Producer: [whose sacks are now being "stuck" by the shirtless sack stickers pulling samples] *So that's the factor? 94? High.*

Leon: *Which means, that—of this coffee—we need 94.15 kilos to yield a 70kg sack of exportable coffee. Out of 100 kilos we'd have 74.34 kilos. Right?* [The phone rings.] *Co-operative, good afternoon. 535,000 pesos. You're very welcome.* [One of the shirtless guys walks over and hands Leon a bowl with the Producer's homogenized sample.]

Producer: *It's good-looking coffee, right?* [Leon expertly sorts the beans into two piles.]

Leon: *This has a Factor of 89.22.*

Leon takes the Producer's Coffee Grower's ID # and makes out a receipt, which the producer can then take around the corner to another office to get paid. Luis walks in and starts recounting his saga with the mechanic. Leon finishes the paperwork and walks over to the coffee maker, where he pours us each a cup of Co-operativa *tinto*, the Colombian term for a cup of black coffee.

If you came from Roberto and would like to return to Coopedota, turn to p. 149

If you came from Alejandro and would like to return to Costa Rica, turn to p. 181

For a conversation with an Antioquian coffee growing family, turn to the next page.

*4C is the Common Code for the Coffee Community, a business-to-business verification code ensuring ethical practices up and down the supply chain. Because it is not a certification, it provides no guarantee to consumers and therefore doesn't appear on product packaging.

Gladys and Alirio

Recorded Wednsday, April 24, 2013, at Finca La Pradera in the Salgar Municipio.

Alirio (Luis's mom's brother), Alirio's wife Gladys and I have all been seated in the kitchen of their house at a table covered with a floral patterned plastic tablecloth, but before we start the interview, Gladys really wants to show me something. Aliro waits at the table while Gladys leads me through a narrow hallway and into what could have been a bedroom if it wanted to be but instead is home to a sprawling nativity scene that covers every inch of the floor.

Streets lined with trees, animals, houses, and smiling figures extend from one corner of the room to another. The paths through the scene were just wide enough for human feet, and I picked my way through all of Bethlehem and up to the manger. Glady's had told me ten times that I could take pictures, so I took pictures, as she stood beaming in the doorway.

Dance company masters famously tell recruiters, "Don't look at the young dancers; look at their parents to see what the young dancers will become." By this point in my odyssey I'd gotten pretty good at not looking at the dancers but instead looking at the parents. Want to know how someone takes care of his farm? Look at the state of his house.

The tiny slumber-suspended town of Bethlehem was orderly and maintained, even though it was April. I didn't have to see every inch of Gladys' farm to know that every inch of it would be as orderly as the nativity. How people do things is how people do things; the care of careful people carries through everything they do, whether it's placing Wisemen figurines or washing coffee cherries.

I tiptoe out of Bethlehem and follow Gladys downstairs to a bulletin board in a sort of "mudroom." Alirio wears a white cowboy hat and Gladys wears a pale yellow t-shirt.

Gladys: *Well, this is like the beginning of the story. Where did it start? [Alirio] got the land from his father, got married, and we had two kids, Adriana, who really likes coffee and takes care of all the paperwork for the farm, the accounting. I do the trainings of new workers, things about the* *environment and sustainability, but she does the accounting. And Hugo helps with the work in the cafetales and the beneficio.*

I want to start with the human part and then with the environmental part. This is what we've learned so far: to notice things from the very smallest to the very largest. We don't sleep to rest, rather in order to dream. We follow the values star [gestures to painted star on the wall] *which includes respect, discipline, dedication* [and love, honesty, sincerity, responsibility, effort, and honor]. *We also realized that it's important to take care of the environment, before even thinking about the product. Because one should take care of the soil, and follow good agricultural practices. Because we take so much care of nature here, we have lots of animals living with the coffee. For us it's not just about "money, money!" Rather, we consider that taking care of the natural environment means that we get much more.*

These [motions to framed plaques on wall in hallways leading to a mud room with a large bulletin board on one wall], *these are all from UTZ and some from Rainforest too. Our diplomas. We also have an internal control; this is the main regulation of the farm. It says, "Whoever loves and works will be happy." So many times there are big conflicts over nothing. We say that things that are too small to fight over are the things that bring us together.* [The bulletin board is covered in handwritten signs on colorful paper, decorated with flowers and designs in marker and paint. They read:

"You are incredibly rich. Wealth does not just refer to material goods. You cannot be judged poor if inside of you exists the power of love, capable of overcoming all difficulties. You cannot call yourself poor if you have health, intelligence, and most of all faith in God the creator. Profit creates imbalance. You may want to raise your level of well-being, but never put money as your first priority. There are millionaires who would like to be where you are, full of life, health, and joy. Be conscious of the wealth God has given you."

"Of all the paths that lead to good forturen, the most sure are perseverance and work."

"A good cafetero plans, organizes, directs, and monitors."

276

"Love and work and you will be happy."

Gladys explains that they have signs outlining values, but also the necessary signage indicating any dangerous machinery or materials. Certifiers are big on signage.

They lead me around the finca, explaining as they went. There was fresh picked coffee from the morning sitting in the hopper at the top of the depulper, and they tried to show me how it worked, but when they flicked the switch nothing happened. "*Se fue la luz!* The power's out! It'll probably come back," they told me. Sure enough, three hours later it did, and I watched the cleanest machinery I've seen anywhere spit out slimy depulped coffee like a pro.

They also showed me the guestbook, which every visitor to the finca had signed. There were names from people from the local co-op, from UTZ, and from neighboring communities. I proudly signed my name in the handmade book, the cover of which was covered with more intricate flower designs like those on all the posters and signage.

Gladys continued to explain the mentalities she and her husband share, mentalities which have lead them to produce prizewinning coffee.]

Gladys: *The key story of us is here. We've always liked to work like this, with things done well, mostly because of Alirio, who always liked to make good coffee. Quality. And very well washed. That's where all his comes from. To just end up with any old kind of coffee is not something he likes to do, right?*

Alirio: *For as long as I can remember I've liked to have coffee that's washed right. So much so that I never let any worker—or anyone else—use the [depulping] machine, because no one else can do things as well as I want them done! I'm always on top of the coffee. How it's washed, depulped. And I'm watching how it's picked. Everything.*

Gladys: *His perseverance and painstaking care has always been something I've admired in him. So what has helped us more than anything to keep moving up and continue to manage our coffee production even better? The* *trainings. And the assistance from the Co-op and the practical workshops that the Federation holds in the Coffee Axis.*[Landscapegoats p.404]

  They've given us very, very good support. They have their areas of expertise. One used to just show up, pick the coffee, depulp it, and wash it. But, as one becomes more educated, with trainings and workshops, in these steps, you start to see that final product improves. These have been five years where people are saying, "Oh look, you're certified," *but to us it's not really about—like I said—"Money, money!" Rather it's about learning and then being able to apply it to your very own soil, to your very own cafetales, your trees. That's what's carried us. Perseverance on one hand and on the other hand because we like it. We like living in nature, and we like doing things well in order to see the positive results.*

Alirio: *And it's such a great thing to walk into the Co-op with really good coffee, right? People will come over and look at the coffee; when it's on the scales everyone is saying, "Wow, look at that good-looking coffee!"*

Gladys: *We get to be very proud. People ask us, "How do you do it?" And we're always thinking, more than anything, about the client. The person who's going to drink it, whether it's you or someone else. I have the peace of mind that this coffee is well made. This is fundamental, not thinking about money, rather about whether or not people like it. That they can drink it and say, "What delicious coffee! How did they make this?" And that it's as natural as possible. That it doesn't have many chemicals; that's the idea. We don't like to use anything that will harm the soil.*

Rachel: *It's been five years that you're certified. Did you start with one, or go for all four [certificatons] at once?*

Gladys: *With one, right? UTZ, no, 4C! The Common Code [for the Coffee Community]. Then UTZ, and Rainforest, and [Starbucks C.A.F.E] Practices. Rainforest has a lot to do with the environment. We like having this certification because we support biodiversity within the cafetal. Everything that has to do with animals and taking care of the fruit trees and the hardwoods. So we said, "We might as well go for Rainforest too, because we like taking care of nature so much." And it's gone very well.*

Rachel: *And because you're part of the Co-op—well, you have to pay to be certified, right? Do they pay the cost of certification or do you have that cost?*

Gladys: *No. On the contrary; they've helped us a lot. With everything from latrines to draining wastewater from processing. And more than anything, with the understandings we have. That's key.*

Someone who's going to certify to make more money is better off not doing it. These are organizations, and what's more valuable than an organization? For example, we're right now—Alirio and I—basically alone on the finca. Because our son's out picking coffee. So for all this, for cleaning and maintaining the machinery, it's just the two of us. So because of that I'm part of several groups. Because I like talking to people. I love people. It gives me great happiness to be able to help people.

Rachel: *What inspired you to first participate in the Rainforest cupping competition?*

Gladys: *Ahh, the competitions at the Co-op.*

Rachel: *They also hold competitions between Co-op members?*

Gladys: *Yes, yes. Within the Co-op. In Concordia. And then there's also the one with Rainforest. This is the third place award from Concordia.* [Gladys walks across the room to get a small plaque with a large coffee bean etched into it.] *This was the first competition we ever participated in. And we won third place. And then it was the Rainforest competition, which is held over there in the U.S., and ours was one of the ten best from Colombia*. And we won 250,000 pesos [roughly $125], and the Co-op gave us another 250,000- no! 300,000.* [She sets the plaque from Rainforest on the table as well.] *And the Co-op also gave our daughter a job.*

Rachel: *That's great! And do you sell all of your coffee to the Co-op?*

Alirio: *Most of it. But the price isn't guaranteed and sometimes it's pretty regular. Once we sort out the pasilla we'll usually sell it there. They're all about quality.*

Rachel: *And do you drink your own coffee here?*

Gladys: *My sister's the one who roasts it—she'll show you! Want to see?*

Rachel: *Yes, in just a minute! I'm just wondering what kinds of coffee you have planted.*

Alirio: *There's a part that's Caturro, but very little, only 1,000 plants. And then there's Variedad Colombia; I also have Castillo, but just a little. That's what I'm planting. The majority is Variedad Colombia.*

Rachel: *Lots of people in the U.S. are asking me about roya in Colombia. Have you been affected by it here? By broca?*

Alirio: *The roya affects the Caturro a lot. Which is why there's very little left; the roya destroyed most of it. And the broca, yes, there's always some.*

Gladys: *There's some, but we try to control it by thoroughly stripping the trees [of their cherries at the end of the harvest]. We go out and look at the lots, and pick everything up off the ground and take even the over and underripe cherries.*

Alirio: *When I go to the Co-op—every time I've sold to the Co-op there's been zero broca. I also select it very carefully.*

Gladys: *He selects it. Because we first start controlling in the lots and then sort it once it's processed.*

Rachel: *Well, that leaves me with just the final three questions I ask everyone: What's been the biggest challenge? The biggest success? And what would you like people who drink your coffee to know?*

Gladys: *The biggest challenge to overcome? You know, I'll tell you. The most difficult is to get people to understand the importance of taking good care of things. It's hard for everyone to understand. To get people to understand their own worth and to value what they do is very, very hard. Certifications make very harsh criticisms—unfortunately—some of those were of our own neighbors. Our very own neighbors don't want to be a part of what we wish everyone could work together towards. This part has been hard. Everything else has been doable, but for people to understand has been hard.*

Alirio: *Tell her that we started as a hundred, a hundred families, and at the end there are seven of us certified. Only seven families out of a hundred.*

Gladys: *So it's very sad. We'd like everyone to be a part of the journey that is so wonderful and amazing. But, unfortunately, this is what hurts us the most.*

Rachel: *And the biggest success?*

Gladys: *The biggest success! Oh, to feel so satisfied knowing that people who drink our coffee are drinking it with all the guarantees that what we're doing is as low impact as possible.*

Alirio: *Knowing that I grow the best coffee in Antioquia!* [He breaks into a big smile and laughs.]

Rachel: *And lastly, what's something that you'd like someone drinking your coffee somewhere to know?*

Gladys: *Let's see, well, that they know that we really are doing things the right way so that they can be happy. We're not lying. It's true what we're doing. It's a coffee that's created with lots of work and lots of love. We really are working towards something bigger.*

Gladys lead me into the kitchen, where her sister showed me the big wooden *pilón* where the peel the parchment paper and the pan they use to roast it on either the stove or the *fogón*. Then pan looks almost like a popcorn popper, with a special handle that keeps the beans constantly rotating. She roasts coffee and then lets me grind it in the same hand crank grinder used for corn for arepas. I pass it through the grinder several times to get a nice fine grind. While we're waiting for the water to boil to make coffee, I tell them about things people grow in New York. I describe green roofs and wall gardens and explain how people are even reclaiming abandoned lots. They're delighted to hear that people are developing new ways to produce.

The sun is setting and it's time to go. Painted signs decorated with flowers and designs like those on the bulletin board continue all the way up the driveway to the main road, reminding me of the proximity between spirituality, religion, faith, and growing things. Maybe their interconnectedness stood out to me here because putting a prayer on the wall of a business in New York would be taboo and controversial, but here the social guidelines are different. Maybe work and tasks and doing your job can somehow take on different qualities when the beliefs behind them are overt, pronounced, and decorated with hand painted flowers.

Where does Alirio and Gladys' coffee go?

Alirio and Gladys are members of the local Salgar co-op, Coocafisa. If they sell to the Co-op, their coffee could go the path similar to other coffees sold to Colombian co-ops. It could be bought by the FNC's Almacafe and exported with coffees from all over the country, or it could be purchased by roasters, including Starbucks, looking for coffees with the qualities particular to the Antioquia region.

If you came from **Gerardo Aguilar** and would like to return to **Turrialba**, turn to p. 48

If you came from **Henry** and would like to return to **Nicaragua**, turn to p. 113

If you came from **Minor** and would like to return to **Los Santos**, turn to p. 165

If you came from **Graciano** and would like to return to **Panama**, turn to p. 240

For a conversation with **Alirio's sister**, turn to the next page.

*Alirio and Gladys' coffee won 10th place among Colombian coffees at the 2012 Rainforest Alliance Cupping for Quality competition held in California. To date, they're the only top ten coffee to be certified with the four seals of 4C, UTZ, Starbucks C.A.F.E. practices and Rainforest Alliance.

Doña Rocío

Recorded Thursday, April 25, 2013, at Rocío and Guillermo's finca in the Vereda of Punta Brava up in the mountains above Ciudad Bolívar.

It's early afternoon and Rocío and I are seated in white plastic chairs, the kind that populate every café and cafeteria in the country, at the dining room table on the finca. The table should probably more appropriately be called the open air corridor table, since that's where it is. Rocío wears a navy blue t-shirt.

Rachel: *Just anything you remember about your dad's finca, about where you grew up.*

Rocío: *What can I tell you… it was a small finca. We lived as a family, ten of us. Ten kids. Four women and six men. All the boys helped my dad. Well, the older ones. And all us girls helped my mom, in the kitchen. We'd work with her a lot. We always wanted her to peel the bananas for us, so she would.*

And that was what we lived practically; my dad raised us all from that small farm—small but well managed. For example, we'd help him wash the coffee and dry it. What else? My mom passed away, and my dad had to hire employees to help. He was tired of working on the farm, so he and one of my sisters left, another employee came, my dad got very sick, and divided the land up between us, everyone got some.

For example, we all have what he gave us. We haven't sold anything. I have, in my little lot, about four thousand trees. My brother [Alirio]—where we were yesterday—he takes care of it.

Rachel: *So wait, then your coffee is also part of the coffee that won all the awards!*

Rocío: *Well, no one really ever put it like that, but I guess so.*

Rachel: *Because your four thousand trees are contributing!*

Rocío: *Well, no one mentions things like that to me…The majority of my lot is just overgrown, because my piece is fairly good sized. It's too bad you didn't get to go over there yesterday! But you saw the little house that's on it;*

it's from there up, up, up the hill to the road, and then down in front too. It's practically its own little finca, because it has a small beneficio, a house, electricity, water; it's practically it's own finca.

Rachel: *And where the working beneficio is, the house that we were at yesterday, is that where you grew up, where your family lived?*

Rocío: *The one that's right across from my brother's house; that's the one where we grew up. That's all empty now. We thought about walking up there yesterday, but we ended up not having time to go because it got late.*

Rachel: *Oh I see. So there are lots of houses on the property then.*

Rocío: *Um hm. Because, you saw, my brother's house is really two houses connected. The house for the workers, and then the big house with two floors.*

Rachel: *Did you have other crops too, or just coffee?*

Rocío: *There were bananas, yucca—because on the fincas there was always a lot of yucca. And pineapple. We also planted a lot of pineapple.*

Rachel: *You said you helped wash coffee? In canals, or how did you do it?*

Rocío: *Um hm, like in the beneficio here. I would wash it; I know how to wash. Depulping really doesn't have any science to it, you know, it's very easy. Washing it, well, I learned how to do that. To dry it in the sun. To turn it and recognize when it was dry. I never had to pick coffee. I was in the kitchen helping my mom cook for the workers. Making arepas. Milling corn.*

Rachel: *During the harvest how many workers did the finca need?*

Rocío: *Ten, twelve.*

Rachel: *Lots of arepas, then.*

Rocío: *Oh yes! Because the workers plus us. So it was about two kilos [of corn] to grind every day. Back in those days we made the arepas a little differently. As a snack. For example, when the workers came back in the afternoon we'd give them something, chocolate*, coffee with an arepa and* *butter, an egg—people used to eat more than they do now! They'd have a snack between three and four while we were finishing getting dinner ready.*

Rachel: *Alirio's the oldest of your siblings, right? And where are you?*

Rocío: *I'm the youngest! Well, the youngest girl. I have one brother younger than me. He's forty-three and I'm fifty-three. So I'm the ninth. We used to hull coffee in the same pilón we used for corn. We'd peel it and roast it. You know what, Raquel? In those days my grandmother liked to mix the ground coffee with burned panela. And it didn't taste good! It takes away from the taste of coffee. But my grandmother made it that way because she said it tasted like wine! [Laughs]. And I said, "No! It's better without it!"*

Rachel: *And did the cafetales used to be like they are now, with nothing else planted in between?*

Rocío: *No, it used to be—when the coffee was small—we'd plant yucca in between the rows. When the coffee is small we planted yucca, beans, corn. Like the lot, where Guillermo is right now, like that. You were there. It has young coffee [seedlings] and corn. And yucca. But we don't have any corn now, because a boy came by and left his horses up there, and the horses ate everything! Every last shoot that had come up! The mules love that stuff. And the yucca! Everything!* [Pause. Rocío goes into the back kitchen to shoo away the chickens and stir the soup cooking on the fogón.]

Rachel: *There's another beneficio at the top of this property, right? I think Luis mentioned something when we passed it yesterday.*

Rocío: *Oh yes. But that one is horrible—terrible! We had to depulp the coffee by hand, with the crank, and by the end our hands were blistered.*

Rachel: *You help with a lot of stuff.*

Rocío: *Um hm. If I have to wash the coffee, I'll wash it. It's very important to know how to do as many things as possible in this life. You never know. You end up by yourself, without a husband, in the end, and have to do things. I wouldn't falter. I'd wash the coffee like normal. A little while ago [Guillermo] was very sick, and so I would go with Luis to wash the coffee and put it up in the casilla to dry.*

285

Rachel: *Has there been any year that stands out in your memory?*

Rocío: *Ahh. Well, the year before last, for example, was a very good year. The coffee gave us a profit with its good price. And this year it has been really bad. It's the same for all the cafeteros. We weren't able to pay the debts we had. People all going to the Co-op, the bank. Because of the price. Right now the price doesn't help us with anything.*

Imagine—last year we'd bring in a carga and it would get 1,000,000 pesos. 900,000. Imagine. Now bringing in a carga to sell for 500,000. [A carga is] two sacks, and it takes a lot of coffee to fill two sacks, like nine bucketfuls of ripe cherries! That's eighteen full buckets per carga! You have to pick a whole lot of coffee to fill two sacks, to then go and sell it for nothing. At half the price, practically, half the price.

Rachel: *It's hard because the price changes often, and often it changes a lot. And you have all the costs...*

Rocío: *Of fertilizers! Of the herbicides, all that, stuff for broca...*

Rachel: *Do you remember, on the finca when you were a kid, was there roya and broca and all that?*

Rocío: *No, no, there was no of that. All that is now.*

Rachel: *So you didn't have to spray?*

Rocío: *No, I don't remember my dad doing that. Nope. Or having to use herbicides. No, he used a hoe and machete to keep the weeds and undergrowth from choking the coffee. And now they use weed killer to keep it from growing. I don't remember any of that from when I was little. That's why people are saying now that they're hurting the soil, with all the herbicides. That they're sterilizing it.* [Pause. Chirping birds. Winged chatter.]

Rachel: *Did your dad buy the farm? Or was it from his family?*

Rocío: *No, he bought it.*

Rachel: *Was there coffee on it or did he plant it?*

286

Rocío: *Well, I suppose he planted it. There might have been some coffee there. When you're little you don't really pay attention to those kinds of things. We had lots of gardens. Because the house is empty now the gardens are abandoned. When you come back you can help with them!*

I laugh and tell her I will help even more the next time I come back. The day before, Luis, Guillermo and I had planted a small vegetable garden near the beneficio. Rocío loves plants and flowers; pink and red geraniums planted in old cooking pots hang around the entire perimeter of the house. There are even a couple planted in old rice cookers sitting on the ledge in the open air corridor. Chickens squawk. I follow Rocío into the kitchen to finish helping with dinner.

If you came from Lucy and would like to return to Turrialba, turn to p. 59

If you came from Ronulfo and would like to return to Puriscal, turn to p. 77

If you came from Haydee and would like to return to Panama, turn to p. 215

For a conversation with another woman who knows how to do many types of finca work, turn to p. 115

For a conversation with Doña Rocío's husband, turn to the next page.

*basically hot chocolate that isn't hot. Or chocolate. The biggest national brand is Milo, a Nestle product. A generation ago people would make their own hot chocolate from cacao that grows in tropical forests. But now powdered instant chocolate drink is a staple grocery store purchase.

Don Guillermo

Recorded Friday, April 26, 2013. Guillermo and I are seated at the same kitchen table where his wife Rocío and I talked the day before.

My phone sits between us on the green plastic gingham tablecloth. The radio plays the news softly in the background. Guillermo wears his wide brim Costeño hat with a pattern woven in black straw.

Guillermo: *My name is Guillermo. I was born in the corrigimiento of Alfonso Lopez, outside Ciudad Bolívar. I've been a coffee grower since I was a kid. I studied until fourth grade. At age twelve I started learning about— and working in—coffee. When we started growing coffee there was coffee that we called "pajarito." And Bourbon. There were both, both types of coffee.*

They were all tall; the pajarito was tall. Bourbon was also tall; you had to prune the Bourbon. And…what else can I tell you… so I started as a caficultor at twelve. I started working in the cafetales. And, for example, coffee was planted much differently than it is now. Before, we planted coffee "en escoba." An "escoba" is a tree that's born right out there in the woods, and we pulled up the "escoba" and planted the coffee seedling right in the same hole.

Then Caturro arrived. So we worked with Caturro for a while, until the roya showed up. And so we had to change to a variety more resistant to roya. Well, from there we had to change to the Colombia Variety. The Colombia Variety is good against roya. And so we've had to live with all the plagues that affect coffee. We've had to deal with, for example, broca, also, which is also an aggressive plague. It affects us a lot because it damages the cherry. For roya we used a different chemical. The one we used for broca kills rats, was dangerous for people, very bad. What else can I tell you?

Rachel: *You said you learned at age twelve. Was that from your dad?*

Guillermo: *No. Look. When they took me out of school, I left the house. I went to live with an aunt. My aunt lived out in the mountains. My family lived in San Gregorio, because if you're in school, it makes sense to live in town. Well, from there I learned to work with coffee. To make almacigueras, all the techniques up until now. There were some varieties that I didn't have to plant. I did see them, because as a kid you see what's already been growing. And now, everything's very modern, developed. So back at my aunt's I* *learned to weed, to prune, to fertilize, everything you have to do to a coffee plant.*

And I'm still a farmer. All my life I've lived from coffee. Coffee's given us good horizons. We've also had rough years, where it didn't leave us much, but it's given us something to eat, gracias a Dios. It's given us something. One goes into debt growing coffee. It's hard.

But coffee—it doesn't create wealth but it does create a lot of jobs. So, naturally, because we have lots of coffee, we have to work with it, to live with coffee, which is what we've done.

You know what impresses me the most about coffee? It's the only tree that has faith in it. [In Spanish, the word for coffee is "café." The word for "faith" is "fe."] *Right? For me coffee is a mystery. It's a mystery. It carries faith. And you can ask any coffee grower and no one will tell you what I'm telling you about faith. We, as Catholics, have a belief, we believe in God. And it's for something that we're in awe of Him.*

Rachel: *You're right. I've never realized that about "coffaith" before.*

Guillermo: *Because no one else has realized it either! That coffee has the name of faith, what we live from. What did the Lord tell Peter? Live in faith. And look, we're living from coffaith. It's true; it has the name of faith.*

It's the only one! And look at it, you see a cherry on the ground and you just have to pick it up. So it, I don't know, it has something. You pick up a coffee bean, just one bean that's drying, and you peel it and you pop it in your mouth. Just because. It's provocative to people, right? Unique. There's nothing better than waking up in the morning and having a good cup of coffee. Nothing. [Pause. Hum and buzz of mountain insects.]

Rachel: *And your aunt? Is her finca near San Gregorio too? Because where we are now is your dad's finca or…?*

Guillermo: *Look. My father had another farm near San Gregorio. Our family's caficultura comes from my grandmother. From both grandparents; we had two fincas. My grandmother, named Nieves, her father had a farm. She left that farm to my father. My father sold that farm to buy this one. And there, at my aunt's, I went to work on that finca. I left at fifteen. I went at twelve and left at fifteen; I stayed three years.*

So I came here. And I kept working. I kept going to my aunt's too, visiting there. And when I was eighteen I saw my wife in San Gregorio and I convinced her! And I married her, thirty years ago.

And I've lived all my life on this farm, all my life. I've left some—I've also had other endeavors, but I went bust and came back to the farm. So I'm living with coffee and living from it. And from it they've been able to study. I have five children, four girls and one boy. And they've all finished high school. With the change from a few coffee trees. [Pause. The news has changed to crooning *corridos*, lamenting love songs and stories of woe. Guitar strings.]

Rachel: *A while ago you mentioned that you built this beneficio when you won the lottery?*

Guillermo: *Oh yes! My father liked to keep things really small. There was a little canal—imagine, with all the coffee from here, just one little tiny canal. So, I won some money from the lottery in Ciudad Bolívar: 250,000 pesos* [$125 dollars at today's conversion rate]. *Imagine, with that I made a nice little beneficio. But when I won the lottery the finca wasn't mine, it was my father's. I was administering his farm alongside him.*

And it was very, very useless—well, let's not say useless—difficult, to process the coffee because there was always a lot and there wasn't room to ferment it, so there was always lots of pasilla, and we had to sift it all—lots of stuff. So I, seeing this, said, "Dad, I'm going to make a real-deal beneficio when this is mine, so that we can process well, so that the coffee comes out better." Which is what I did. And it worked well for us, the beneficio. It was easier to wash the coffee because there was more space. And it came out better. The coffee was better. I built it with casilla. With an "elda," that's called an "elda."

And the dryer, I bought the little dryer, to dry the coffee. In the question of processing, we've been improving a lot. Because we used to have such a small canal space [for fermenting and washing the coffee]; it was hard. My father told me, "Man, what are you going to do with such a big canal?" And I told him, "The finca is big. One day we'll fill it with coffee and so we'll need a big tank." And he was like, "Oh, when are you ever going to fill this farm with coffee?" And look. Full it is.

It's that my father—he wasn't much of a coffee grower. He had the finca but he never worked it; my father never even picked coffee or anything. We all ran the finca together. From when I got here at fifteen I've been

290

working and working, and like I said, I got married here. And I organized everything very well on the finca, I had it all very organized, all little improvements and such, because I also liked to plant corn, and yucca… plantains were never lacking!

When you renovate [replant or chop down the majority of the tree to let it regrow] you can also plant corn, beans—while the coffee's growing—and yucca, plantains, everything. So you get food and coffee. And you know how to work. You have to know how to work with coffee, to manage it very well.

I'm telling you, a farm; it's a business. A lot of us live together from it. For example, we live together as a family, plus the workers. You have to give workers a lot of morale, so that they work well. Give them good food, a good place to sleep. You have to treat the workers well so that they can work. If you have a worker who hasn't slept well and who's hungry—he's going to be complaining all day instead of working. So if you treat your workers well, things go well for you too because they have nothing to complain about.

Rachel: *And if you have happy workers, they stay longer. Instead of having new people every month, you have people for a while.*

Guillermo: *You know, you've been staying here with us; the food we eat's not bad. We eat the same thing as the workers. We don't give the workers something else because they're workers. No. We eat from the same pot. In lots of places the owner eats from the little pot; he eats something different. Here, no. We all eat from the big pot. Because we're all the same. A worker is like part of the family. I respect him. I don't go around saying nasty things to my workers, no. I don't have problems with workers in this respect because I know how to manage people well.*

For example, there are people who show up in the cafetal, to make the rounds, and they start yelling at everyone in general. No. You have to make the rounds row by row, and if you see something wrong talk to exactly who did it wrong. So that there aren't problems, you have to know how to treat people well. Because… you need to have the workers you need. I would never fire a worker as an enemy. No. They always leave on good terms. I have a saying, "El sabado para mi es sagrado. Y lo llamo el San Valentin. Porque salen con el vale, o con el maletín." *["Saturday for me is sacred. And I call it St. Valentine's Day. Because workers either leave with paystubs or with suitcases."] You might need that person back. So you have to treat people well. And what else can I tell you? Let's see…*

Rachel: *Well, you're a member of the co-op?*

Guillermo: *Look. I'm a member of the co-op in Bolívar [Cooperativa de Caficultores de los Andes, Coopeandes]. I joined thirty-eight years ago, before I was married. Because I had the finca and all. I planted coffee, but "en compania." Did they tell you this story already? So I planted coffee with our neighbors, but my neighbor ended up with the coffee and didn't give anything to us. He told us, he told me and one of my brothers, "We're going to change that lot of land for the lot of coffee you planted." And I said, "Ok, let's go ahead and swap them." However you look at it we planted the coffee; it was ours. And my brother eventually changed it because I had the final say. He sold his part. So I bought that part and I bought another part from my other brother. And so I was the only one left on the farm, and I had my own coffee trees, and so I decided to join the Co-op.*

I joined at eighteen. Imagine, I'm fifty-three. So I'm no ordinary member. [Laughs.] Sometimes it's been good, other times bad, but I stay a member because sometimes one isn't able to fulfill all one's duties, to make all the payments one needs to, so... so in the end the co-op offers good services, for example when my kids got sick they gave me a little bit of money, I had a loan for the orthodontist, so yeah, they offer a lot of support.

Rachel: *They offer a lot, but they also don't offer the highest price.*

Guillermo: *Exactly. For example, if the price for coffee at an agency [middleman]—for example—if the price at the agency is 550,000 [pesos per carga], the price at the co-op might be 520,000. So sometimes you have to sell some in one place, some in another. Especially when the price of coffee is low. I've never been particularly stuck to the co-op.*

Rachel: *Right now how many hectares are there to the finca?*

Guillermo: *In coffee, there are five. Because the finca is like seven or eight, but you have the valley, where the house is, so more or less five hectares. So there are probably 30,000* coffee plants.*

Rachel: *And now you have which varieties?*

Guillermo: *We have variedad Castillo...first there was Caturro, then Variedad Colombia showed up. And then after Variedad Colombia it was*

Variedad Castillo. So you have to switch. Because everything turns, even the sun turns! So we had to turn. It's that with the techniques for growing coffee, and with the broca and all that we've had to deal with, we've had to technify the farms more. To survive. Because if we didn't technify we wouldn't have been able to survive.

The roya got here first. And that's when we switched to Variedad Colombia. Because the roya attacked the Caturro, and Colombia is more resistant. And then the broca was on us. Which is worse because it eats the fruit itself. Well the roya's also bad because it knocks off the leaves. So the tree doesn't have any leaves for the coffee to be able to ripen.

Rachel: *And how many years ago did the broca show up?*

Guillermo: *Broca…more or less twenty years ago.*

Rachel: *So when you were a kid it wasn't there?*

Guillermo: *No, no, no. There wasn't any of this. Roya either. For example, when the roya first showed up I was twenty, I had already been working with coffee here for five or six years, when we first saw roya. For it to really be a problem took a while, because it came slowly. We would spray a little fungicide, and she stayed moving slowly. But it doubled in force. So then we had to switch varieties, to the Variedad Colombia. And now to Castillo. It's a change.*

Castillo, for example, isn't just about plagues. It gives a bigger fruit than the other varieties. But I've just started working with this, so I don't know how productive it is. Because Variedad Colombia was productive. After Caturra it was the most productive variety I've ever seen in my life. We're improving with this, with this kind of coffee. We'll see if it works out better for us, in terms of quality. Because the quality can be better, having a bigger cherry and all.

Rachel: *For you, what is do you like more about coffee; working in the field or in the beneficio process?*

Guillermo: *I like to plant it. And weed it. And fertilize it. And process it. Not pick it. I don't know, it never worked out for me. Because I wanted to be so careful with the tree, I would go along picking one little cherry at a time. And to pick coffee, people have to be a little tricky for it to be worthwhile.*

Pick coffee with lots of leaves, things to add weight. But I would go picking one by one—

Rachel: *And never manage to fill your basket!*

Guillermo: *No, no—I'd fill it! For example—with Caturro, because Caturro is a plant that matures all at once, you could pick it in three big passes. And then there wasn't any left. One time I went to pick coffee and I picked twenty-five bucketfuls—I picked a lot of coffee! And the other guys picked thirty-five to forty. So I picked nothing.*

So I've picked it and everything, but I wasn't any good. I'd rather weed it, plant it, fertilize it, and process it, in the beneficio. For example, during the harvest, I don't have time to go pick coffee because I'm busy with the beneficio all day. I like to process it to then see how it turns out. Because in the beneficio you can also determine how much output you get from coffee. If you know how to do it, you get mostly coffee, and a little bit of pasilla, a little bit of corriente. You get lots of types of coffee; the good stuff, the corriente, and the pasilla. And you sell them separately.

Rachel: *And what's your process? Depulp, ferment, and wash? You depulp one day...*

Guillermo: *...and wash it the next. I depulp it, then early the next morning I wash it and then put it out to dry. To get a good quality. Because if you let it "turn vinegar" [overferment] it doesn't... Well, we had to technify ourselves with coffee so that it wouldn't have defects like overfermentation, so that it would give a clean cup. We can't be producing a...contaminated coffee, because it's something that people drink. So you have to be careful.*

It's a food. Food. It's something people drink daily; it's consumable. And the problem with coffee is that it absorbs everything. From when it's on the branch to when it's drying; it soaks up everything. And even when it is dry! So you can't put it on a dirty floor, or it will be dirty too. And you can't put it somewhere inappropriate for storage because it will take on bad odors. Coffee is a product that you can't really store. You can't really save it for a long time unless you have someplace really good to store it. Like the big co-ops have, or the big buyers who have everything. One doesn't have the facilities to store coffee.

Rachel: *Of all the steps to producing coffee, which step is the most expensive?*

Guillermo: *The most expensive is the fertilization.*

Rachel: *How many times a year do you have to fertilize?*

Guillermo: *Two fertilizations. I fertilize in November and in May. Those are the two times I fertilize because you have to apply fertilizer during [moderately] rainy periods, and those are the rainiest months of the year. May and November. In our area.*

Rachel: *And why do you fertilize during rainy months? So that it's absorbed?*

Guillermo: *So that the soil takes it in. And it gets to the tree. It's not the tree that's being fertilized; it's the soil. That's where we're mixed up. If you ask a caficultor if he's fertilizing the ground or the tree, he'll tell you, "The tree." But it's really going to the soil. So that the soil passes the product on to the tree. You have to know to know when to apply. Because if you apply it when it's too sunny you're just wasting it, because it's a chemical. And it will evaporate. So the tree will get very little. On the other hand, in the rainy season, it immediately gets taken up by the soil, and the tree gets the fertilizer.*

I also have a theory, I don't know, that, for example, in November the tree is full from the harvest you're picking. And it starts to flower in February, March, April. So that when it gets to that point it's already well-fed so that it flowers well and the cherries are good, well fed. So it'll come out—well, I have faith that it will come out—a quality cherry. Because it has all the nutrients.

Rachel: *And the trees are flowering all year round; is there a little something to harvest all year?*

Guillermo: *Now that's a question of climate. The climate where we are, it grows all year, this far up in the mountains. With the varieties we have now, I don't know if it will still be producing a little bit all year. Because the varieties act differently. Like I told you, the Caturro gave a harvest once a year and that was it. In three months you picked everything, and the rest of the year there was nothing at all to harvest. When there's something on the* *trees all year, there's food for the broca. It has something to eat all year round. But with Caturro, it didn't.*

For me, I don't know. For example, these plagues are...complicated. There never used to be plagues that showed up from one day to the next. As soon as a plague sets in there's a product for it. I don't know if it's a question of sales... It just used to be that you just planted coffee and fertilized it and that was it. You would fertilize two times a year if you could afford it. Two, no more. This was when coffee was just growing with all the undergrowth.

But now, you have to keep it free of weeds, very fertilized, and keep it very well sprayed [with pesticides]. It's very different. Right now it's more difficult for the caficultor. Because of the plagues and all. There's ICA [Colombian Department of Agriculture] so I don't know... if there's no plagues then there wouldn't have to be any products to sell...so it just looks like there might be a connection...

We have to learn to live with what's in front of us.

Rachel: *And try to survive one way or another.*

Guillermo: *And not give in as defeated! That's the case with human beings. A defeated man is a dead man. Fight—in order to live—fight until you overcome. Because, because if not, you're already defeated. It's hard.*

My son is doing some work with caficultura, but sons lives are very different from their fathers.'

Rachel: *The way things are now is very different from how they were when you were his age.*

Guillermo: *Caficultura could get to the point of disappearing. Why not help out coffee growers? It's getting to the point—*

Rachel: *Do you think it'll get to a point where it's not profitable?*

Guillermo: *No, it'll still be profitable, but there won't be anyone to do it. Because kids already don't like working the land. So, I don't know. I don't know where that leaves the culture of growing coffee. And even the big estates, they could disappear too if there's no one to work them. Disappear, no, because rich people—because the owner has money and he can fill it with cows and—voila! But the poor will have to fight for the little they have.*

Rachel: *Having a small finca has its challenges, and having a large finca has others. It could be that things change. I guess we'll see. This land is good for coffee; you can grow really good coffee here.*

Guillermo: *We're in the optimal location. 1600 meters above sea level. Ideal for coffee. It produces well. It's not too hot or too cold. We're at a mild temperature. We're at a very profitable point for coffee. Because if it's too cool it's not worthwhile. Neither if it's too hot. And we're halfway up the mountain range. The finca is very well placed. But growing coffee is still hard. Which is why a lot of people don't want to get into it. Or help it and support and keep up the morale. Because if not, caficultura will disappear. Is there anything else you'd like to know?*

Rachel: *Well, what would you like coffee drinkers to know? The majority of the people who drink coffee have never seen a coffee plant. We don't have cafetales in the United States. Because, like you said, it needs the kind of climate and land you have here. And there we have colder colds and hotter hots, but we don't have this optimal climate for coffee.*

Guillermo: *But you drink more coffee than we do!*

Rachel: *We do; I think we do! We drink a lot of coffee.*

Guillermo: *It has to be grown because so many people drink it.*

Rachel: *Exactly. I think coffee growing culture will never disappear because there are so many people who love drinking coffee so and will always keep buying it, so there will always continue to be a demand. Maybe it will change, but I don't think it will disappear.*

Guillermo: *But it might disappear from here. Because a lot of times they punish us, because they can get coffee cheaper from other countries, where the costs are lower. And it costs us a lot to produce. And in other places it costs them less, so they can sell it for less. But then they pay us that lower price. Because there are a lot of places producing coffee, and some of them have virgin soil, land where there isn't broca or roya or anything! The land is pure! Just add a little fertilizer and it'll give you coffee for days.*

But for us, our land is tired. It's spent a lot of years producing coffee. And we're competing with people with new brand new land, just producing coffee for the first time. And so it goes really well for those people. Which is how it was for us, when we had land that had never produced coffee, had been pasture or whatever. Because the land had never had coffee on it. But now that we've had it for years, renovating and replanting, renovating and replanting, the soil is tired. And so we've rotated and rotated so that the soil can rest, but after so many years of coffee, coffee, coffee, the soil is worn out.

Rachel: *It's true. Colombia has spent a lot of years producing a lot of coffee.*

Guillermo: *We also have the problem of highways. Now there are big highways everywhere. You have a finca, and they just build a highway right down the middle. Cutting up the land. All this contributes to soil becoming more sterile.*

Rachel: *Which is why, in some places—I don't know about here, there are people who are replanting forests to try to refertilize and renew the land and the soil. Planting more trees of various kinds.*

Guillermo: *So that the land becomes more fertile? When we first got our land there was still rich soil...*

You'll remember what I said about coffee being the only tree with faith in it? Peter's faith. Because we live from faith. And we live from coffee.

I turn off my phone and start to pet the three dogs who've just come running up to me. (I call them "the herd.") Guillermo looks at the phone and asks, "So it's there? The interview?" I tell him yes, and that I will also put a copy on my computer and one on the Internet to be sure I don't loose it. He looks skeptical. "Can I listen to it?" I tell him of course, and press play. He leans in intently, focused on the screen even after it goes black. I walk into the kitchen to help with dinner. Forty-five minutes later he walks into the kitchen, and says, "Raquel, it's a good interview, no? I think it's a good interview." I tell him that I think so too.

If you came from Silvia and would like to return to New York, turn to p. 25

If you came from Rodolfo and would like to return to Costa Rica, turn to p. 73

For a conversation with another lifetime coffee grower, turn to p. 151

For a conversation with a lifetime coffee grower's son who took on the rest of the production chain, turn to the next page.

Where does Don Guillermo's coffee go?

If he sells to Coopeandes they could export it themselves to any major roaster or trading company, or to Almacafe, the commercialization arm of the FNC who then sells to roasters and importers. If he sells it to a middle man they then could also sell it to a roaster or trading company, probably one of the big guys who buys large volumes, like Louis Dreyfus Commodities or Olam or even Neumann and ECOM.

---

*6,000 plants per hectare is an average density in Colombia.

Pedro

Recorded Thursday, May 2, 2013, at Café Pergamino in Medellín.

It's a gorgeous morning inside Café Pergamino, tucked on one of Medellín's prettiest tree-lined streets in the city's trendiest neighborhood: Parque Lleras. Pedro invites me to sit at the corner table in the back of the café, where the sun from the skylight streams past the art on the walls and onto the blonde wood of the bench seating. He orders a French press and a Chemex* from the barista. He wears a pale green Oxford shirt and black thin-rimmed glasses.

Pedro: *Well, I'll tell you a little. Café Pergamino is part of a company called Café Santa Barbara. It's a company that produces and exports green coffee. My family, my father, has been cultivating coffee for more than thirty-five years. Our farms are divided between Santa Barbara and Fredonia, but the production is principally in Santa Barbara.*

We're one of the few companies of our size to be vertically integrated. We used to sell to the Federation and private exporters, the large ones who have a presence in Antioquia. And three years ago we started this, here [gestures around him to coffee shop, motioning to the point in the past that was the start of the journey away from purely producing and towards a diversified, integrated business]. *And when we started exporting, we did it, more than anything, because we had enough volume to make the whole chain work. We do the agriculture, the shipping logistics. No one touches our coffee until it's at the port ready to leave.*

And when we started to export, we started to discover a world of high quality coffees. At the beginning everyone was saying, "Your coffee's not that good, your coffee's not that good. Your fincas are pretty and everything, but…" And we're very happy that we were able to finally produce specialty grade Colombian coffee. We hope to get to know more about specialty markets, meet more medium sized roasters, ones who want to know everything about the finca. [A Pergamino barista approaches the table, French press in hand. Pedro pours the coffee into our chocolate colored ceramic cups bearing the Café Pergamino logo.]

This is coffee from La Palma, which is very close to the finca we use for Loma Verde coffee, but coffee from La Palma is processed differently. It's almost been aged like wine, so that it has more notes of red fruit and red wine. It has the profile of a very good typical Colombian coffee. A lot of chocolate,

300

caramel, very intense, smooth, and sweet. [Pedro's phone rings and he quickly takes a call].

So, we got to know roasters and importers of specialty coffees; we started to significantly change what we were doing on the farms in order to improve the taste in the cup. And we now export 100% of our production** and we export it at different qualities. For example, we have Santa Barbara Estate, which is our bulk coffee, which is better than the average Colombian, but it's still what we produce in bulk. And then we have batches from various fincas and lots— [Pedro takes another quick phone call].

So we started changing what we were doing on the farms, in terms of processing the coffee and controlling quality. When all of our coffees leave the beneficios they go to the dry mill, where they're hulled, separated, and cupped for quality, and then they're ready for sale.

Last year, after we'd spent two years working with small and mid-sized roasters, we decided to open our own café. This is our only location. We have coffees from all over, right now we're serving three but sometimes we have four or five, right now there's one from Ethiopia in the ports, tied up—because everything gets tied up. We also have different Santa Barbara coffees.

The level of the baristas here is superior to what you'll find at any other establishment. All these guys—some have studied with SENA and are trained. To be a barista here you have to be trained for five, sometimes six months. And the drinks they make—the lattes and cappuccinos—come out with latte art, which is not very common here. And they can tell everyone the stories of the coffees. If someone asks them why La Palma is different, they'll tell you. You can learn as much as you want to know.

We have free cuppings once a month. We're starting to turn it into almost like a coffee school. So we're a family business, and this is us. Anything else you'd like to know?

Rachel: *You said you started exporting directly three years ago. What was the impetus for doing so?* [The same barista brings over a Chemex of Loma Verde. Pedro pours it into our mugs.]

Pedro: *Like I mentioned, the decision came from the size that we are. We are a fairly large farm, and we have the volume necessary to maintain the logistics of exporting. We had enough money to build a trilladora [dry mill], etcetera. The initial intention was to take advantage of the export margin. It's a margin that varies but is significantly more than the prices of coffee. Yes, this margin is important. But, once we started studying the model, we decided* *that the goal was to earn a premium on the price of coffee, because this price dictates the price we're paid [per pound].*

Rachel: *So you're paid the [New York "C"] market plus a premium, versus a fixed price?*

Pedro: *Exactly. There are tiny producers who have buyers who say, "We'll buy everything, your whole harvest, for this price, for five years." But those kinds of negotiations, now, are basically non-existent. No one will buy two thousand sacks—or ten thousand—at a certain fixed price every year. That doesn't happen. So, the idea behind all of this, is to try to—balancing the different premiums we have, some that are huge because they're for five sacks of the very best coffee we have, others that are small because they're for one or two thousand sacks—is to try have these [premiums] at an average that gives us a cushion on the market price. It might not be a huge cushion; it might not make us rich, but at least it will keep us out of debt.*

The final goal of the whole business, from export to roasting and the cafe, is the desire that coffee—in all its forms—and stabilize its own prices. Because if one time in ten years there are good prices, we'd be spending the cushion all at once just to maintain the fincas. So we try to maintain sales, which fluctuate, but which fluctuate much less than the market price fluctuates. So that's our first and central goal. Sustainability.

Often, the things people talk to us about are environmental and labor policies. But what people, especially the certifiers, don't understand is that sustainability is based on the income producers earn. From there, you can be environmentally and socially sustainable—whatever you want. But if you don't have a stable price, if a small producer has nothing to eat, he's never going to care about where his residual wastewater from processing is going. Or where the fermented cherry skins are being dumped. Or anything. And a producer with a mid-sized farm, who doesn't have enough money to maintain his land, isn't going to be worrying about how he's paying his employees.

The base of any kind of sustainability is—and therefore should be the base of any certification—is economic sustainability.

Rainforest, who certifies lots of farms—we had Rainforest for five years, we're about to recertify a few fincas—Rainforest gives you $0.06/lb. That won't sustain anyone—anyone at all! This is a little tiny extra, but not enough to do anything with. And they come and the make sure one tree is so many meters from another or you won't get the stamp. A lot of times, these *certifiers focus heavily on the environmental and the social before the economic. Sustainability starts at the economic level and then goes where you take it.*

Rachel: *Which is why a lot of roasters now say that they don't need the certifications, that they'd rather come see for themselves.*

Pedro: *Exactly. And the biggest thing they're then certifying is that they're buying coffee. They're not buying the New York Stock Exchange or a middleman. They're buying coffee.*

A few days later I accompany Pedro to Compania Santa Barbara's finca in Santa Barbara, located between Medellín and Ciudad Bolívar. Santa Barbara's land is divided between multiple finca's. We visit some with young Typica and Bourbon, others with mature Variedad Colombia, and three separate beneficios.

On one finca a group of men are picking, including Jair, a local man who's been working for Pedro's father, and now Pedro, for over a decade. Forty percent of Santa Barbara's employees live in houses provided by the company. On another finca a foreman, who's worked for Pedro's father for years and has watched Pedro grow up, asks when the next inter-finca *fútbol* game will take place. Apparently last year's was quite eventful, and people have reputations they'd like to maintain.

One beneficio is in a converted stone barn and has special fermentation tanks where Santa Barbara employees can monitor the process of fermentation and measure temperature and pH. The lofty ceilings and shiny, spotless steel machines seem more the like stuff of a bourbon distillery or beer brewery. Outside the stone beneficio a giant peacock roams between the piles of dried coffee pulp that will be used for making almacigos. The peacock belonged to Pedro's grandmother, and when she passed away, the peacock stayed as a sort of beneficio mascot.

Where does Pedro's coffee go?

Pedro sells to direct trade buyers worldwide, including Mercanta "Coffee Hunters" of London. Some of his coffe goes to Brooklyn Roasting Company in the Dumbo neighborhood of Brooklyn. If you visit their café/roastery you might even see a bag of Santa Barbara beans stacked in front of the roaster, waiting for its turn to become the coffee in your cup.

If you came from Francisco and would like to continue to Nicaragua, turn to p. 93

If you came from Henry and would like to return to the mountains of the Matagalpa region, turn to p. 113

If you came from Wilford and would like to return to Panama, turn to p. 238

For a conversation with someone else who runs the chain from ground to grounds, turn to p. 177

For a conversation with someone who worked in at the FNC's science labs and in their coffee freeze drying plant, turn to the next page.

*Chemex…trendy form of "pour over" coffee preparation, consisting of putting a paper filter into the top half of an hourglass shaped "coffee beaker," pouring near-boiling water over the grounds in the filter, removing the filter, and serving the coffee.
**Well, almost 100%. The majority of the coffee sold in Café Pergamino is from the Santa Barbara fincas. What isn't from their fincas is from other countries, making Pergamino one of the few places in Colombia that imports coffee from other countries, since the rest of Colombia is drinking some grade of Colombian coffee. Because here, coffee can be a local crop, so importing it from Africa makes about as much sense as New Yorkers importing apples from Chile. Which we do. But for us it's actually more cost effective because the labor in Chile is so much cheaper than labor in the U.S. But there's no real advantage for Colombians to buy coffee from Kenyans since everyone who's growing it everywhere is getting paid pretty close to the same bare minimum. Unless they're growers like Pedro, who are seizing specialty markets by the horns.

Caldas

The Department of Caldas is a geographically much smaller department than Antioquia, but as a department holds much more administrative importance. It is part of the Coffee Axis ^{Landscapegoats p. 404} and home to many important FNC offices, including Cenicafe, the world's best-funded coffee science research center*. Cenicafe is responsible for developing the varietals that fill the Colombian coffee mountains and for generating all maner of agronomic recommendations that are issued via the country's network of Extentionists, who are instantly recognizable by their bright, bumblebee yellow polos.

The FNC owned and operated freeze-dried coffee plant producing the brand Buencafe is located in the city of Chinchiná and is guarded round the clock by a team of German Shepards and Rotweilers living in little yellow doghouses.

Just outside of Chinchiná, not far from the labs of Cenicafe and the smokestacks of Buencafe, is another FNC institution: the Fundación Manuel Mejia, the FNC's program for rural education. The FMM is responsible for creating and disseminating materials for school aged children through to adults covering topics related to coffee cultivation for use at workshops both at the FMM or out in the field.

The capital of Caldas is the city of Manizales, a city high in the mountains with a sort of bizarre cable car running through the middle of it. The FNC Departmental Committee of Caldas is located just outside of Manizales in a sprawling park known as The District of Thought. Caldas has a reputation as having the most active departmental committee, and in unrecorded conversations with committee members that work in the District of Thought, they shared a presentation showing all the work they've done to certify every co-op in the department with at least one certification, ensuring that all coffee coming out of Caldas is somehow differentiated and thus worthy of a premium.

The cafetero who's assumed the role of Juan Valdez, ^{Juan's World Part 1: A Sombreo, a Poncho, and a Mule p. 376} acting as the FNC's character-in-the-flesh international coffee ambassador, also hails from Caldas, adding one more point to the long list of things the Department is proud of.

*Cenicafe will host the 25th Annual ASIC conference in fall 2014.

Jaime Mosquera

Recorded Friday, May 10, 2013, at the Mosquera household in
Chinchiná.

I'm seated at the kitchen table (because it's close to the
internet router). Hum of the new refrigerator. Otherwise, silence.
It's Friday night and everyone's out doing Friday things. Jaime,
the cousin of my Couchsurfing host David, has just come in to
get some leftover dinner, which is sitting in pots on the stove. Of
course being curious as to who is the foreigner sitting at a laptop
at his mother's dining table, he offers me a cup of reheated *agua
panela* and sits down to talk. Turns out, he has a lot to say about
coffee. He wears a white t-shirt.

Jaime: *When did I work at Cenicafe? That must be, let's see, fiteen years
ago? I worked there for a while when the Federation was just trying out, was
trying…was doing research. I don't really know what happened, because they
eventually closed the lab, and I had to find work elsewhere. Another job.*

Rachel: *But the lab with the wasps and the broca, is that in Chinchiná too?*

Jaime: *Yes, there were two labs there. There's only one now, I think. I
think there's just one in the country and it's there [at Cenicafe].*

Rachel: *What was your job with the wasps? What did you have to do?*

Jaime: *Well, this was—well, I had to look for coffee [cherries] with
broca—out in the finca. So we went and found, oh, let's say two or three
cargas worth. Or eight or ten sacks. And then we put them in a screened cage.
And the broca comes out in the evening. They come out when it's warm, to
mate. They're looking for new "houses" for themselves. And because they were
enclosed we could collect them. We collected those little bugs alright, scooped
them into a jar. They'd fly out of the cherries and against the glass—sticking
themselves to it looking for a way out.*

*And then you also had to pick A1 coffee, the best of the best, zero
broca. And put it on a tray, oh, 30 or 40 by 80 cm. And then we'd
introduce a certain quantity of broca, so that they'd live there. They had a
process of, I think it was, twenty-two days. And they would start to bore [into
the coffee] to make their homes, to put their eggs in. And so every, every eight
days, marked with the date and everything, we'd put them in lockers. And*

307

after eighteen days, the broca's eggs weren't out yet, but they were almost formed.

So then we moved them to another room, where the wasps were. We tossed them in there with a bunch of wasps. And we'd just introduce wasps once, because they'd start mating too and maintain themselves [by eating broca eggs].

And people would come to the Federation with their application and ask, "Oh, it's that I need this or that much because I'm infested with broca." And so we'd take a bunch of the eighteen-day-old coffee, which had already been in with the wasps, and then start the process of breeding the wasps, which was different.

So, these wasps were born at around eighteen days. And so we pulled, let's say…one hundred wasps. And after eighteen days there'd be, depending on their fertility, three hundred, five hundred. So we'd collect them and release them into another screened cage. And before the broca came out of the coffee, we'd take a jar full of the wasps and bring them out into the cafetal. And they, by nature, would go looking for coffee with broca. So that was the cycle. And we worked with a huge number.

And every day the same thing. Because every day we had to do the ones for that day, so that every day there'd be some that were at the twenty-second day. More and more and more—nonstop.

And we did that for five years.

Rachel: *For five years!?*

Jaime: *All the agronomists from the Federation would come and take samples; they'd take some from every tray, a few cherries. And they'd put the cherries under the microscope and make the tally, "Broca's at sixty percent, seventy percent."*

And according to this tally the Federation paid the lab, which was private and subcontracted. [The Federation] paid the lab for the costs of the chemical inputs and all that. And for the workers.

And the wasps maintained consistent numbers, but the number of wasps compared to broca never reach the ratio the Federation was looking for…

The broca's a pretty nasty plague. Very hard to control. In another lab they were working with rice, with a fungus. It's been a while since I've worked in the lab. But those guys have a lot of money to work with. Have you seen what they have in Naranjal? At the Fundación Manuel Mejía?

Rachel: *I haven't been there yet, but I'm going next week. Today [your cousin and I] went to a talk at Cenicafe about costs of production. But that was at the main buildings, not at the labs where they do the actual research.*

Jaime: *I also worked as a janitor at the freeze-dried coffee plant here in Chinchiná. Where I had to clean machines. And then after like three months, they put me on cleaning but in the cold rooms and the roasters. There, the trash isn't trash like it was at the beginning, just sweeping the hallway and such. You have all the grime on the machines and the fermenting chaff from the roasting machines. The chaff is light so it flies around everywhere and you have to collect all of that.*

There something called a "Greco," which is where they cook the coffee to get the extract, and those drip. And they're as big as this kitchen table, and you had to keep it all clean.

And the cold room, that was at like -40 degrees Celsius (-40 Fahrenheit). The coffee entered the room through a tube. It fell onto a conveyer belt and after two minutes—wow!—it was stone cold frozen. [Knocks on table]. *Before it gets to that point it goes through a mill that grinds it. And a vacuum room that extracts all the humidity. But I'm sure you're familiar with this process?*

Rachel: *No, I've never seen any of it. I don't think we have this kind of factory in the U.S.*

Jaime: *Well, in this little chamber that collects the coffee that's* [knocks on table] *as if it were a stone; it falls into there and then it's ground, so it ends up as a powder. And the other thing this chamber does is siphon out all the humidity. About 10 kilos at a time go into the chamber, which is about the size of this fridge, and schuuuuup it absorbs all the water, and it comes out the other end as a powder; that's the process of freeze drying.*

Rachel: *So they freeze it, extract the water, and grind it?*

Jaime: *Um hm. And there are other rooms where they do it with organic coffee, decaf coffee—where they extract all the acidity [caffeine], and one that's natural, that people like the most. But it's also an elegant process.*

When you're in the cold room you can't work for more than an hour. You have to put on a suit like an astronaut. You always work in teams of two; one person can't work alone. Always two.

Rachel: *Ah, because if something happened...*

Jaime: *Exactly. We always worked in pairs. One pair goes out, another goes in. An hour later, another two go in, and the two that came out rest for an hour. And that was how we spent our day's shift, eight, nine hours. Resting one, working one.*

And it wears you out. After two months you're thin... you have to do a lot of—sometimes the tubing that comes into the cold room, that's carrying the hot liquid coffee extract, would burst and gush liquid, and as soon as it hits the floor it's frozen. So we had to, with an ice pick and a hammer, chip at it to get it up. And sometimes it would cover the floor. And we were wearing those suits! Super, super thick ones! With a pair of giant glasses, giant gloves, and we had to grab a chisel to clean it up. That was hard.

Rachel: *-40. Wow.*

Jaime: *You put a glass of water in there and in two minutes it would be frozen solid. And there were people who after five or ten minutes in there would faint. And we'd have to take them out; they just couldn't do that job. Because you could die.*

I was only there for a year, at that job. Because all the sudden the engineers would start saying, "Oh I know this guy or that guy," and they would bring in their friends, and so wheeesht! We were out.

But the process is impressive, elegant.

Rachel: *And how does it work, since the coffee's just been roasted? Do they let it cool before they freeze it or take it right out of the roaster and into the cold room? Does it have to rest at all?*

Jaime: *When it's ground coffee, for making drip coffee, they roast it to a certain temperature, and then grind it. And then they sell it to you, just like that. So they roast the coffee, and then they cook it, in what I told you was called a "Greco." It's like the size of this table, round, almost three meters tall, like cooking something in a [stainless steel] pitcher, except it's macro.*

And then this concentrate starts flowing out, through the tubes, hot. And it falls on the conveyer belt, which carries it into the cold room. And then it's frozen.

When they cook it it's like a pressure cooker, but giant. And so it has chimneys on top, and this where the borra *[dirty dust] comes out. And the coffee ends up cooked, as they say. And the waste goes to another part of the factory where they extract the oils. And the rest they did throw away. We also had to clean the chimneys, all of it.*

It used to be that the only way to get—a resident of Chinchiná, well this was years ago, must have been like fifteen years ago—to get a jar of freeze-dried coffee you had to know someone who worked there who could give you one. They didn't sell them in the grocery stores here. It was all for export. And then sales went down and the international price of coffee was low, so they started selling them in our grocery stores. And now they sell a lot.

People really like it. They make this coffee in proportions of 100 to 0. What do I mean by 100 to 0? 100% pure coffee, 0% filler. But other brands, like Colcafe from Medellín, they have coffees that are 80 to 20, so 80% pure coffee 20% broca eaten coffee or coffee parchment paper and hulls. But Buencafe is pure—they don't mix in anything. But some people don't mind coffee that's less than 100% pure, because they mix it with milk anyway.

For every cup of coffee you drink, someone stood out in the rain to harvest it. For every cup of freeze-dried coffee you drink, someone wore an astronaut suit, elegantly, to chip away at spilled coffee extract frozen to the factory floor.

If you came from Fernanda and would like to return to Costa Rica, turn to p. 151

For a conversation with someone else who works in the more industrial side of coffee, turn to p. 205

For a conversation with people who work at another FNC operation, turn to the next page.

David and Albello

Recorded Tuesday, May 14, 2013, at Fundacción Manuel Mejia outside of Chinchiná.

The Fundación Manuel Mejia is the FNC's rural education and training division. David and another agronomist have just given me a full tour of the facilities. The FMM has a full working finca that serves as a learning lab for caficultores who come to attend workshops and as a practical space for training trainers who will be the ones to carry out workshops around the country in the future. David and I stand in the patio in front of the entrance gate. David wears a blue Fundacción Manuel Mejia monogrammed polo.

David: *Ok, so I studied at the University of Caldas in Manizales. The major's called Agronomic Engineering. It used to just be called Agronomy, but to give the title a little more clout they changed it to Agronomic Engineer.*

Rachel: *You were telling me that you had to do an internship; can you choose where or does it depend on the type of agronomy you're studying—like are people studying agroforestry out in the jungle, or—?*

David: *The University gives us options. I could have also chosen to study palm oil or bananas, other crops cultivated in Colombia. But I've always really liked coffee, so I made the decision to do my internship here. My expectations are to keep working in coffee, in another coffee growing institution. Cenicafe, the Foundation, Almacafe, all that.*

Rachel: *And the courses you take in agronomic engineering, are they more specific to coffee or are they more general?*

David: *In the major, you learn, more than anything, general topics that can be applied to any crop. For example, we'll look at soils. PH, micro and macro elements, toxicity, all that. The part that I focused on while in university was phytosanitary and had to do with plagues and diseases. Fungus, bacteria, viruses, nematodes, all that affects a plant.*
Here at the Foundation, since I've arrived, I've been reinforcing that knowledge, everything about integrated pest and plague management. With the understandings I brought from the university and the support of the

professionals who work here, I've learned many technical things very specific to coffee.

Rachel: *Does your family have coffee; did you know anything about coffee before you started working here?*

David: *My family—well, my grandfather had a farm in the Risaralda Municipio. A coffee farm. But my grandfather died, so there were some problems in the family and all that, so we lost the farm. Right now, an uncle who had a part of the farm still grows coffee on it. So that's my family connection to coffee.*

Rachel: *Once you earn your title of Agronomic Engineer, what jobs, what positions, will be available to you?*

David: *Agronomy is a very broad field. That's one of the things I knew about it going in. You think that going into agronomy the first thing you'll do is start looking at plants. Not so. The first thing you do is math, calculus, chemistry, physics, botany, administration, rural politics. So what positions can you work in? Whatever you want. The truth is, in whatever position you want.*

If someone says, "Can you calculate the costs of this farm for me?" you can, because you're an engineer and you're capable; you have to be capable. "Can you evaluate the affect of a certain product on a given disease?" You can; you've done it before. "I need you to go commercialize this coffee!" You can, because you're an engineer and you've studied international markets. That's how it is. You leave the university with a sea of knowledge that's a centimeter deep, as they say. So what are you missing? Some depth in a field.

For me, I'd like to work on the research side; I'd really like to be in Cenicafe. I'd be doing research to then give recommendations.

Rachel: *Have you also studied hybrids and how they do the crosses and all that?*

David: *That's another part that we touch on; it's another whole discipline called "phyto improvement." So that's what I mean when I say that it's a really broad major. A minute ago I was explaining that the trees we saw were a hybrid of such and such varieties. While we were walking I forgot to mention that there were some trees that were taller, those are Tabi [Typica* *and Bourbon cross]. And because Tabi is a variety [versus a homogenous line like Caturra or Catimor] you see different types of plants. Others are Variedad Castillo, another variety, which are taller.*

For example, this lot in front here is Variedad Colombia. What impresses me is that it's planted on a wall.*

Rachel: *Um hm, because Variedad Colombia is also a cross between Caturra and Timor Hybrid.*

David: *Yes, just fewer generations of crossing.*

Rachel: *I was reading that the Variedad Castillo is an F5…*

David: *It's the product of crossing sixty-five genetic lines. And Variedad Colombia was like half the number. When Cenicafe started this study, they didn't stop at Variedad Colombia because they knew that they needed horizontal resistance and vertical resistance [to roya]. There is one that was stably resistant, and so they kept researching until they got to a variety that demonstrated all the desired traits of resistance.*

Rachel: *Someone told me that the reason to move from Variedad Colombia to Castillo was because the leaf rust mutated and started to attack Variedad Colombia.*

David: *Yeah, imagine that you have a fungus that reproduces in logarithmic quantities. In a little beaker you have four times the world's population in spores. So of course it's going to mutate. The same happens with insects and their resistance to chemicals. You show up and you kill all the susceptible ones, then the resistant ones are left alive. And within the resistant ones they cross, and that's where you start losing.*

Rachel: *Um hm, that's why they're always innovating agrochemicals.*

David: *And that's why it's always more recommended to opt for biological controls.*

Rachel: *But for the roya is there a biological control? Really, there isn't one, right?*

David: *Genetic improvement. After genetic improvement, chemical.*

Rachel: *Right, so there really isn't a biological option. And the people who have Castillo and varieties that are more genetically resistant, do they still have to apply preventative chemicals?*

David: *No, no. Because they have that genetic resistance. If you do apply chemicals you're just throwing away your money. But, if you do get roya it's a really hard problem to manage. What other questions do you have?*

Rachel: *Well, you mentioned that you'd like to work in Cenicafe. In research. So in plagues and diseases, trying new products...?*

David: *I like the entomological part. The part that has to do with insects. If I had the opportunity to work in that department, that would be my preference. Apart from broca there's* minador *[leaf minor]...* Minador, palomilla, cuchintas arenosas, *and also there's research in insects as biological control, like the wasps.*

Rachel: *Oh, and is it very common to see people using* beauvaria bassiana? *Are there a lot of people who make the most of it as a biological control? I understood that you have to mix it in a lab so that the proportions are correct for it to actually work and be effective.*

David: *No, look; what you'd buy from a lab is a concentrate. It'll say the concentration on the package. It comes ready, in powder. And what does the powder do? The powder includes all the spores. Right? So what do you have to do? An agronomist will recommend to the producer, so that the fungus establishes itself well in the fields, that they mix it with an agricultural oil. Why? Because these fungi are very susceptible to light, to solar radiation. Another thing is when you apply it. If you apply it at high noon—and without an oil, you're not doing anything. The oil functions like a filter with sunscreen. So the product, the oil, and the concentration make up the effectiveness.*

For example, if it rained, and after a little while the lot is mostly dry, and it's still cloudy and maybe even a little bit chilly out, that's the ideal moment for application. You also have to think about wind speed. You can look at the movement of the branches. Right now, it's at around 4-6km per hour. So these are acceptable wind conditions for application. For the product to work well you need a set of optimal conditions. You need good sprayer equipment, a worker with some knowledge of what he's doing, temperature, light, wind, dosage. You have to account for all those variables.

Oh look—some of the workers are just coming back from the fields. Would you like to interview them?

Rachel: *Sure!* [David calls over one of the foremen, Albello. He wears a light red plaid shirt, a white baseball cap, and black work boots. I introduce myself and ask him how he got started in coffee.]

Albello: *I started working outside because I was born in the mountains. I was born caficultor. They gave me a plot of land, and I learned everything I know through working her. And I've been working here fourteen years.*

I was born, I grew up, and my studies were very few because my parents had to work, and so I also had to go to work in the fields.

And right now, [here at the Foundation's fincas] we're planting coffee. I'm transplanting, and I know how to transplant and plan out a lot, following the contours of the land, all that. We're planting, and so they put me in charge of transplanting seedlings, so I'm in charge of transplanting seedlings.

We started the process yesterday, and before we actually put anything in the ground we first had to apply an herbicide. So that the ground is clear. To move the seedlings, dig the holes, and plant them! And you when you plant you have to mix in some lime with the soil. Some lime to mix with the soil, to sow the plant.

You mix it with the soil you've taken out when you dug the hole, then those 50 grams of lime are mixed with the soil used to fill in the hole with the plant. And then after about twenty days you give it Da, a special fertilizer for seedlings, about 20 grams per tree. And then after two or three months, you apply 25 grams of the same fertilizer, so you go along upping the dose. After about eight to ten months after planting, you can give it Da and urea. And then it will start to sprout little buds, meaning it's near flowering, and then it starts producing. It takes, more or less, eighteen months after you plant coffee for it to produce fruit. Eighteen months for it to produce. And then you can start to harvest. Eighteen to twenty months in this part of the country, because it's pretty warm here.

Rachel: *And do you also do all the work to prune, select regrowths...?*

316

Albello: *To clear lots, prune—partial and total, to select, clean, I also know how to weedwhack, all that. And right now I have to clearcut and pull up old trees. The part that you saw down below, I had to clearcut everything with a chainsaw to be able to plant the new stuff.*

But ripping it up and replanting is a different way of renovating than a zoca *[pruning down to stumps], because with a* zoca *you leave 20cm of the trunk, so that the tree will regrow its branches and produce higher volumes again. And it's up to you how many new trunks you leave on the pruned tree—three, two, one. But on the majority you leave two, one on each side. On one lot over there is a* zoca, *where were now selecting the regrowths. We keep the ones that are the healthiest looking, one good looking one on each side. We're already thinking about how the trees will be in terms of feasibility for picking.*

Rachel: *Out of all the jobs you've done in coffee, which is the most challenging, and which do you like the most?*

Albello: *The most difficult? Well the truth is that everything is habit; because I'm used to doing them all, none of them seems difficult to me. I'm accustomed to planting, transplanting, clearing with machete, everything; it's all what you're used to. When it's hot out it is hard. The thing that kills you more than anything else is the sun, whatever job you're doing. Out fighting the sun all day, that will wear you out more than anything. But it's all what you're used to. And when you grew up in the country, well, what can I say?*

Rachel: *So then on the other hand, what do you like the most, out of all the work you do?*

Albello: *What do I like the most? Drinking a cup of coffee when I'm at home and done working!* [Alirio belly laughs and grins. Laughter from small crowd that had slowly assembled to listen to the interview.]

Really, what I like to do the most is weedwhack. It can be a little dangerous, but still. Or applying herbicide. You just put on the sprayer backpack and go up and down the rows, nice and comfortable. That's one of the easier things to do. Some jobs are easier than others. When I was pulling up the old coffee—that's a question of having a good back, because you're out there with the chainsaw, bent over to get to the base of the trees. So to be in

317

that position all day, you need a strong back. It's tiring. But it's a question of being conditioned, too.

Rachel: *Have you also worked in all the processing jobs?*

Albello: *That too. From receiving it from the producers and weighing it, depulping it, putting in in the sun or the silo to dry, all that. And I've worked in construction.*

Rachel: *To build casillas?*

Albello: *Yes, I've done that too. Everything you learn how to do will serve you.*

David: *Another thing the Foundation does is to train [workers] in new equipment and tool maintenance, like chainsaws, etcetera. And managing toxic chemicals—remember we did that last week? The idea is that the workers stay updated and trained in those topics.*

If you came from Karole and would like to return to Turrialba, turn to p. 51

If you came from Jose and would like to return to Nicaragua, turn to p. (Henry)

If you came from Don Pachi and would like to continue to Colombia, turn to p. 257

For a conversation with someone else who works in South American agronomy, turn to p. 90

For a conversation with someone involved in the private sector of Caldas coffee production, turn to the next page.

* The term "wall" (*pared* in Spanish), is used to describe a particularly steep slope, one that's almost vertical, where coffee is planted. As in, "I'd never want to pick on Don Ramon's farm; half of his coffee is growing on a wall!"

Doña Gloria

Recorded Wednesday, May 15, 2013, at La Meseta's dry mill in downtown Chinchiná and the company's fincas just outside of town.

La Meseta's dry mill is a large facility almost in the center of town. The massive hulling machinery is surrounded by stacks and stacks of varying grades of coffee waiting for export. Gloria has spent the morning showing me the company's wet mill, dry mill, and various fincas, a process that included (but was not limited to) worm composting, caged mastiffs, penned ostriches, rain, mud, a golfcart, and homemade popsicles.

Gloria's wears a black t-shirt with a painted image of the Virgin Mary outlined with several halos of colored beads and sequins.

Rachel: *If you could just say a little more about what you were telling me before, about how your family got started, your mom's dad…*

Gloria: *Raquel, we've now been doing this here for thirty years. It was property that my mother received. My grandfather's name was Manuel Castaño, and he had, at that time, the finca called "La Meseta." At the time of his death those lands were divided between six children, and so my mother received a piece.*

From that, my brothers started with a sod house, with no light, no water. They got there and there was nothing—barely a few banana trees.

Over time, they started planting a little coffee here and there. In the year 1985, with the explosion of the volcano Nevado de Ruiz, a few acres of land on the edge of Finca La Meseta were for sale.

The people who bought it didn't know how to administer the fincas, they didn't know how to process coffee, therefore my brothers—on Finca La Guamera, which is part of La Meseta—started buying their coffee at this time, in 1986, from the people who came after the volcano Nevado de Ruiz.

At this time they then started to process and dry it. And more people started hearing about it, neighbors from the area, that Finca La Guamera was buying coffee.

They started, my four brothers Jorge Fernan, Jose Fernando Muñoz, Juan David Muñoz, Carlos Alberto Muñoz. And at that time, all the veredas that correspond to the Municipio of Villa Maria—which are like twenty neighborhoods, with good altitudes of 1800, 1900 [meters above sea level]—started to sell all their coffee to Finca La Guamera.

And so they started to work really hard. They had to pack up the coffee, dry it—and all in very difficult conditions with little old machines that were practically all manual, working with their hands, drying [the coffee] in the sun. This created the need to build the first silo. Then another one, and another, and another, and from there they kept growing—in the purchase of coffee. From there they started to buy farms abutting the original farm that was my mom's inheritance. When my mother got her inheritance it was seven hectacres, now the farm is one hundred hectacres, all planted with coffee. [A passing car honks and Gloria waves. She's a known personality. Perhaps a local celebrity?]

It was my brother Fernando who, from one moment to the next, said, "Well, why don't we keep looking? We're growing more—we should try to be exporters! We have enough coffee here!" And they bought La Insula. La Insula is the largest wet mill in the Department of Caldas—and I think in all of the Coffee Axis. La Insula consists of thirty silos, coffee from all over Palestina, La Esmeralda, Manizales, Trebol, El Triunfo arrives there. They dry the coffee there too and also send it to the trilladora [dry mill].

After La Insula Fernando Muñoz decided, "We have to build a trilladora! For ourselves, to not have to go to a middleman." We started with a teeny, teeny tiny one. And then we started growing, and people knew about us, and people came from Medellín, from the east part of Caldas, to sell us coffee. And now we buy coffee from Huila, the east side, Medellín, all the Coffee Axis. Everyone brings us coffee. And right now we export to seventeen countries. That's, well, that's the story of our family.

In total, we're four men and two women, and we all work for the business, which is called Compania Cafetera La Meseta.

Rachel: *And your mom's siblings, do they still have fincas around here? From when they also inherited land?*

Gloria: *No, only one—no two—two still have their fincas. Only two were left with farms. Right now. Only two ended up with farms, but they really only use them as retreats.*

Last year, Compania Cafetera La Meseta, was the ninth largest [coffee] exporter in Colombia. And this started, well, in '86, when they bought the first coffee cherries at Finca La Guamera. And we're still in the same business. We're a very united family, and we continue to fight in order to move onward.

Rachel: *I can see a lot of collaboration between you all.*

Gloria: *Lots of collaboration. We're very committed to what we do.*

Rachel: *And of all the work that has gone into the journey from '86 until now, what has been the most difficult, and what has been the biggest success?*

Gloria: *Well, the most difficult, I'd say, was, were, the last three years. Because in the last three years the climate has not helped us. There's been a lot of rain. The harvest has been down by a lot. And also, the prices have been very difficult. Last year the prices were very low, so, I say, of the big crises we've seen in the past thirty years, we can count the last three years among the worst crises. And, of the good stuff, it also started with the hard part of last year. Even with such low prices, Compania Cafetera La Meseta was the ninth largest exporter.*

Perfect timing. As she puts the period on her sentence she pulls the car to the intersection where the pickers and the foremen and the big truck full of cherries are waiting for la medida.

Where does Doña Gloria's and La Meseta's coffee go?

La Meseta exports to twenty six countries in North America, Europe, and Asia. The coffee from La Meseta's own fincas, and some of what they buy from other producers, is UTZ certified, making it attractive to European markets. Follow @coffeelameseta to stay connected.

If you came from Jose Cruz and would like to return to Costa Rica, turn to p. 43

If you came from Alex and would like to return to Panama, turn to p. 199

For a conversation with a farm administrator who sells his coffee to La Meseta, turn to the next page.

Aldemar

Recorded Thursday, May 16, 2013, at Finca San Lukas just outside of Chinchiná.

Aldemar and I have just finished drinking *tinto* from small china cups. He leads me down the mud slick driveway to the beneficio and *bodegas* adjacent to the house at the entrance to the finca. The air is thick with post-rain humidity. It is the most conventional form of tropical hot and sticky. Aldemar wears a khaki shirt and a dark brown leather cowboy hat.

Aldemar: *Be careful, it's slippery! In the United States they don't grow coffee?*

Rachel: *Nope. It's either too hot or too cold. Our land is mostly either desert or frozen part of the year. We don't have this perfect climate. And so you manage the whole process—*

Aldemar: *Everything. Every single thing. I bring the seedlings for planting.*

Rachel: *Do you guys do almacigos here?*

Aldemar: *No, Lukas [the owner's son and current decision maker] buys them.* [We cross the threshold ^{Eyelashes and Thresholds p. 389} into the shadow of the beneficio]. *Look sweetie. Here is the depulped coffee and the depulpers. Here is where we select the coffee. If you want I'll show you how it looks once it's washed.* [He opens a burlap sack to show me the dried coffee in parchment inside.] *This comes out [of the depulper] without mucilage.*

Rachel: *Oh the machine washes it?*

Aldemar: *The machine has one of those demucilagenators on it. And this is one of the [drying] ovens. We'll turn it on every couple days at this point.* [I grab a few handfuls of dried coffee in a sack next to the oven.]

Rachel: *It looks really nice.*

Aldemar: *Yes, the coffee comes out looking good. And this is how we take it to the buyers, looking nice like this. Want to see how the best of it looks* *when it's dry?* [Rustling sacks and sounds of crumpling beans-in-parchment.]

Rachel: *And how did you learn how to do all this?*

Aldemar: *Well sweetie, I spent all of my life in the mountains. Learning. And on top of that I have a good boss; Lukas's dad knows a lot about coffee. And I've spent a lot of years—twenty-seven years—working with them. So I've learned from them too. And the guys from the Committee come and they show you some little things—how to plant, how to fertilize, how frequently to fertilize, all those little things. So one keeps learning. And you just know what you have to do.*

Rachel: *And you started learning as a kid? Did your family also have coffee?*

Aldemar: *Well I'm from Tolima [in the southern part of the country] and all my life we've worked with coffee. Toda la vida. This is the only thing that brings in the bread.*

Rachel: *In Tolima there's a lot of coffee too, right?*

Aldemar: *Yes, Tolima's also cafetera. It's cafeterito. It's got some coffee. Twenty-seven years ago I came to work for Luka's family. Lukas was just tiny, tiny—a newborn!* [Chuckles and smiles] *Coffee is very involved—it has a lot of expenses. Spray for one disease and then another—a lot of diseases attack coffee—right now the roya is really damaging us. It's a really bad time for roya right now. But what can you do; you have to try to control it. God helps but you still have to do the work. And the broca, too. That's another thing that you have to be very vigilant of.*

Rachel: *And I'm guessing this has changed a lot—the types of diseases and how you control them.*

Aldemar: *Today, yes. They sell lots of different products for controlling pests and plagues. I say, because of all the diseases that can befall coffee these days, it's very difficult to grow organic coffee. Right? It's very difficult, because— take the broca—if you're not super vigilant with spraying, it will get* *everything. And organic coffee, I'd imagine, would have to be very well selected, very high quality.*

We worked with hanging traps, and with the little wasps, which [the Committee] also brought us, but, but, it's always tricky, and Lukas's dad was using them for a little while, and we were doing some fertilizing with organic stuff, but we ended up not doing it—the broca takes advantage of you. That's why growing organic coffee is so difficult. Very hard.

Rachel: *It is. And right now, what work are you doing?*

Aldemar: *We're spraying weeds. I have a few other guys picking, getting the last few cherries. And I go through selecting the regrowth from the trees that were pruned. Taking off the little* chupones. *It's important for fertilizing and all that. That's the work of taking care of the finca, keeping it clean, making sure there aren't diseases attacking the trees.* [Rooster crows.]

Rachel: *In the twenty-seven years you've been here, have you done different jobs or always the same thing?*

Aldemar: *I've worked with coffee the whole time. Planting, spraying, fertilizing—the routine is always the same with coffee. There is one lot where you need to do one thing, another lot where you need to do something else, that's how we spend our time.*

Rachel: *And how do you know Don Jorge, Lukas's dad?*

Aldemar: *Through two family members who were living with them and working with them. And so I came, and gracias a Dios, I'm still here working, very well. I'm grateful that everything is going so well with them.*
That's my little sister-in-law's house [connected to the beneficio]. It's just me. By myself. It's six years now that I'm a widower. I have my kids, they live in Chinchiná, but I keep working, you have to continue living, right? Life is to keep living.

Rachel: *Very true. Of all the years that you've been working with coffee, what has been the biggest challenge to overcome, and what has been the biggest success?*

Aldemar: *Well, let me see, what can I say? The success would be that we have good production. And this year there was a good amount of coffee, gracias a Dios. There was coffee, but there was no price. We've had pretty stressful moments with the broca, the roya* [A bunch of dogs that had been barking in the distance fly down the hill and leap on to Aldemar. I start petting them as they also try to jump all over me. We all walk out of the beneficio and into the sun, looking towards the coffee growing up and down the hills.] *This dog is crazy!*

Lukas really likes dogs; he's a master of all the animals. Yes, mi niña, *we've been through some tough times with the broca. You catch a breath for a minute and then it starts choking you again. But, gracias a Dios, we keep going. I don't know how we sustain ourselves, but somehow we always do. The one thing you can always do is make sure there aren't too many costs.*

Rachel: *During the peak harvest how many pickers do you have here?*

Aldemar: *At the height we probably have twenty-five, thirty. Because the property is divided up into so many little lots. Everyone who picks is paid by contract; the ones paid daily are the ones spraying, macheteing. Daily workers are the ones who spray, who prune. Every single picker is paid by contract. They're paid by [a fixed price per] kilo.*

Right now we're at 380 [Colombian pesos, equivalent to $0.21 at time of interview] per kilo. That's because there's been a huge lack of workers. Everywhere. Tolima, Quindio, Valle. People leave. Here the harvest in October is really easy. In October there are a lot of people to pick. But right now it's hard to find them.

There are people who come and the next week are gone. To find another finca. There are other people who stay with you for longer. You know there are people who like to always be on the move. And looking for the best money, because one finca has a lot of coffee, another doesn't, so people go. They leave. This is a big process. They'll leave if the coffee's not giving them an advantage.

Rachel: *Um hm. And what varieties are those?* [Pointing to the coffee on the hill in front of us]. *What types do you have on the finca?*

Aldemar: *We have Variedad Colombia. And we have a tiny, tiny bit of Caturro, you can see that lot over there that was pruned. And right now we're* *planting Variedad Castilla. We're cultivating a lot of that—on the other lots too. We have all kinds of coffee.*

Rachel: *For you, what part of the process do you like the most? What job do you like to do plant, prune, work in the beneficio?*

Aldemar: *I go with Lukas to check out the other fincas, and so I dedicate myself to* deschuponando *[selecting the emergent regrowths post-pruning]. That's what I'm doing right now. Any time I have, that's what I'm doing. But I have to be paying close attention to the guys I have spraying weeds, spraying the seedlings.*

Every year the Extensionists come according to the regulations to make a visit. They look and see how much coffee you've cut down, how much you've pruned. We don't invite them, every area just has their person from the Committee who gets sent.

Lukas comes down the muddy driveway, his German Shepard, Kaiser, at his heels. Once Kaiser has licked all our hands (and boots) and tried to leap up and lick my face, Aldemar, Lukas, and I set out to hike up to the top of the finca. It had just poured the night and early that morning, so everything is slick with mud. We zig zag through the various lots, peering down into the valleys and across to other hillsides where we can see moving dots that are people picking coffee.

Where does Aldemar's coffee go?

Lukas sells the finca's coffee to La Meseta. La Meseta exports it to roasters in over twenty countries around the world.

If you came from Gerardo and would like to return to Costa Rica, turn to p. 33

If you came from Felipe and would like to return to Panama, turn to p. 249

For a conversation with Aldemar's cousin, continue to the next page.

326

Hilberto

Recorded Thursday, May 16, 2013, at almost the highest point on Finca San Lukas, in the shadow of the radio towers of Chuscal.

Hilberto and I stand in the small grassy area in front of the house where a few finca employees live, almost at the top to the Chuscal mountain, which the finca runs up the side of. The dogs play around us and bark incessantly. Hilberto wears a brown plaid shirt.

Hilberto: *What can I say? We start by planting little coffee plants, really with the little seed, making seedbeds. And then we plant the little plants, and all the way to picking the cherries off the trees and everything.*

Rachel: *And on the finca you do all those jobs?*

Hilberto: *Yes, controlling the weeds, everything. Spraying, fertilizing, everything.*

Rachel: *And right now you're…*

Hilberto: *Picking. And spraying weeds too.*

Rachel: *And have you always worked in coffee or in something…*

Hilberto: *I've been here all my life. For a little bit I was living in Bogota, but all my life I've worked with coffee.*

Rachel: *You learned to do all the jobs by…?*

Hilberto: *As a kid my dad showed me. As a little kid I learned to do everything. To plant it and everything.*

Rachel: *And your family is from Chinchiná?*

Hilberto: *No, we're from Tolima. But now all my family lives in Bogota.*

Rachel: *Ok, in Tolima. And you're family of Aldemar?*

Hilberto: *Yes, we're cousins.*

Rachel: *And did you come up here at the same time he did?*

Hilberto: *No, he was here first. And then I came after as a picker, and then they gave me this finca, which I ended up administering, and now I'm administering both. This and the one below.*

Rachel: *Right, because Don Jorge's farms are all connected.*

Hilberto: *They're all connected. We're all like part of the same family; the fincas aren't separated one from another, rather they're all connected from here down.*

Rachel: *Of all the work you've done with coffee, what job has been the most difficult and what has been the biggest success?*

Hilberto: *The worst job? The worst job is to spray for broca. That's the worst job on the farm, the rest are good.*

Rachel: *And spraying* for broca is the worst because it's difficult, dangerous…?*

Hilberto: *Because…because it's the strongest poison we use.*

Rachel: *And the biggest success, out of all the work you've done?*

Hilberto: *This—all this. I'm still here and everything's working out well for me.*

Rachel: *And is there anything you think that people in New York who drink Colombian coffee should know about?*

Hilberto: *That we depulp coffee, dry it, and there you go. We bring it to the dry mill. At least that's the process I know. I don't know anything about freeze-dried. I just know coffee up until that point, when I sell it.*

Rachel: *I'm guessing you also have coffee in Tolima.*

Hilberto: *Yes, in Tolima we have a little finca. Coffee.*

Rachel: *And does all your family still live there, or here, or…?*

Hilberto: *No, they're all in Bogota.*

Rachel: *Well, this place is really enchanting.*

Hilberto: *Yeah, it's pretty nice here. Great house, great boss, really great owners. And that's why we've worked so well together for so long. But right now is it pretty hard with harvesting coffee. There aren't any workers. The majority of people who were here before have gone elsewhere. And you can hardly find anyone. So you do what you can with the people you have.* [We both turn and watch the dogs wrestling on the grass.] *And did you walk through all of the finca?*

Rachel: *We did! We started down at the bottom by Aldemar's house, and we climbed! I don't really know which lots we went through, but certainly a lot of them. Straight up the steep parts.*

Hilberto comments that this is nothing; parts of the finca have coffee planted on walls. He rallys the rest of the men and they head back into the cafetals.

If you came from Luis Angel and would like to return to Costa Rica, turn to p. 85

For a conversation with someone who sells agrochemicals, turn to the next page.

*Spraying can be a pretty rough job. Another employee who'd just eaten lunch with us was suiting back up to continue spraying the cafetales. He put on a facemask and a long, stiff silver apron that reached down to his feet. It reminded me of the mom sitting in the sun on the sidewalk in *Requiem for a Dream*. Or maybe those things they make you put on before getting x-rays. I wanted to ask him about his job, but Hilberto explained that he doesn't speak. During lunch I had seen him gesture to the woman cooking something about his eye, indicating that he wanted eye drops. Lukas said he'd bring them up the next day.

Julio Cesar

Recorded Wednesday, May 22, 2013, at the Almacén de Café by the Cathedral in downtown Manizales.

Sometimes being a twenty-five-year-old woman means people dismiss me. And sometimes it means people give me lots of free coffee and want to tell me every story they can think of just so they can keep talking to me, because it's not every day a young woman from New York with a strange Spanish accent wanders into the local hardware store and says, "Tell me what you know."

The Colombian *Almacenes de Café* (Coffee Warehouses) are essentially coffee growing supply stores selling agrochemicals, chainsaws, and those life saving black rubber boots (in Colombia called *botas pantaneras* which is the only name for "rubber boots" I've heard anywhere that makes them sound as vitally important as they are).

These Almacenes are run by the nation's network of coffee buying co-ops; they are in fact one of the services the co-op provides: *"Things you need for your finca at prices you can afford!"* You can put everything on your Cedula Cafetera super coffee grower ID/debit card, you can open interest-free lines of credit, and you can get advice from the staff agronomists who know the area, coffee, and you.

The Almacenes are some of my favorite places and like havens in the middle of new cities. They remind me of making Saturday trips to the hardware store with my dad; the shiny orange painted tools and the smells of rubber and fertilizer feel bizarrely familiar and like small town New Hampshire is somehow intimately similar to tropical coffee growing.

I love visiting the Almacenes because even when I show up for the first time, I feel like I'm visiting old friends. I just wait in line—if there is one, if not I just walk right up to the counter—and I start talking to the employees. I usually introduce myself as a "coffee journalist from New York," and ask, "What's going on? What are people doing on their fincas?" The people who work at the Almacenes interact with the area's coffeepeople all day every day, but they don't have to present any glossy figures or give any official report. They are the ideal sources for information because they have a ton of it, have no reason not to be candid, and have enough time to be human.

I visited the Almacén in Manizales on a cold, soggy afternoon right in between downpours. I was the only person in the place, and Julio Cesar and Juan Carlos were happy to oblige my odd requests and pull bottles of pesticides off the shelves, dig up paperwork, and even put a few files about sustainable farm management on my flash drive.

They offered me piping hot cups of coffee (served in my favorite "Café de Colombia" cup 'n' saucer), gave me a little Jet chocolate, and complimented my raincoat. They tried out a few English phrases and finally let me interview them with the simple premise of, "Can you tell me about what you do? What do you know?"

Julio Cesar cleared his throat, and prepared himself To Be Recorded. (If he'd had on a suit he would have dusted off his shoulders and straightened his tie). He wears a blue and green striped polo and a navy blue fleece vest.

Julio: *My name is Julio Cesar Obando Montoya, I'm an agronomical engineer. Right now I'm working for Colinagro [Colombian agrochemical supply company], but for four years I worked for the National Federation of Coffee Growers.*

The experiences I had with broca, here in Caldas, which you could say is part of the coffee growing belt of Colombia, have been mainly in the areas of broca management and sharing information with farmers about how to manage it.

One of the main controls we have to have to handle broca is an adequate recollection. It's one of the general principles we have, as producers, so that the broca doesn't attack too much and we don't have to spend so much [time and money] on chemical applications.

Secondly—wait! First, what does an adequate recollection consist of? Sorry! An adequate recollection consists of a group of pickers who principally emphasize picking first the ripe and then overripe cherries. Ideally we never get to the latter, overripe cherries. Ripe and overripe cherries, if we leave them on the tree or let them fall, constitute the principal habitat for broca.

Cherries left on trees will over ripen and fall off, making chemical controls more difficult, because they're directed at the tree not the ground. One cherry left on the ground can house more or less 121 individual broca, which

331

will be affecting the quality of my future harvests. Which is why we highly emphasize an adequate recollection.

The second process we have to employ to have adequate broca control in terms of work habits is the "re-re" [re-passing and re-collecting]. Which means making passes every fifteen days during harvest periods. Don't wait a month, a month and a half to go back to a lot and pick again. If so you'll have overripe cherries and cherries on the ground.

Another factor we have to have is that, in the process of recollection, the sacks stay closed. After the picker collects his cherries, and he gets to the beneficio where the cherries get depulped, he has to cover the sacks, because at this point broca can also escape.

There is an important document called "Brocarta [Broca Bulletin] 21." This document also indicates how to adequately manage broca when you renovate your cafetales. What does it consist of? When I renovate, if my finca has—just as an example—five thousand coffee plants, ideally I renovate [prune or uproot and replant] a thousand plants every year. So in five years I've renovated my whole finca.

When I renovate, I have to leave some "trap trees" in the lot, so that the broca living in the cherries on the ground will all go to those trees, so that then I can eliminate the broca culturally [pick cherries and burn/bury/drown them] or chemically [spray them]. This will help permit an adequate control of the broca. This is another principal activity.

Secondly, in the process of the beneficio, when the bean comes out in parchment paper for drying, you still need to keep everything covered so that any remaining brocas don't fly back into the cafetales. This is more or less one of the most important variables to have in mind for cultural management of broca.

In terms of biological controls, we've had some good experiences applying a product called Brocaril. It's a product that's made with a base of a fungus that feeds off the broca as a parasite; the base is beauvaria bassiana. Ideally you apply 100g per 200 liters of water. It is applied to the ground, given that the majority of broca are found—come from—the ground, where cherries have fallen.

This control is very effective during rainy seasons. During hotter periods is difficult to control by means of this fungus because it needs some humidity to perform its function. And, as such, sometimes you have to apply chemicals.

You have to take into account something very important; Colombian coffee is of bimodal character, meaning, you find the harvests concentrated in

332

two peaks. One in the first trimester, one in the second. In the first trimester, when is the period of harvest? In May. May is the harvest period. In the second trimester, when is the period of harvest? Between October and November. The principal harvest in almost all of Caldas is in October. But there are regions where the main harvest is in May, and so we refer to them as "May fincas," where the main harvest, sixty percent, is in May.

Now, what do we call these two harvests? The harvest in May is called la traviesa *[the naughty, mischievous (tricky) one]. There's less concentration, and the other is called "the main harvest." And in these two periods is when the major broca controls take place.*

Rachel: *You mentioned leaving a few trees as "traps?" Is that common—to leave trees when you renovate? To attract them?*

Julio: *Exactly. The idea is that after I uproot or prune [down to stumps] all the trees in a lot, for a new planting, the trees that I'm chopping down are old and probably have a few cherries on them, which will end up on the ground, very attractive to the broca. When these broca emerge, they'll immediately head for other lots where everything isn't chopped down. So ideally, the idea is to leave a few trees standing within the cleared lot, so that they lure the broca. Ideally, well, you're supposed to do it. This is from ICA [Colombian Department of Agriculture]. A finca that doesn't do it can be sanctioned by ICA. This is part of the work of renovating. It's also in Brocarta 21, which you can find online.*

Rachel: *Hm. I've never seen anyone do it… Okay, so if you're recollecting all the cherries from the ground, which I've done and they're always super full of broca, what do you do with them? Burn them? Bury them? Drown them?*

Julio: *Ideally, these cherries are buried. That's the ideal. So that they don't reproduce more in our cafetales. It can be a hole half a meter deep.*

Rachel: *Before your work with Colinagro, what job did you have at the FNC?*

Julio: *I was an agronomical engineer with the Federation, as a Technical Extensionist.*

Rachel: *With a yellow shirt!*

Julio: *Exactly. I had a zone here in Caldas, one of the principal coffee zones; it's about half an hour from here, from Manizales. I was responsible for a big zone, five veredas. The Extension Services fills the function of transmitting the knowledge and investigations of Cenicafe to the coffee growers.*

So I had to train the caficultores on things like managing broca, managing roya—chemical dosages, how to make community almacigueros, demonstrations of methodologies, days on the fincas, meetings, all that.

Rachel: *At that point was Castillo around?*

Julio: *Yes, at this point… the truth is that Castillo has been around this part of the country for a while. Colombia has its varieties: we have a very low percentage of traditional varieties, like Bourbon, that are more "original" Arabicas. They're taller, you plant them farther apart, but they're very, very susceptible to roya. So these varieties were changed for Caturro. Caturro is shorter, gives a good harvest, but was still susceptible to the roya.*

After these, the Variedad Colombia variety came out. This variety is a mix between the Caturro variety and the Híbrido de Timor. The Híbrido de Timor is a variety from the island of Timor. It's a variety, that during a period when roya attacked the island, was one little tree that wasn't affected, so they studied it and found it was resistant to roya. So they made crosses, and, through phyto-improvement methods, came up with the Variedad Colombia. And this variety fulfilled a very important initial function in Colombia in terms of managing roya through genetic resistance.

Now, as we talk about "resistance," and not about "immunity," they started creating the resistance of this variety, and with respect to different changes, like those in the environment and the climate, it started to loose its resistance. A few years ago, Cenicafe came out with a super resistant variety, called Variedad Castillo.

Castillo is the same mix of Híbrido de Timor and Caturro, but in this case there are eleven parents of Híbrido de Timor, and the F5 was taken from that mix. It's a very resistant variety. There are also different varieties of the variety for different agroclimatic conditions. Castillo Naranjal, Castillo Rosario—which you see a lot in Antioquia [I did], Castillo Generico.

Part of my job was working with Castillo; it's an excellent variety. It's shorter, with longer branches; it has a bigger cherry. It's a variety that continues conserving the quality of our coffee, which is a mild coffee with an excellent quality, because it comes from the acidity characteristic of Arabica. It's a mild coffee, Excelso, of good quality, with a good cup.

Rachel: *And what do you think that the people in the United States who are drinking this excellent Colombian coffee should know about it?*

Julio: *I think that it's important that they, the people in the United States, know about coffee for several reasons. First reason: there's an entire world of culture surrounding coffee.*^{Agriculture p. 372} *Because we were born into a coffee cradle. The first thing we do every day is work to produce an excellent final product for the most discerning palates.*

We also produce specialty coffees, which are high quality. And we don't even get to drink them so that people in other countries can! There's the case of Nespresso, which has its AAA program. Only ten percent* of the coffee in the world is high quality, and Nespresso wants all ten!

What we drink here is honestly a bunch of pasilla, which could never even be considered good coffee [I disagree. I happen to think that the Colombian coffee I drank for $0.25 in little restaurants all over the country is actually much better than your average NYC deli coffee.]

Second, because we have a strong world of coffee culture, like that all the pickers depend on coffee [to live], lots of people depend on coffee, the economy of this zone depends completely on coffee, we're doing all of the work along the way thinking of quality.

And third because the quality in the cup identifies our coffee as one of the best in the world.

Rachel: *I agree. I'm very much enjoying drinking Colombian coffee in Colombia!*

Julio: *I'm glad!* [I move to turn off the recorder.] *When I show up on ESPN make sure you let me know…*

I let out a belly laugh. Standing in a pair of soggy sneakers and equally soggy jeans (which is the only pair I have to my name at that point), I say that my work and I probably won't make it to network television any time soon. But I do promise that I will give him a copy of the book in which his interview appears. He smiles, commenting that a bestselling coffee book is kind of like ESPN. I laugh again and he offers me another cup of coffee. As I finish drinking it, he reminds me not to forget my umbrella. I look out at the downpour and thank him.

If you came from Fabio and would like to return to Costa Rica, turn to p. 67

For a conversation with a Panamanian agronomist, turn to p. 217

To visit cafetales clear on the other side of Colombia, turn to the next page.

*don't take his word on that. Coffee stats are slippery eels on their best days, and a source like SCAA (Specialty Coffee Association of America) would probably be a more reliable one.

Huila

Hulia is perhaps Colombia's most star-studded coffee growing Department. Every year, the Cup of Excellence program awards more and more top places to coffees coming from Huila. The national Cup of Excellence programs, active in contries throughout Central and South America, invites coffee producers of all sizes to submit lots of their best coffee to be scored by an international panel of cupping judges. Something in the water (or volcanic soil, or microclimates) in Huila makes for especially superb coffee. The region crops up on most single origin menus offering Colombian coffees and is becoming trendier by the day.

Huila is a long (fourteen plus hours) drive south from Caldas, and the highways pass through dizzying mountains and flat, naked desserts. Part of the department itself is desert around the city of Neiva, but the heart of the Huilan coffee lands is the small city of Pitalito.

Pitalito is on the valley floor, and, as is the case with so many coffee towns, the coffee producing hills climb up on all sides around the town, forming a bowl of skirtfolds from the surrounding mountains. Huila may be far from Antioquia, but when you get up into the coffee mountains you can still see from ridge to ridge, watch cars trace the spines of the mountains, and gaze out onto the layers of mountains that fade one onto the other until they're muted by distance. Maybe it's Olympus over there in the haze, or maybe it's just more folded land, ^{Folded Land, p. 363} producing more things to eat and drink.

The small town of San Agustin, about half an hour outside of Pitalito, is home to stone artifacts and ruins, hailing from a time far before the ships that would carry coffee through imperial trade routes were even a dream. Today's coffee grows in the shadows and dust of yesteday's deities.

338

Miller

Recorded Sunday, May 26, 2013, in the car en route to Miller's finca La Esperanza in San Isidro.

It was a Sunday so all the community buildings in the tiny village of San Isidro were shut tight as people spent the day at home with their families. Miller brought me up to the cluster of buildings anyway, partly so that he could show off the new building that combines safe storage for agrochemicals with a composting facility, and partly so he could unlock the dilapidated garage across from the school so that the guy who'd be turning the garage into an additional classroom for the school could take measurements.

En route to the little vereda Miller described the work the San Isidro Association had done with the Fairtrade premiums they'd earned. Being a small association and not a massive co-op, they have only one hundred members and therefore everyone gets to put in his and her two cents about what the Fairtrade premiums should be allocated for. Miller told me that so far the association has used the money to bring in a dental hygienist to peform check ups, to help add grades to the local school such that the vereda's first four high school graduates earned their diploma's this year, and to put up half the money to pay for an FNC Extensionist to work exclusively with members of the association, versus having to share him with thousands of other caficultores. The FNC funds the other half of the cost, and Miller expressed the hope that they'd be able to continue the arrangement for a second year.

The car weaves up the hillside, coffee trees flying past on both sides. Miller wears a white polo.

Miller: *My name is Miller Otoya and I'm a caficultor from the region of San Isidro. I've been a coffee grower for the past eleven years that I've lived in this region, eleven years growing coffee here. But I was born and raised in this region; I went to school here, finished high school, and went to Bogota to continue my studies. Twenty years later, I took the initiative to come back to my father's finca and support my family in their coffee growing.*

From here I was able to, a little later, become a member of Grupo Asociativo de San Isidro, which, when I joined, had been together for just over twenty years. Little by little, I took on leadership roles, according to the goals the group had. And not long after, I was part of the executive committees. And a year and a half ago, the organization took the initiative to create the role of general manager, and they have entrusted this responsibility to represent them, the members of the Asociación San Isidro, to me.

Rachel: *And did you study agronomy or finance or something that…*

Miller: *When I finished my high school diploma I was a little bit unsure of what I wanted to pursue, and there wasn't much money, and I started studying agronomy, but couldn't continue because there weren't enough resources at the time. It turned out it was easier, a little bit later, to study business administration. I have a degree in Business Administration.*

But after I came back and became a part of the coffee growing industry, I went to study Coffee Production. I finished a course in Coffee Production two years ago, and now I'm finishing another course in Sustainable Growing Technologies.

Rachel: *And you said the farm was your father's?*

Miller: *Yes, I came back to my father's farm, and a little bit after he split up the finca between his five children. And between ourselves, we bought pieces. Today, I administer the farm, including the properties belonging to two more brothers. I also bought another farm, close by, and so I also manage that. I have employees who work on the farm, and my wife helps me administer everything. And that's how we work.*

Rachel: *How many hectares do you have in total?*

Miller: *I have two fincas of five hectares.*

Rachel: *And of all the work you've done, what has been the most challenging and what has been the biggest success?*

Miller: *I think that the challenge, and what today I'm most passionate about, is caficultura. It's what motivatd me to study and now I'm constantly thinking about how I can train myself more, for the responsibility I have as manager of the organization, to be able to support this important organization, which today characterizes itself as a national—and international leader—among producers of high quality coffee.*

Rachel: *And the biggest success?*

Miller: *The biggest success, I'd say, is… to have been able to… one second* [picks up ringing phone] *Excuse me. Today, of all the important achievements…there are business developments, representations of the organization on national and international levels. I've had the opportunity to visit Los Angeles, Chicago, and this year I went to Boston for the SCAA fair.*

One feels satisfied that year after year, since 2005, we've been able to participate in the Colombian Cup of Excellence. And we've never won first place, but various members of San Isidro have been in the Top Ten of the Cup of Excellence.

Rachel: *Congratulations! Is there anything else you'd like people who drink your coffee—or at least coffee from Huila—to know?*

Miller: *Yes. Our coffee, for what it is, has been able to captivate national consumers as much as international ones, and it has characterized itself— from in the middle of many coffees—for some sensory profile that marks the difference. It has some herbal, floral notes, high acidity, good body, and…and an aftertaste that sets it apart and characterizes it as coffee from Huila, from Acevedo, known for a profile typical of San Isidro.* [Pause. We both gaze out windows to the sprawling coffee landscape. It's a brilliantly sunny day, with a true blue sky and all the waxy coffee leaves shining. Zig zag highways hug the sides of the mountains, zig zag foot paths climb their way up.]

And from here, from this point on, we're in the Municipality of Acevedo. This mountain, that we see from here, and those over there, are natural reserves that have been saved through the work done by Asociacion San Isidro. Some 300 hectares of forest have been part of studies of oaks, of various birds…all studies done in these mountains.

Rachel: *It's a forest reserve, meaning no one can cut anything down?*

Miller: *Correct. Between us all we take care of it, this reserve. We don't permit anyone to cut down a single tree inside these mountains.*

This is the last farm I visit on my odyssey. The following day I picked 38 kilos (83 pounds) of coffee with four other workers at La Esperanza. By far my personal best but a mere drop in the coffee bucket. I was lucky enough to be picking on a gorgeous sunny day, and the clear, cloudless sky let me gaze at all the surrounding fincas, since we were picking at the highest point on the property.

After a full day of picking my basketfuls yielded a full sack, and perhaps the most daunting part of picking coffee is getting that picked coffee from the heights of the cafetal back down to the beneficio. The men hoisted their sacks full of cherries onto their backs and nimbly trotted down the narrow, vertical path (at least it wasn't slick with mud). I stared at my sack and knew I would not be hoisting it onto my back and nimbly trotting down anything. I started to drag it, and Adrian, Miller's finca manager, just laughed at me, grabbed my full scak by one hand, and hoisted it on top of his sack that was already on his back. Loaded with two sacks, each at least 80lbs, he trotted nimbly down the path in front of me. This is what they original cross fit looks like.

Where does Miller's coffee go?
The Associative Group of San Isidro sells some of its Fairtrade certified coffee via direct trade to Caffe Vita of Seattle, who also recently opened up a hole-in-the wall roaster/coffee shop on Manhattan's Lower East Side.

If you came from Santiago and would like to continue to Costa Rica, turn to p. 121

If you came from Roberto and would like to return to Los Santos, turn to p. 149

If you came from Susy and would like to continue to San Marcos, turn to p. 168

For more thoughts and observations from my coffee odyssey, turn to the next page.

Appendix

The following are posts excerpted from content on whencoffeespeaks.com, the blog I maintained during my nine months of traveling. They are presented in chronological order.

Coffee 101: Coffee Survey Answers

Coffee grows on trees covered with shiny, waxy green leaves. Depending on the varietal of coffee, the trees can be between three and eight feet tall. Higher quality coffee (Arabica) comes from smaller trees, lower quality (Robusta, used for blends) comes from trees that are often twice the size of Arabicas.

The beans that we see when we buy roasted whole bean coffee grow inside a small fruit known as coffee cherries. The cherries grow along the branches of the coffee tree. They start out green, and once they turn dark red, they're mature enough to be harvested.

Coffee grows literally around the world, in what is known as the "coffee belt," spanning the equator between the tropics of Cancer and Capricorn. (Think Southern Mexico to Bolivia). It *can* grow in other places with lots of encouragement, but the only places it's grown commercially fall around the earth's wide waist.

Meaning it's grown predominately in Central and South America, Africa, and parts of Asia. It is not grown anywhere in the continental US, but it is grown in Hawaii. Technically, it's grown in North America because there are coffee farms in southern Mexico, but that's the only place on the continent. There are a few commercial farms in Australia but a globally negligible amount.

The world's top two producers are Brazil (40% of world's production) and Vietnam, whose production exploded as a result of reconstruction investments from France post Vietnam War. African coffee comes predominately from Uganda, Kenya, Rwanda, and Ethiopia, the birthplace of coffee. Some gourmet coffee is still grown in Yemen. India also exports lots of Robusta for blends. Currently, Jamaica is not a major producer, but their Blue Mountain coffee made a name for itself. The Pacific Islands are home to many gourmet coffees, most notably Indonesian Sumatra. Many exporting nations are working with minimal infrastructure and technology, so market info and trading stats don't necessarily show the whole picture of production. Part of the coffee "game" is also storing quantities in warehouses and waiting for market prices to be just right before buying/selling.

Even though Europe purchases and consumes a massive portion of the coffee grown worldwide (Finland and Norway jockey for highest annual national per capita consumption), no coffee grows there. No Italian espresso actually comes from Italy. The climate just doesn't support it.

The most important climatic restriction for coffee is that it can never see temperatures below freezing. Even a day or two of frost can severely damage or kill a plant. Because coffee plants produce for up to forty years and are not uprooted after each harvest, one frost can disrupt the entire life span of the plant. Coffee's second demand is consistent rainfall. It won't grow in desert climates.

Robusta and some Arabica varietals can take full sun, but many Arabica varietals prefer shade. Coffee sucks up lots of nitrogen from the soil, so shade grown coffee benefits from fertilization by decomposing leaves falling from other vegetation as well as partial shielding from the sun.

Robusta coffee grows at low altitudes and in flat spaces (much more similarly to other industrial agriculture crops), but Arabica needs the cooler temperatures found at higher elevations in order for its sugars to develop slowly, completely and complexly. Arabica particularly thrives in volcanic soils, making South and Central America ideal commercial growing locations for a crop native to the other side of the world.

Soil composition directly affects the flavor of coffee, so anything that affects the soil indirectly affects the flavor. Coffee coming from rainier regions is distinctly different from that grown in sunny regions. Soils at different altitudes have different make ups, and interplanted species deposit different organic matter (leaves, flowers, bugs) into the soil to decay, thus affecting the overall soil composition and "food" the coffee plant takes in.

Unless coffee says specifically where it's from, there's a good chance it's a blend of Arabica and Robusta, Robusta being the filler, Arabica bringing the flavor. Most Robusta comes from Brazil, with Vietnam offering up more and more every year. Companies like Folgers, Maxwell House, and Dunkin Donuts constantly adjust where they buy from based on price and availability in order to maintain a consistent flavor. Even coffee that's labeled by country comes from numerous places. Colombia is a big place, so is Kenya, so coffee labeled "Colombian" or "Kenyan" will include beans from all parts of the country.

345

"Gourmet" roasters/cafés/vendors are now selling "estate coffees," meaning all the beans in the bag came from the same single farm.

Coffee is a truly international product in that it's either grown, processed, or sold between almost every single country on earth. If you drink decaf it's likely that it was sent to Mexico, Canada, Switzerland, or Germany to be stripped of its caffeine. Some coffees are roasted "at origin" near where they're grown, but most U.S. distributors buy "green" unroasted beans and roast them according to a carefully calculated formula to maintain a distinct brand flavor.

As you can see, there are no simple answers to any questions about coffee. Grounds for thought over your next cup!

Posted October 3, 2012

Pura Montaña

After Gerardo and I had toured the rows of coffee and the sugarcane planted above, Gerardo still felt like he hadn't shown me anything worth seeing, so he offered to take me up to the top of the mountain to a cow pasture that looked down onto the town where we'd all gone for the *futbol* game last weekend. Never one to turn down a good jaunt through the jungle, I nodded, "*Si, por supuesto!*"

Turns out, we were both unprepared. I was quickly reminded of the two cardinal rules of the jungle 1) never leave home without your snake/mud proof rubber boots. (You might end up knee-deep in the jungle.) 2) Never leave home without your machete. (You might end up knee-deep in the jungle. Where you might run into someone else with a machete).

I was only wearing sneakers and shorts. The coffee rows are not particularly rugged, and the roads up and down the mountain to the farm are actually in pretty good shape; sneakers were certainly sufficient. I also see weekends as a welcome vacation from my boots (which are like wearing Goodyear tires on your feet. One of the other volunteers on the cow farm calls

346

them my "Batman boots" because they have a yellow strip along the bottom.) I really hadn't considered wearing them. But, after the rows of sugarcane ends, the *"pura montaña"* starts. We were following a "path," which was essentially the route someone had cleared with a machete once upon a time, (watch out for the poisonous spiders that build webs between the trees!) But, the ground of the "path" was the same as in the rest of the jungle— still the ever sliding mud that I'd experienced on my last *pura montaña* excursion. Not only were my sneakers far from ideal for trying to leap from slippery rock to slippery rock, but my exposed legs were being pretty much massacred by all the slicing leaves and mosquitos and biting fighter ants (which I learned today are called *chopas*). I was actually not bothered by that, as long as a snake didn't attack me at the ankles.

At a few points as we climbed I thought I heard cracking branches or falling vines behind me, but here everything sounds like footsteps, rain plopping on *malanga* leaves or especially dead banana leaves brushing against the trunk of a banana tree. I was mostly focused on not stepping on all the malicious snakes that were surely waiting to get me in this vulnerable moment. A few times Gerardo turned around to make sure I was alive, commenting things like, "Sweating like this is good; that's why people have little holes in in their skin- so all the fat can come out," or, "If you did this every day you'd be so skinny when you get home that no one will recognize you— like a Barbie!"

Finally, the ground leveled out and we saw a pile of cow dung, so I figured we were near the picturesque pasture. As soon as we turned to follow the cow tracks, we heard what were definitively crashing footsteps, a machete slashing through jungle growth, and a man's loud shout. Gerardo turned to me, "Eh, that must be the owner of the land that joins ours. Sometimes he's ok with us using his path…but sometimes he gets mad." The man shouted again, and Gerardo shouted back, something like, "Hey there neighbor!" About six seconds later, the jungle to our right started to fall away, and a man emerged onto the path, machete brandished. My first thought was of General Zaroff.

This jungle was not *pura montaña*; it had nothing on this guy. HE was *pura montaña*. I thought the men who worked on the finca were gritty campesinos, and they are, but this guy was an entirely different level of rural. I've read literary descriptions of things as "sinewy," but this guy was in fact the definition of sinewy. Lifetime outdoor labor-tanned skin stretched tight over lean muscle, but mostly sinew, stuck out of his grungy sleeveless t-shirt. I could see every tendon of his arm articulated as he swung his machete to slash away a vine. A threadbare red bandana was tied around the back of his neck and a flattened straw cowboy hat hung against his back. He had a scraggly gray mustache and a scragglier, grayer head of hair. His face was all creases of even tanner skin, with light, darting eyes.

Behind him were his sons. The first to emerge was probably fiften and looked like the psycho kid in every movie I've ever seen (think the one who kills the dog in *The Butterfly Effect*). He immediately thrust his machete into the mud as he stepped onto the path and glowered through a thick black unibrow. The second was probably ten, also wielding a good 16-inch machete, but he didn't have quite the poker face of the other two. The instant he saw me his jaw dropped, and for the duration of the conversation between Gerardo and the mountain man, he stood and gawked at probably the last thing in the world he ever expected to see on the cow path at the top of the mountain: a gringa wearing shorts, sneakers, and an orange LL Bean fanny pack.

Gerardo immediately identified himself to the man as Jose's nephew, which seemed like a good line to open with. The guy was pretty much calm as soon as he saw who we were, because the first thing he said was, "I thought you were the hunters!!" Quite clearly, I'm not hunting anything. They had a conversation I couldn't quite follow about what Jose was doing lately, the evil hunters who've been on this guy's land (although hunting what I couldn't catch), and someone selling off pieces of a nearby farm. Gerardo gained his blessing for us to take pictures in his pasture, and we turned down the path.

A few (muddy) minutes later, we climbed through the barbed wire and into what really was a beautiful pasture, made even more beautiful by the fact that it was surrounded by the starkly contrasting *pura montaña*. As I clicked the last frame of my 360 panorama and took the camera away from my face, I saw the younger son standing three feet in front of me. By now he'd managed to close his mouth. He just looked at me. Without taking his eyes off me, he swung his machete back and forth, just slicing the top off of the short pasture grass. It was like a slow motion Western scene, so I gave him a look that clearly said, "Don't worry, I know who wins this fight." Gerardo turned around and, surprised, paused before asking about the weather. The boy then escorted us out of the pasture, leisurely swinging his machete and slicing the grass as he went.

After making sure that we did indeed start down the "path" back toward Gerardo's farm, he disappeared in the other direction. All I could think to myself was, "Holy shit. Those guys are the real deal. People who don't work for a gringo, who don't sell stuff to tourists, who haven't heard of Britney Spears, and who live every single day to make sure that their land is protected and productive." This is the jungle, and if you own the land in the jungle, you have to *own* the jungle. Those kids are not being raised to do their homework and brush their teeth before bed; they're being raised to keep hunters (and ill-clad gringas?) off their land.

Living in New York and selling large slices of one's soul every month for a 10' x 15' room, we tend to forget what it means to lay claim to land. Laying claim to the corner of a mildewy fifth floor walk up is hard enough; establishing ownership of the jungle is far from a picnic.

As the trail looped back to the farm, there were several excellent photo ops; I could even see the house where I was staying in little cluster of buildings known as Esperanza nestled below. Gerardo certainly felt that he had shown me something more interesting than coffee. My sneakers and ankles were entirely caked with mud, but Gerardo's mother still invited me in the house for lunch (leftovers, we'd been gone longer than expected). While I munched on *arroz con verduras*, I thought about my earlier prediction. I had been partially right; Gerardo had wanted to talk about something less trivial than soccer uniforms and less romantic than living with the rhythms of the earth. He wanted to show me, a foreign visitor, something he deemed more worthy of tourism than boring, mundane coffee plants. I still happen to think that coffee plants are cool, but I certainly did see something out of the ordinary, even for Costa Rica. I think it's a safe bet to say that plenty of people living in San Jose and working for Pfizer have probably never run into anyone holding a machete.

But if you drink coffee you need coffee farmers. And you need coffee farms. For that, you need land. And to own land, you should probably have a machete. Because your neighbors do. And they have sons.

Posted September 19, 2012

Trampa

Trampa— (n. f.) trap, snare. *Hacer trampas.* To cheat.

Farmers can't cheat. If stuff doesn't grow, stuff doesn't grow. At pretty much any point later in the supply chain of any agricultural commodity someone can be paid less, corners can but cut, costs can be reduced to increase profits. But when you're dealing with coaxing consumables from the loins of the earth, you can't cheat anyone or anything to get more. Yes, fertilizers and chemicals can be used to increase yields, or they can be eliminated to cut costs, but at the end of the day you don't have control.

Sure, farmers could add sand to grain bags or leaves and twigs to coffee bushels to juke their production stats, but at the end of the day farmers can't fake what the earth produces. It's risky business knowing you're simply not in control and never will be. Yes, significant sway can be exercised, but the final say still is still out of human hands. Which is a little bit daunting and scary.

Thursday I picked coffee with the Aguilars. Some trees just didn't have many leaves or cherries, while those around them were full of foliage and fruit. Why? That little patch of soil just didn't have as much nutrients. Rain washed away the good stuff. Wind blew away the good stuff. Animals and insects ate the good stuff. If you get stuck on "why?" you'll go crazy. There are too many reasons. But one row over the plants had been looking feeble, so Geraldo put a bunch of manure, leaves, and twigs all around the roots and between the rows. Now the plants boast big, juicy, ripe cherries. People aren't in control, but they do make a difference.

The response to not being in total command is not to say, "Oh well. That just means I won't do anything. Why bother?" The response is to keep trying things. Sometimes they'll work, sometimes they won't. But you keep trying. Because sometimes they do.

*for more thoughts on believing in coffee, turn to "In Coffee We Trust" on p. 356.

Posted October 11, 2012

If the Suit Fits...

Some people talk about getting stuck in jobs they hate, about ending up in a field in which they have no interest. That's a little bit of a misnomer. If you don't do your job well you won't be stuck there for long. To be stuck in a given line of work you at least have to be somewhat good at it.

However, it is true that by being just good enough you can spend a long time in a job that has little relation to your skills, talents, and interests. I've met quite a few people who work in fields from foodservice to education who do their jobs, get done what needs to get done, and have no affinity for any of what they do every day.

That is not the case with coffee. I've spent the past 48 hours trying to decide what made the two coffee conferences at which I spent the last two weeks so fundamentally different than all other "work events" and conferences I've ever been to. I think I've got it. Everyone who works in coffee is impeccably suited to their jobs.

David Neumann says coffee is not for the weak of heart, and he's right. It's not easy at any level, and it's not a place you'll end up if you're only "ok" at what you do. Every single trader, banker, exporter, roaster, farmer, chemist, geneticist, agronomist, and processor I've met seemed to be tailor-made for his or her coffee job.

Not only are the coffee people I've met suited to their jobs, they're practiced at them. Maybe because I have a

351

background in dance, but I inadvertently watch how people move. And I can tell how deeply people's work is ingrained in them by the way they carry themselves. Muscle memory doesn't lie.

For evolutionary reasons our tools have had to become extensions of ourselves in order for us to survive, and nothing reveals as much about people's knowledge, skills, and history as how they manage their tools.

When I first arrived in Costa Rica I headed straight for a mountain farm. There I worked in the vegetable gardens and was daily impressed to speechlessness by the way the men worked with machetes. They could chop down banana trees, cut the cow grass, clear a path through dense jungle, whittle branches into spears, and even peel an orange with an effortless grace and skill. They manipulated their tool as naturally as they manipulated their own limbs.

Not all tools have to have blades to be wielded with sharp precision. At the two conferences in San Jose I was reminded how an iPhone can become a part of a person. People often put "iPhone" at the top of the list of things they could never live without, and, as a tool that connects a man to his business, it does in fact represent a means of ensuring a livelihood. Watching the way these traders and CEOs handled their phones, literally watching the pattern of movement form pocket to palm to ear, observing the micromovements necessary to effectively use a touch screen proved just how practiced they are with their tool. I could tell that these guys use their phones as many hours a day as the men on the farm use their machetes.

Maybe it seems like using a cell phone wouldn't be that noticeable or remarkable of a pattern of movement. But think about when your grandparents try to use a touch screen phone. I've often watched people with a generation or two on me put the phone on the table in front of them, scowl at it, and peck at it like it's about to explode. The subtle ways in which people connect with their tools, literally fit them into their hands, reveals exactly how much consistent repetition they have in using them.

Muscle memory is infinitely fascinating; there is so much our bodies can do without any input from our consciousness. Muscle memory is the reason why I can touch type, why my friends can play the piano and the guitar, why top chefs can get their mise en plase ready with primetime-worthy speed and precision. When you do something enough you can stop thinking about it. But getting to the point where muscle memory takes over takes time and practice.

I find one of the most fascinating parts of spending time in a new culture to be discovering what muscle memories are necessary to make that culture tick.

For example, Lucy told me about her work as an *envueltadora*, a coffee seedling wrapper. Her job no longer exists, but when she was younger she worked on hillside coffee seedling plantations. She and other women would sit in rows and wrap the root balls of uprooted coffee seedlings in sugarcane leaves for transportation to farms. For hours a day, six days a week, she would perform the same motion to tie the leaves around the baby plants.

Even though this was over thirty years ago, as she described her work, she mimed the motion with her hands, and from that miming I could tell how many hours, days, weeks, months she had spent wrapping coffee plants. People use the phrase, "I can feel it in my bones" to imply instinct, and I propose that we should start saying, "I know it in my muscles" to imply a knowledge that is far from superficial, knowledge that can only come from sheer volume of time and the intimate relationship of practice.

Evidence of just how much we can know something in our muscles is most apparent by contrast. At first glance it might not seem like that waitress is doing anything special, but as soon as you try to pick up those five plates and whisk them off the table the way she did, you realize it actually takes some skill. Watching dads play with their daughters and try to put the clothes on a doll, it's instantly evident that this is not what dad does all day. He is awkward and slow and has to think about how in the world to wrestle with the tiny armholes of the dress. When you compare someone who has the advantage of muscle memory to someone doing that same task for the first time, it is indisputable that our muscles have a mind of their own, an involuntary inventory of finesse.

Observing muscle memory in action, noticing the deep ingraining of motion into people's nervous systems, might even be the most impressive aspect of travel. Watching Costa Rican grandmothers make tortillas is as stunning as watching ballerinas pirouette; both exercise the art of knowing a movement so completely and so perfectly as to execute it immaculately every time. In theory picking coffee is simple and easy; you pull a ripe cherry off a branch. But I've watched lifelong pickers in action, and what they are doing is not simple; it is an individual art particular to cultures that cultivate coffee. Every picker has his or her certain way of manipulating the branches, of using every finger, armpit, chin, shoulder to navigate the tree and remove the fruit as efficiently as possible. This is not something you learn in a day. And it is anything but easy.

People can dress up in different clothes and adopt new accents, but muscle memory doesn't lie, and our movements will always communicate what we're still learning and what we really, truly, know.

Posted November 21, 2012

Shapes of Coffeespace

The goal of *When Coffee Speaks* is to share the stories that coffee growers (and other coffeepeople) have been generous enough to share with me, so I'm constantly recording conversations. Some people get very, um, well, just rather… careful knowing that I'm recording what they say. But there are some things you can't hide whether you keep your mouth open or shut.

One is the use of space.

Lots of things about coffee are fuzzy, some tending towards downright scuzzy, but at Co-opedota the use of space is clear, completely unique, and utterly fascinating.

What first hinted to me that something different is going on here was the flash on my camera. Usually when I go to take pictures inside *beneficios* in the bright light of a Costa Rican morning (decidedly the best hours for taking pictures anywhere in the country are between 7 and 9am), the flash on my camera automatically pops open. Because even though the sun is shining, the interior of the beneficios is normally dark. I don't like the translation of beneficio to "mill," and less accurate would be "factory" or "plant," but beneficios do encompass the industrial qualities of those words, and therefore they also embody the dank ceaseless churning that goes with doing anything industrially. But at Co-opedota the beneficio is built in a way that involves significant amounts of natural light (perhaps as a contributing factor to their title of first certified carbon neutral coffee ever), and I could shoot the machinery without a flash.

The physical space that Coopedota occupies continued to set itself apart and to indicate the relationships among people involved in the co-op and the values of the co-op as a business.

The next morning was the culminating barista "test" for the fifteen high school students completing a two-year course on coffee, seed to cup, run through the Co-op in conjunction with the local high school. The test, a competition against the clock and each other, followed the international barista challenge rules, with spotless espresso machines and elaborate place settings for the four espressos, four cappuccinos, and four original recipe drinks each "contestant" must prepare within the fifteen minute time limit. But instead of being held in a hotel conference center, restaurant event hall, or even school auditorium, it was held in the dry mill section of the beneficio, in the immediate shadow of silos storing coffee beans in parchment. The projector screen was propped in front of where the hard hats hung, and behind the espresso machines loomed the dormant coffee hulling and sorting machinery. Call it unconventional, but perhaps there's no more fitting space in which to prepare gourmet coffee drinks than in a place where you can't forget how many earlier steps are necessary to make that espresso possible.

While they prepared their drinks for evaluation, the students stored their backpacks in the same cupping lab that transnational corporate representatives use to taste microlots when they visit the Co-op. The lab is also used to hold cupping and quality courses for which co-op members can sign up, and, similar to the high school program, learn more about the technical sides of the product they grow, from ground to grounds.

Above the cupping lab, the Co-op runs a cafeteria, which has a large window looking into the dry mill below and down onto the same silos storing beans. The menu offers gourmet drinks equivalent to any café in New York or Europe, the majority prepared by employees who graduated from the same barista prep course whose newest graduates I watched that morning. Producers, after turning in their coffee cherries to the mill, often come into the cafeteria- clad in muddy boots, stained jeans, and sweaty hats- and no one bats an eye. They might enjoy a cappuccino with fellow growers, made from the coffee they grew, at the table next to the co-op CEO, who's meeting with international clients.

The Co-op's main agronomist has his office in the Co-op's hardware store, adjacent to the *beneficio*. When producers come in to stock up on supplies they can peek their heads in to ask questions or just say hi. His office door is only waist high.

Tracing the equitable distribution of funds through the veins of a co-op is one of the places where coffee starts to get fuzzy, but the use of space at Co-opedota demonstrates the ease and comfort with which participants in all activities of the Co-op moved between spaces often segregated and staunchly maintained as separate in businesses operating under a more hierarchical corporate structure.

Coffee warehouse as community center. Local factory as interdisciplinary education hub. Fertilizer aisle as collective troubleshooting forum. Not only are such division-defying models possible, they're thriving as real uses of coffeespace.

Posted December 13, 2012

In Coffee We Trust

If your coffee comes with a tag of organic or fair trade or single origin, do you believe it? If you do, who does that mean you're trusting?

No matter how direct trade gets, coffee drinkers in the United States will never be able to watch how their coffee is grown and processed. It always happens far away. And even if we go there once, we aren't always there.

Which means people can tell us whatever they want about the coffee we drink, and it's up to us to decide whom we believe.

We can go to the grocery store and buy a can that says "100% Colombian," and we have to decide if we trust the company that labeled it as such. But we probably care about the label in the first place because we want the coffee to taste a certain way, not because we have a particular concern about whether or not every bean was actually grown in a certain country. It's not hard to believe the label because we can confirm its claim when we taste it. We're trusting something we can more or less measure, not a set of principles about which we feel conviction.

But if we do have convictions about principles of sustainable agriculture, we can look one shelf up and reach for a bag that has the USDA logo on it and claims to be certified organic. Which means that now it's not just the brand making a claim, a third party agency has also vouched for it, in this case a third party that is in turn backed by the US government (and the US government's participation in international organic agricultural standards). So when we decide whether or not to believe that the coffee in the bag is in fact organic, we have to decide whether or not we trust the brand, the actual auditor contracted by the certifying agency, the certifying agency, the government department that gave the certifier its right to certify, and the set of standards against which all parties are checking.

Which means we have to trust that the certifier's auditors did in fact test the soil and the water like they were supposed to; we have to trust that the items on the list were really checked, not just checked off. And then we have to trust that the growers are still doing those things the other 363 days that the certifier's auditor isn't there "checking," because just like we aren't there to see what's going on, most of the time the certifiers aren't either.

And now there's a little more at stake; it's not just that we want our coffee to taste a certain way (like we want coffee labeled as Colombian to taste like other coffee we've had that's labeled as Colombian), we want assurance that the coffee in the bag complies with our convictions. Agricultural management is something we ourselves can't measure, so we have to trust that someone else is in fact measuring it and reporting those measurements truthfully.

So is coffee in a bag that's labeled as 100% organic actually all organic? Probably not. But there's also a good chance that coffee in a bag labeled as regular has some organic coffee in it too.

If we have a hard time trusting packaging, we can now also, increasingly, go to coffee shops that sell direct trade coffee. We can see the list on the chalkboard that says that the coffees come from certain regions in certain countries, or even from certain farms or families. We can see the framed pictures of the owner posing next to farmers in far away coffee fields, we can read the shop's online travel blog, we can watch their Vimeo channels about sourcing trips. We can buy their roasted coffee that has a "farm profile" blurb on the back of the bag. We can ask the baristas to tell us about the coffee they're brewing, and maybe they'll tell us about microclimates and the mountains on which the farmers grew it. And we can decide whether or not to believe that any of it has anything to do with what's actually going on in those far away fields—or what's in our to-go cups.

Maybe we do trust every single story, conversation, and video. That then would mean that we also then have to decide whether or not we trust that the guys who run the mills didn't mix up the signs on the bucketloads of ripe cherries or on the warehouse piles of bagged green coffee, and that the guy at the port didn't load coffee from the wrong truck into the wrong container, or the wrong container on to the wrong ship. And then we have to decide whether or not we trust that the labels on the coffee in the domestic warehouses also didn't get mixed up, that the roaster didn't put the wrong labels on the roasted coffee either, and that the guy brewing it also didn't mix up the labels (or mix the coffee together) after he ground it. We have the choice to start or stop trusting whenever we want.

I can tell you that I've watched farmers painstakingly apply truckloads of organic fertilizer; I can tell you that I've seen farms in the middle of bird-filled forests and show you pictures of happy families picking together in the cafetales surrounding their homes. I can report that mill owners watch every truck pull up to make sure the right cherries go in the right place and that there's a quality control engineer who stands watch with a clipboard every time a truck is loaded with sacks headed for export. I can talk about how the bags of beans are stamped with lot numbers and how quality controller check every bag. I can list the names of people whose full time jobs are to trace the chain of traceability. But you have to decide whether or not to believe me.

Sometimes coffee from one family's actual chemical-free farm all the way in the highlands of Costa Rica or Ethiopia really does make it to your cup in a New York coffee shop unadulterated and bearing its real name. Which is an incredible miracle— a miracle generated by a lot of meticulous work, backed by strong conviction, and coupled with a serious dose of luck. But sometimes it doesn't.

There really are families toiling honestly on mountainsides growing organic coffee. And there really is coffee in your cup. How much you trust in the literal connections between the two is up to you.

Posted February 11, 2013

Barista's Burden

Coffee is in many ways comparable to wine, but it separates itself as the more labor intensive of the two beverages in the final stage: preparation.

When a vintner corks a wine bottle, his work remains intact until you uncork it and drink it. There is no "wine preparer" needed to be the final link in the wine chain, but the professional coffee preparer, the barista, is arguably the most crucial link in the coffee chain just because his or her job comes at the end. If a barista messes up, all the work that's gone into the coffee up until that point is lost.

I usually make my coffee in some version of a drip percolator, or buy it from a corner deli making it that way. I pretty much considered baristas as adding unnecessary flourish to a task that could be accomplished quite simply. I mean, how hard is it to make an espresso? I worked at an Italian restaurant in high school and served a few cappuccinos for dessert; it certainly didn't seem like rocket science. But the more professionally prepared espresso drinks I've had in Costa Rica and Panama, the more I've been able to say, as a long-time non-believer, that, "Wow, now *that* tastes different."

The more baristas I meet, the more I'm also learning that not only does their work take practice and skill, they don't take their jobs lightly. Their role is not inherently necessary; coffee does always require one more step than wine, in that roasted beans have to be prepared by someone somehow, but they can be converted to drinkable coffee with less machinery and manipulation than that of espresso. But there are some aspects of coffee flavor, body, and aroma (all those same qualities you look for in a good wine) that you just don't get without the craft of a barista.

And baristas feel this burden; they know it is on them to unlock all the flavors and body that a particular coffee has to offer. One Dutch barista visiting a coffee farm for the first time told me, "It takes around twenty seconds to make an espresso. From the time the coffee plant flowers until the time I put the roasted beans in the grinder usually takes around eight months! I have twenty seconds to get it right to not ruin all the work the people before me have been doing for the better part of a year." And much longer if you start the timer from when the coffee tree seed germinated.

Baristas are cognizant of the responsibility they have to all the people who've put in devoted work beforehand.

The people who tended the seedlings.
The people who pruned the trees.
The people who harvested the cherries.
The people who transported them.
The people who depulped and washed them.
The people who dried the beans.
The people who hulled and sorted them.
The people who shipped them.
The people who roasted them.

And after all that the barista has about twenty seconds to do it right, or all that work will be in vain. The fact that high quality coffee even makes it to baristas' hands is a bit of a miracle in the first place, considering that if someone makes an error in any of those steps it would not reach that highest level of quality.

So when baristas have near-miraculous coffee in their hands, they feel the burden of not being the weak link that screws it all up.

Baristas and their creations might be the most elaborate iteration of coffee preparation, but at the root of all the flourish is an understanding that the meticulous (sometimes damn near obsessive) treatment of coffee is done out of respect for all the people who've put in so much work beforehand.

Posted February 19, 2013

Personalidades de la taza

En el mundo de la venta y compra de comodidades, como el café, todo se maneja con tramites y papeleria. Hace muchos años hemos avanzados de las épocas de confirmar un contrato con un handshake; ahora vivmos en un tiempo de formularios digitales, acuerdos legales, y regalamentos internacionales.

Pero con todo esta sistemización, creemos mucho espacio por errores y fallas. Cuando certificaciones piden una audita, resulta que la cosa mas importante al final es que toda la papeleria del auditor sea en orden para que los productores puedan recibir el sello. Puede ser que el auditor, en realidad, no miro nada. Pero si la papelería dice que todo está bién, está bién.

Entendiendo que, como sociedad, ponemos tanto valor en los documentos y prodecimientos oficiales, yo quería conocer las personas detrás de esta pared de formalidad. Porque da igual la cantidad de sistemas y procesos que desarollamos para compra, venta, y certificacion; las sistemas son siempre manejado por personas, y todas estas personas tienen personalidades únicas.

En realidad no son las sistemas de regulacion que diterminen si la gente roba o se comporte de manera justa, si miente o dice la verdad, son las personalidades de la gente misma. Y nunca se podrá conocer estas personalidades por leer estatisticas de cuanto café se importa a los eeuu o revisar listas de los requisitos que un café tiene que cumplir para llevar una etiqueta de sostenibilidad- hay que ir para conocer las personas cara a cara.

Y llevo mas que seis meses haciendo exactamente esto. Y cada día de estes meses recuerdo de nuevo nunca habrá espacio en ningún formulario para la riqueza de las personalidades detrás de una taza de cafe.

Esta semana pasé unas dias dentro de la selva de Hornitos en Fortuna, Panamá. Es uno de los lugares mas bonitos que he conocido en Centroamerica, pero no podía aprovechar esta belleza al principio, porque la lluvia cayó y el viento sopló sin parar, hasta el punto que se fue la electricidad y el agua de mi hospedaje rústica.

Con casi ningún batería en mi celular, llamé a Don Cune, un caficultor de la zona quien hace un trabajo muy especial, y todo el mundo me recomendó hablar con él. Fijamos una hora de encontrarnos aquella mañana, y pusé mi abrigo para bajar de mi hospedaje, cual fue ubicado dentro de la jungla.

Llegué a la carretera principal, y por un especie de miscomunicación, pasé una hora esperando en una casita de autobus, bajo la llovina y una brisa tan fuerte que casi me llevó a David. Al final logré a hablar con Don Cune para averiguar que pasó; casi no le podía escuchar por el viento. Le dije, "Estoy en la casita al lado del super La Mina—" y la llamada cortó. Seguí esperando (Centroamerica me ha enseñado tener mucha mas paciencia), mirando los carros y buses en su camino curvoso por la carretera.

Despues de otro quince minutos sin recibir una llamada de vuelta, vi a una persona caminado por la carretera hacía el super. Fue un hombre con una camisa de cuadros y botas negras, el típico traje agropecuario. Él camino directamente a donde estuve de pie, y-sin decir ninguna palabra—me dió una abrazo grande y fuerte. Me soltó, me miró a los ojos y me dijo, "Raquel, al final nos encontramos. Vamos caminando, que dices?"

Contesté en el afirmitivo, y empezamos a caminar por donde el acabo de llegar. *Esto* es la personalidad tras una taza de cafe. Cuando él di cuenta de que yo estaba en otra casita (despues de diez minutos caminado pasamos por una casita azul, en la entrada de su pueblito, donde debo haber estado esperando), vino a buscarme y llevarme—sin queja y con mucha sonrisa.

Al pasar la casita azul empezamos a bajar por un valle con vistas de lomas verdes verdaderamente increíbles. Inmediatente al entrar en el valle salimos de la lluvia y de la brisa, y el tiempo se convertó en un día precioso, con sol y cielo celeste. Al bajar mas, llegamos al pueblo de Don Cune, con flores y árboles brillantes en frente (y encima) de cada casa.

Enseguida al llegar en su casa, Done Cune me senaló una silla a la mesa en la sombra bajo la casa. Tenía el café puesto, y me ofreció una taza de café que él mismo ha sembrado, cosechado, procesado y tostado, para tomar mientras me contó la historia alrededor de su trabajo con cafe.

Me dijo, "algunas personas son productivas, otras comerciantes. Yo tengo las dos cualidades, tengo la suerte," y con estos cualidades pudo superar la epoca de précios muy bajos que pasó en los años 90, porque él hizo una cosa que nadie mas hizo— empezó tostar, empacar y vender su cafe para venta local.

Don Cune es una persona con la personalidad de resolver el problemas. Cuando yo no llegué a la casita azul, me vino a buscar. Cunado no ganó suficiente dinero con él café en grano, empezó a agregar valor y venderlo de otra manera.

No se que resumen daría un reportaje sobre la producción y ganancias de su finca, pero la personalidad detras de una taza de Cafe Issa (como llamo su cafe por su nieta), es familiar, innovador, siempre muy feliz, y puramente la del único Don Cune.

Posted March 8, 2013

Folded Land

Disparate themes seem to converge in coffee more and more the further I continue on this odyssey. I've been following Costa Rica's grassroots resistance to the entry of Monsanto and GMO corn in the country because I find it interesting and relevant to the type of sustainability writing I did in New York, but I never thought it would have anything to do with coffee. Turns out, there is a place where coffee and GMOs cross paths: folded land.

Part of the rationale for the development of genetically modified crops is that the current food supply and systems of food production will not be able to feed the world's growing population in the near future. Plants like corn and soy are already producing at max capacity; scientists moved to transgenic research because they had exhausted all avenues of maximizing plant production through fertilizers and pest/plague control and resistance. One impulse behind the research— and planted application— of genetically modified crops is that plants need to produce more in order to feed more people.

But I wonder if there aren't other ways to think about the question of feeding a lot more people. If we need more food, instead of having plants that produce more, we could have more plants. But we then need somewhere to plant them. And there are lots of ways to think about arable space. Perhaps it isn't possible to tack another couple hundred acres onto existing megafarms, but what if we could supplement the production of those farms with food grown in other places? People are already doing really amazing things with turning lawns into gardens. And the number of homes with sprawling green grass in front of them adds up to a whole lot more land area to plant, if we think of it as such. Maybe real estate development did encroach onto former farmland, but what if land that's been developed doesn't have to take a uniform bite out of that arable land; what if it's sprinkled with small, highly productive plots?

When we think about ways to increase production, instead of thinking about altering the genes of a plant, maybe we can think about growing up. We already have cities with skylines of towering buildings. What if they could become vertical fields? People are already proving that they can be. Hydroponic growing systems and wall gardens give us new ways to think about using the space we already have. Instead of looking for arable land, we can look for arable space. Impressive technology and innovative people are showing that any office or classroom wall can be such arable space, producing food in unlikely places.

We have thousands of existing buildings begging to become arable. It's not as though we need to build up to then plant up; the buildings are already up. They just need to be tweaked a bit to become productive places. Many vertical spaces (walls) serve active functions of storing things in shelves or displaying things on screens, but the majority of walls are idle, white space with nothing better to do than be converted into vegetable patches. Genetically modified foods are uncharted territory in that we don't know what effects they might have on people, now or generations down the line. But growing up provides no potential for cancers or allergies; it provides the opportunity to shift the ways we think about the surfaces and directions in which we can produce food.

Nature already grows up. Arable mountain land shows us that the bird's eye square mileage of a country is not the same as its total arable land area. Mountains are essentially folded land, crinkled to fit more surface into a smaller space. How can you make a sheet of 8.5x11 paper the same size as a post it? Fold it. The surface area is still there, but its footprint shrinks. A mountain with a two square mile footprint boasts much more land area on which to plant than two square miles of flat land.

Coffee shows us just how significant the potential of folded land can be. Brazil has pretty much always been the world's largest producer of coffee. Which makes sense, because Brazil is massive. Sprawling coffee fields disappearing into the horizon crank out a good portion of the world's supply. But right behind Brazil in production, holding the number two position for decades, is Vietnam. Vietnam has no sprawling fields extending in all directions; it has mountains. Neither country has the advantage of producing coffee with genetically modified plants; both countries grow Robusta and Arabica, and both have many varieties of each. The intensity and efficiency with which the land is managed of course differs, but the reason tiny Vietnam is able to consistently come in as runner-up to massive Brazil is because Vietnam grows up.

Coffee can also remind us how many different things can grow together at the same time. The diversity of stuff that can come from one hectare of coffee includes bananas, avocados, beans, corn, yucca, and oranges. You can get a lot of food out of land that also grows coffee. The food production capacity of existing land can be increased not only by the genetic manipulation of the seeds we plant on it, but by the choices we make in what to plant and how to organize it.

Coffee grows in the mountains and can therefore take advantage of nature's vertical space, but other crops can't. What if the time and money and investigation devoted to looking at ways to genetically modify grains to increase productivity were instead

devoted to looking at new ways to use existing spaces, like
horizontal lawns, highway medians, edges of sports fields and
vertical spaces like office walls, parking garage ledges, and mall
rooftops, as arable and productive places?

We can't make more folded land, but we can keep
planting and growing up.

Posted March 22, 2013

Putting Things in Boxes

Metaphorically, coffee defies boxes, being more than a
commodity or a beverage, being a plant, a lifestyle of production
and consumption, a competitive sport, a delicacy, a right.

In reality, all coffee comes in boxes. Literally, it all arrives
wherever it arrives in a box.

The majority of coffee consumed in the world is
consumed in countries other than those where it is produced.
Often those countries are far away from each other (think the
distance between Rio and Stockholm). Sometimes the distances
are shorter, like between Vietnam and Japan, but all coffee travels
and most of it travels pretty far to get from where it was picked
and processed to where it's roasted and served.

And it always travels in boxes. If coffee travels overland
(like from Southern Mexico to the US or from Peru to Argentina),
it travels on a truck, packed into the box that is the tractor trailer.
Plenty of coffee travels in truck boxes, but the real box that
moves coffee is the 40ft metal shipping container.

Shipping is the bottleneck of the coffee chain; the
narrowest point through which the commodity must pass to make
it from point of origin to point of consumption. Coffee is grown
in a wide belt of places wrapping around the world, and it is
consumed there and everywhere else. To get in between, green
coffee gets packed into bags which are packed into boxes which
are packed onto ships and sent across the open seas.

The same is true for almost all electronics, many cars, lots
of fruit, and most of the clothes we wear. If a product has a
"made in" tag that says anything other than USA, Mexico or
Canada, it came to our shores on a container ship. A few things

are air freighted because they demand speedy delivery in order not to jeopardize freshness (think Colombian roses and Panamanian orchids), but anything with a shelf life gets stuffed into a container and stacked on a ship and sent from one port to the next.

It doesn't seem that impressive, until you consider that every single cup of coffee consumed in Europe had to get there on a container ship. One coffee origin could suffer climactic or social crisis and produce next to nothing for a year, and we'd still have coffee. Several major roasting conglomerates could go bust and we'd still have coffee. But if the the shipping lines Hapag Lloyd, Maersk, MOL, or Hamburg Sud disappeared overnight, we'd have to ration the little bit of beans in domestic warehouses, because coffee would have no way to get to our cup.

Part of the reason shipping is the bottleneck of the process is because the number of ports and shipping lines is not as easily amplified as the number of roasters or hectares planted with coffee. It's also interesting that a bottleneck represents a sort of monopoly, a place with the fewest hands controlling the entire volume. Which is why it's further interesting that Hapag Lloyd and Hamburg Sud are German, Maersk is Dutch, and MOL is Japanese. Looking at the imperial history of the coffee trade, it's interesting that producing countries don't ship their own anything. Shipping lines are still run by people going to get things they want, rather than by people selling things they have. But for all the potential to be inflated, as industries with few hands are wont to be, container shipping is actually pretty affordable. Depending how far your farm or mill is from the port, it can easily cost more to get the coffee from the producing mountain to the port than from the Panama Canal to Oakland.

The low cost of shipping comes in part from its inherent efficiency. As Maria Ruiz of Panama's Café Ruiz said, "Whoever decided to start putting things in boxes forever changed the way we do everything." When you put things in boxes, it's easier to stack and store them, and your machinery for stacking and storing can be uniform across the world when everything gets sent in exactly the same size box.

Metaphorically, we put things in mental boxes for the same reasons we put things in physical boxes; it's easier and safer to deal with them. It's easier to put people and ideas in boxes inside of our own heads in order to fit lots of pieces of information in close quarters to one another, and it's safer because things stacked in boxes are stable and don't topple when shaken. Mentally categorizing things into this or that 40ft box lets us process the world as efficiently as a container ship loading cargo.

But because we are not in fact container ships and the mental cargo we're stuffing is often incredibly resistant to boxes, we often have to work harder than a crane mindlessly stacking contaners and find ways of storing things outside of boxes. Putting things in mental boxes is not as reliable as setting a container of coffee on board a ship.

But unlike slippery ideas, coffee does particularly lend itself to being shipped in boxes because it's the ideal commodity for packing. The technical term for filling a container for shipping is "stuffing," and coffee in fact can be stuffed. When a container of coffee is stuffed there is no wasted space; the container contains coffee front to back, floor to ceiling. 60kg bags fit one on top of each other, row of piles next to row of piles, for a total of 300 bags per container, summing to around 37, 500lbs of pure coffee cargo, generating the unit in which green Arabica coffee is traded on the New York "C" market. Because it's the bottleneck, the shape of the shipping industry dictates the unit of the commodity market.

The shape of the shipping industry is in turn dictated by its own internal bottlenecks. The shipping industry is the narrowest point on the coffee chain, and the narrowest point of the shipping chain is the Panama Canal. The dimensions of the Canal dictate the shape of any ships that need to pass through, and shipping lines have entire fleets of Panamax ships that are the exact maximum width that can pass through the locks of the Canal, with just inches to spare on each side.

Currently, the Panama Canal is undergoing expansion, originally slated for completion just in time for the celebration of the 100th anniversary of the completion of the original Canal in 1914. The completion date has been pushed back to April 2015, due to lots of logistical hangups, like relocating baby jaguars found on construction sites, and extracting five meter long crocodiles that have eaten all the fish- and then started eating each other- in the lake that formed in abandoned construction sites from previous expansion attempts.

Turns out that building wider locks is no small task, even with a hundred years more technology to work with. An engineer and construction foreman working on the expansion said, "We're just widening the entrances to the lake. At least the hard part is done for us." Even though the hard part was done a hundred years ago with much less technology and immigrant labor forces that spoke dozens of languages, the Canal's location itself presents the same inherent and ever-present challenges of stifling heat and humidity, often dangerous (and now endangered and thus protected with lots of red tape) wildlife, plants the size of buildings, and the sheer force of the planet's two biggest oceans tugging at each other.

Panama is full steam ahead in the face of these difficulties, determined to continue to demonstrate that the nation is not only capable, but also innovative and pioneering, in its management of the Canal in the fourteen years it has administrated operations completely independent of former U.S. control.

Widening the bottleneck of bottlenecks means that the effects ripple out, creating other opportunities for expansion. Atlanta is dredging its port in order to dig deeper; wider locks mean bigger boats; bigger boats mean deeper harbors. Maersk is building the world's biggest ship: the Triple E. You can watch the construction—and hear stories from the people involved in the process, in a very "when container ships speak" way—in a six-part Discovery Channel mini series.

The dimensions of the shipping industry might change, but the concept won't. Because it works. Putting things in boxes replaced lines of men tossing sacks of coffee from to one another to load and unload cargo from the "break bulk" hulls of massive sailing ships. It might have eliminated jobs and some of the romance of ports-of-call, but it did work better for ensuring that entire loads of cargo didn't fall into the ocean, and provides a little more assurance that the contents of a container are sealed from departure to arrival.

But putting things in boxes isn't perfect. Container theft is still a problem. When things are neatly stuffed into a box, it's easier to steal the whole box. Putting things in boxes might be easier than other transport methods, but it's still not magic. When coffee gets shipped in a box, the empty box has to make it to the coffee. When a roaster in the US wants a load of coffee from origin, say, Boquete, Panama, the roaster sends the coffee mill shipping instructions, stating the shipping line and boat departure date.

It's then the mill's job (and usually cost) to go and get a container from that shipping line (or send a trucking company to go get one) and bring it up to the mill in Boquete, stuff the container with coffee, drive it back to the port, where the coffee sellers wait until the goods (coffee in a box) have been loaded (by crane) over the ship's rail, so that the shipper can give them the bill of lading, proving coffee-in-a-box-on-board, that the coffee makers can then send to the buyer in order to get paid. That one piece of paper speaks for a box of three hundred bags, rather than trying to ensure that three hundred individual bags each made it over the ship's rail.

Coffee cargo sits snugly together and doesn't waste the container space a car does, but it also has a high moisture content (and the ability to absorb more), potentially changing the quality of the final product delivered. As the International Marine Office official guide on container stuffing says, "Bagged cargoes with high moisture content, such as coffee and cocoa beans, may require dressing of the container ceiling and walls with moisture and condensation absorbing paper, and the hanging of so called Moisture Absorbing Materials (MAMS) bags in the container's corners."

Coffee travels pretty well, all things considered, and if it's passing from the Pacific to the Atlantic—or vice versa—it might even be offloaded at one end of the Panama Canal, put on a train, and then reloaded onto a waiting ship at the other side of the Canal, to avoid time and cost of getting a ship all the way through the Canal. In addition to being able to turn a shipping container into the back half of an eighteen wheel truck, putting things in boxes also makes them instantly convertible into train cars.

Putting things in boxes makes them stackable, shippable, trainable, truckable, and still a little mysterious, because you never quite what you'll get when you open a container. Hopefully it's coffee—the coffee you want it to be.

Posted March 31, 2013

The Significance of Being Statistically Insignificant

In 2012, Panama produced around 100,000 bags of coffee and exported around 50,000 (according to the International Coffee Organization). Whether those bags are 60kg or 70kg, it doesn't really make a difference. Either way, Panama's coffee production is globally pretty insignificant. Coffee numbers are particularly tricky numbers to pin down, but 50,000 bags out of several hundred million is a drop in the bucket.

So what does that mean for the people who grow coffee in Panama? Do they work less hard than people in a coffee producing country with statistically significant export numbers? Is it any easier to fertilize and prune and transplant when you're part of a statistically insignificant coffee growing population? Is it any harder?

Panama's government essentially ignores coffee growing; growers have free reign and don't have to comply with as many regulations as in Costa Rica or Colombia, but it also means they don't have the support producers in those countries see. Want a soil analysis? Get it on your own; there's no ICAFE or Cenicafe office for you to turn to.

When you're statistically insignificant, you have to differentiate yourself in ways that don't show up in the spreadsheet, ways like superior quality and extra special and unique attributes. Panama hit the goldmine with Geisha.

But for people who work on or own goldmine farms, is the quotidian process of growing coffee any different than for someone on a not-so-special farm in a place with statistically significant production?

A little bit. Goldmine farms demand different attention to detail to make sure all those specialties stay intact. So working on a tiny, specialty small-lot exporting farm in Boquete is different than working on a farm that's part of the Colombian powerhouse.

It's a little different, but it's not all that different. Because as much as we differentiate coffee, coffee is still coffee, and the work is still work. Panama doesn't register on the radars of exporters and traders and the commodity market yo-yo because it simply isn't statistically significant enough to.

And that's the problem with conventional valuations of commodities. They forget that the sweat of someone growing coffee in Panama is just as sweaty as that of someone growing it in statistically significant Brazil.

To attempt a more humanistic valuation of coffee is to look just as closely and carefully at people in places that barely register on the bar graph as at those in places that dominate it. And then of those fish in that little pond, to not look just at the big Specialty fish, but also at the little fish in the little pond, coffee growers whose coffee doesn't even make it to export, or who export such small amounts they're barely even on the Specialty radar.

Humanistic valuation of a commodity means spending time to get to know both the individuals who comprise the norm and those who defy it.

April 3, 2013

Agriculture

Agri*culture* is termed as such because growing things is a way of life. When you earn a living for yourself, and often your family, by growing things, you build your life accordingly; the way you dress, what you eat, what you care about, and how and why you get together with other people follows the patterns of farming. When an entire region, or the better part of a nation, makes its living from growing things, the way styles evolve, what everyone eats, the themes of songs and movies and books and TV shows, the laws and structures of government, and how and why most people gather communally is dictated by the shape of the agrarian life.

In Colombia there are approximately 566,000 families who grow coffee (figure currently touted by FNC—National Federation of Coffee Growers— and all subsequent parties who work with them). Most of these families also grow other things, and of course there are even more thousands of agraian families who grow exclusively other things. Of a country of almost 47 million, coffee growing families make up a fairly small percent, but the land they grow on occupies a much greater percentage of the nation's land area.

At past points in Colombia's history there have probably been much higher percentages of the population belonging to coffee growing families. The figures aren't particularly important because towns, cities, and entire regions are still today bursting with culture rooted in the agrarian life, particularly coffee culture.

In Spanish, the word *caficultor* is used for someone who grows coffee, who cultivates it. The "culture" of agri*culture* and the root of the word "cultivate" are connected; and in Colombia a coffee cultivator is synonymous with a coffee culture maker.

Colombian coffee culture looks a lot like Juan Valdez. Men wear crumpled old wide brim hats while working on the farm during the day and crisp clean ones when they go into town or to visit their neighbors (or even to sit out in front of the two stores at the intersection and maybe have a beer or an ice cream) in the evening. The men wear folded white ponchos, often with the three yellow, red, and blue stripes of Colombia, over one shoulder. Most people do own horses and mules and ride the horses, with the mule obediently trotting in front or behind, with some sort of cargo strapped to his back, maybe coffee, fertilizer, firewood, cement for construction, groceries, or even furniture.

Most women of coffee growing families seem to occupy more "traditional" roles, and the way *caficultores* eat, and therefore the way the women cook, is certainly different than that of Medellín or Bogota. Every morning, the women start the day making *agua panela* and arepas. *Agua panela* is made by simply placing a *panela,* a block of the molassesy sugar that forms from the cooled and hardened "honey" of fresh pressed sugar cane, into a pot of boiling water. The result is a very sweet, almost molassesy, tasting hot beverage that people drink straight, or use as the base for their coffee, most of which is still instant and *tinto*.

In many cases this is prepared on a *fogón*, a wood-burning stove, usually with three openings that can be covered with metal disks to create burners, that is often fueled entirely with trunks and branches of pruned coffee trees. The arepas are often prepared one "burner" over. After soaking and grinding soft corn kernels by hand to get a sort of corn dough, women patt out the arepas by hand until they look like thick tortillas (which they kind of basically are), which they then set on the special wire arepa cooking griddle that sits over the *fogón* and facilitates flipping. The food side of coffee culture includes lots of staples that can be grown on the same finca as coffee: yucca, bananas and plantains, corn, beans, complimented by store bought rice by the bagful.

In Colombia coffee culture means living on the finca, which is often pretty remotely up in the mountains, and while most people have electricity, not all have refrigerators. Which means that meat gets salted, milk is powdered, cheese is delivered every now and then by a neighbor and finished in one meal, and the only chicken or eggs you eat will be ones gleaned from the coop out back.

The culture of picking coffee is its own subsection of the coffee producing culture. Most landowners who have enough land to need to hire workers therefore don't end up picking much of their own coffee themselves. The coffee picking culture includes hanging a flat black AM/FM radio around your neck (often in a plastic bag in case it rains) to listen to as you work. Most people (men and women, though the majority of pickers are indeed men) wear a t-shirt over their heads, with their faces peeking out the neck holes, looking like they started to put on the shirt then stopped, with the sleeves tied at the back of their head, making a sort of protective turban against sun and bugs and scratching branches and the way dirt glues itself to coffee cherry goo and forms a sticky, caked layer over your skin.

In Nicaragua people harvest with woven baskets, in Costa Rica with plastic laundry-looking baskets, in Panama with five-gallon buckets, and in Colombia with bins that look a bit like trash cans, but still with the same belt fashioned from a folded fertilizer bag or extra piece of webbing. One cross cultural constant of picking coffee is the way pickers fold an extra fertilizer bag for hauling picked fruit and stick it inside one of their rubber boots.

The culture of growing things extends beyond those who grow to those who buy what is grown, transform what is grown, and resell what has been grown and transformed.

The men who work in the "points of purchase" (co-ops or middlemen's warehouses) of dried coffee in parchment spend their days hauling coffee: off trucks, onto scales, and up the stockpiled mountain of coffee where they slice open the sacks and empty the coffee onto the growing pile. The men are all shirtless, with a piece of cloth tossed over their heads, necks, and shoulders and held in place with their teeth in order to eliminate the abrasiveness of the coffee sacks as they lug them and flop them down somewhere else. They all hold metal hooks to facilitate grabbing the coffee, bringing to mind Peter Pan. The other bizarre tool of the points of purchase is the "sticker," a hollow metal pointed rod used to stab each sack to extract a sample to determine quality of the lot, and therefore the price the grower gets for the day. The process is a bit like a coffee blood test.

Just getting coffee to these points of purchase is a culture of its own. Colombians still use quite a few beasts of burden to move coffee to and fro, both as fresh picked fruit and as dried beans-in-parchment. Some deliver it on horseback/muleback to point of purchase, but most use some sort of vehicle. For those who don't have their own, they pack coffee onto a public *carro, chivero,* or *linea/chiva.*

The *carros* are gritty Jeeps, which often have a bunch of bags of coffee tied to the roof, a bunch of women and children packed onto the benches inside, a bunch of men hanging off the back, and maybe a couple teenagers sitting on the roof on top of the coffee, their feet dangling onto the windshields. Even more coffee can be stuffed into the *linea* (also called *chiva* which is also the slang word for goat...), which are essentially a species of public bus but look like what would happen if a Mac truck, a trolley, and an intricately painted art project somehow mated. In Colombian towns shaped by coffee growing culture, the form of public transit is designed to transport coffee as much as people.

Colombia's coffee culture is being amplified and diversified as more of the good stuff stays home. For decades Colombia exported 100% of its tastiest coffee, leaving Colombians to drink not quite so tasty variations of instant coffee or to home roast and grind the leftover *pasilla* beans, the ones gnawed by insects, overfermented, underripe, or broken. Some *caficultores* have been roasting their own coffee for home drinking for years, but now Colombian roasters are preparing the country's finest beans for domestic consumption in cafes, restaurants, and for sale by the pound. Colombians have always known they have awesome coffee, but now their coffee culture extends to include drinking that awesome coffee, prepared awesomely.

Today's agri*culture* is not the stuff of storybooks, with just a man and his land, toiling in honest harmony with nature. Today's culture of growing things includes labs of cloned hybrids, monitors refreshing commodity reports every three minutes, pickup trucks and retrofitted flatbeds, upscale eateries and international gourmet tastings. But, in Colombian coffee growing agri*culture*, the donkeys and the hats are still there.

Posted April 14, 2013

Juan's World Part 1: A Sombrero, a Poncho, and a Mule

The story of Juan Valdez is the story of one of the world's most successful marketing campaigns. The National Federation of Colombian Coffee Growers (FNC) did something that no one had ever done before: they branded a country. And they did it with astounding success. There are books written about the startling effectiveness and sheer vastness of the Juan Valdez campaign, of how "Colombian" became synonymous with coffee. One of the campaign's most impressive features is its longevity; the campaign that was developed before I was born has never needed an aggressive rebranding overhaul; it has simply evolved organically with both the people it represents and those it sells to. The character of Juan Valdez was done right enough the first time that he has never had to sell out in order to survive. He doesn't drive a Toyota and he's not wearing Nikes. In 30+ years he's still a mustached coffee farmer with a sombrero, a poncho, and a mule.

But you can follow his blog. And you can order his coffee in lattes at kiosks in the mall in Panama City. You can like his new chocolate drizzle *granizado* (Frappuccino equivalent) on Facebook.

Back in high school, when I was gearing up to head off to Spain for a year as a foreign exchange student, people would say, "Oh! Like Fez from *That 70s Show!*" And my answer was always, yes, like Fez; I'm going to be the awkward one with the accent. When I was gearing up for this year on coffee farms, people would say, "Oh! Like Juan Valdez!" And my answer was always, "Yes, like Juan Valdez;" I'm going up into the mountains where people still carry things by mule.

But I didn't realize how much *like* Juan Valdez Colombia was going to be.

Juan Valdez is pretty much the original voice of coffee speaking. He gave the North American coffee drinking masses a narrative to apply to the sourcing of their coffee. He wasn't just a logo; the campaign gave him a life, a personality, and most importantly, a human name. The FNC forces behind the campaign were spot-on in finding a narrative that not only effectively spoke to consumers, but one that effectively spoke for hundreds of thousands of Colombian coffee growers. Juan Valdez, though a figure developed for advertising, is in fact a pretty accurate representative of Colombian coffee growers. Which is a hard thing to get right.

When you have a representative it's tempting to forget that the representative is not in fact the same as every member of the group that he is representing. A representation is not the equation of one part of the whole with every part of the whole; a representation is the understanding that a part of the whole is in some ways similar, comparable, to other parts of the whole.

Representations work differently with different wholes. A randomly selected sample of soil from a uniformly mixed batch should in fact be the same as any other randomly selected sample from the same batch. A handful of coffee from a bag of Excelso grade should in fact be the same as any other handful from that bag (in theory...more on coffee trickery— by the seller and the buyer— in Juan's World: Factor 90). But when you have a person acting as a representation of a group of people, he or she is not an equation to the rest of the people in the bag, but rather a representation of certain commonalities among individuals who still retain marked differences.

The concept of representation is particularly important in the case of Mr. Valdez, because the agency that created him, the FNC, is itself a representative body. The Federation is indeed a Federation, with representatives elected to serve in the FNC congress and make decisions about things that affect every single coffee grower, like what to do with resources allocated to the Federation by the government.

People as representatives are tricky because it's important that the members of the group they represent feel ok with the fact that that specific person is representing them (which is the idea behind voting). But, when you develop a representative who is not in fact elected, the members of the group still have to like the representative enough that they're all ok that said rep is not exactly the same as they are. They have to like the rep enough that they're willing to accept that he's also different in some ways.

Part of the reason Juan Valdez has been able to endure as a representative, without having to change himself, is that his representees like him. They've always liked him and will continue to like him because they like the parts of themselves he represents.

Juan Valdez is a hard working, honest gentleman. He doesn't get drunk, he doesn't steal, he doesn't go wooing women, he doesn't beat his animals, he doesn't grow drugs, and he certainly doesn't neglect his coffee trees. He gave Colombian coffee growing men an admirable archetype to aspire to. At the same time, he reflected realities they all knew: to get good coffee you have to grow it way up in the cool mountains, it takes a lot of work, and you move it by beast of burden.

All these years (over a generation!) after the campaign first hit the screens and pages of domestic and international media, Juan Valdez remains largely unchanged because the people he represents are still involved in an activity that is fundamentally the same. Coffee growers now have cell phones and many a Facebook profile, but they are still growing things, a job that requires getting hands-on dirty and interacting with plans and animals, even when other technologies are involved. (The farm I'm staying on uses a mule to move sacks of picked coffee within the property—from the trees to the beneficio—then uses a car to drive it into town, for example).

Even the style, perhaps the most iconic element of Mr. Valdez, is still pretty accurate. Plenty of middle aged caficultores still have thick handlebar mustaches and wouldn't be caught in town without a crisp white poncho over one shoulder and a crisp hat on their heads. I even saw a guy in his 20s wearing jeans, a t-shirt, and a crisp hat and poncho as he posed in front of a monument in Medellín, with his girlfriend, dressed in a Victoria's Secret "Love Pink" florescent sweat suit, snapping the picture. The traditional coffee grower formal attire is still a common style, common enough that even though most of the youngest coffee growing generation does generally wear jeans and t-shirts, they still respect the style of their parents and grandparents.

But more fundamentally, coffee growers as a group remain largely unchanged because growing coffee is largely unchanged, even after a generation. It's true that since Juan's inception Colombian coffee growing has become exponentially more technified, and if Juan were to represent the full reality of growing coffee he should have a *bomba* pesticide-spraying backpack on and be dressed in the regulation agrochemical application outfit: orange hooded jumpsuit, goggles, facemask, rubber gloves, and boots.

The intricacies of coffee cultivation have certainly evolved, but at its core Colombian coffee growing today is similar to Colombian coffee growing a generation ago because it is still widely done on the family scale; land is still owned by individual people, not corporations (or exporters or trading houses or roasters). Even if families have hired workers, individuals hold titles to the land on which coffee is grown. Of course there are sprawling "plantations" that do in fact resemble plantations in their organized monoculture and forces of modestly paid employees, but it's the smallholding Juan Valdez's of Colombia that make Colombian coffee happen.

At the second session of an eleven-session free course on coffee production held by the National Learning Service (SENA) in conjunction with the FNC, the professor asked the twenty plus attendees who they thought would outlast who in the Colombian coffee arena: the big guy or the little guy. Attendees' answers were mixed. The instructor's official prediction: the little guy. Why? The price of labor with respect to the market price of coffee. Coffee is falling off the trees because there's no one to pick it. The smallest growers, families who do everything themselves without any hired help, are immune to this cost because they never have to pay it. When the largest landowners are losing their harvest, the little guy is collecting 100%: like always. The future of Colombian coffee might have to cede everything back to the Juans in order to continue.

But for now, it's more or less business as usual. Juan Valdez still serves as a dashing representative in ways that the cow in the field with a red barn in the background on your package of Hillshire Farms burger patties doesn't because Juan is as many parts accurate as he is idealized; there are in fact still hundreds of thousands of families with sons and fathers and brothers who all put on their hats to block the slanting afternoon rays as they strap overstuffed sacks of coffee to the backs of their mules to haul coffee through the Colombian mountains every day.

Posted April 24, 2013

Juan's World Part 2: Organization of a Coffee Country

Of Colombia's some 47 million inhabitants, there are roughly 560,000 coffee growing families. In its recent history, Colombia's government- and the country as a whole- has been through some stuff, to say the least, and the country's highways are dotted with billboards that read things like, "Where coffee grows, first comes development, then the flowering of peace."

The source of all the country's coffee taglines is the FNC *(Federacion Nacional de Cafeteros Colombianos,* The National Federation of Colombian Coffee Growers). The FNC is not a government agency or officially a part of the government of the Republic of Colombia, but the two are certainly in bed together. Not because they're siblings that grew up having to share things, but because they've mutually consented to form a union as love/hate as any.

The FNC has a presence in 364 municipalities across fifteen coffee growing Departments (equivalent of US States). Every four year the country's *cafeteros* (coffee growers) elect representatives to serve four year terms as Departmental committee members and members of the National Congress of Coffee Growers. The last elections were held in 2010 and reported a 64% participation rate among eligible voters. An eligible voter is a coffee grower who's part of the national coffee paper trail, meaning they've registered their finca's stats in the national Coffee Growers Information System (SICA) and registered themselves to hold a "Smart Coffee Grower ID," a nifty little card that serves as identification *and* a debit card to which the FNC can transfer funds from things like subsidies. It's not linked to a bank account nor is it contingent on holding any other type of ID. The FNC is proud to say that it reaches places in the country that the government still doesn't. So, in paper trail terms, you can be off the government's radar, yet receive government subsidy funds administered by the FNC through your Smart ID. In bed together enough to split the bill, but not enough to merge contact lists.

FNC initiatives are almost always referred to in the media as "guild activities," using a delightfully medieval vocabulary to remind everyone that coffee growers are dignified craftsmen, not just your average farmers. One of the main prerogatives of the FNC has been, and still is, promoting the image of Colombian coffee growers, both domestically and abroad, as one of dedicated artisans working tirelessly to better their craft and foster domestic tranquility. In what translates to English as an almost corny hippie- reminiscent refrain, the words "coffee" and "peace" are never far from one another in Colombian press.

In the March/April edition of one Departmental coffee growers' newspaper, an excerpt from a press release by the FNC General Manager Gerardo Nuñoz in response to the recent strike concludes a paragraph with the profound, "The path to peace in Colombia passes through a cafetal."

In the February edition of another regional paper, a quote from a coffee grower participating in the strike reads, "we call this [strike] the Movement for Dignity of Coffee Growers because the dignity begins with us ourselves, and for that we insist that our members always behave admirably, that they don't generate violence. We're an example of peace because we demonstrate it, because peace is in the countryside; we're the builders of peace."

The FNC has been preaching coffee growing as a peaceful enterprise for generations, and coffee growers are proud to make that the reality and remind the government—and themselves, and everyone—of it.

Marketing has always been one of the FNC's fortes, but it is far from its only function. It's other main task it to take the funds from its government bedfellow and put them to use. One of the main destinies for such funds is to be funneled into one of the country's many co-operatives to ensure that those co-operatives can continue to offer a full guarantee of purchase, all year long, every year, to any member who shows up with any amount of any quality of any coffee. This is huge in the agricultural commodity world, and it ensures that small-scale production will continue to be viable even if larger producers spring up in the same area.

This guarantee of sale does not mean that farmers will get the same price if they turn in stellar coffee or moldy, insect-riddled beans, but they at least won't ever be turned away and loose that harvest completely. The FNC converts the market's dollars per pound into pesos per kilos and then transfers between 90-95% of that price to producers.

The "presence" the FNC maintains in those 364 municipalities across fifteen departments is manifested in departmental and municipal committees, also determined by popular vote. The FNC uses its own money, generated from things like selling instant coffee domestically and Colombian coffee internationally (30% average of national annual production is exported via the FNC's Almacafe), to operate offices in each of these municipalities, where it offers extension services like sending out soil analyses and helping farmers read them to determine next steps, distributing *roya* resistant seeds (often gratis), receiving the necessary paperwork so that subsidy money can show up on growers' Smart IDs, and sending extensionists into the field and onto the farms to troubleshoot and collect data firsthand about things like levels of insect infestation and erosion to feed into a national database, which in turn helps inform unified plans of action against widespread challenges like pests, plagues, and climate change.

Local FNC committees also collaborate with co-ops to offer trainings, courses, and workshops, which range from single session to many months. Municipal level educational content is usually geared towards the basics of production and processing (think planting, maintaining, depulping, and drying), but departmentally the FNC works with the free National Learning Service (SENA) and departmental governments to offer courses about more "elective" topics like coffee cupping and barista-style beverage preparation.

At both the municipal and departmental level the FNC also works with SENA to offer more continuing education around budgeting, finance, and administration. Sometimes international non profits get involved, too.

These collaborative educational experiences can take place in the church of a tiny town up in the mountains, in the lobby of a local co-op's office suite, or in conference room of the departmental committee. The FNC really gives the word "outreach" a run for its money. If there's a tiny pocket of people growing coffee anywhere up in the mountains, the FNC knows about it. Colombia is a place where a grower can go over a soil sample with a FNC extensionist in a municipal office and be able to say, "You know, it's the part of the lot up by the road, where we planted the seedlings in between the pruned trees," and the extensionist actually knows what he's talking about.

The FNC is in an imperfect— but committedly intimate— relationship with Colombian government, but it has a lot going on the side. And everyone gets with everyone, such that the "Basics of Coffee Production" course held "in the field" at multiple locations across the country is the love child of the FNC and SENA, while the ongoing monthly Coffee Promoters course is the spawn of a Spanish non profit and a local co-op (but members also get a free annual soil sample through the departmental FNC committee), and the Antioquia Cup of Excellence belongs to the Government of the Department of Antioquia, the departmental FNC committee, and all four of the department's co-ops.

In Juan's world *cafeteros* know nothing of the simplicity of a two-parent household; they're privy to the joys of growing up in a place where it takes a village to raise a coffee grower.

Posted April 24, 2013

Juan's World Part 3: Factor 90

When coffee speaks it says, "You have no idea what I'm worth." When you buy a cup of coffee the number of things that purchase has to pay for are pretty numerous and diverse. People more numerically inclined than myself have made all kinds of pie charts to try to figure out where that money goes. But wondering whether or not those pie charts are accurate seems to be the wrong question: coffee pricing has so many layers that it splitting up a circle just doesn't cut it.

Part of the reason straightforward division is overly simplistic is because coffee comes from so many different places, and in each of those places everything is completely different. In Costa Rica, coffee is measured by volume and sold as fresh picked cherries. Farmers are paid in colones. In Colombia it's measured by weight and sold in dry parchment, basically as a grain. Farmers are paid in pesos. In Costa Rica quality is assessed by cherry color and density and deductions are often made on a whim (as in, "there seems to be a lot of green in here. I'm taking two *cajuelas* off the *fanega*-and-a-half you're selling me." In Colombia it's assessed by a physical evaluation and deductions are made based on the precise percentage of defect-free green beans (as in, "out of the 162g remaining after we hulled the initial 200g sample, 12g of beans were defective.") Coffee is grown in over fifty countries. And each one has its own system.

So making a neat pie chart of where that $3.50 from your latte or $1.25 from your gas station coffee "really" goes is a little bit wishful thinking. Who gets what cut of the price of coffee, at any point, can depend on which middleman you go to, which co-op you sell to, and which currency is being converted to the US dollars of the New York ICE Futures market (which is used as the base to then determine the price of most Arabica sales) and the London LIFFE Euronext Futures market (which is used as the base to then determine the price of all Robusta sales).

Just figuring how much to pay coffee growers when they walk into the points of sale (co-op or middleman) is itself a lesson in algebra, financial speculation, exchange rates, unit conversions, and some good old weights and measures. (It took me three visits to the co-op to feel like I really understood the process of selling/buying coffee in Colombia. As I left the first visit I thanked the buyer[Leon, p. 268] for the "math lesson." My notes literally looked like high school algebra. I went over them, did a "sample problem" by weighing and sorting defects in a batch of coffee on the farm, and then brought in my "homework" for the buyer to review.)

In Colombia, coffee is exported in 70kg sacks. On the New York ICE Futures Market (operated/regulated by the New York Mercantile Exchange and known as the "C" Market) coffee is traded in dollars per pound. The price is updated every three minutes and represents the movements of trade for "future contracts" in five contract months. If you want to check out what's happening with ICE coffee futures, you can look at a scary chart, which shows all the movements for all contracts months. Or you can look at ticker, which tracks the price *right now* for the nearest contract month.

From this constantly fluctuating magic number, the buyers (co-ops and middlemen) set prices paid to producers. Only the presidents/owners/top dogs of the co-ops and middlemen (which is a bit of a misnomer because every "middleman" is in fact a business with lots of employees, versus a single rogue dude loitering in the shadow of the saloon with his hat pulled low and cash wadded in the inside pocket of his coat) know the formulas for getting from those dollars per pound to the price posted in local currency per kilo. In Colombia that formula takes into account exchange rates, transportation, milling, sorting, and exportation costs which include taxes and licensing and inspections by Almacafe, the arm of the FNC charged with Colombian coffee quality control and transfers between 90-95% of the C Market price to producers.

If we're still trying to keep a pie chart in mind, futures and physicals traders certainly clean up with a healthy slice compared with that paid to producers, but their portion of the coffee pie is overtly calculable by the differences between the prices at which they buy and sell— whether what they're buying and selling is actual coffee or just imaginary contracts. But the one party at the table with the most mysterious portion seems to consistently be the first person who gets the coffee after it leaves the farms, be it a Costa Rican *beneficio* buying ripe cherries by volume or a Colombian co-op buying parchment coffee by weight. Everyone claims to "use the market as a base," but how these origin buyers get from New York market dollars per pound to local currency per local unit is certainly not common knowledge and seems to leave a lot of room for greedy bites.

In Colombia, the price to producers is discussed in terms of *cargas* (125kg) or *arrobas* (12.5kg). The zone I'm in works in *cargas*. So when a coffee grower rolls into the co-op the price, he sees posted on a *tablero* (sign board) outside is in *pesos* per *carga*. If he's not selling a full 125kg, then the price just gets divided by 125 to become the price per kilo and multiplied by what he has.

But it's not quite that simple. Because the coffee the farmers are bringing in is *en pergamino*, in parchment paper. And coffee is exported as hulled green beans, free of parchment paper and ready for roasting. And obviously the buyers won't pay for the weight of the parchment paper. Coffee is also exported at differentiated prices based on its quality. And obviously the buyers won't pay the same price for a *carga* of awesome beans or for a *carga* of crappy ones.

So Colombians work it all out as the following (the main goal being to figure out how many kilos of the specific coffee a given farmer shows up with are needed to yield 70kg of defect free, export quality [Excelso] green beans):

1) The grower shows up at the co-op and loads sacks of coffee in parchment onto a scale, where they're weighed in kilos.

2) An employee then *chusa* "sticks" every sack (with a cool hollow coffee sack sticking rod) to pull a representative sample (five sacks, five mini samples. 500 sacks, 500 samples. I've been told that the buyer also stabs the sacks to make sure there's nothing else hiding in there to bolster

386

the weight or alter the quality. So theoretically you wouldn't get away with putting a sack of crappy coffee inside another sack and then just putting pretty coffee on the top. Which apparently people used to do a lot.) The guy with the "sticker" then will usually open and empty all sacks in front of the seller before handing him/her the receipt.

3) The bowl containing all the stab-fuls pulled from the sacks is then emptied into a "homogenizer," a nifty machine that looks like it belongs in Dumbledore's study. Stab-fuls from only a few sacks will just be mixed in the bowl by hand.

4) The buyer weighs 200g from the big sample bowl to use as the representative sample from which he'll determine the price the producer gets. (Why 200g? Because 100g isn't quite enough to get a good representation, but 300g makes kind of a big pile of beans to hand sort through. So the norm is 200g.)

5) He then hulls the 200g grams and reweighs it. He usually gets around 160g, meaning around 18-20% of the weight is parchment. Let's say he gets 162g.

6) The buyer removes defects from green beans. That means pulling any bean with broca bites, discoloration, missing chunks, or a weird shape out of the pile.

7) He weighs the coffee again. Let's say there's 150g, meaning 12g of defective coffee.

8) He completes the following equation: (Let Y equal grams of defect-free beans) 14,000/Y= Factor. The Factor is (another) magic number that finally gets to the goal and determines how many kilos of this specific coffee— accounting for weight of defects and parchment— it will take to yield 70kg of defect-free exportable Colombian coffee. In this case, 14,000/150 gives us 93.3, so the Factor would be 93. That means it would take 93.3 pounds of this coffee to get 70kgs of exportable coffee. (Why 14,000? The grams of defect-free beans [in this case 150g] are out of a sample of 200g. This means that 75% of the weight of the representative sample [and therefore— theoretically— 75% of the total weight on the

scales] is exportable coffee. So we want to find 75% of what number will give us 70 to know how many kilos of this coffee we need, if 75% of it is exportable, to end up with 70kg. To find 75% of what will yield 70kg we could do find the following: $.75 \times Y = 70$. And good ole high school algebra tells us that's the same thing as saying $Y = 70/.75$. Which is the same thing as $7000/75$. Which is the same thing as $14000/150$. Which is much faster to do because you just pop the "150g" off the scale after you've weighed the defect-free hulled beans to get the magic Factor).

9) The buyer then plugs the Factor into the computer to yield the price paid per *carga*. (Although this formula is also clandestine, and set by the co-op, you can in fact trace it by plugging in different Factors and seeing the prices it spits out.) The publicized price is usually expressed in terms of Factor 90. This is not the average Factor, but because it's low, it looks good and is an "attractive price to put on the board." During my "math lesson" visits, the price was hovering around 535,000 pesos per *carga*, Factor 90. So my Factor 93 coffee might fetch around 522,000 pesos per *carga*.

10) Once the computer formula gives the price per *carga* accounting for the Factor, the buyer can then figure out the price per kilo and determine how much to pay the producer.

11) The gofer guys (who are all kinds of badass and do the lifting and hauling of sacks of coffee off the trucks and onto the scales) slash the ties off the sacks and dump them into the big piles of coffee. Mission accomplished.

Things work pretty much the same at the middleman's as at the Co-op, except most middlemen don't have nifty Dumbledore homogenizers, and middlemen always offer higher prices than the co-ops (while the Factor 90 at the co-op is 535,000 pesos per *carga* it's 550,000 at all the middlemen in town). Middlemen don't offer services like trainings and workshops and school supplies for your kids, meaning they also don't have the costs to cover. So why sell to the co-op? Because middlemen don't offer loans and lines of credit. Only co-op members who've been selling to the co-op consistently are eligible for those juiciest of benefits. Middlemen also don't offer premiums for certified coffee.

There are some certified growers who are active members in every event and training and are all around co-op die hards who sell 100% and don't even look elsewhere. But pretty much everyone is a member of Ciudad Bolívar's one co-op, and yet twenty-some middlemen stay in business in the same town. Most growers split their sales and take advantage of the benefits of slightly better prices while remaining in good enough standing to also take advantage of longer-term co-op benefits.

Did Juan ever mention he was good at math? If you're an algebra teacher looking for new "real world application" material, make all your word problems about coffee.

Posted May 1, 2013

Eyelashes and Thresholds

In Spanish, the word for a tab on your internet browser is *pestaña*, which translates to "eyelash," which I think is the best online language imagery I've heard in any language (even though "surfing" and "spam" make for some good ones).

If tabs are eyelashes, then my computer consistently looks like the vending machine full of those green aliens fearing "The Claw" in Toy Story. All eyes. There's no Cyclops here; my computer, and I, are always peering in dozens of directions.

On a given day my "eyelashes" can be looking into plant genetics, latte art competitions, and maps of rural Panama. If someone were to peer over my shoulder and interrogate me about all those open eyelashes, the conversation might go something like this:

Interrogator: Why are you checking futures market prices?
Me: Coffee.
Interrogator: And Instagram pictures of "mug" shots?
Me: Coffee.
Interrogator: And NPR's newsfeed?
Me: Coffee.
Interrogator: And bus schedules to Manizales?

Me: Coffee.

Interrogator: And definitions of hybrids and F1 vs. F5 seeds?

Me: Coffee.

Interrogator: And corporate press releases from Germany?

Me: Coffee.

Interrogator: And a Smithsonian African music album?

Me: Coffee.

Interrogator: And soil pH charts?

Me: Coffee.

Interrogator: And Todd Carmichael's article from Esquire?

Me: Coffee.

Interrogator: And guidelines for measuring carbon footprints?

Me: Coffee.

Interrogator: And container ship specs?

Me: Coffee.

Interrogator: And those Peace Corps project updates?

Me: Coffee.

Interrogator: And the Economics section of a Nicaraguan newspaper?

Me: Coffee.

Interrogator: And Melbourne conference listings and Nice event tickets?

Me: Coffee.

Interrogator: And that Facebook group about grassroots political resistance in the name of land rights?

Me: Coffee.

Is all this stuff at every end of so many spectra— finance, biology, pop culture, gourmet foodie trends, international trade, local politics, global environmental concerns, and personal photo albums all really related to coffee? Yes. Does it all really have anything to do with the black liquid in my cup? Yes. Does it really connect to the bag on the grocery store shelf and the stuff in the pot at the diner? Yes.

How? How do we get from potassium levels in a volcanic mountainside to the closing bell of the exchange to the wet grinds left in the filter every morning?

We blink. As quickly as eyelashes go from open to closed, coffee crosses thresholds, and on either sides of these thresholds it is transformed to the point of being unrecognizable from what it previously was.

The process of coffee from "seed to cup" has been explained and illustrated in books and comics and photo series and YouTube videos. It's no mystery how coffee physically transforms from being a seed to a tree to a bean to a drink, but how does it get from being a tree to a commodity? A commodity to a fad? A fad to a livelihood? A grocery staple to a coveted treat? A Petri dish culture to an international event? Where are the thresholds for conceptualizing and experiencing coffee?

They're tricky to catch. But they tend to lie where coffee changes hands or changes measurements.

When coffee changes hands the transfer is physical. When a container of coffee passes from buyer to seller it, it crosses a threshold of physical transformation different than that when it passes through the depulper. It has literally crossed the threshold into a new space and therefore new ownership. (Most FOB contracts determine this as the moment when the coffee "crosses the ships rail." The container, swinging in midair from a loading crane, is set on board, and suddenly it's different, even though molecularly it's exactly the same. In an instant it has changed from being a Colombian export to an American import).

When coffee changes measurements the transfer happens in the blink, somewhere between the eyelashes. Neuroscience tells us we can never look at two things at once; we can only look really quickly back and forth between them. But, no matter how quickly we look, our brains have a limit. That fascinating proof is in the pudding of the experiment where subjects read lines of text on a computer, but as they read the previous lines are changed. And yet the changes are undetectable because during the "between" of looking between one thing and another, we go momentarily blind.

And that's where coffee changes: during that instant in which we are blind. Coffee can be kilos of grain on a scale. But when we punch those kilos into a formula to yield a price, it comes out on the other side of the equal sign as a tradable commodity. We can look back and forth— really, really quickly— between the number on the scale and the number on the receipt, but we can't see both at once. While coffee in reality doesn't cease to be a bunch of grain once we've put a futures market price tag on it, we can't think of it as both at once, and so we have to choose which one to think of it as, and thus we choose how to treat it.

When the sack of coffee physically crosses the threshold from discrete jute sack to indiscrete part of the middleman's coffee pile, it has crossed the threshold of ownership, and thus become something different. Its value has changed. It will no longer be valued in pesos of pergamino but in dollars per pound of green beans.

When coffee crosses visible thresholds or blind blinks behind eyelashes its value transforms. Sometimes these value changes coincide with changes in form; roasted coffee is valued differently than unroasted coffee because it is in fact different. But other times when the values change it's because we blink. The value changes not because the coffee in parchment is actually any different when it's in the bag strapped to the roof of the Jeep bouncing down the mountain than when it's in a pile at the co-op; it changes because we assign it a different worth. Those shifts in value are purely the product of how we choose to see coffee; and the changes happen as fast as we blink, as fast as that imperceptible blindness.

But even though that blindness is imperceptible, it runs deep. It happens so quickly that it doesn't seem like we could be missing that much, but as soon as we dump the coffee into the pile it stops being the result of the intense labor of one farm, one family, one team of workers, and starts being the lucrative plaything of someone else.

The same phenomenon can happen in reverse. When we pull one lot of coffee from one harvest of one farm and roast and cup it all by itself, it stops being part of the commodity playing field and starts being auctioned, prized, and savored. And yet a top Cup of Excellence lot could be mixed into the swirling mass of commodity coffee and the market wouldn't notice. It wouldn't drive up the price or make any difference at all, even though the actual beans are still physically the same: special-enough-to-be-loved.

Coffee biologically and chemically crosses transformative thresholds in its path from plant to drink, but we also push, pull, drag, dump, coax, cajole, and heave it across mental thresholds of our own design, thresholds that can hold all kinds of implications that we just don't see at the times of crossing.

Posted May 10, 2013

Worth

Coffee pricing anywhere along up the line is pretty much guesswork, but comparing numbers up and down the production chain and from place to place gets even more dicey.

The reason that all coffee pricing is pretty much guesswork is that most of it is loosely based on a convoluted supply/demand market mechanism, and the rest of it is set in circumstances where people don't even know their operating costs.

There's also a lot of morphing between units and currencies, making things even more convoluted. I have a personal aversion to putting everything into dollars, because the shock-and-awe tactics of "people who live on a dollar a day!" are too over/misused. Here I'm putting things into dollars so that they mean something to you, but I'm also including indicators so that you have actual points of reference for how much that amount is worth in a local context. *¿Listo?*

Determining what coffee is worth depends on the form it's in and the place in which it's in that form. Let's take a cup of coffee.

A 4oz cup of *tinto* costs 500 Colombian pesos, roughly $0.25 (that *buñuelo* is another $0.50). Minutes on your cell phone cost between 100-200 pesos and for 6000 pesos you can get a full lunch. A cup of brewed coffee in New York can cost anywhere from $0.75 to $4. That's 1400-8000 pesos.

A pound of roasted whole bean coffee can cost between $6-18 dollars in the US. Here in Colombia roasted whole bean coffee is only recently being sold per pound and runs around 10,000 pesos ($5).

A pound of green, unroasted (Arabica) coffee is the global crux of every other coffee price that comes before or after it. The price at which a pound of green coffee is traded determines the money the growers and processors make and can thus pay their employees. It determines how much it costs for roasters to buy it to then sell to consumers. And the price per pound for this green Arabica coffee has nothing to do with coffee.

It is no way connected to the cost of production any of the fifty plus countries where coffee is grown. It has to do with how many people are buying and selling contracts for coffee, but because you can just sell one contract to buy another one and never actually end up with any coffee, just a rotation of contract trades, it then also has to with how many people think (speculate) that other people will be buying or selling coffee. And how much. And exactly when how many people will buy how much.

At 16:59 EST Friday May 17, 2013, a pound of green Arabica coffee was trading at $1.37. The New York price per pound is then what local coffee co-ops/middlemen plug into their magic formulas to determine what they pay producers for the coffee in parchment that they then turn into green coffee for export.

But if you're operating outside of the market, a pound of this green Panamanian Geisha can be worth upwards of $100/lb. Last year's top Panamanian Geisha auction price was $ 90.25/lb, with the record breaker in 2010 at $170/lb. The 2013 auction takes place in a few weeks.

"Direct Trade" sales aim to pad traditionally low market prices by offering a "market plus x" premium for exceptional coffees. Some direct traders even sidestep the market altogether, by buying coffee at a fixed price based on the cost of production. But because most coffee farms aren't selling direct trade and aren't run like businesses, a surprising number of farmers don't know the cost per kilo of growing the coffee they sell.

With Friday, May 17th's market price— which holds through the weekend—125 kilos of coffee in parchment is worth 500,000 pesos ($272.50) per 125kg. The price could differ depending on the Factor. Then, in parchment a kilo is worth 4,000 pesos ($2.18/kilo, or $0.99/lb). For 4,000 pesos you can get a kilo of potatoes (800), two empanadas (1,000), a pack of five arepas (1,000), and at least 30 minutes of internet (1200).

In Costa Rica, a picker makes between 800-1500 Colones per cajuela (1 sq ft, roughly 13 kilos) of ripe cherries. That's between \$1.60-\$3 per cajuela, meaning between \$0.12 and \$0.23 per kilo, or \$0.05- \$0.10/lb. A top notch picker can pick upwards of 30 cajuelas per day, so at five days a week that's 150 cajuelas, or between 120,000-225,000 colones a week. A beer costs 1,000 colones, I got a cheap duffle for 7,000, and local bus fares are around 500, with long distance rides at around 8,000 or 10,000.

Picking Panamanian Geisha will earn you a daily wage far above per volume/weight payouts. Some pickers even sign a contract for the season.

Picked Colombia cherries are worth between 380-500 pesos per kilo, which is roughly \$0.21-\$0.27 per kilo. It's the end of the harvest and Colombian pickers are picking about 120 kilos per day, for 45,600-60,000 pesos a day, for 228,000-300,000 pesos a week. A soda costs 2,000 pesos, a beer 1,400, a pack of cigarettes 2,000, and the all-important jumbo batteries for the portable radio, 2000 for a pack of two.

Let's review! These are the current average (mode) prices per **kilo** of Colombian coffee in all its different forms.

Cherries (price paid to pickers by owners)	\$0.21 (380 pesos) (\$0.09/lb)
Parchment (price paid to owners by co-op)	\$2.18 (4,000 pesos) (\$0.99/lb)
Green coffee (price paid by importers to co-op/exporter)	\$3.14 (\$1.37/lb)
Green coffee (price paid by roasters to importers)	Depends on market price at the second in which the deal is made
Roasted coffee (price paid by consumers to roaster)	\$22 (\$9.99/lb for Colombian French Roast on freshdirect.com)
Prepared coffee (price paid by consumers to vendors) for 16 oz cup of cofee	\$2.40

Kind of like the integrity of Juan Valdez, what coffee is worth really depends on whom you ask.

Posted May 18, 2013

Ingenuity is Sustainable

Sustainability doesn't mean tree-hugging (although trees are extremely sustainable). Sustainability means being able to keep doing something for a really long time. Fasting is not sustainable because you'll die. Competing in Nathan's hot dog-eating competition daily is not sustainable because you'll also die. The activities that are the most sustainable lie somewhere between extremes.

Sustainability is often discussed in terms of actions; is eating a single hot dog sustainable? Is driving your car to Coney Island to get one sustainable? Is taking the bus? Is biking? Is walking? Is swimming from Breezy Point?

Sustainability is not often enough discussed in terms of thinking. Our actions don't act themselves; they come from our mindsets. And some mindsets are more sustainable than others.

"I want that!" is not a particularly sustainable frame of mind. "I want that NOW!" is even less sustainable. We can't think like that 24/7 because we'd take candy from babies, punch our bosses in their faces, and shoplift every pair of fly kicks we saw in the Niketown display window.

"I don't need anyone or anything" is just as extreme and unsustainable. You won't make it very long sitting cross-legged and naked in the middle of the forest by yourself.

"Do I really need that?" is a more sustainable way of thinking about things. "What can I do with what I already have?" similarly so. Sustainable ways of thinking are those that come in the forms of questions, because when we ask questions we're analyzing things; we're looking at them closely and critically to figure them out. And that is something you can keep doing forever and ever.

All creativity comes from some sort of necessity; artistic creativity comes from the absolute need to express something. Practical, inventive creativity comes from the need to get something done. We're inventive not when someone tells us to be; we come up with ideas when we have no option but to do so.

Artists will tell you that the need to be creative is every day. For people living in challenging circumstances, it's the need to create things also presents itself every day because no mindset yields as unprecedented creativity as, "How can I survive?"

If you need a place to live and the road dead ends at unused railroad tracks running along a river, saying, "I can't live here," is not going to sustain you very long. Asking yourself, "How can I live here?" is what will keep you going.

It is what will lead you to build *marranitas*, homemade transportation schemes that run back and forth along the tracks. It will inspire you to attach wheels to a wooden pallet/sled and propel yourself along with a long bamboo pole, or to cut a hole in the sled/pallet to fit the wheels of a moto into so that they're riding on one of the rails and thus propel the sled along, and then you can still just pop out the moto and use it as a moto. It will inspire you to use a bike instead of a moto and pedal yourself and your cargo (or children or chickens) down the tracks. It will inspire you to build a little plastic roof over the sled and screw in some benches to create a shuttle to and from the nearest town, charging a dollar each way. And then you can build houses and buy groceries and commute to school and work and it doesn't matter that there isn't a traditional road, because you figured out a creative solution to the problem because you needed a place to live. And you ended up with riverfront property and almost zero carbon footprints. Creativity has its fringe benefits.

Complaining that, "Picking coffee is really hot and buggy! I'm just going to sit down under the trees and mope," will get you kicked off the picking crew and thus booted from your room, board, and source of income. Asking yourself, "How can I make this sweaty, insect-laden job more bearable?" will lead you to find ingenious ways of tying a t-shirt around your head so that there's no skin for the sun to burn or the bugs to bite. It will lead you to cut a custom plastic "raincoat" for your radio that you've creatively hung around your neck so that it doesn't bump into your basket or get in the way of picking. Discomfort is inspiring.

It seems like being comfortable would be a sustainable human state, but when we're comfortable we have a tendency to be less creative. Is, then, the most sustainable human state being in a state of moderate need (and thus discomfort) because that's when we're at our most ingenious? It might not be quite that simple. We're always creative when we're in need, but do we have to be in need to be creative?

Can we predict future need and states of discomfort and be just as ingenious? Can we catapult ourselves into creativity while we're still comfortable; can we be creative before we get to a place of dire need? Can we all be like the guy who built the electric car way before anyone ever thought we'd actually reach the bottom of the oil barrel?

I think so. Because once you start asking questions and thinking of creative ways to answer them, you usually start to think of more questions, and your creativity fuels itself. But this kind of hypothetically prompted creativity is harder, because the need is projected rather than present, and if the theoretical need/discomfort is a tricky problem to solve, it's tempting to just throw in the towel and say, "Well sea levels haven't *actually* risen two meters so we don't *really* need to do anything about preparing for that to happen because they might never rise at all."

The reason creativity in the face of pressing need is so downright genius is because it's the product of having no other choice but to solve the problem at hand. Even if the dilemma is tricky, you just keep creating until you figure something out. Because that's all you can do. Unless you just curl up in a corner and cry defeat. Which humans are not known for. Maybe you cry for a few hours and then think, "this is silly," and get up and figure something out.

Complacency is unsustainable in the way that stagnant water is unsustainable; it's not immediately lethal but overtime it will yield enough mosquitos to eat you alive. Ingenuity is sustainable in the way that a river is sustainable; water tumbles down gravity's tug just like ideas roll off one another until you're treading in the swirling pool at the bottom of a waterfall of ingenuity.

Posted May 19, 2013

The Coffee Shelf

No direct trade coffee farm is complete without the coffee shelf. The requisite installation includes bags of beans from all the roasters who buy directly from the farm. It's the coffee grower's trophy case: a lineup of all the places his coffee has reached, packaged with his farm's name, a nice big Direct Trade or Single Origin label, and sometimes even the story of his family.

In order to become direct trade coffee sellers, growers have to convert themselves into industry experts and beverage aficionados, learning to cup and determine firsthand the quality of their coffee. This is also usually the foray into becoming something of coffee collectors; and so the coffee shelf includes bags of beans and grounds received as gifts or picked up in travels to other parts of the country or the world.

The first coffee shelf I saw was at La Candelilla in San Marcos de Tarrazú, Costa Rica. The Sanchez family proudly displays Starbucks bags boasting their beans and an entire Korean line of Single Origin coffees.

Coopedota has a pretty healthy collection too; their coffee shelf also includes all the coffee they package and label for private collections. They have a "coffee table" next to the coffee shelf that showcases all the different iterations on Co-opedota's own coffee, from (an admittedly quite unexciting) generic blend sold in local grocery stores to their Dota Fresh micro lot line, which is on the short list of the best coffees I've tasted anywhere on this trip.

Henry Hueck's coffee shelf at Ramacafe in Nicaragua is an ample assortment of Central American coffees and includes a Starbuck's Reserve: Nicaragua Black Diamond Limited Edition vacuum-sealed coffee brick containing 70% Ramacafe coffee.

Exclusive Coffees, being Costa Rica's exclusive direct trade exporter, has a loaded coffee shelf, with coffees from Costa Rica's best micromills transformed by roasters across the US, Canada, and Asia.

In Volcán, Panama, the Hartmann family's coffee shelf is inside their cupping lab; all the bags of coffee are lined up like a row of sentinels stationed above the picture windows.

The Janson family's coffee shelf occupies a corner of their coffee lab and includes as many of their own coffees as those of others.

In Boquete, Ricardo Koyner's Kotowa coffee shelf is brimming with extravagant packages of all the places his prized Geisha lots, including a Japanese "Gran Cru" champagne bottle.

Wilford Lamastus's coffee shelf is inside his Bajareque coffee house in Casco Viejo, Panama City and has just as many coffee books and back issues of *Tea & Coffee Trade Journal* as it does bags of beans.

Looking at people's coffee shelves is one of my favorite things about visiting farms, cupping labs, and even people's homes. It's the kind of thing you can't see on the website or in a marketing brochure; in order to brush the dust off the bags lining someone's coffee shelf you have to actually be there.

Specialty coffee is a pretty small circuit, and direct trade coffee is an even tighter circle of people who all know each other (whether they work together in harmony or just gossip...) Checking out people's coffee shelves becomes like a scavenger hunt to see who's been where, who has whose coffee, and where the overlaps are. (Phil and Sebastian Roasters of Canada, for example, buys from both Exclusive in Costa Rica and the Hartmann's in Panama. I know this because both had the stylish blue Phil and Sebastian's bags on their coffee shelves).

The coffee shelf is a point of pride and a right of passage. It's personal and human and I wasn't really expecting to find one in the land of technified Colombian milds. But I did.

Every Department of Colombia that grows coffee has a Departmental Committee with a main office in the department's capital. On Monday I visited the Department of Risaralda's main office in the capital city of Pereira to talk to the Coordinator of Extension Services (from which I walked out with the magic coffee pricing formula!) I had spoken to countless Extensionists at other small offices across various departments, but this was the first time I was visiting someone this high up the FNC food chain. I could immediately tell that he was a higher up not because his office was bigger or because it was on the second floor with a separate secretary; I could tell because he had a coffee shelf.

He was the first person other than direct-trade-growers I'd met who had a coffee shelf, so of course I was extra curious. I was picking up the bags and skimming the labels of lots of unfamiliar names— and of course a few Juan Valdez— when I saw a black bag with a peeling paper logo reading APOT.

No way. I grabbed it, brushed off the fine layer of dust, and it was indeed a bag of coffee from APOT, the Association of Producers of Organic Coffees of Turrialba, Costa Rica. Here in an office building in Risaralda, Colombia was a bag of coffee from the very town where I started this whole trip. Here was a bag of coffee that had beans from Marie's organic farm at Monte Claro and Fabio's finca in San Juan. I was ecstatic. Somehow, this coffee had made the same trek I had.

Grinning, I showed the lead extensionist the bag, saying, "I've been here! I know them!" He half looked at it and said, "Oh, I don't even remember where I got that from." I didn't care that he didn't care. It was too cool that APOT coffee was sitting on the coffee shelf of an FNC office.

When I was in Turrialba in October the members of APOT were trying to resurrect it from the ruins of a corrupt former president. They weren't even processing their own coffee, let alone roasting it or selling it. And they might never again. So the bag of APOT coffee on the extensionist's coffee shelf was something of a collector's item.

I don't even have a bag of APOT coffee. I wish I did, but in my first month I was trying to refrain from collecting more things to carry (but once I realized that I was going back to NYC for a week I immediately amassed my own sort of portable coffee shelf, which turned into me checking an extra 35lb "coffee backpack.")

Coffee reaches around the world's girth in growing regions from Turrialba to Risaralda to Vietnam and Burundi. And then it reaches around the world thousands more times to get to micro and macro roasters and then all the way into your travel mug. It's massive and complicated and tangly.

Which is why I love the coffee shelves. Even if you don't remember how you got that bag of APOT coffee gathering dust on your coffee shelf, it's there. It's real and it's tangible and it's there. It represents the work of real people growing real coffee in a real place. If you keep your eye on the coffee shelf you can follow a few threads through the tangled coffee fabric, and by following just a few it reminds you that all those threads you're not following also correspond to real people growing real coffee in real places.

Coffee is drinkable and transient and as baristas know and sweat about, over all too soon. But coffee can also be deified: mounted over the fireplace just as majestically as the antler's of the season's biggest buck. Coffee can be sipped and spent, or it can be put on a pedestal and revered as a symbol of taste or struggle or success or exoticness or whatever it is that its collector most wants to revere.

Posted May 29, 2013

Collective Regurgitation

Tell me your story. Don't retell me what someone else has said about you, has told you about yourself, tell me what you know about you, what you've seen and done, not someone else's interpretation of it.

We hear a lot about ourselves from the outside world. Media shows us representations of groups we belong to. We overhear and participate in conversations where individuals we know (teachers, bosses, friends, family) make claims about groups we belong to, or even about us specifically. The world is a constant, fragmented mirror reflecting back disjointed images of who we are. Our job then becomes to fit those fragments together, to sort the actual reflections from the exaggerated, the exaggerated from the plain inaccurate. We end up with a constantly evolving narrative perception of ourselves gleaned from the people bobbing and yapping in the concentric circles radiating out around us.

My mom said this about me. My brother said that about me. My friend said this about me. I overheard my neighbor say that about me. My teacher said this about the class; I belong to the class. My minister said this about the congregation; I belong to the congregation. The police sergeant said that about local farmers; I'm a local farmer. The mayor said that about the city; I live in the city. The president said this about Costa Ricans; I'm a Costa Rican. The *ranchero* ballad says that about single men; I'm a single man. The TV show said that about Latin Americans; I'm a Latin American. The movie said this about people who live in the campo; I live in the campo.

The emerging narrative that we subconsciously gleaned from all those external evaluations that we apply to ourselves— often without realizing we're doing the synthesizing and applying— is something we then regurgitate. If someone walks up and asks this hypothetical Costa Rican coffee farmer about himself, there's a good chance he'll give some piece of a summary he's amassed from all those piecemeal reflections from varying proximities (immediate :: mom, distant :: mass media).

This regurgitation can often become collective. All these outside sources say things about Costa Rican farmers, I've heard other Costa Ricans repeat some of them about themselves, and because I'm also a Costa Rican, they must apply to me as well. This is the source of the collective regurgitation of narratives constructed by someone else— by someone elses— and therefore really by no one at all.

Which makes them empty generalizations that don't actually apply to any member of the group, even when members of the group readily apply them to themselves.

We have so many opportunities to be unwittingly collecting data on what other sources—both informed and ignorant—are saying about us that we rarely have an opportunity to take a minute to think what we actually know about ourselves.

When I ask people to tell me their stories, I'm asking them to do something apart from what they normally do (regurgitate some piece of a collective narrative in order to consider their own experiences); I'm asking me to tell me what they've *actually* done, seen, felt, and experienced, even if it doesn't comply with some fractured, floating narrative of best fit.

I'm asking people to go outside (Inside? Next door to? Underneath? Beyond?) the collectively regurgitated narrative of "this is my family's land; I learned to farm coffee from my father, and now that's what I do. Everything I have I have because of coffee," and tell me the specifics of their individual lives.

And a lot of people don't know how to do it. Because they've never done it before. They've also never seen or heard anyone do it. Lots of people don't realize the stories they have to tell, don't realize that they are brimming with unique experiences because they've spent so long finding the parts of their life that *do* fit with the collectively regurgitated mass narratives of the groups they belong to.

The exceptions make us human; they're what make us individuals who have to face coincidence, luck, misfortune, challenge, and opportunity. Some people are more inclined to tell stories than others, but telling stories about what has made and is making us who we are is never simple, it is never easy, and it is always something we can (and should) keep learning how to do.

Written December, 2012
Posted June 4, 2013

Landscapegoats

People become what you tell them they are, and if someone tells people that they live in the land of the Colombian Coffee Landscape World Heritage Site, they will turn around and tell you how great it is that they live in the land of the Colombian Coffee Landscape World Heritage Site, even if they've never seen a coffee plant themselves. Which, even in the land of the Colombian Coffee Landscape World Heritage Site, is not uncommon. City people don't usually do rural things. That's a premise that is fairly universal.

Plenty of urban Colombians told me they'd love to read my coffee book so that, "I can learn something about coffee, because I really don't know anything." And yet when you give people a title to hold onto, they sometimes use it as a scapegoat for actually seeing or doing what the title refers to.

In 2011 UNESCO declared Colombian Coffee Cultural Landscapes in four of the country's coffee growing departments as a collective World Heritage Site. This declaration is trickling down through Colombians in the form of some interesting sentiments.

The first is resentment. Because only four of the country's twelve coffee growing departments were included in the declaration, people who work just as hard growing coffee in the other eight feel a little bit bitter. They feel like somehow their work has been slighted by being omitted. (I'm a little bit inclined to agree. The farms I saw in non-World Heritage departments were just as impressive and with just as rich a cultural heritage as those that fall within the Heritage boundaries.)

The second is trickling sentiment is pride. Of course knowing a large part of your country has been declared a World Heritage site will make you proud, considerably more so if you live within the site's boundaries, but pride without knowing what you're proud of can look a little funny.

People become what you tell them they are, and we all have an incredible capacity to be part of collective regurgitation. Groups also become what you tell them they are, and one by one people spit back out the labels you've applied to the groups they belong to, until you have the whole group enthusiastically claiming to be what you told them they are.

I found that people would repeatedly tell me, "This area is part of the Cultural Landscape World Heritage Site!" and when I told them that I'd just spent the past few days hiking in the mud and the rain through the very cafetales that constitute the Site they'd then reply, "Wow, really? I've never actually been to a cafetal."

The cycle of Colombian coffee narratives is a complex one, and the declaration of the World Heritage Site gave people who were not part of the long standing Juan Valdez narrative a way to suddenly be included in the Colombian coffee story. To be included as part of the Site the Departments had to meet a ten point list of requirements including everything from preserving water sources to architecture styles (which seems a little arbitrary because even after looking at the list I really don't see any marked differences between departments that made the cut and those that didn't). One of the requirements was to have an "Urban Heritage," and it's true that one cool feature of the Coffee Cultural Landscape is that its principal cities are on high hill tops above coffee growing land.

This simple inclusion of the word "urban" beckoned city dwellers to also include themselves the Colombian coffee family. So now you suddenly have city people excited about the Coffee Cultural Landscape, even though many of them have only seen it from the window of a passing bus.

A third cultural trickle down from the declaration is a cool nickname. The regions included in the Site are known as the *Eje*

405

Cafetero, the Coffee Axis. This already cool nickname often gets cut to just the even cooler "the Axis," making the Coffee Cultural Landscape sound like an important place to be just by referring to it.

I was sitting at the kitchen table on the Herrera Araque finca (probably eating an arepa) when this conversation happened:

"Luis, you should take Raquel to the Coffee Axis!"

"But there's lots of coffee here."

"I know, but it's the Axis!"

"But there's actually still a lot of coffee she hasn't seen in Antioquia."

"Well, she should still go to the Axis."

Because the Axis sounds important, it seems like it should be prioritized, even if it has no other superlative qualities (like Cup of Excellence winners or greatest percentage of national production volume). How often do we do things because we're collectively regurgitating their priority rather than actually thinking about whether or not they're really important to do?

Just naming the landscape and talking up its coolness can let it become a scapegoat for actually going and getting to know the place behind the cool name and the crop behind the reason for the cool name in the first place.

If you're Colombian I recommend going to see the coffee growing in all the areas it grows in your country, be they as close as your own back yard or as far away as the Axis. I recommend walking through the tangled rows, feeling the waxy leaves, checking the berries for broca, and noticing if the air smells different.

If you're not Colombian, I recommend considering Colombia for your next vacation and taking a trip that is not as empty as baking on the beach in Cartagena. Check out a cool crop grown by cool people. Whether the fincas and cafetales you visit are technically part of a World Heritage Site or not, it will be worth your trip and I promise you will never drink another cup of coffee the same way again.

Posted June 5, 2013

Endnote:
The Stories Behind
the Stories

The catalyzing inspiration for the form of this book comes from Jonathan Safran Foer's *Eating Animals*. Before I'd picked up *Eating Animals,* Foer was already on my shortlist of favorite fiction writers because I trust his renditions of people and the worlds they experience. In the case of *Eating Animals* I further trusted his candid motivation for crabwaddling from fiction over to nonfiction; what more honest inquiry is there than that of a parent who wants to know what to do for his child? I also trusted the facts he presented not just because of the motivations and methods with which they were acquired, but because they came paired with discussions of the real life questions that eclipse, in practicality, any fact sheet: questions that no one was asking about the social tethers that bind us to eating flesh.

I'm no stranger to materials about the benefits of the all-veg life and the horrors of the meat industries, but they always seemed a bit like one-sided rabble. But *Eating Animals* turned me into a vegetarian for the six months before I left on this odyssey. (While traveling I did eat meat. Rogue Traveler 101 is that when people open their homes and tables to you, you immediately get over any picky eater tendencies).

For me, the most compelling aspect of *Eating Animals,* what really convinced me to make a change, was the collection of letters from farmers. Reading the words of the people who know live animals and dead meat best cut through that rabble in a way that no other text or documentary had. I've always loved the way Foer manipulates form to find ways of taking characters and readers to places no one else can seem to put their fingers on, and the ingenuity in form of *Eating Animals*— the treatment of social questions and particularly the inclusion of unadulterated first person accounts— was enough to jolt me out of my carnivorous stupor.

Thus, for my own book, I decided to take my favorite part of *Eating Animals* and do more of what Foer had done, gather first-person accounts, so that the voices of others could be the bulk of the book, and my voice would be there to leave the breadcrumbs to help readers navigate the stories of others.

Just like we're eating animals, we're drinking people. And as a drinking person I want to hear from the people whose livelihoods I consume every day of my life.

So I turned on the Voice Memos Utility of my Airplane Moded iPhone and started recording.

And once I got going I realized I'd actually been channeling another of the writers who most changed me as a person.

At age fifteen I read Joseph Campbell's *Power of Myth*, and it changed the way I thought about everything. I was fascinated that he had done something so simple; look closely at all the work of other people who'd looked more closely at one thing. What he found couldn't be more heartening; there are more things that unite us as humans than those that divide us.

At fifteen I wanted to do what he'd done. I wanted to survey everythings from everywheres and look at the big picture of a sweeping horizon. I knew I could never just sit and analyze one cave painting to death because I'd be too busy wondering what other cave paintings looked like.

I started this odyssey in a literary mindset; I planned to collect stories from coffeepeople, expressing in their own words who they are, what they do, and what's going on where they live. I had no intentions of paying attention to industrial trading, commodity markets, plant genetics, international politics, or flavor profiles, but that's exactly what I ended up doing. I somehow ended up channeling Mr. Campbell, looking at coffee everything, and finding coffee with a thousand faces.

In the process of writing this book I've become some kind of homemade nomadic agronomist, commodity analyst, market researcher, ambassador, coffee cupper, and occasional manual laborer.

I never thought I'd be a chemist, but I've again surprised myself, because that seems to be what I've also become.

As I translated and transcribed the interviews I recorded, I transformed audible words into readable ones; sound into text. With the application of a little heat and pressure (or was it just a solid keyboard and a good pair of headphones?) words changed form. I've condensed word vapor into textual water, put the water in a glass of pages, the glass on the bound tray of a book, and am serving stories in consumable form.

As a chemist, I sometimes get creative with my role as transformer, adding a touch of food coloring to the water or a lemon wedge to the glass. Sometimes I just put a fancy napkin on the tray. But the vessel still holds water, water born from curling wisps of steam.

This vessel still holds stories, stories born from transient curls of sound. Steam and conversation are fleeting, evaporating before you can really be sure that you've caught them. Water in a glass and pages on a spine are much easier to save, share, and swallow.

This book is titled, *"When Coffee Speaks"* because the premise of this project is that, in order to best understand the process of producing the coffee I pour into my body every day, I should talk with the people whose lives and work make coffee possible.

This is about listening, not about proving a hypothesis. So I listened. And I funneled transient sound through ones and zeros into a microprocessor on my smartphone.

These stories have crossed the thresholds of medium and language, but they make it across intact.

Cheers to coffeepeople.

Indicies

Interviewees, in order of appearance

Interviewees, by first name

Interviewees, by job type
Agronomists

Employees

Entrepreneurs

About the Author

Rachel was born and raised in New Hampshire's White Mountains. She earned her Bachelor of Science in English Education at New York University's Steinhardt School of Culture, Education, and Human Development and proudly taught in New York City's public school system for several years. She lives between Brooklyn and her backpack.

Contact Rachel and read more at rachelnorthrop.com and whencoffeespeaks.com

Photo Credit: Nina Raman